Understanding Ireland's Economic Crisis

Prospects for Recovery

Edited by

STEPHEN KINSELLA AND ANTHONY LEDDIN

BLACKHALL
Publishing

Published by Blackhall Publishing
Lonsdale House
Avoca Avenue
Blackrock
Co. Dublin
Ireland

e-mail: info@blackhallpublishing.com
www.blackhallpublishing.com

ISBN: 978-1-84218-198-0

A catalogue record for this book is available from the British Library.

Printed in Ireland by ColourBooks Ltd.

Acknowledgements

Thanks to Lisa Hickey for her excellent research assistance, to Eileen O'Brien and the team at Blackhall Publishing for their expert help in preparing the manuscript and to Ailbhe O'Reilly for suggesting the book in the first place. Thanks also to the contributors for their articles, without whom there would be no book. We dedicate this book to our teachers, past, present and future.

Contents

Contents

About the Contributors

Michael O'Sullivan, Author of *Ireland and the Global Question* (Cork University Press, 2006) and editor, with Rory Miller, of *What Did We Do Right?* (Blackhall Publishing, 2010).

K.P.V. O'Sullivan, Postgraduate Student, Department of Government, London School of Economics and Political Science.

Morgan Kelly, Professor of Economics, University College Dublin.

Ronan Lyons, Postgraduate Student, Department of Economics, University of Oxford.

Colm McCarthy, Lecturer in Economics, University College Dublin.

Michael Taft, Research Officer, UNITE.

Anthony Leddin, Senior Lecturer in Economics, Kemmy Business School, University of Limerick.

Eoin Gahan, Head of Regulation, Trade and Policy Foresight, Forfás Ireland.

Edward Nell, Malcolm B. Smith Professor of Economics, New School for Social Research.

K. Vela Velupillai, Professor of Economics, CIFREM/Department of Economics, University of Trento.

Stephen Kinsella, Lecturer in Economics, Kemmy Business School, University of Limerick.

Brendan Walsh, Professor Emeritus, Department of Economics, University College Dublin.

Introduction

It may be the conceit of every age to believe that its experience is unique – that somehow this time is different. Though the fortunes of every economy will necessarily rise and fall over time, in the 88-year economic history of the Irish state, no set of challenges have presented themselves as starkly as those to be overcome in 2010 and beyond.

The aim of this book is to critically analyse and interpret the roots of the current economic crisis from differing perspectives, in order to provide possible solutions or strategies for recovery. The hope is that this book will provide a platform for debate on the diverse challenges facing the Irish economy in the medium term. *Understanding Ireland's Economic Crisis* contributes macroeconomic, microeconomic and theoretical perspectives on the same theme – just how small, open economies might prosper in the medium term, following a domestic and international economic downturn of historic proportions.

The Scale of the Problem

The period from 1994 to 2007 is often described as a 'game of two halves'. The first half, from 1994 to 2000, was largely an export-led boom that has been tagged the 'Celtic Tiger' years. Following a series of adverse shocks in 2001, export-led growth was replaced by debt-financed capital spending, as cheap credit and demand for housing led to a property and construction bubble,[1] However, deceptive as it now appears, by 2007 the Irish economy appeared to be in good stead. The figures for economic growth, unemployment and inflation were 4.4 per cent, 4.6 per cent and 4.9 per cent respectively. The respective figures for 2009 are now estimated by the Central Bank of Ireland's *Quarterly Bulletin* as -11.3 per cent, 12 per cent and -4.5 per cent. By any standards, the economy has been hit by an unprecedented set of adverse economic shocks.

The reasons for this downturn will no doubt be assessed and debated by economists and commentators for many years to come. Indeed, many of the chapters in this book provide an assessment of what went wrong. The broad bones of it is that 'irrational exuberance' with regard to house prices, a massive inflow of cheap money from the inter-bank market, a failure of the regulatory system and an unwarranted belief in free market ideology combined to create a housing and construction bubble. This bubble peaked at the same time as the international recession and financial crisis of 2007. Once the flow of interbank credit froze the property bubble burst and this precipitated a domestic banking crisis and the sudden unavailability of bank credit. The result was a dramatic fall in house prices and in bank equity prices and a significant negative wealth effect. When we add to this negative wealth effect a general lack of confidence and poor expectations about the future (the 'fear factor'), and years of lost price competitiveness, the overall result is a severe downturn. The Central Bank of Ireland estimated a *fall* in consumer spending and investment of 7.2 per cent and 34 per cent respectively in 2009.

The downturn resulted in a large fiscal deficit as tax revenues collapsed, and spending on social welfare increased. Constrained by the European Union's Growth and Stability Pact, the government could not embark on any form of Keynesian fiscal stimulus and was, instead, forced to introduce a number of deflationary measures. In 2009, public sector workers were subject to income and pension levies and, in January 2010, cuts in gross pay. It is estimated that public sector salaries are down by between 13 per cent and 21 per cent over the twelve months to January 2010. This deflationary fiscal policy has undoubtedly compounded the recession, but the hope is that the downward movement of wages and prices will help restore competitiveness in the medium term. So far the only form of stimulus is borrowing to bail out Ireland's banking system with the creation of a 'bad bank', the National Asset Management Agency (NAMA). (This borrowing is being kept off the national balance sheet through the creation of a 'Special Purpose Vehicle'.)

The road to recovery will be protracted and will involve further reductions in standards of living. It is in this context that our chapters are written. Ireland faces stark choices, and it is hoped that the views and opinions presented in this book provide policymakers with a balanced, and thoughtful, insight into understanding the economic crisis and designing strategies for recovery.

Chapter Synopses

Michael O'Sullivan writes of Ireland's 'great transformations', from Celtic cub to economic miracle to burst bubble. O'Sullivan traces the transformation in Ireland's economic and social fortunes through its long history and relative to the booms and busts of other economies. He highlights how Ireland has so far failed to answer 'the global question': how do small states survive and thrive in a globalised world? With the next ten years in mind, O'Sullivan underlines the need for deep-seated reform and rejuvenation of Ireland's key economic, political and social institutions, leading to a 'Second Republic'

K.P.V. O'Sullivan focuses on the financial supervisory regime in Ireland, encompassing regulation and corporate governance. He shows that while the Irish banking crisis stemmed from the contraction in domestic property and the US sub-prime crisis, its roots can be found in the inadequate risk management practices of Irish banks and the failure of the Financial Regulator to supervise these practices effectively. He recommends that the Financial Regulator should adopt a meta-risk regulatory framework in the future and reorganise the institutional structures associated with financial supervision to facilitate better risk management practices in the Irish banking system.

'We have turned the corner', Finance Minister Brian Lenihan told the Dáil, Ireland's parliament, while delivering his December 2009 Budget. Morgan Kelly's chapter on the Irish credit and property market, however, makes it abundantly clear that we have not, as yet, turned any corner toward recovery. Facilitated by easy access to funding from the interbank market, Irish commercial banks significantly increased lending to the property sector from the mid-1990s onwards. This, in turn, was the primary reason for the dramatic rise in property prices over the next ten years. When the property price bubble ended in 2006, the Irish commercial banks quickly found themselves facing a solvency crisis as a large proportion of property-related loans ceased to perform. Kelly argues that while the government-backed bad bank, the National Asset Management Agency, may address the problem of large losses on development loans, it does not deal with the problem of heavy reliance on interbank funding and the potentially large losses on mortgages in the future. He argues that the commercial banks have little option but to shrink their balance sheets by repaying debt and this can only lead to further falls in bank credit. He paints a picture of the commercial banks in the future relying on government guarantees and the forbearance of the European Central Bank (ECB) and 'committed solely to reducing their own debts'. However, as the economic recession worsens and mortgage defaults rise, it could be that the 'Irish banking system is too big to save' as the government has exhausted its resources rescuing the losses on development loans.

Ronan Lyons describes the evolution of Ireland's property market from boom to bust, and argues that poor quality of information in the property market contributed in no small part to the severity of the early twenty-first century boom and bust in Ireland. He contends that better information in the property market in Ireland will contribute to more sustainable economic growth in the future, citing examples from other key economic systems that show the potential for a twenty-first century approach.

Colm McCarthy compares Ireland's first fiscal crisis in the 1980s with the second, and current, crisis in 2009–10. He points out that the two periods are very different as, contrary to the first crisis, there is now a banking collapse, a worldwide credit crunch and a contraction in world trade. His re-examination of the first fiscal crisis causes him to challenge some well-worn myths. He argues, for example, that the 'slash and burn' fiscal policy of 1987, which is frequently cited as a factor underlying the Celtic Tiger economy, never really happened and is, in effect, 'journalistic invention'. Instead, the devaluation of 1986 and the tax amnesty of 1988 were pivotal factors in turning around the economy. The 'economic bubble' that prevailed from 2001 to 2007 was due to failures in public expenditure control and the management, regulation and supervision of the banking system, and to the international downturn. Also, after entry into economic and monetary union (EMU), Irish economists focused more on microeconomic issues and less on macroeconomic issues such as external balance and budgetary policy. Following the bursting of the bubble, the deterioration in the public finances was extremely rapid as tax revenue collapsed while real current spending continued to increase at a rapid rate. The main lesson from the first fiscal crisis is that little will be achieved in delaying fiscal adjustment. Given the financial forbearance of the ECB and the wholesale markets, the European Commission has allowed the government until 2014 to get borrowing back to 3 per cent of gross domestic product (GDP). It is not in the country's best interest to spin out the adjustment until 2018 as debt service costs could increase and the exit debt–gross national product (GNP) ratio would exceed 100 per cent. What is required is to re-balance the economy by bringing tax and expenditure shares in GNP to that prevailing ten years ago. On the expenditure side, consolidation has to entail significant cuts in public sector pay and possibly social transfers.

Michael Taft shows that there is another path to recovery. In a stimulating chapter, he debunks many of the myths promulgated in defence of fiscal contraction, arguing that such strategies, have, and will continue, to depress output and employment. Instead, he shows that a combination of investment stimulus and restructuring can achieve the interrelated goals of economic growth and fiscal stabilisation.

The chapter by Anthony Leddin uses the pay awards under the various national wage agreements to construct a new wage index. This index is then used to examine the interrelationship between wages, unemployment and inflation in Ireland and the role of domestic factors in the inflation process. Both the New Keynesian Phillips Curve (NKPC) and the Triangle Phillips Curve (TPC) models were estimated and variables representing inertia and persistence effects and lagged real earnings were found to be important determinants of nominal wages. A seminal point in the process occurred in October 1999, when Irish inflation increased from 1.4 per cent to over 7 per cent. This provided the catalyst for a standard Phillips curve wage–inflation spiral after this date and, combined with an appreciating Euro exchange rate, a significant loss of price competitiveness. This left the economy in a very vulnerable position when the recession hit in 2007. It is argued that a key element in any 'strategy for recovery' should be the adoption of a specific policy relating to inflation targeting and ultimately price competitiveness.

Eoin Gahan's chapter returns to the theme of competitiveness, but Eoin looks at the longer-term opportunities and threats for Ireland's competitiveness. Eoin shows convincingly that Ireland needs sustained investment to prosper; and investment in increased infrastructural capacity must continue to be a priority, particularly in energy and telecommunications. He points to the importance of policy analysis and foresight in an increasingly complex and competitive global economy, and stresses the need for enhanced capacities in order to allow good decisions to be made quickly. As next-generation networks (NGNs) develop, he emphasises their crucial role in competitiveness for the future, and advocates action in this field, using state assets as the basis for an NGN, in order to develop the advanced services that are enabled by NGNs.

Edward Nell explores the theory and implications of an employer of last resort (ELR) scheme, which has not been tried in Ireland to date. With unemployment rising rapidly over the 2007–10 period, and full employment a stated long-term societal goal, the idea of an ELR set of policies is timely and warrants serious consideration.

Vela Velupillai describes the theoretical shortcomings of the currently fashionable crisis theories of Hyman Minsky and his adherents. Velupillai shows that 'Minsky moments' are nothing of the kind, and in a wide-ranging and historically informed chapter, he shows how Minsky's theory may not complete the Keynesian vision of capitalist crises. The relevance for Ireland of Velupillai's analysis is simple: the costs of a theoretical mistake transformed into a poorly applied policy may be severe.

Stephen Kinsella's chapter on cycles, crises and uncertainty highlights the role of high levels of personal debt in potentially stalling an economic recovery and a return to balanced growth.

Brendan Walsh examines the relationship between demography and Ireland's economic growth, past and future. While recognising the importance of feedback effects, he takes issue with the view that economic growth in Ireland has been to any great extent exogenously driven by population growth. Instead, based on a long-run perspective, he argues that net migration is responsive to economic conditions in Ireland and in neighbouring economies. The rate of natural increase, although subject to the secular forces that have influenced it in other rich economies, has also shown responsiveness to the country's economic performance. In terms of the current economic crisis, he assesses the impact of demographic fundamentals on the housing market and concludes that the ageing of the population will reduce the net growth in demand for housing over the next fifteen years. If net emigration resumes on any significant scale, the demographic determinants underlying the housing market will further weaken.

Ireland's Bubble: The Great Transformation

Michael O'Sullivan[1]

The Great Transformation, Again

It is some time since Ireland has experienced a recession, let alone an economic depression. To younger generations this experience will be shocking,
and will jolt their expectations of the kind of wealth and lifestyle they can
hope to enjoy in the future. To older generations, the onset of recession is a
reminder that the totality of Ireland's economic history is one of underachievement. Indeed, in the long-run of history, the boom of the past
twenty years looks nothing more than a bubble, or a boil. The key question
is whether it was an anomaly, or the start of more promising era.

The view here is that the bursting of Ireland's economic bubble is a necessary coming of age and that the current downturn must provide time and
reason for reflection and a renewal of the institutions that make up the
state. Ireland is a developed country with an adolescent economy, and awk-
ward and sometimes ugly growing pains are to be expected. At the same
time, we need to keep a careful, strategic eye on the future and accept that
some very profound structural changes are necessary in order to meet future
challenges. Above all, the political and policymaking infrastructure has to
change, if it is not to act as a handbrake on economic, social and human
development.

Ireland's economy and society have undergone a 'great transformation'
in the past twenty years, of which two broad stages can be identified. The
first 'catch-up' phase involved a coupling of the country to the very powerful forces of globalisation (e.g. US multinationals), while the second saw

the flourishing of the domestic economy with the tailwind of low real (inflation adjusted) interest rates.

While the first phase saw Ireland grow in confidence, the second arguably witnessed it becoming complacent, uncompetitive and dazzled by its own unexpected success. This is standard behaviour in economies that are in the full throes of an economic bubble, though at times the real estate frenzy, showy materialism and careless policymaking reached excessive levels.

In this respect the catharsis of a recession should help to bring expectations and behaviour back down to more normal levels, and, it is to be hoped, will make Irish people more appreciative of their long economic (as opposed to political) history and their policymakers more focused on the long-run economic and social future.

A less optimistic view sees the collapse of this economic bubble and the policy response to this now threaten a second, negative 'great transformation'.

This chapter tracks Ireland's first 'great transformation' from a long-run underperformer to 'miracle' model economy, and then examines its credentials as a contender for the pantheon of asset price bubbles. The collapse of the Irish economy has brought a number of slow-moving changes into sharper focus, not least Ireland's position as a poster child for the Anglo-Saxon socio-economic model.

In the changing post-credit-crisis world, we argue that Ireland needs to examine its position with respect to emerging nations and new economic trends, and where once it was held up as the example for others to follow it needs to learn from the lessons of others. In many respects, Ireland now needs a third 'transformation', starting with a rescue of its economy, building an economic recovery and profound institutional reform that embody the notion of a 'Second Republic'.

Reversal of Fortune

Irish economic history from the Middle Ages to as recently as the 1980s has been a tale of sustained and painful economic underachievement. Though a good deal of this can be ascribed to its political status up to the early twentieth century, Ireland's economic underdevelopment persisted for at least fifty years after independence. For instance, going back as far as 1500, the ratio of Ireland's gross domestic product (GDP) per capita relative to that of Britain was 0.74 times, which then fell to 0.63 in 1600, contracted further to 0.57 in 1700 and reached 0.51 times in the immediate aftermath of the Famine in 1850.[2]

One hundred years later there was no discernible improvement in this relationship, which remained close to 0.5 times until the 1970s, meaning that for most of the last three centuries, Britain was twice as wealthy as Ireland on a per capita basis. Comparisons with other European countries reveal a similar, though slightly less unequal, picture over time.

Yet from the late 1980s onwards something unexpected happened. Growth took hold and has continued uninterrupted ever since. Having lagged the British and other European economies by so much for so long, Ireland caught up quickly, with the ratio of Irish output to that of Britain jumping from a level of 0.74 in 1975 to 1.15 by 2001. By 2003 gross national product (GNP) in real terms was five times the level it was at in 1960).[3]

Although many of the factors that are now perceived to have laid the foundations for this period of growth (which labours under the cliché of the 'Celtic Tiger') are now well documented, there were few signs in the late 1980s that Ireland had such a promising economic future and very few, if any, policymakers and politicians behaved as if this would be the case. Indeed, the initial surprise of Ireland's growth spurt is hinted at in the language used by economists to explain the turnaround in Ireland's fortunes.

The long-awaited flourishing of our economy begs a number of important questions, most of which have an important bearing on the future of the Irish economy and society. Did Irish policymakers discover a policy elixir that drives impressive rates of growth and that can now serve as a model for many other countries, or, more simply, is Ireland's phenomenal growth a benign accident and mostly attributable to external, global factors?

If Ireland's economic growth spurt is largely the result of Irish policy-making genius then we have little to fear, safe in the knowledge that policymakers have the ability to successfully navigate future challenges. If, on the other hand, Ireland's economic miracle is more attributable to (overdue) luck combined with the positive influence of deep-seated international forces like globalisation then we have more to worry about, as this relatively small, open economy is very much at the mercy of the forces of globalisation.

The view here is that the credit, or perhaps blame as some might have it, for Ireland's economic miracle falls somewhere between unintended domestic policymaking 'genius' and the invisible helping hand of international economic, political and financial trends. It might well be argued that the same policymakers are using the opportunity of the credit crisis to rid themselves of the burden of the 'genius' label. What has become more clear in recent years is the way in which these factors have combined to supercharge the Irish economy and mark its coming of age such that, gorged by cheap capital, it has fed off itself and produced an Irish version of the many asset bubbles that have popped up through history. While Ireland's boom and bust economic profile may seem unique to many Irish people, its profile fits increasingly snugly over that of economic bubbles throughout history.

Was John Law Irish?[4]

In 1841 Charles MacKay, a Scottish writer, published a book entitled *Extraordinary Popular Delusions and the Madness of Crowds*,[5] which chronicled and analysed the history of asset price bubbles going back as far as the impact of the Crusades on goods and land prices in eleventh century France.

The organising theme of the book is that asset bubbles share a common and very human template, a thread that has made it through to research by modern economists and central bankers.[6] Yet MacKay must have hoped that having read his tome the public would be enlightened as to the causes and pitfalls of asset bubbles and that these would cease to re-occur.

In that respect he would have been disappointed but perhaps unsurprised by the credit crisis of 2007–09, and arguably if he were alive today he would be furiously scribbling down details of the Irish property bubble, which, like Ireland's economic ascent of the past fifteen years, places it to the vanguard of the latest global economic trend. A key figure in MacKay's book and indeed in the pantheon of asset price bubbles was John Law, a Scotsman whose programme of economic and financial innovations reflated and then nearly obliterated the French economy during the Mississippi Scheme bubble period of 1719–21.[7] In general, asset price bubbles involve a large degree of collective failure of reason and judgement, though the Mississippi Scheme bubble is a rare case where the actions of a single individual were of enormous consequence.

MacKay wrote of John Law that 'the personal character and career of one man are so intimately connected with the great scheme of the years 1719 and 1720 that a history of the Mississippi madness can have no fitter introduction than a sketch of the life of its great author John Law'.[8] Other connoisseurs of asset prices bubbles, such as Garber[9] and Velde,[10] also rank Law's scheme as one of the 'mythical early bubbles'.[11]

What makes John Law fascinating today is that there are parallels between his actions and policies and those enacted in Ireland in recent years, and the lessons that the Mississippi Scheme and many other asset price bubbles have to offer Ireland and other countries are also important.

Arguably the most attractive parallel between John Law and recent Irish economic history is that both cases have in common very contradictory qualities. Law was a mixture of genius and rogue, and without too much analytical difficulty we can break the Irish economic 'miracle' into two contrasting parts: the policy-based catch-up of the period 1990–2001 (genius), and the hubristic bubble years of 2002 to present (rogue). For instance, Law's turnaround of the French economy from 1719 onwards (from 1715 it was mired in a deep recession) was referred to as a 'miracle which posterity will not believe' by one commentator[12] in much the same way as a leading (French) economist had heralded Ireland's economic leap forward as a 'miracle'.[13]

The authority on John Law is an Irishman, Antoin Murphy,[14] and he writes of Law as a gambler[15] who led a rollercoaster life (on arrival in France Law's first brush with authority saw him spend time in jail in Caen[16]), a man whose financial genius made France the most innovative country in the world with respect to banking and finance and who could be seen as a very early architect of the move away from commodity-based money (Murphy notes the resonance between the birth of Law in 1671 and the breaking of the gold standard in 1971). Similarly, MacKay underlines that Law 'understood the monetary question better than any man of his day'.[17]

Law would later be celebrated by renowned economists like Schumpeter, who placed him in the front ranks of monetary theorists of all time, but derided by others such as Montesquieu, who disdained Law's practice of 'catching the wind in balloons, which he then sold to travellers' and his entrapment to the 'blind god of chance'.[18] Karl Marx reflected that Law was 'the pleasant character mixture of swindler and prophet',[19] a remark that echoes Engel's comment that 'the worst about the Irish is that they become corruptible as soon as they stop being peasants and turn bourgeois'.[20]

Besides the vivid human parallels between Law, the few Irish policymaking geniuses and the many showy Irish oligarchs of the recent boom, there are a number of reasons why we draw parallels between Law and the Irish property bubble.

First of all, both cases show how a nation can surrender its mind and soul to an economic bubble. Beyond the vivid colour of human folly and subsequent miseries one strand is that great shifts in economic performance, and innovations in economic policy, eventually produce imbalances and externalities.

Another very important factor is the interaction between human or behavioural factors and economic theory. Simple greed, the triumph of irrationality over the rational, overconfidence, loss aversion and denial are some of the increasingly well-established facets of behavioural finance theory that were evident in France in 1720 and Ireland in the early 2000s.

More specifically, the economic changes and financial innovations sparked by Law in 1720s France have echoes in Ireland of the 2000s. Law secured the rights to collect tax revenues for the government through his Compagnie d'Occident and he later effectively securitised the potential revenues from this. The price of the Compagnie d'Occident had the high octane ingredients of both a potentially risky, derivative claim on a land and commodity development project in French Louisiana and a lower cost of capital with the conversion of its short-term debt into long-term debt.

The bubbles of the 1720s also illustrated the effects of lop-sided distribution of information, manipulation of facts and figures, and insider trading – all have featured in modern bubbles and financial crises. Moreover, human behaviour during the bubbles of the 1720s – in terms of propensity toward greed, denial and appetite for leverage – also strikes a chord with recent bubbles. Similarly, one study of Law notes a series of examples of gauche materialism, with 'the new rich serving soup in a church offertory basin, sugar being dispensed from an incense burner and salt from chalices'.[21] This could well be a satire of the Celtic Tiger.

By the time Law had silver for paper currency, the viability of the Scheme was contingent on asset prices (paper shares) remaining high. A similar pattern is evident in the United States (US) and to an extent the Irish housing and mortgage markets in the past ten years, where financial 'innovation' created enormous amounts of debt and derivatives based on inflated house prices.

Law's Scheme came undone because the growth in money supply and in asset prices was not matched by real economic growth and the failure of the economy of French Louisiana to live up to expectations. This led Law to conjure support mechanisms where low interest loans were given to investors (very similar to that at Anglo Irish Bank in 2008), with shares in the Company used as collateral.[22]

Like property prices in Ireland during the 2000s and asset prices (like equities) in other asset bubbles, share prices in 1720s France were wildly overvalued. Velde estimates that the scale of overvaluation of share prices was between two to five times their true value.[23] As Law's financial world fell apart, the price of 'Compagnie' shares collapsed by close to 90 per cent (from a peak in December 1720 to a low in February 1722), which is comparable to the decline in value of US collateralised mortgage debt from 2007 to late 2008.

The wreckage of Law's Scheme took some time to clear away. The principle vehicle employed here was called the Visa – a structure that today's economists would recognise as a 'bad bank' vehicle.[24] The aim of the Visa was to extract the paper liabilities of Law's company from the economic system and convert these into bonds, which in turn would introduce liquidity back into the parched financial system. In total, of 2,800 million livres issued through Law's Scheme, 2,200 million ended up in the hands of the Visa agency and were later converted back into bonds. The Visa paid a significant discount for the livres – between 20 and –25 per cent of the original issue value. Ireland's National Asset Management Agency (NAMA) aims to do something similar, though it is paying a comparatively small discount for property loans.

With the future of the Irish economy in mind it also must be noted that Law's Scheme wrought long-running structural changes in the French and British economies. For instance, having initially copied the Bank of England Company and East India Company models, Law's legal, financial and corporate innovations were themselves copied by the British with the incorporation of the South Sea Company. The subsequent collapse of the South Sea Company then led to the Bubble Act of 1720, which, like some of the regulatory changes proposed today, signalled the encroachment of the state into the business world and a desire to limit speculation, as well as create large 'national champion' companies. Similar legislation was enacted in France to make 'entrepreneurship' more difficult.

Anatomy of a Bubble

These patterns have been repeated over and over though history, key examples being the railroad bubbles in England in the 1840s and in the US at the end of the nineteenth century, the Florida property bubble in the mid-1920s, the US stock market bubble of the late 1920s, Japan's stock market and property bubbles of the 1980s, and more recently the Asian equity and currency bubbles of the late 1990s, not to finally forget the dot.com bubble, which ended some six years ago. This long and colourful history of bubbles provides a template which we can fit over the Irish economy of the past ten years.

The first stage in a bubble is what we can call 'the favourable shock'. In many cases it is a dramatic change in economic policy or a technological shift that heralds the arrival of a new economic regime or technology. For example, the Mississippi bubble was born out of the creation of paper money and the opportunities offered by the New World (America), while railway booms in the United Kingdom (UK) and US in the nineteenth century were led by technology change and infrastructure build. More recently, the dot.com bubble of the late 1990s was driven by technological change and de-regulation in the telecoms industry. In Ireland the favourable shock was the initial wave of growth driven by foreign direct investment into the country.

One of the key changes brought about by a positive economic shock is that it lifts expectations of future economic and earnings growth and, with these, expectations of prosperity. Rhetoric matches these developments, with some economies referred to as miracles (in Ireland's and Law's cases), or 'Number One', as was the case of Japan in the 1980s.[25]

This first phase of a typical bubble can be classified as a boom or growth period, and not strictly a bubble. What helps to turn a boom into a bubble is more often than not the supply of easy money (excess liquidity), in the forms of expansionary monetary policy, lax credit standards and direct lending to speculators. In this way cheap money and easy credit are the monetary equivalent of throwing petrol on a fire, and there are relatively few bubbles where easy availability of money did not play an important role. Law's alchemic experiment in turning commodity-based currency into paper currency set free the genie of money supply, especially as further money growth had very weak foundations.

Cheap money (and rising asset values) allows companies and households to take on more leverage, and this process is often aided and abetted by a general lowering of credit standards. Easy credit often leads to the clustering of bubbles so that equity and house market bubbles often crop up in the same place (such as Japan in the 1980s; a 2003 International Monetary Fund (IMF) study[26] is particularly detailed on this point).

In Ireland, real interest rates (measured by the money market rate less consumer price inflation), averaged 0 per cent from 1998 to 2001 and fell to close to -4 per cent in 2000, having been as high as 10 per cent in 1985 and 15 per cent in the period around the first Gulf War.[27] This 'free money' and the expansion in credit (Central Bank figures show growth in credit card and mortgage debt in the high 20 per cent levels for much of the past ten years) that allowed it to flow through the economy go a long way to explaining the boom in the domestic economy over the past ten years. In a more conventional monetary policy framework interest rates would have been much higher but during this period the European Central Bank was effectively setting interest rates for the sluggish economies of Germany and France rather than Ireland, and in Ireland regulation of the banks and their credit policies was poor.

Bubble Trouble

The next typical stage of a bubble is when euphoric appetite for risk chases high returns and investment becomes speculation. A quote from J.M. Keynes, written some eighty years ago, sets out this change of mood and could well describe the Irish economy of the past ten years:

> [T]he position is serious when enterprise becomes the bubble on a whirlpool of speculation. When the capital development of a country becomes a by-product of the activities of a casino, the job is likely to be ill-done.[28]

As the typical bubble gathers momentum, people come to believe in the arrival of a greater fool (i.e. other investors would take the over-valued assets off their hands at a high price). Such a belief, together with specious supporting arguments such as 'the world has changed' or 'this time it's different'[29] permits a ratcheting upwards of expectations, and sets loose 'a mood of exhilarant optimism and wild speculative frenzy', as J.K. Galbraith termed it.[30]

At this stage emotion and giddy expectation are the drivers of investment and consumption. The bubble is fully formed, gathers momentum and, like the Irish property bubble of the past ten years, acquires a logic of its own. One very pointed example of this was a statement from former Taoiseach Bertie Ahern that those warning of the property bubble should 'commit suicide'.[31] Equally, a few warnings in the French parliament during the Mississippi period were ignored.[32]

Unsurprisingly, Law's bubble is also peppered with examples of this kind of fervour and apparently throughout France in 1720 there was 'no sort of extravagance of which even a wise man was not capable of.'[33]

The existence of the typical bubble is often confirmed by evidence of its side effects (as one author notes, 'a housing boom in Houston is an oil boom in drag';[34] in Ireland's case its economic boom was a housing boom in drag). To return to the time of the Mississippi Scheme, those who had succeeded in their speculations spent wildly, and the prices of silver, tapestries and jewellery rose rapidly. This orgy of consumption showed the rich to be 'very fond of luxury, which has never been indulged in to such an extent as it is at present'.[35]

As a result:

> [T]he looms of the country worked with unusual activity to supply rich laces, silks, broad-cloth, and velvets, which being paid for in abundant paper, increased in price fourfold. Bread, meat and vegetables were sold at prices greater than had ever before been known ... new houses were built in every

direction; an illusory prosperity shone over the land and so dazzled the eyes of the whole nation, that none could see the dark cloud on the horizon.[36]

The wave of materialism that has taken hold in Ireland in the past fifteen years is not unlike the conspicuous consumption that gripped early eighteenth-century France.

When a bubble is in its final stage it becomes very difficult to meaningfully act against it or stop it. Rational voices and analysis based on fundamentals find little audience. The herd mentality[37] goes into overdrive and this stage often sees the sharpest and most bewildering rise in asset prices.

While bubbles are hard to define and identify, crashes are not, and to an extent one might say that you know them when you see them.[38] There is no one cause associated with the ending of bubbles, though tighter monetary policy or credit policies are often the culprits. Instead, bubbles seem to reach an end simply when a series of factors synchronise. In Ireland's case it seems that the tightening of credit conditions brought about by the global credit crisis was the decisive factor.

If history is again a guide the unwinding of the Irish property market bubble is likely to be as brutal as the expansion was giddy. IMF studies show that on average house price corrections tend to last for four years. By the standards of the UK and Japan, which have experienced severe property bubbles in the past twenty years, it is likely that Irish property values, and activity in the construction sector, will be depressed for some time to come.

It is inevitable that the fall from grace of the Irish economy will bring into question many of the factors that are thought to have driven its growth in the first place. This long overdue introspection will be healthy, provided it does occur in a sensible fashion. Too often, sharp economic downturns breed economic nationalism, protectionism and a nervous adherence to short-term policymaking.

What Did We Do Right?[39]

One starting point in such an analysis is to ask how the Irish economy broke from its long pattern of underperformance in the first place. Looking back on the past twenty or so years we can divide the Irish 'miracle' into two broad parts: the first wave based on investment in Ireland by foreign multinationals and increasingly stable investment climate, and the second the flourishing of the domestic economy as aided and abetted by low real interest rates.

The latter part is easier to understand, and as the earlier sections have outlined, it has largely respected the patterns of previous asset price bubbles. The first part is more difficult to analyse, as it is hard to spot a single factor that ignited Ireland's economy after so many years of slumber. A salad of economic factors, both domestic and international, seems to have combined to drive the turnaround in Ireland's economy. At this stage a consensus has emerged that identifies the main domestic factors in this mix as Ireland's education system, credit growth, the role of the Industrial Development Authority (IDA), Ireland's membership of the European Union (EU) and its flexible labour market.

What is interesting from the point of view of those who look to Ireland as an economic model is that most of these factors were in place during some of the bleakest years for the Irish economy, as well as the best. To a large degree they were catalysed by outside factors, principally by a falling cost of capital, the trend toward the opening up of international markets and trade, diminished geopolitical risk and the advent of new technologies – all of the ingredients of what are now taken to drive economic globalisation.

At the same time, there is very little evidence to suggest that Irish policymakers foresaw the boom in growth that started in the 1990s as the state of physical infrastructure, institutional development and microeconomic policies all lagged developments in the economy. This suggests that Ireland's politicians were neither the architects nor masters of its economic destiny, and this issue should be one of the central political economy questions in Ireland for some time to come.

What Ireland's policymakers did manage to create, often with a leaning toward social and political goals, was a country with a high-quality intangible infrastructure.[40] Intangible infrastructure is 'the set of factors that develop human capability and permit the easy and efficient growth of business activity'.[41] Adam Smith puts it in more colourful terms:

> Little else is requisite to carry a state to the highest degree of opulence from the lowest barbarism but peace, easy taxes, and a tolerable administration of justice: all the rest being brought about by the natural course of things.[42]

Finance is a good case in point of the power of intangible factors. Laws (e.g. Glass-Steagall in 1933, Sarbanes-Oxley in 2002, both in the US), regulations and standards (e.g. international accounting standards) drive the way financial systems evolve and are decisive in determining why some countries and cities have strong financial sectors and others weak ones. Also, important issues such as investor protection, transparency, political stability and regulation are by nature intangible but nonetheless vital in determining the strength of banking systems and flows of capital into countries.

The Bigger Picture

At a very broad level, the rising relevance of intangible infrastructure is driven by globalisation. If we define this as the growing interdependence and integration of markets, economies and societies, then by nature much of globalisation rests on the spread of 'intangible' factors like international institutions, the diffusion and patenting of ideas, financial innovation and the diffusion of cultural trends. Amongst other things, globalisation breaks down barriers to the flow of services and information, and helps to relegate geography as a driving factor in economic development. Globalisation means that many economic and cultural activities are increasingly played out in the world as a single place, rather than within national borders.

While the nation state is still very much a viable entity, power is increasingly placed in the hands of unelected policymakers, and this is reflected in a number of quarters, such as the standardisation of accounting and financial measures. Institutionalisation increasingly seems to be replacing the role played by the gold standard, Pax Britannia and the ideological consensus that prevailed in the nineteenth century. It is manifest in bodies like the EU or IMF, and has, broadly speaking, been beneficial in preventing and resolving crises (for instance the magnitude of the role that institutions like the US Federal Reserve have played in the credit crisis has been remarkable), and in particular in placing a premium on negotiating skills rather than military power. Also, many states increasingly barter their sovereignty in return for economic benefits, the leading example being membership of the Eurozone monetary union.

What is particularly convincing about the case for 'intangible infrastructure' is that the broad trends in demographics, economics, society and geo-politics that point toward the rising importance of intangible factors are now increasingly supported by the academic literature on economics and development. In turn, this is filtering through to the policymaking and political levels and to, a large extent, countries like Sweden, Singapore and Korea are the economic poster children for this line of argument.

With its very stable political climate, business-friendly economy and general respect for 'intangibles' like the rule of law and education, Ireland had fitted well into a globalising world where, though this is now a well-won catchphrase, we hear of the 'death of geography', and 'softer' rather than hard forms of power (i.e. military strength) are more influential.

Ireland's intangible infrastructure (i.e. an educated workforce, low taxes and an uncomplicated approach to doing business) rather than its physical infrastructure is what appears to have attracted a large number of (mostly American) multinationals. In this respect, advocates of low and simplified taxation systems who point to Ireland in support of their case miss the bigger, more complicated picture. As a number of Eastern European countries have found, low taxes themselves are not the sole means of attracting foreign direct investment; they need to be coupled with a variety of other factors, such as the rule of law. Furthermore, this view is also embedded in the Lisbon Agenda, which underlined the EU's goal to become 'the most competitive and dynamic knowledge-based economy in the world, capable of sustainable economic growth with more and better jobs and greater social cohesion'.[43]

The important point here is that in the aftermath of the credit crisis, high leverage and de-regulation will most likely be replaced by more regulation and lower leverage. This means that the Irish economy will have to move away from a bubble- or casino-type economic model towards one where companies make and sell things and, importantly, innovate. In short, Ireland and its policymakers will have to revisit the notion of intangible infrastructure.

The leading example of how this goal can be achieved, at least in the minds of European policymakers, is the Nordic model. In many respects this model is shorthand for investment in the knowledge economy, education and the power of 'intangible' factors such as social contracts.

The 'Nordic model' reflects the success of longstanding socio-economic systems across the Nordic countries (Denmark, Finland, Norway and Sweden) that are founded on the values of social justice, a commitment to full employment and comprehensive welfare services. Most of the factors that support the Nordic model are specific to the region and are deeply embedded in its culture, society and politics. For instance, in Denmark, the foundations of its flexible labour market were laid over one hundred years ago (in the 1899 'Septemberforliget').

Likewise, Sweden's concept of 'the people's home' (or 'Folkhemmet') arose during early twentieth-century social democratic politics. Though many of these intangible factors are very specific to the Nordic countries, they help to illustrate the way legal, cultural and political factors can shape economies. Note of course the way in which the Swedish banking bailout model of the early 1990s has recently become fashionable.

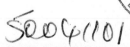

What Have We Become?

The Nordic model, though itself under pressure from globalisation, is generally seen as the 'idealised' political economic model; the others being the relatively more aggressive Anglo-Saxon one (UK, US, Australia), the more staid and safer Continental European one (France, Germany), and the perennially troubled Mediterranean one (Greece, Spain, Portugal and Italy).

Ireland is interesting in this regard in that it began the 1980s firmly in the Mediterranean category of underperforming economies, then gravitated more toward the Continental European model as policy packages like social partnerships and Eurozone membership were put in place, and since then it has taken on the trappings of the shinier free-dealing Anglo-Saxon model. In good times the Anglo-Saxon model is typically composed of a vibrant economy built at the expense of social development and cohesion, or the inverse of the European social model, though in bad times, as Ireland is now finding, it is a ramshackle debt-laden economic model subsisting in the context of relatively low social development and cohesion.

The inconsistency in Irish people's resoundingly positive views on both globalisation and Europe is that in many continental European countries the path that Ireland has pursued in its economic progress would be regarded as neo-liberal and contrary to the European social model. Irish people display very little of the aversion to globalisation that is manifest in some other European states, and their attitude does not reflect the concerns of those who are discontented with globalisation. However, the embrace of the Anglo-Saxon form of globalisation by Ireland is only now beginning to register itself politically, most notably in the rejection of the first Lisbon Treaty referendum in June 2008.

Indeed, one interesting and so far relatively unremarked upon aspect of Ireland's successful engagement with globalisation is that it has done very well in all of the areas that anti-globalists love to hate. It is a pro-American country, hosts many of the world's largest multinationals and has made a success out of a Washington consensus-style package of economic policies.

Boston, Berlin or Birmingham?

The issue of the competing influence of the Anglo-Saxon and Continental European worlds on Ireland has received little serious attention in Irish public life. At the popular level, this issue is referred to as the 'Boston or Berlin' debate, meaning whether Ireland is politically and culturally closer to the US or Europe.

In recent years, Ireland has unambiguously moved closer to the Boston end of this spectrum. For example, economic policy (e.g. deregulation, credit growth and tax reduction), government spending patterns and foreign policy (within the EU for instance) have followed the paths beaten down by the large Anglo-Saxon countries and Ireland much more resembles the Anglo-Saxon countries than the continental European ones when issues like labour market regulation and income inequality are taken into consideration.

Given these trends, placing Ireland in the Anglo-Saxon camp is appropriate, though to compare it to Boston is to flatter it. Boston is known for the excellence of its well-funded educational institutions, the high levels of research and development of its industries and its decent transport infrastructure, all of which are notably absent in Ireland. Instead of drawing parallels with Boston, perhaps a more accurate comparison is with a middle ranking region of Britain.

Though anti-Britishness is often widely and loudly expressed across Ireland, we seem more than willing to import and hungrily consume the more ugly aspects of British cultural and social life, from its popular culture to a litany of social problems like binge drinking, poor diet, large income and wealth inequalities, anti-social behaviour, drug-related crime, house price bubbles and rampant consumerism to name a few that are not manifest to the same extent in most continental European countries.

The Irish high street resembles that of Manchester or Glasgow rather than Paris or Madrid, choked by the spread of UK chain stores. There is a strong sense that Ireland has become more materialistic, a trend that is supported by evidence from consumption patterns and levels of indebtedness. The Irish and English have an increasingly shared popular culture. From boy and girl bands, to the intake from the Murdoch media, and a common appetite for the output of the US entertainment industry, the differences between the cultures are closing.

Where Are We Going and What Needs to Be Done?

Overall, a number of strands come together to support the view that socially and culturally, even though there is an Irish exception in terms of its indigenous culture, it is increasingly influenced by the Anglo-Saxon world, especially as globalisation advances. Even if Ireland is European culturally, then it is best categorised as a 'New' rather than an 'Old' European country.

One pitfall here, that is perhaps only beginning to come to light as the credit crisis deepens, is that there appears to be a very low level of awareness of the downside of Anglo-Saxon cultural and social norms, even though these are beginning to manifest themselves in a less fraternal and more unequal and ugly society. The lack of a serious debate on whether Ireland is more Anglo-Saxon or European belies the lack of a vision as to the kind of society that is desired in the long term. What is its peer group in a post-credit-crisis world? Is Ireland happy to resemble a region of Great Britain, or does it have more ambitious designs on a new peer group? The need for such a debate is all the more important in the light of the great transformation ongoing in Irish society and public life.

There is a strong sense then that Ireland has backed itself into an economic and cultural corner, from which a clear and dignified exit may be difficult. What compounds this is that any direction and leadership from political classes, the media and some commentators is lacking. A focus on the tactical at the expense of the strategic is a recurring weakness here.

It is ironic that at a time when the lazy cliché of the 'Celtic Tiger' has become a model for so many other countries (China, Chile and Bulgaria, amongst others, have sent their wise men and women to Ireland to study its economy), Ireland itself is badly in need of a lodestone to guide both its economy and its society. Indeed, as this awe has evaporated amidst the decimation of our economy by our policymakers, bankers and builders, we have become hypersensitive to what people in other countries think of us.

Who's Watching Now?

This tendency has been made worse by the fear-based nature of the campaigns in the Lisbon Treaty referenda (on the 'Yes' and 'No' sides), and by the threats advanced by the architects of NAMA that international institutions and capital markets will shun Ireland unless it undertakes this most damaging and regressive of policy options.

Taking the global view has never been easy for our political class – consider how warnings over the past five years from the Organisation for Economic Co-operation and Development (OECD) and IMF on our property and banking sector went ignored, though Irish taxpayers are now threatened with the arrival of the cost cutters from the IMF.

With very few exceptions, policymakers and politicians have responded to the economic crisis by becoming more inward-looking, rather than use the example of what other countries are doing to shed light on our own problems.

Economic and financial crises often produce this head-in-the-sand reaction, but the present danger is that Ireland is not only squandering the lessons that other countries can offer it (look at how Swiss banking regulators have navigated the financial crisis, or the way in which the American version of NAMA, the Troubled Asset Relief Program (TARP), was radically rethought), but is also losing ground in a very fast-changing post-credit-crisis world.

The brutal irony in our paranoia about Ireland's image is that very few nations outside Ireland are watching us; the rest of the world is busying itself with recovery (for example, interest rates are already rising in Israel and Australia) and driving on with finding its feet in a very changed geo-economic landscape. We need to pay more attention to this.

Before the credit crisis the world was effectively uni-polar, but the collapse in markets and in the familiar political economic geometry has crystallised a number of changes that have been building over the past decade and that are leading to a multi-polar world.

A small group of countries that we still refer to as 'emerging markets' will make up nearly half of global economic growth in the next five years. The likes of China and Brazil have learnt the lessons of their own crises in the late 1990s and now have strong balance sheets and fast-growing economies. This is in contrast to the debt-laden developed world (mostly Anglo-Saxon countries like the US and UK), where high government, banking and household debt levels will constrict growth for at least the next five years.

In some respects we can begin to think of the new world along the same lines as George Orwell, who described three zones: Oceania, Eurasia and Eastasia. Oceania is the debt-laden Anglo-Saxon world where high unemployment may struggle to recover, where consumers will be more measured in their spending patterns and where economic growth will be tame, as structural issues from run-down infrastructure to crippled regional economies (e.g. California) act as economic handbrakes.

Eurasia consists of the larger, healthier economies of the Eurozone, returning slowly but surely towards trend-level growth rates. It is a zone where the state and markets can co-exist, albeit in a dawdling fashion.

Most exciting of all is Eastasia, the vast band of emerging economies with China as its economic epicentre. The political and economic effects of 'Eastasian' growth are felt in spheres as various as African commodity countries, Australian property prices and Brazilian banks. China in particular is seeing radical changes in food tastes, land use and consumer financing. The Chinese now buy more cars than the Americans, not to mention heavy trucks and tractors.

To a growing extent, the story of China's re-emergence has echoes of other economic bubbles (in 1820 it had 32 per cent of global GDP). Remember the way people referred to our economy as a 'miracle', or to Japan in the 1980s as 'No. 1', or the way in which commentators rationalised the dot.com bubble as 'it is different this time'?

In this respect it is to be hoped that the Chinese as well as officials in the relatively new G20 body will lean against the long-held view of developed-world central bankers that asset bubbles are hard to spot and harder still to deflate, and that the best way to tackle them is to clean them up once they have burst.

One new development here is that the shock and awe of the credit crisis is sparking a debate on this issue and, importantly, spurring new banking legislation. Unfortunately, there is very little rigorous analysis of this, or different scenarios for the level and nature of global growth, or what the indebtedness of the UK means for us, or the implications of the weak dollar, in either the NAMA business plan or the government's economic analysis.

Instead of obsessing about the outside world looking in at us, we need to pay more attention to the new trends and rules of the post-credit-crisis world.

What does this mean in practice? We could, for example, partially outsource regulation of our banking system to bodies like the European Central Bank (ECB), OECD or Bank for International Settlements (BIS), allow new and foreign financial institutions to operate in Ireland, rethink our assumptions of what multinationals will look like and where they will invest, learn from financial crises in other countries and use foreign expertise to make infrastructure projects more efficient.

Since the onset of the credit crisis we have been victim to a series of grave policy errors, mistakes that will leave a nation partitioned by wealth inequalities and moral perspectives. In particular, the passage of NAMA will produce a structurally weak economy and a darker society that will cast us adrift in a faster-moving, speedily changing world. The last thing we should worry about is our image abroad, but what lessons we can still learn from others.

In this respect there are three challenges: first, to rescue Ireland from its bad banks, 'property entrepreneurs' and politicians while managing the deflation of its bubble economy; second, to lay the ground for a meaningful and durable economic recovery; and third, to profoundly reform the existing institutions of the state while building new ones that equip Ireland to act independently in a globalised world.

Rescue, Recovery and Reform

Allowing the Irish economy to adjust and de-leverage from its bubble in an orderly manner is going to be hard. Entrenched levels of denial need to be broken – denial that there was a bubble in the first place, denial that high levels of growth will not quickly reoccur. As the history of bubbles past shows, the breaking of denial usually comes when markets inflict overwhelming pain on policymakers and consumers. In the Irish context, it is unfortunate, though likely, that expectations will be only be 'normalised' once a very sizeable correction in the housing market is behind us, and once indicators like bankruptcies and unemployment have risen to levels probably not seen since the 1980s.

Policymakers do not yet appear to be attuned to a post-bubble Ireland. The majority of policy actions to date, such as the banning of short selling, the issuing of guarantees to all of the Irish banks, the nationalisation of Anglo Irish bank and the establishment of the National Asset Management Agency (NAMA), have been reactive, myopic and have more generally displayed an air of overconfidence that each bold action had saved the day, and a blustering assurance that the worst was over and the recovery is in sight. Over the course of the credit crisis, the litany of policy failures in Ireland is in contrast to the more successful strategic thinking adopted by other small countries.

The attempted rescue of the banks has merely shifted risk from their balance sheets to that of the state. Indeed one could suggest that the establishment of NAMA institutionalises the logic of the housing bubble in that it mistakenly aims to extract bad property-related loans from bank balance sheets. A national bank or even single, large 'nationalised' bank may well have been a more elegant way forward here.

The ongoing tendency to focus on the property sector is dangerous. Economic history and recent studies from bodies like the IMF[44] show it is rare that bubbles can be successfully reflated and that most often they need to be allowed to fully unwind. Thus with regard to the property sector, the government must avoid bailouts of any kind – particularly for builders, who are keen to unload some of their debt and housing stock. The exception is at the lower end of the market, where a steep, prolonged fall in house prices could sow the seeds of future social problems. Infrastructure such as public transport and schools needs to be built around new housing estates and conurbations, where developers' zeal has led planners' aptitude.

Some but not all of the rescue of the Irish economy will depend on external factors, such as the recovery in global trade and the alleviation of the stresses in the global banking system. However, high levels of government and household indebtedness mean that Irish economic growth over the next five years will have a low correlation to global growth, especially growth in emerging economies.

In this respect, the second challenge of generating a meaningful recovery and pinpointing Ireland's place on the political economic map will be more difficult. Ireland's economy no longer has the support of many of the factors that drove its super performance in the last twenty years, and in particular many of the multinationals that provided the initial bedrock of support for Ireland's economic spurt will themselves change in structure and focus in the post-credit-crisis world.

Ireland must also rediscover its competitiveness, which has deteriorated as the hubris in its property and construction sectors has helped inflate prices and expectations. In this regard, bringing down high public expectations of the kind of lifestyle, wages and economic growth people can enjoy is going to be a very difficult but critical test of political leadership.

An important and related issue is how the balance of power within the economy needs to be changed. At one stage, the property and construction sectors accounted for nearly 30 per cent of Ireland's output, although the real estate market is arguably more of a 'casino' economy than a real and productive one. Ireland's economy needs to be weaned off this sector. And while remaining cognisant of the role of foreign multinationals as pistons of its economy, Ireland needs to focus on expanding the number of domestic industries that have relatively high organic growth. These include software and green technology firms.

In this respect, one advantage for Ireland is its pragmatic and entrepreneurial business class and business-friendly investment climate. Yet Ireland needs to spend more money and intellectual energy on encouraging more innovative and research-intensive industries. At the same time, important segments of the economy such as the financial services sector need to be pushed up the value chain to avoid the threat of competition from countries like India. Ireland should be attracting investment managers, for example, not back office functions for hedge funds.

A further challenge for Irish policymakers and academics here is to solve the puzzle of long-standing private underinvestment in Irish industry and enterprise and excessively high investment is the speculative property sector.

If Ireland's economy is to grow durably into the future then its economic policymaking framework needs a complete remaking. Again, this must be done with the guidance of international economists and institutions like the ECB and with the wider involvement of domestic academics, business-people and foreign multinationals operating in Ireland. Functions like regulation and governance need to be 'outsourced' to multinational bodies. The overall goal should be to achieve stable, broad-based economic growth while managing the economic side effects of international markets and trade on Ireland.

Specifically, one institutional innovation that is badly needed is that fiscal or microeconomic policy needs to be adapted to offset the effects of Eurozone interest rates. When these are too high, fiscal policy and regulation need to dampen down its effects, such as slowing the flow of credit in the economy, or reining in specific economic activities where growth is simply too high. It is easy to say so with hindsight but such an approach could well have halted the bubble in the property and construction sectors.

On the other hand, when interest rates are prohibitively high, tax and export credits, labour market incentives and capital market development are just some of the measures that can re-invigorate growth in certain areas of the economy.

This approach is new and complex, and has relatively few precedents. One could point to the individual states and municipal authorities across the USA, though their situation is nothing as complicated as some of the smaller Eurozone nations. At the same time, countries on the periphery of the Eurozone, like the Baltic states, or the Gulf states, who themselves are planning a currency union, could have much to learn from such an approach.

In practical terms, this kind of programme would be run jointly by the Central Bank and the Department of Finance, with, say, the Central Bank having some formal role in indicating whether Eurozone interest rates are too 'hot' or 'cold' for the Irish economy, and the Department of Finance, or another independent, transparent body (a type of Council of Economic Advisors) recommending specific microeconomic policy actions. This might also take some of the politics out of policymaking, though this is an entirely different problem, and well beyond the scope of this chapter.

The basic goal here is to avoid a boom–bust type economic cycle and to foster a more stable economic profile under which organic service and industrial sector growth can stem. A necessary condition of putting a plan like this into action is that Ireland has complete freedom over fiscal measures like corporate taxes and not less, as some of its Eurozone neighbours would prefer. Loss of monetary independence has created its own problems, and loss of fiscal policy would make these a lot worse.

Reform – The Second Republic[45]

Major economic crises often provide the context and motivation for fundamental philosophical and institutional changes in policymaking – from

Meiji Japan in the 1860s to the Thatcher era in 1980s Britain. In a similar respect, Ireland needs reform. The bursting of its bubble and the lacklustre political response to it underline the need for a large-scale reassessment and renewal of political values and structures.

It may not be too much to say that Irish society and public life have lost touch with the values of those who established the Republic. Ireland's economic depression is exposing further the hubris of the recent past, and the many social, political and economic problems that have gone unattended in the past ten years. This, together with the lack of a convincing strategic response to the crisis, suggests that a renewal of our republic is needed. In short, we need to start thinking about what a second republic might look like.

In more detail, some of the reasons why our republic needs to regenerate are that many long-standing institutions are malfunctioning, various pillars of excellence are crumbling and the values of Irish society have become less republican in the traditional sense.

From an institutional point of view, the failure of the Irish banks and of the institutions and mechanisms that were supposed to oversee them is the one that stands out. A deeper failure is the lack of serious strategic thinking on the part of the political and policymaking classes, not just in the past six months but in a habitual way. By and large, the skills and incentives of our political class draw them toward small, local issues and leave them unprepared for 'bigger picture' ones. The political havoc sown by the smaller political parties during the Lisbon Treaty debates was a warning signal of where the abilities and motivation of the mainstream political class lay.

There is also a sense that the moral paradigm shift that took place in Irish politics from the 1970s onwards has now caught up with us. Moral courage, accountability and leadership are in short supply.

At the same time, many of the institutional successes that drove our economic success are themselves beginning to falter. For example, education is widely accepted to be one of the bedrocks of Ireland's economic success, though in recent years the state has invested less in it, relatively speaking. Educational standards, especially in maths and science, are unremarkable by comparison to most other European and many Asian countries.

In addition, long-held satisfaction with our status as an EU member state has become embittered in recent years, and is set to be severely tested by the stresses brought on by the credit crisis. In general, from the points of view of foreign policy and economics, it is not at all clear that Ireland is well prepared for a post-credit-crisis world.

From a purist, traditional republican point of view, Irish society has ducked and dived away from the values of equality, fraternity and liberty over the past twenty years. The cohesion of a previously fraternal society is breaking down as trust in institutions withers, and as levels of crime and anti-social behaviour rise. Despite the wealth created by Ireland's economic boom, its distribution has changed little in thirty years. Serious inequalities remain and on many socio-economic measures Ireland is more comparable to some of the poorer Mediterranean states than the 'model' Nordic countries.

If we really do want to live in a republic, how do we get back on track? A good starting point is the definition of a republic by the (Irish) philosopher Philip Pettit as simply 'a state where citizens are free from domination'.[46] This definition is particularly relevant in the context of today's credit crisis as it points toward a type of republic that is able to shield its citizens from powerful external forces such as financial markets or even global organised crime, or potentially where the state acts to check the forces that might lead its citizens to be dominated by speculation and rising expectations of wealth, as has happened in Ireland in the recent past.

While this sounds theoretical, the practical implications of a second republic are increasingly apparent. Here are a few proposals: a smaller Dáil that focuses on 'big picture' national and international issues; a Presidency with more power and resources; elevate local politics to the provincial from county level, and attract better qualified and more accountable local politicians.

We must also institute an unambiguous legal framework to oversee political corruption and to govern the interaction between commerce and the state. Upgrading the technical skills of politicians and policymakers is also very important. Both groups need a deeper grounding in technical areas like economics, the sciences and management, for example. Something along the lines of a 'Grand École' is an option here, together with cooperation with international universities and institutions like the OECD.

The overall idea here is renewal and evolution of our institutions and values, rather than revolution. Public agitation at the causes, effects and lack of remedies to the credit crisis is growing across Europe, and in Ireland frustration, mistrust and falling confidence are more and more visible.

While relatively little can be done to alleviate the short-term effects of the recession, for the sake of the longer term we need to begin a debate on the renewal of the institutions and values of the Republic.

Many policy issues in Ireland have been treated with a far greater dose of pragmatism than careful strategic thought. Ireland is at a crucial juncture with regard to the next stage of its economic development, its place in the world, the well-being of public life and the structure of its society.

The pre-eminent historian of modern Ireland, Joe Lee, wrote that 'small states must rely heavily on the quality of their strategic thinking to counter their vulnerability to international influences[47] and this essentially is what Ireland's policymakers need to do in the future.

2

Financial Supervision in Ireland: Where to Now?

K.P.V. O'Sullivan

Introduction

In 2008, Ireland experienced a deep financial crisis, stemming from a contraction in property prices and domestic output together and the spillover effects from the subprime crisis in the United States. However, the roots of Ireland's crisis can be found in the inadequate risk management practices of Irish banks and the failure of the Irish Financial Services Regulatory Authority (IFSRA) to supervise these practices effectively. Given the country's current predicament, we are likely to see significant changes in the financial supervisory system in the near future.

While several articles have dealt broadly with the Irish banking crisis,[1] few have been written exclusively with financial regulation and corporate governance in mind. This chapter will address this lacuna, attempting to inform current policy debates surrounding the overhaul of both these forms of financial supervision. The study's aim will be parsing out the weaknesses in the supervisory system and delineating a number of solutions to address these weaknesses. The objective being, in part, not to reiterate the facts of what happened in an idiographic sense but rather to place the Irish banking crisis and the failure of its supervisory system in a wider regulatory context.

The chapter is structured as follows: the next section presents a brief rationale for financial regulation and describes its development in Ireland in terms of its evolution and current institutional design. A similar structure of analysis will be deployed in the third section, but this time corporate governance provisions will be under review. In the fourth and fifth sections, the contribution of regulation and corporate governance to the banking crisis will be examined, particularly principles -based regulation (PBR) and banks' internal controls. Following this, I will critically evaluate the measures the government intends to introduce to reform supervisory practices in Ireland. I argue that in some instances, these changes are neither necessary nor sufficient. Instead, in the following section, I will introduce a number of measures, which should address these concerns, including the adoption of a meta-risk regulatory approach by IFSRA together with a number of institutional reforms to facilitate this transition. Finally, the eighth section concludes the chapter.

Rationale for Financial Regulation

A well-functioning banking system is said to 'oil the wheels of the whole economy'[2] through efficiently allocating resources, increasing capital formation, stimulating productivity growth and acting as a repository of national savings.[3] Therefore, as banking crises can result in serious negative consequences for the wider economy,[4] governments have sought to carefully supervise banking institutions in order to limit the probability of failure. Regulation has become the favourite interventionist policy tool in this regard, and two main types have been promulgated: conduct of business and prudential regulation. Conduct of business regulation is concerned with the protection of bank customers. In many cases this relates to the establishment of guidelines and rules of acceptable behaviour and business practices between banking institutions and their customers. Conduct of business regulation deals with unsolicited contact, advertising, complaints and, in some jurisdictions, levels of service provision and profitability.[5] Prudential regulation focuses on the factors that are essential to the stability of the financial system. Its aim is to minimise the possibility of a breakdown in the financial sector and prevent any adverse effects on long-term growth in the economy. Issues such as liquidity provision, licensing and ownership control, risk management requirements and entry restrictions are, in most cases, regulated.

Evolution of Financial Regulation in Ireland

Financial supervision was first institutionalised with the establishment of the Central Bank in 1943. The authority had a number of specific powers and duties, the most important being to safeguard the integrity of the currency. Its role was not as expansive as in other countries, in so far as the Central Bank was not the banker to the government,[6] had no legislative powers to control credit in the economy, and did not hold the cash reserves of commercial banks. However, with the passing of the Central Bank Act 1973, it started to systemically engage in the regulatory process and acquired the role of custodian to the banking system. Following this Act, the Central Bank became statutorily responsible for the direct licensing and supervision of most financial service providers in Ireland. Throughout the 1970s, the authority introduced strict credit restrictions on bank lending, deposit requirements on net capital inflows and liquidity ratios for licensed banks.[7] After Ireland's membership of the European Economic Community (EEC) and the passing of various EEC financial directives, the regulatory tools and techniques available to the Central Bank were greatly enhanced. By the mid-1980s, the authority created a banking system which was characterised as being one of the most 'intensely regulated' in all developed countries.[8] At that time, an interest rate cartel existed as a key factor inhibiting competition. Additionally, the Central Bank controlled new entrants in the banking sector and entry was practically unattainable except by way of takeover.[9]

In the last few decades, the financial regulatory regime has undergone significant structural change and liberalisation.[10] In the late 1980s and early 1990s, many of the regulatory provisions which were designed to protect the stability of the banking system were either removed or relaxed.[11] Recent 'better regulation' initiatives[12] following the Organisation for Economic Cooperation and Development's (OECD) report on *Regulatory Reform in Ireland* in 2001[13] led to the enactment of the Central Bank and Financial Services Authority of Ireland Act 2003, which mapped the institutional arrangements for financial supervision. The Act created a single Irish Financial Services Regulatory Authority (IFSRA) operating within the Central Bank's legal structure, with overlapping board members. This 'curious regulatory hybrid' structure[14] was effectively a compromise attempt at implementing the main recommendation of the *McDowell Report*, which suggested that the Regulator should be a 'completely new organisation outside, and independent of, the Central Bank'.[15] The report outlined that there was no significant international precedent of imposing a regulator with such a large range of responsibilities within a conventional Central Bank, suggesting, 'no EU member state has done so or proposes to do so'.[16] Many suggest[17] the reason for situating IFSRA within the sphere of influence of the Central Bank was due to intense lobbying from the Central Bank and the Department of Finance. However, in line with good practice, the newly created institutional arrangements did fuse together all conduct of business and prudential supervisory practices into one authority. Previously, supervisory authorities were separated on the basis of activity and type. This gave rise to a complex and multifaceted matrix of regulatory processes, which was inefficient and cumbersome.[18] In terms of responsibility, the 2003 Act mandated IFSRA to achieve a balanced regulatory framework with strong enforcement provisions. To this end, IFSRA introduced a principles- and risk-based approach to financial regulation.

The New Regulatory Regime

Following the example of the British Financial Services Authority (FSA),[19] and in accordance with government policy,[20] IFSRA (the financial regulator) adopted a principles-based approach to regulation following its establishment. With principles-based regulation (PBR), a regulator sets out basic principles or desirable outcomes in a number of different areas, such as solvency, governance and consumer protection. It then allows banks the flexibility to determine the compliance provisions on each of these principles. The objective being, in part, to create a regulatory structure that isn't 'overly bureaucratic'[21] and where its regulations are followed to the *spirit* and not just the *letter* of a rule. The PBR regime is a 'decentred' form of regulation,[22] with many supervisory functions transferred to multiple stakeholders within the system. In particular, the integrity of the Irish PBR regulatory regime rested on the 'ethical behaviour' and 'transparency in business dealings' of board members at banks.[23] PBR facilitates the inclusion of senior personnel in financial institutions in the compliance sphere, as principles are much more accessible than a complex handbook of prescriptive rules. Therefore these officials, with knowledge of the complexities of their own operations, are made directly responsible and accountable for compliance. However, the effective application of PBR requires a high degree of mutual trust between participants in the supervisory framework.[24] It does not work with individuals 'who have no principles', as the chief executive of the British FSA recently stated.[25] Instead, the PBR system of governance relies on self-observing and responsible organisations within its framework.

To buffer against the negative consequences of PBR, the Financial Regulator designed a risk-based enforcement regime to monitor the activities of directors and senior management. The risk-based framework adopted by IFSRA was very much influenced by Basel II's 'risk weighted' approach.[26] IFSRA's internal risk rating system represented the kernel of the framework, supporting the efficient allocation of the authority's resources, especially in its monitoring and enforcement functions. The system represented a 'consistent approach' to evaluating risks inherent in the financial sector, allowing the authority to concentrate its resources on areas of the greatest risk to customers.[27] The Regulator adopts a different approach depending on the type of institution and sector, as risks tend to fluctuate. However, this process is fluid and the Regulator's risk profile can alter depending on political or societal pressures. The banking crisis in 2008 and the use of state funds to support the financial system is evidence of how the Financial Regulator became much more risk adverse in a short period of time.

The risk rating system evaluates financial service providers under a number of general and specific headings. General headings include supervisory complexity, structure, corporate governance, capital, contagion and related party transactions, business risk, regulatory risk, operational risk and foreign exchange risk. The specific risk categories promulgated by IFSRA include credit, funding, liquidity and market risk provisions. The authority also evaluates the potential impact that financial institutions have on a number of different stakeholders before assigning a final risk score. In weighting overall categories of risks, first and foremost IFSRA attempts to make certain the integrity of the Irish banking system is protected by ensuring that solvency and corporate governance standards conform to international standards. Information which supports this process is acquired through various sources such as prudential returns, on- and off-site visits and financial statements. On-site visits are a 'critical element' in ascertaining whether financial institutions are in compliance with IFSRA's supervisory standards and requirements.[28] The on-site visits enable the Regulator to evaluate the corporate governance system in place and assess the general culture at the financial institution under investigation.

The enforcement regime adopted by IFSRA is heavily dependent on the risk rating system to highlight breaches of principles or rules. Since 2003, the Irish Regulator has acquired new powers strengthening the sanctions it can impose for prescribed contraventions of laws or regulations. Specifically, the Regulator's powers include the abilities to refuse an application for authorisation, to establish an inquiry to determine whether or not the financial service provider is committing a contravention, to impose monetary penalties on financial institutions or senior management and to revoke banking licences from incumbent financial service providers.[29] However, in practice, the Regulator has only in very rare cases availed of any of these measures, despite countless instances of overcharging in the banking system in recent years,[30] and is very much associated with weak enforcement practices. Instead, it tries not to impose sanctions where appropriate given the large costs and resources required to investigate cases.[31] Before it decides to pursue sanctions, it first determines the availability of other regulatory actions available to it. If pursuing sanctions, the Regulator's strategy is, first and foremost, to try to promote a culture of compliance in the financial services industry but not at a significant cost to the taxpayer. Influencing the adoption of this 'light touch' enforcement regime was a belief in strong corporate governance provisions in Ireland, a matter we will investigate further in the next section.

Rationale for Corporate Governance

The shift towards PBR in Ireland resulted in a greater reliance on corporate governance arrangements. For the new regime to work effectively, it was essential that banks had properly functioning internal controls and risk management systems. The underlying rationale for corporate governance arises from agency problems due to the separation of ownership and control in firms. As such, small stakeholders frequently lack the proficiency to monitor managers. Additionally, the large costs associated with this task may induce free-rider concerns, with small stakeholders relying on each other, which may result in little managerial oversight. Therefore, corporate governance provisions have been introduced to protect the interests of minority stakeholders. These mechanisms attempt to monitor and evaluate the performance of managers and represent a system through which the objectives of a company are outlined and the methods of achieving and monitoring performances are formulated. The process of realigning the interests of managers with other stakeholders can take many forms, including managerial remuneration packages, concentrated ownership structures and the use of non-executive directors in boardrooms. Independent non-executive directors are an essential element in any corporate governance system, and are usually given a number of explicit responsibilities such as strategic decision-making, identification of corporate goals, recruitment of key personnel and the provision of managerial oversight. Specifically, they are required to review and analyse risk management procedures and ensure that these practices are consistent with previously fixed policies and agreements. Benefits accruing from effective internal corporate governance provisions are not just concentrated on the part of small stakeholders and may result in lower equity and debt capital cost for a company, a reduction of labour costs and a higher value in products and services from clients.[32]

Ireland's Corporate Governance Landscape

Corporate governance systems, and the regulations and laws encompassing them, can be geographically segregated into two main ideological viewpoints, the Anglo-Saxon model and the Continental model. In its simplest sense, the Anglo-Saxon model is based on the fiduciary relationship between shareholders and managers. It is centred on market dynamics, the belief that the market can self-regulate itself in a balanced and efficient manner. In contrast, the Continental model is associated with the stakeholder theory of firms. In this model, the stakeholder, such as employees and trade union groups, plays an active role in a firm's decision-making process. However, even within these ideological viewpoints, no two national corporate governance systems are alike and general rules and practices have developed over time to suit each country's individual legal, political and economic environment. In designing national corporate governance systems, regulators should seek to maintain the integrity of financial markets through strong monitoring and enforcement practices, particularly in relation to the level of disclosure, risk management, and accounting and reporting standards. However, it must strike a right balance between legal, regulatory and voluntary provisions to help foster a suitable environment for businesses to grow and develop as well as attract international capital.

Ireland conforms to the Anglo-Saxon model of corporate governance, mainly due to our historical relationship with Britain. The Irish Stock Exchange annexed the British Combined Code of Corporate Governance to its listing requirements in 1999, making Ireland one of the few European countries to adopt another one's regime. Henceforth, Irish listed companies are required to report on how they applied the Combined Code in their annual reports and justify any instance of non-compliance to their shareholders (comply or explain). The Combined Code sets out general standards and principles of good practice in relation to areas such as board composition, director remuneration, internal control, accountability and audit functions. It combines the recommendations of five separate reports: *Cadbury* and *Greenbury* on corporate governance, *Turnbull* on internal controls, *Higgs* on the role and effectiveness of non-executive directors and the *Smith Guidance* on audit committees. Central to the code is the creation of an effective and accountable board with clear division of responsibilities between directors, preventing situations where any one individual becomes too dominant. Additionally, proper and transparent procedures in relation to the appointment of board members should ensure that the correct people are appointed. Apart from issues related to director remunerations, the

Combined Code is said to have had an overall positive impact on corporate governance in Ireland.[33] However, the majority of companies in Ireland regularly disclose 'comply or explain' information on a general basis.[34] Explanations for deviations mainly relate to the boardroom appointments and remuneration policies.

The government has enacted a number of its own measures to fortify the Combined Code. Primarily, the Company Law Enforcement Act 2001 and the Companies (Auditing and Accounting) Act 2003 have set the general tone of its philosophy in this area. With the Company Law Enforcement Act 2001, the establishment of the Office of the Director of Corporate Enforcement (ODCE) – a regulator separated from the relevant ministry or department (in this case the Department of Enterprise, Trade and Employment, now the Department of Enterprise, Trade and Innovation) – has strengthened and concentrated the enforcement of company law in Ireland.[35] Chiefly, the office is responsible for improving the compliance environment in Ireland. It has the power to initiate a fact-finding company investigation and issue fines or refer cases to the Director of Public Prosecutions, where appropriate. However, following the Enron scandal and subsequent reservations about the integrity of the international auditing profession, the government enacted further legislation in the form of the Companies (Auditing and Accounting) Act 2003. This led to the establishment of a new institution, the Irish Auditing and Accounting Supervisory Authority, to oversee the auditing profession and outlined stricter requirements in relation to audit independence and the establishment of audit committees. Broadly, audit committees, under the Act, are required to review accounts and compliance statements and monitor the work and independence of external auditors. One of the most controversial provisions of the Act relates to the requirement for directors to prepare, approve and review a written compliance statement under various legal and tax obligations. Particularly, the compliance statement must describe the company's system of internal financial controls. Additionally, directors must acknowledge their responsibility in securing compliance and confirm that they have reviewed their internal control systems on an annual basis. External auditors are mandated to review these statements each year to determine whether they are fair and accurate. Unfortunately, during the Irish property bubble (2003–2007), directors, senior managers and auditors failed to uphold their responsibilities, whether in relation to the Combined Code or specific legalisation provisions enacted by the government. Moreover, weak monitoring and enforcement practices by the ODCE further diluted the effectiveness of corporate governance. In such cases, regulation should step in as the next line of defence and offer protection to bank shareholders, creditors and customers. However, the Central Bank, Department of Finance and Financial Regulator failed to recognise the inherent vulnerabilities in the banking system. The negative shock in the form of the failure of Lehman Brothers and the dip in domestic property prices were to fundamentally change everything and ultimately bring Irish banks to the brink of near failure.

Failure of Regulation

As noted above, in the new regulatory regime financial service providers were given discretion to expand their operations with little regulatory oversight. Irish banks applied this discretion to exercise a profit maximisation approach by ramping up their credit outflows. This is evident from the excessive appreciation in the aggregate loan book and asset base of Irish banks from 2004 to 2007, compared to the previous 54 years (see Figure 2.1). The majority of this expansion was property-related, either through the financing of commercial developments or by the provision of mortgage credit to the personal sector. Increases in these sectors were atypical and vastly outstripped other areas of lending, such as in the agricultural or manufacturing sectors, where growth in credit remained relatively incremental during this time period (see Figure 2.2). The euphoria surrounding property lending was supported by a number of factors, such as full employment, favourable planning laws, a tax system which was biased towards home ownership and property development, and historically low and even negative real interest rates. Banks funded this lending through disproportionately high borrowing from the interbank lending markets, as their deposit accounts could not keep pace with the huge growth in lending they experienced (see Figure 2.3). More worryingly, amid aggressive competition,[36] and pressures to maintain growth levels, the terms associated with lending were loosened to widen the pool of potential customers. For example, with regard to mortgage finance, 5 per cent of the total stock of mortgage lending in 2004 related to 100 per cent loans; by 2007 this increased to 15 per cent. Similarly, the amount of loans greater than 31 years increased in this time period from 10 to 33 per cent and the size of mortgages greater than €300,000 grew from 7 to 23 per cent of the total stock of mortgage lending.[37]

Figure 2.1: Growth in Total Assets and Customer Loans of Retail Clearing Banks, 1948–2008

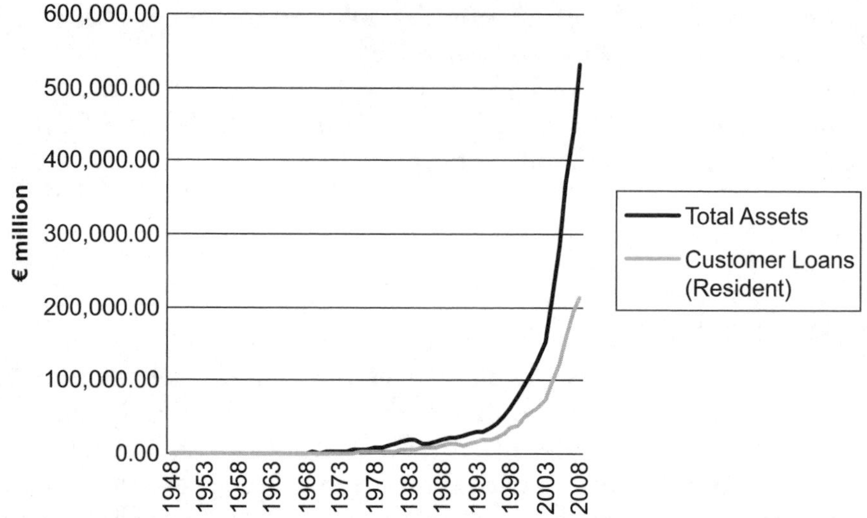

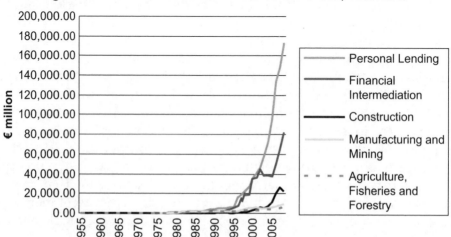

Source: Central Bank Annual Reports/Monthly Bulletins (1948–2008)

While these practices increased the banks' profitability, their fortunes became inextricably intertwined with the property sector, resulting in greater vulnerability to market cycles, both nationally and internationally. However, the Central Bank was not concerned about the changing nature of the banks' risk profile.[38] This despite continued warnings from the Inter-

Figure 2.2: Sectoral Growth in Private Sector Credit, 1955–2008

Source: Central Bank Annual Reports/Monthly Bulletins (1955–2008)

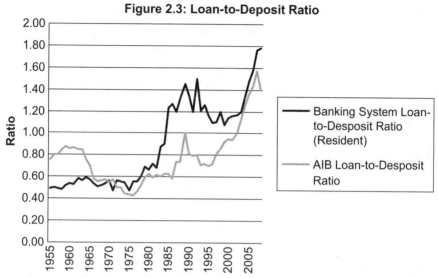

Figure 2.3: Loan-to-Deposit Ratio

Source: Annual accounts of Munster and Leinster Bank, Royal Bank of Ireland, Provisional Bank of Ireland (1955–66); Annual Accounts of Allied Irish Bank (AIB) (1967–2008); Central Bank Annual Reports/Monthly Bulletins (1955–2008).
Note: AIB figures prior to 1967 relate to the aggregate values from the Munster and Lenister Bank, Royal Bank of Ireland and the Provisional Bank of Ireland; some author calculations included.

national Monetary Fund[39] and *The Economist*[40] on the dangers on the Irish banking system's overreliance on the domestic property sector. In its *2007 Stability Report*, the Central Bank concluded that banks were 'appropriately capitalised' and 'solvent' and the system was well placed 'to cope with emerging issues'. The Financial Regulator's assessment of a well-functioning and robust banking system was tenacious. Patrick Neary, its then Chief Executive Officer (CEO), speaking in the days preceding the government's guarantee, stated that 'by any estimate the Irish banking system is so well capitalised compared to any banks anywhere across Europe and I am confident that they can absorb any loans or any impairments'.[41]

However, banks are now operating in a very different landscape and the consequences of the economic recession have exposed its poor risk management procedures. After more than fifteen years of continuous economic growth, the economy contracted by between 1 and 2.5 per cent in 2008 and declined by a further 8 to 10 per cent in 2009. The downturn was caused by a sharp correction in the property market which has been further exacerbated by the international credit crunch. Since 2008, the market for property in Ireland has been on hold, with prospective buyers waiting for prices to reach their nadir and the economy to come out of recession. Highly leveraged property loans were built around fast-exit strategies and in the new environment of minimal sales, property developers are finding it difficult to meet their debt obligations. Consequently, banks saw a significant increase in credit defaults in 2008 and the prospect for further impairments and bad debt charges loomed large. Events were further exacerbated following the collapse of Lehman Brothers in the US in mid-September 2008, and the freezing of money markets, a critical element of short-term finance for Irish banks. Interbank rates were set soaring and Irish banks were seeing substantial outflows and volatility in funding. Sean FitzPatrick, former chairman of Anglo Irish Bank, outlined that there was 'no money available on global markets' during this time.[42] In light of growing concerns about access to credit and a potential run on a number of Irish banks, the government has been forced to issue a guarantee scheme, recapitalise its two main banks and establish the National Asset Management Agency (NAMA) to cleanse the banking system of its non-performing loans.

Due to the government stake in the financial sector and purchase of much of its risk, Irish society will have to deal with the consequences of imprudent and high risk lending for the foreseeable future. These consequences have been far-reaching and the regulator's two main goals – to establish a robust and solvent banking system and to protect the interests of customers – have not yet been reached. Particularly, IFSRA failed to curtail the lending boom, which saw the loan book of Irish banks double in only five years (2000–05). This despite the established evidence between lending booms and banking crises.[43] Consequently, the banking system is currently on 'life support'.[44] Its binge on property-related lending has resulted in its capital base being destroyed, and years of steady progress and integrity have been eroded in just a few months. Market sentiment, nationally and internationally, is very low and the share price of Irish banks has fallen by over 90 per cent since mid-2007. The rapid deterioration in the state of the banking system is also reflected by their dismal financial performance. In March 2010, Anglo Irish Bank announced a loss of €12.7 billion, the largest in Irish corporate history, for the fifteen months to December 2009, after writing off €15.1 billion in bad loans.

Both Bank of Ireland and AIB have announced huge falls in profits and increases in bad debt charges for 2009, primarily due to higher losses on development- and property-related loans moving to NAMA. A similar picture is evident for Irish building societies, such as Irish Nationwide, which recorded a pre-tax loss of €280 million for 2008, after it was forced to write off nearly 5 per cent of its loan book.

In relation to IFSRA's second goal, safeguarding the interests of bank customers, many individuals have been left vulnerable due to a failure in financial regulation. Nearly one in three households are facing negative equity by the end of 2010.[45] Heightened bank lending has also driven private sector credit to 215 per cent of gross domestic product (GDP), one of the highest in the OECD area, which is likely to stunt any future recovery in the economy. The Financial Regulator's own consumer watchdog, the Consultative Consumer Panel, recently announced that most financial consumers had 'lost substantial sums of money' due to the 'inadequate' performance of the regulatory regime.[46] It pointed to the failure of IFSRA 'to dampen the bubble' by introducing measures such as greater capital provision for riskier lending. Governance was viewed as existing 'entirely within regulated institutions' and not the shared responsibility of the Financial Regulator, Central Bank, Department of Finance and the banks themselves.[47]

However, failure is not just limited to the Financial Regulator and should be apportioned accordingly across the multiple agents involved. For example, private customers are expected to manage their own financial risk,[48] and some failed to grasp the dangers associated with easy credit, particularly in times of low interest rates and cycles of property appreciation. Moreover, many property developers failed to effectively evaluate their own risk profile and instead pursued highly leveraged and speculative property deals which ultimately became unstuck following the crash in property prices. Auditors failed in their job of ensuring that financial statements were correct and true reflections of the state of the financial institution at a given point in time. Shareholders of banks, particular institutional investors, did not uphold their duty to protect the interests of their shareholders. However, a greater responsibility must rest within financial institutions themselves. For instance, bank directors approved strategies of short-term risk-taking and accelerated growth instead of pursuing more prudent and sustainable long-term growth. Management failed to introduce appropriate risk management procedures and internal controls during the property bubble. The breakdown of these systems ultimately resulted in banks rapidly expanding credit, increasing the probability of credit quality deterioration. Moreover, at an operational level, bank employees failed to help consumers make informed decisions which were in their best interest in accordance with IFSRA's Customer Protection Code.[49] In the next section, I will examine the effectiveness of corporate governance arrangements at banks more closely by looking at internal controls at Anglo Irish Bank, specifically in relation to the director's loan controversy.

Failure of Corporate Governance

In order to understand the failure of corporate governance at banks during the property bubble, it is necessary to get a detailed description of a department within an Irish bank with responsibility for an element of internal control. However, before I begin with this, it is necessary to provide a brief overview of one instance of corporate governance failure,[50] in this case the director's loan controversy at Anglo Irish Bank, which will be the subject of further analysis in this section. This issue relates to the 'inappropriate treatment' of Sean FitzPatrick's loans over an eight-year period.[51] Mr FitzPatrick, then chairman of Anglo Irish Bank, temporarily transferred loans of between €87 million and €122 million to Irish Nationwide prior to his own bank's year end, thereby concealing this information from auditors and shareholders. The Financial Regulator's office became aware of this circle transaction in January 2008 when it conducted a routine examination of a quarterly report from Irish Nationwide but failed to take any corrective action and communicate this information to its (IFSRA's) board. Instead, it blamed the external auditors, Ernst and Young, suggesting that 'a lay person would, I believe, expect that issues of this magnitude and nature would be picked up [by the auditors]'.[52] Fallout from the incident resulted in the resignation or retirement of the CEO and chairman of Anglo Irish Bank together with the CEO of Irish Nationwide and the Financial Regulator. Additionally, the board of directors at Anglo Irish Bank apologised for the incident, indicating that it was not aware of this circular transaction. But given the bank's perceived compliance with the provisions of the Combined Code,[53] and the various safeguards that this affords, how could have this been the case?

Speaking to an all-party committee on regulatory affairs in February 2008, the head of the internal audit[54] department at Anglo Irish Bank, Walter Tyrell, explained that the role of the internal audit department was to provide 'assurance to the board' in relation to the daily operational risks faced by the bank.[55] It also ensures that appropriate controls are in place to deal with identified risks. Its annual plan and operations are approved by the audit committee, which is composed of non-executive directors. Until December 2008, it reported directly to the chief executive and independently to the audit committee. Conforming to guidance from the Institute of Internal Auditors and international best practice, the department approaches its work through 'a risk-based approach based on a hierarchy of risks' looking at, first, the impact on the bank and second, the likelihood of the risk occurring. The department completes between 70 and 90 audit reports each year and an 'essential' part of its work is to follow up on these reports to ensure that its recommendations are complied with.[56] In relation to lending, it undertakes a number of tasks to ensure best practice procedures are followed. It inspects the bank's loan approval framework and the processes involved in acquiring loan security. However, it is not concerned about the risk profile of the loan but rather that it went through the proper application process and was approved by the credit committee 'in a full and frank manner'.[57] Therefore, issues such as the size of the loan book or it concentration in a particular sector are not under its remit but rather the responsibilities of the credit risk department.[58]

The internal audit department uses a 'statistical sampling basis' in selecting loans for detailed examination. While directors' loans are part of the overall population under investigation, Mr FitzPatrick's loans were never selected. Defending this, Mr Tyrell outlined that the chairman's loans had normal commercial terms attached to their provision and, therefore, were less likely to be selected.[59] In fact it never occurred to him that the department had extra responsibilities with directors' loans and that 'any corporate governance issues' applied. While the internal audit department was aware of the chairman's original loans, it had no knowledge of the short-term refinancing arrangements with Irish Nationwide, as it was the responsibility of the credit committee[60] and the external auditors to review such transfers. However, the credit committee was not aware of these transfers either, as non-executive director Mr Frank Daly outlined: 'movements in or out of the bank would not have come to the attention of the [credit] committee' but rather individual lending executives.[61] In retrospect, Mr Tyrell admitted that the internal audit department should have examined Mr FitzPatrick's loans, suggesting that it was 'wrong' and the organisation is now in the process of reforming its structures to ensure that 'this does not happen again'.

While Anglo Irish Bank's corporate governance framework appears to be designed and operated in accordance with the *spirit* of the Combined Code, clear failures to control corporate risks and in the provision of adequate directors' oversight are evident. Particularly, the presence of information silos was evident from Mr Tyrell's account, probably influenced by the complex internal controls arrangements adopted by the bank.

Departments and committees seemed to be governed by their own individual functions, which are not clearly understood, with little attention given to the *big picture* in the bank. For example, the annual approval of the temporary transfer of Mr FitzPatrick's loans to Irish Nationwide might have been acceptable to the credit committee based on its limited terms of reference. However, other committees might have taken a different stance given issues such as corporate governance and reputational risk. Commenting on the divergent roles and responsibilities of the various departments associated with internal controls and risk management, Senator Shane Ross indicated that he was completely 'lost'.[62] Moreover, Mr Tyrell suggested that probably ten individuals at the bank were aware of the chairman's annual transaction with Irish Nationwide. Therefore, the presence of organisational silos between some committees or departments was also evident. Whether this was due to poor corporate governance arrangements or because these transactions were associated with an individual who had significant power, as the bank's previous CEO for nearly two decades and current chairman, is difficult to determine. In the wake of these revelations, the government needs to engage in a root-and-branch review of the supervisory regime, to provide real and lasting changes to regulation and corporate governance in banking. In the next section, I present an overview of the main reforms proposed by the government and critically evaluate their likely impact in terms of changing behaviour and ensuring a similar crisis is less likely to happen in the future.

The Government's Response to the Crisis

In response to the Anglo Irish Bank debacle, the government is proposing to put the principles of the Combined Code of Corporate Governance on a legislative footing for all banks. While this is positive, evidence from the previous section suggests that full compliance with the code is not enough. Therefore, the government is likely to add a number of specific conditions to the code in the future, such as in the areas of board composition and independence, not allowing the CEO to become chair and the provision of direct roles and responsibilities for non-executive directors. However, specific provisions in relation to the growing complexity of financial institutions must be integrated into a new system of corporate governance.[63] For example, wider concerns, such as the failure of corporate governance arrangements to dampen the rapid growth in lending, cannot be ignored by the government. Additionally, following the 2008 crisis, questions remain as to the ability of non-executive directors to perform their roles adequately and the government has failed to take any action in this regard. In a normative sense, banks should only employ directors with knowledge and experience of the banking sector.[64] However, they can find it difficult to secure the necessary skill set and a mix of backgrounds and competences on a board may be seen as positive. Therefore, the government should seek to examine the prevailing 'fit and proper' test promulgated by the Financial Regulator for non-executive board members.[65]

With regard to regulatory structures, the government is planning to establish a Banking Commission which incorporates both the monetary responsibilities of the Central Bank and the supervisory functions of the Financial Regulator (IFSRA). The creation of a single fully integrated institution follows the establishment of IFSRA in 2003, after a government inquiry into the widespread use of offshore bank accounts, and the failure of the incumbent regulator (the Central Bank) to effectively monitor and supervise these accounts.[66] A parliamentary inquiry in 1999[67] concluded that the Central Bank did little to prevent the widespread evasion of deposit interest retention tax (DIRT) over a twelve-year period. The inquiry reported that the relationship between the Central Bank and its regulated entities was 'particularly close and inappropriate' and suggested that it was perhaps 'too mindful of the concerns of the banks, and too attentive to their pleas and lobbying'. IFSRA's aim was to restore what the Competition Authority noted as the 'shattered' public confidence of the banking system.[68] However, it failed do so and the government is now falling back on an old and tarnished structure to restore international confidence in the Irish financial system. It is naive to think that this approach will make much of a difference, especially as the Central Bank concluded in its *Financial Stability Report 2007* that the 'the Irish financial system's shock absorption capacity remains robust and the system is well placed to cope with emerging issues'.[69] The Financial Regulator and the Central Bank were always closely associated, both legally and operationally; the government's new arrangements will simply formalise this relationship.

Specifically with regard to regulation, following the state guarantee, IFSRA has initiated a more 'intensive and hands-on' approach to its prudential supervisory duties. It has placed greater emphasis on reviewing business models and strategies adopted by banks and the risks facing their operations.[70] It has sidelined its PBR approach to supervision, suggesting that the turmoil in financial markets has highlighted the inadequacies of this regulatory approach, both at home and aboard.[71] Patrick Honohan, current Governor of the Central Bank, indicated that PBR represented a 'code for deferring to the preferences' of banks, an ideology, he indicates, that will not be present in the future.[72] IFSRA has also increased the resources in the prudential department and has recruited a number of staff to enhance the organisation's skills base. Specifically, it has created a new supervisory unit to deal with state-supported banks, given the increased compliance requirements under the guarantee scheme. It has overhauled its reporting obligations for financial institutions, increasing the scope of information required and the frequency of submissions. Staff from the Regulator's office are now also located on-site in the main Irish banks, periodically attending various management meetings (e.g. audit, credit and treasury). It has also 'tightened' reporting mechanisms around governance, increasing the number of meetings with compliance officers and requesting more information on issues raised by the audit committees.[73] Finally, there will be 'renewed emphasis' in relation to enforcement in the future, even at the risk of greater legal costs associated with unsuccessful cases. This should hopefully reduce 'socially harmful risk-taking' on the part of regulated entities.[74]

While most of the measures presented above are constructive, they don't deal with the core failures highlighted in this chapter. Instead, the Financial Regulator's reaction has been to ratchet up its monitoring, control and information-gathering functions in an unsystematic and haphazard fashion. Yet, during the boom in credit, IFSRA had enough information to recognise that lending was dangerously excessive (see Figures 2.1, 2.2 and 2.3) and saw that corporate governance practices were unruly without taking corrective action (see above). Two explanations can be posited for a lack of intervention. Either the regulator was *captured* by the lending bubble or it lacked the authority to make any reasonable intervention. Evidence suggests that we can reject the latter assertion as in mid-2007[75] the regulator did introduce a number of measures to slow down credit in the economy. However, these measures were influenced by the international sub-prime crisis and not by domestic concerns and in any event were too late and 'insufficient'.[76] The first explanation that the regulator and its entities were *captured* by the exuberances of the property boom and lacked the risk management capacity to recognise this seems more likely. Similar international examples have also been demonstrated recently, particularly in the United States and Britain. In the next section, I will present a number of novel approaches which could reduce the probability of such an event reoccurring and attempt to rebuild the scattered confidence of Ireland's banking system.

Meta-Risk Regulation and Institutional Reform

There is significant political and societal will to change the prevailing supervisory regime. IFSRA itself has accepted its strategic approach to regulation was inappropriate, suggesting that it was constructed in a 'benign environment' where many of the current issues were not foreseen.[77] Particularly, its reliance on senior managers and directors to construct appropriate risk management systems and internal controls was 'misplaced'.[78] Therefore, by inference, new arrangements of financial supervision in Ireland are likely to give the Financial Regulator a central role in evaluating risks and overseeing corporate governance provisions. With this in mind, the overall objective of reforms should be to strengthen the competence of the Regulator and senior personnel at banks to detect and forestall occurrences of imprudent risk-taking. Such an approach would be positive, and has been captured in the literature in terms such as 'reflexivity', 'partnership', 'smart regulation' and 'meta-regulation'.[79] While these terms broadly encompass the same ideals of a sophisticated and collaborative form of regulation, the unique properties of meta-regulation make it particularly interesting for the banking system.

According to Parker, meta-risk regulation is defined as the 'regulation of self-regulation'.[80] Modifying this definition slightly to include risk, in a meta-risk regulatory (MRR) regime the regulating authority moves from monitoring individual risks at firm level to evaluating the firm's risk management system. The idea of regulation as a proxy for risk management is well established in the literature, particularly with the growth of the 'risk society'.[81] Governments are being increasingly assessed in terms of their ability to identify, assess and manage risks.[82] In a MRR regime the objective is to improve the 'self-monitoring' capacity of entities[83] by monitoring and evaluating their self-regulatory techniques.[84] The regulator ceases to be concerned about direct controls and proscribing the behaviour of firms,[85] and rather shifts to a proceduralization strategy,[86] encouraging firms to put in place 'processes and management systems which are then scrutinised by regulators or corporate auditors'.[87] Therefore, in this approach the monitoring of compliance at the organisation is undertaken in three layers: firstly, at an operational level in the workplace, next, by the directors of the company, and, finally, by the regulator itself.[88]

This approach recognises the limitations of the state actors (and non-executive directors) to acquire sufficient knowledge to regulate an industry independently in a 'centralistic' fashion.[89] Furthermore, a move to meta-regulation is particularly suitable in volatile and complex environments,[90] enabling regulators to respond to changing market conditions and address shifting priorities in their regulatory agenda.[91] The lack of information inherent when designing regulation has in the past posed problems in formulating appropriate rules or standards.[92] Moreover, difficulties can arise in relation to compliance, as ill-conceived rules may not only fail but may also lead to 'creative compliance' on the part of the regulated entity.[93]

Regulators have come to recognise the potential of steering the internal controls of an organisation 'as a means of securing control indirectly'[94] to achieve regulatory objectives. The classic example being in the nuclear power industry following the Three Mile Island crisis in 1979 in the United States, where, following the incident, state investigators concluded that plant controllers' over-reliance on basic compliance was a contributing factor to the event.[95] When something occurred that was not covered in their rulebook, they lacked the ability to strategically react and manage the event. Following this observation, government inspectors moved from intensively inspecting compliance of rules to evaluating risk management systems at these plants, seeking to establish if controllers had the 'risk analysis intelligence' to understand the safety systems of their nuclear facilities.[96] Under the new regime, each nuclear plant saw itself as a 'unique distinctive system' with its own clear rules, principles and peer review support.[97] The idea of reducing systematic risk in an industry by improving and monitoring the risk management capabilities of individual firms, and not just assessing whether specific rules were adhered to or not, represented a significant change in ideology and was ultimately successful.

The benefits of meta-risk regulation have not just been observed in the nuclear power industry; they have been adopted across the spectrum of societal arrangements, from the taxation and health sectors to the financial services sector. In financial services, regulators have had a quasi meta-risk regulatory responsibility since the introduction of the Basel II accord in 2004. Under this framework, banks were free to impose their own minimum capital requirements based on their risk management systems, but only subject to prior, and continual, monitoring by the regulator of these risk management systems.[98] However, the Irish banking crisis and the subsequent liquidity problems is clear evidence that IFSRA failed in this regard. This is not surprising as IFSRA never saw itself as a meta-risk regulator and lacked the institutional arrangements to effectively act as one. However, as managing and controlling risks are likely to play a central role in the Financial Regulator's future mandate, the authority needs to modify the way in which it interacts with banks by shifting fully towards meta-risk regulation. To support this transition, I propose a new institutional architecture in Irish banking (see Figure 2.4), which hinges around the relationship between two newly established institutions, the Corporate Risk Department (CRD) at banks and the Risk and Compliance Unit (RCU) at the Financial Regulator.

Firstly, in relation to a bank's internal structures, I propose the creation of a Corporate Risk Department (CRD), responsible for formulating company-wide internal controls and risk management procedures.[99] Specifically, the CRD should seek to control and monitor risks in banks by, for

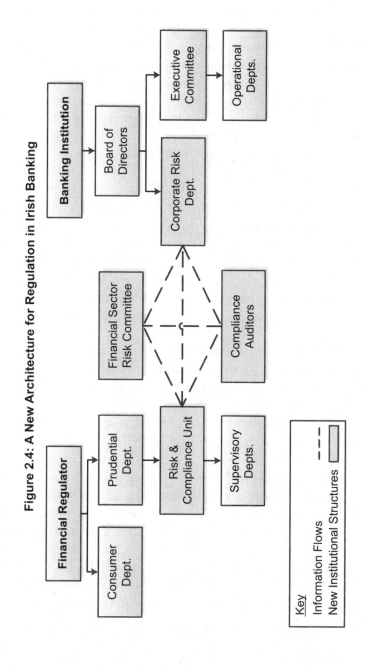

Figure 2.4: A New Architecture for Regulation in Irish Banking

example, introducing mechanisms to limit excessive balance sheet growth. The CRD would represent a nexus merging the operations of the risk management, credit and internal audit departments into a horizontally integrated department. This should help the department make more informed decisions, with greater access to information. The CRD should reduce the problem of organisational silos, which was apparent in the director's loan controversy at Anglo Irish Bank (see above). The adoption of this approach will also improve accountability in the organisation, as only one department would be responsible for monitoring risks. However, establishing these institutional arrangements will not work unless 'the transmission of information is through effective channels'.[100] Therefore, I believe that the head of the CRD, the Chief Risk Officer (CRO), should have a seat on the board of directors. This should facilitate the proper dissemination of information in the boardroom of Irish banks. I also argue that some protection mechanisms must be built into this position, such as its resources being assigned by a group of non-executive directors, to ensure a level of independence and separation from the executive board at the bank (see Figure 2.4). The Regulator should work closely with this department to make sure firm-level internal controls are operating effectively. Also, it should have the power to veto any inappropriate appointment to the CRO position.

In relation to the Financial Regulator's current institutional structure, it is necessary to superimpose a new Risk and Compliance Unit (RCU) above the market and banking supervision departments. This would institutionalise a move towards meta-risk regulation. Under the new regulatory regime, it is envisaged that the RCU would be responsible for monitoring and evaluating the risk management systems promulgated by each CRD, given the bank's compliance requirements. These requirements could be defined through principles, rules or any other instrument the Regulator deemed appropriate. The RCU would take a macro perspective to the regulation of banks' risk management practices, given the interconnected nature of the banking system. Information from both the market and bank supervision departments would feed directly into the RCU on a daily basis, to ensure that it had adequate knowledge to evaluate risks. If a particular CRD was not performing its risk management functions effectively, the RCU at the Financial Regulator should have the power to step in and introduce temporary command and control measures, until the system is corrected. The same allocative principles should apply in the new regime as with the current risk rating system, but 'ability to manage risk' would be heavily weighted. However, meta-risk regulation should not be the Financial

Regulator's only concern and specific best practice rules or principles should remain, particularly in relation to consumer regulation. However, the core current prudential requirements applicable to banks, such as capital adequacy ratios, should be integrated into the new meta-risk regulatory framework.

To support the RCU's bourgeoning informational requirements, I propose the banks should be subjected to yearly risk management or compliance audits.[101] The compliance audit should be required as an enforceable undertaking, funded by the banks themselves. It would be similar to compliance audits in the environmental sector and conducted by an independent auditing firm.[102] Its objective would be to determine whether the risk management systems and internal controls at banks are consistent with the prudential principles and rules imposed by the Regulator. The compliance report would be sent directly to the Financial Regulator and the board of directors of the bank. Its purpose would not be to punish inappropriate compliance procedures but rather to identify problems early on, to create greater awareness about the importance of internal controls and to help foster better risk management systems. While the compliance auditor should examine the work of the CRD, it should separately review the risk management practices in the bank. While the correct policies and systems might be propagated by the CRD, creative compliance in the operational departments is always a danger. In essence, this arrangement would represent an additional layer in Parker's meta-regulatory framework[103] and should add greater protection for the Regulator and the non-executive directors. Interestingly, the Central Bank has already taken some action in this regard and its supervisory teams will be supported by a panel of external risk advisers in the future. This panel will assist the Central Bank in assessing governance, risk management and internal controls at regulated firms. It will also provide a resource for evaluating business and commercial risk faced by banks. However, this chapter suggests that a bottom-up approach, through the compliance audit, is much more appropriate given the inherent complexities associated with banking.[104]

Finally, institutional arrangements should be established where the various stakeholders associated with risk management can interact with each other. The implications of the near failure of Anglo Irish Bank in 2008 indicate that Irish banks depend on each other and a failure of one institution could have serious repercussions on the stability of the entire banking system. Internationally, this type of symbiotic relationship was also evident following the collapse of Barings Bank in 1995 and the fall-off in confidence in derivative trading that ensued. In response to this, J.P. Morgan, the largest derivative trading house at the time, decided to publish its own proprietary risk management model to help smaller companies with less sophisticated systems to manage their risk.[105] Braithwaite argues that J.P. Morgan understood it was in 'a community of shared fate'.[106]

To formalise a similar community in risk management, we propose that a Financial Sector Risk Committee (FSRC) should be established, chaired by the Financial Regulator. While banks' risk management systems can be a source of competitive advantage for firms, mitigating against systematic vulnerabilities in the financial system should override competitiveness concerns. As with internet browser platforms (such as Mozilla Firefox), the movement towards sharing underlying codes usually results in better functioning systems. In fact, in December 2009, electronic voting machine manufacturer Sequoia published its own source code in attempt to, firstly, promote public confidence in the robustness of their systems, secondly, facilitate a shift towards a common methodological format in the e-voting industry, and, finally, to help improve their underlying code.[107] This could also be applicable to the banking sector, as the sharing of risk management systems would create greater scrutiny and, through feedback and consultation, help identify and fix any problems associated with particularly risk management practices. It should also foster greater international confidence in the Irish banking system, if the risk management procedures promulgated by banks are in line with best practice. Members of the FSRC would include the CROs from each bank, officials of the Department of Finance and the Central Bank, and the compliance auditors. It should meet on a quarterly basis, providing stakeholders with the opportunity to disseminate risk management policies and engage with supervisory authorities, as well as set down best practice codes and rules. Additionally, this forum would give banks the opportunity to learn from each others' mistakes, which is essential for any 'smart' regulatory regime.[108]

Conclusions

In the future, regulators who can effectively identify risks in their industry are likely to be more successful than ones who have developed the best rules or principles. It is hoped that the measures presented in this chapter will facilitate greater debate around the issues of regulation and corporate governance in Ireland. Counteracting the root problem of the banking crisis – an inability to understand risk – is not going to be easy, and there are various options open to the government. However, as a regulatory system will always lag behind changes in the marketplace, introducing new rules or principles to counteract a build-up of risk in banks is likely to fail. Furthermore, such regulations will result in unintended consequences, damaging service delivery, competition and innovation in the banking system. This chapter has presented a different approach, suggesting that the most effective way IFSRA can reduce risks in the financial sector is by working closely with senior managers and directors, helping them identify and understand the risks inherent in their own balance sheets. This requires the regulator to meta-risk regulate in the future by evaluating the risk management systems of its regulated entities.

But a move toward MRR will not work in isolation, as a financial regulatory philosophy is only as good as the institutional structures underpinning it. Therefore, this chapter has introduced various measures which should facilitate the gathering and sharing of information in the financial system. Principally, I argued for the creation of a Corporate Risk Department at Irish banks to monitor and control firm-level risks. This department would encompass all other compliance and risk management functions previously separated in complex institutional structures. Additionally, the creation of a Risk and Compliance Unit at the Financial Regulator should facilitate both an operational and a cultural shift towards meta-risk regulation. Finally, the introduction of compliance audits and the establishment of a Financial Sector Risk Committee are likely to further protect the MRR regime.

While these changes are far-reaching, the Irish banking crisis of 2008 should represent a new epoch in financial regulation. Through the banking guarantee, nationalisation and the recapitalisation programme, the Irish government has acquired a significant stake in the majority of Irish banks and now has an obligation to reduce the probability of such events reoccurring. Strengthening risk management procedures at banks and moving to meta-risk regulation should help in this regard. This has worked in the past, most famously with regard to the nuclear power industry in the 1980s. As Ireland's financial system experienced its equivalent to a Three Mile Island incident in 2008, such a change in ideology is required, and, hopefully, when the next future shock hits the economy, the financial system will aid in its recovery rather than inhibit it.

3

The Irish Credit Bubble

Morgan Kelly

Introduction

During the 1990s, rising employment resulting from improved competitiveness caused Ireland to experience rapid economic growth.[1] As Ireland converged to average levels of Western European income around 2000 it might have been expected that growth would fall to normal European levels. Instead growth continued at high rates until late 2007, since when it has turned sharply negative.

The proximate cause of the boom and bust in Ireland since 2000 is well known: construction. Ireland went from getting 4–6 per cent of its national income from house-building in the 1990s – the usual level for a developed economy – to 15 per cent at the peak of the bubble in 2006–07, with another 6 per cent coming from other construction. This construction boom led to an employment boom that drove wages in all sectors of the economy to uncompetitive levels, and generated the tax revenues that funded substantial rises in government spending.

However, driving the construction boom was a less recognised boom, in bank lending. As Figure 3.1 shows, in 1997, Irish bank lending to the non-financial private sector was only 60 per cent of gross national product (GNP), compared with 80 per cent in most Eurozone economies and the UK.[2] The international credit boom then saw these economies experience a rapid rise in bank lending, with loans increasing to 100 per cent of gross domestic product (GDP) on average by 2008.[3]

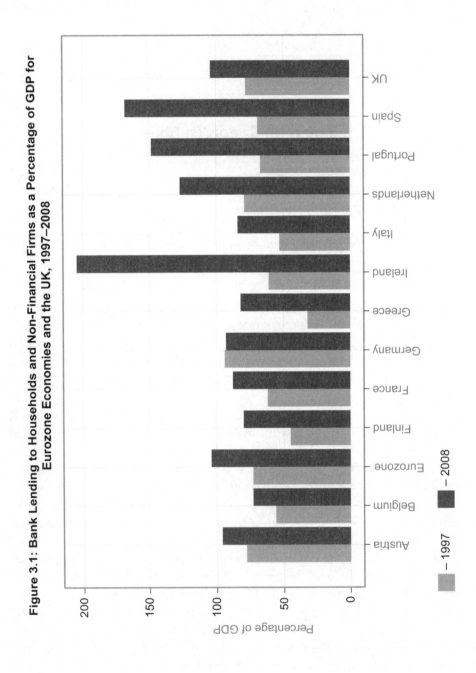

Figure 3.1: Bank Lending to Households and Non-Financial Firms as a Percentage of GDP for Eurozone Economies and the UK, 1997–2008

These rises were dwarfed, however, by Ireland, where bank lending grew to 200 per cent of national income by 2008. Irish banks were lending 40 per cent more in real terms to property developers alone in 2008 than they had been lending to everyone in Ireland in 2000, and 75 per cent more as mortgages.

This more than tripling of credit relative to GNP in eleven years created profound distortions in the Irish economy. The most visible impact was on house prices. We show below that the rise in Irish house prices has little to do with falling interest rates and rising population, and is almost completely explained by increased mortgage lending. In 1995 the average first-time buyer took out a mortgage equal to three years' average earnings, and the average house (new or secondhand, in Dublin or elsewhere) cost four years' average earnings.

By the bubble peak in late 2006, the average first-time buyer mortgage had risen to eight times average annual earnings, and the average new house now cost ten times average earnings, while the average Dublin secondhand house cost seventeen times average earnings. These rises in mortgages and house prices became mutually reinforcing, with larger mortgages driving house prices higher, while rising house prices made banks willing to grant larger mortgages.

As the price of new houses rose faster than the cost of building them, investment in housing rose. Ireland went from completing around 30,000 units in 1995 to 80,000 in 2007: one new housing unit for every twenty households.

Like any bubble, the rise of Irish property prices contained the seeds of its own collapse. Property bubbles grow as long as buyers are willing to borrow increasingly large amounts in the expectation that prices will continue to rise. This process inevitably hits a limit where borrowers become reluctant to take on what start to appear as impossibly large levels of debt, and the self-reinforcing spiral of borrowing and prices starts to work in reverse.

In Ireland, buyers started to become nervous sooner than most observers imagine: the number and average size of mortgages approved (to all categories of borrower – first-time buyers, movers and investors) peaked in the third quarter of 2006. By the middle of 2007, the Irish construction industry was in clear trouble, with unsold units beginning to accumulate.

This property slowdown was bad news for the Irish banking system, which had lent heavily to builders and developers to finance projects and to make speculative land purchases. Share prices of Irish banks fell steadily from March 2007, with the crisis coming to a head in late September 2008, with a run in wholesale markets on the joint-second largest Irish bank, Anglo Irish. After aggressive denials that the banking system faced any difficulties, the Irish government has been forced to respond with a sequence of increasingly desperate and expensive improvised measures.

It guaranteed all deposits and senior debt in the six Irish banks in September 2008; was forced to nationalise Anglo Irish Bank in January 2009; invested €3.5 billion in preference shares in the two large retail banks, Aillied Irish Banks (AIB) and Bank of Ireland, in February 2009; and established the National Asset Management Agency (NAMA) to buy non-performing development loans from banks in November 2009.

It is currently proposed that NAMA buy loans with a face value of €70 billion for €55 billion. However, even assuming that the government's forecasts of interest costs and the recovery of property prices – which appear to lie in the upper tail of optimism – prove correct, the situation of the Irish banking system will remain difficult.

The business model of the Irish banks for the last decade was to borrow heavily in wholesale markets to lend to developers and house-buyers. The collapse of this model leaves them with three interrelated problems:

1. Large losses on loans to builders and developers
2. Heavy reliance on wholesale funding
3. The likelihood of considerable defaults on mortgages

While NAMA is intended to repair, for now, the damage to the asset side of Irish bank balance sheets from developer loans, their liability side appears unsustainable. The aggressive expansion of Irish bank lending was funded mostly in international wholesale markets, where Irish banks were able to borrow at low rates. From being almost entirely funded by domestic deposits in 1997, by 2008 over half of Irish bank lending was funded by wholesale borrowers through bonds and interbank borrowing. This well of easy credit has now run dry. In the words of Bank of England Governor Mervyn King:

> But the age of innocence – when banks lent to each other unsecured for three months or longer at only a slight premium to expected policy rates – will not quickly, or ever, return.[4]

As foreign lenders have become nervous of Irish banks, their place has increasingly been taken by borrowing from the European Central Bank (ECB) and short-term borrowing in the interbank market. Payments from NAMA will allow Irish banks to reduce their borrowing by a trivial amount.

Without continued government guarantees of their borrowing and, more problematically, continued ECB forbearance, the operations of the Irish banks do not appear viable. Borrowing in wholesale markets at 5.6 per cent[5] to fund mortgages yielding 3.5 per cent is not a sustainable activity, and Irish banks face no choice but to shrink their balance sheets by repaying debt and returning to their earlier state of being funded mostly by deposits. It appears likely that the leverage of the Irish economy will return to normal international levels, with bank lending in the region of 80–100 per cent of GNP, back where it was in the late 1990s.

While the stock of credit to the Irish economy will contract by at least half, when we remember that loans equivalent to 80 per cent of GNP are tied up in mortgages (most of them of recent origin with terms of 35 years or more), the flow of new lending will contract even more sharply. It follows that property prices that were inflated by bank lending will drop steeply.

Should lending criteria return to their late 1990s standards, our results indicate that the prices of new houses and commercial property will return to an equilibrium two-thirds below their peak levels, with larger falls possible for secondhand property. This means that, supposing residential prices have already fallen 40 per cent from peak, prices still have to fall by about half from their present levels. Were prices then to grow in line with real incomes, at around 2 per cent per year, it will take about 50 years for real prices to return to their 2006 peaks.

The third problem of the Irish banks is their mortgages. Recent United States (US) experience highlights two factors that rapidly increase the likelihood of mortgage default: falling house prices and, most importantly, unemployment. Both have become realities for many Irish borrowers in the last year. In September 2009, 14.4 per cent of US mortgages were at least one payment past due or in foreclosure; while in Florida, whose investor-fuelled housing bubble closely resembles the Irish one, the figure is 25 per cent.[6] Dealing with the financial and, more importantly, human cost of widespread mortgage defaults will be the next, and far more challenging, step in the Irish banking crisis.

By pushing itself close to, and quite possibly beyond, the limits of its fiscal capacity, the Irish state has succeeded in rescuing Irish banks from their losses on developer loans. Despite this, these banks remain as zombies, entirely reliant on continued Irish government guarantees and ECB forbearance, and committed solely to reducing their own debts.

While bank capital levels are, probably, adequate for the markedly smaller scale of their future lending, we will see below that even fairly modest losses on their mortgage portfolios will be sufficient to wipe out most or all of that capital. Having exhausted its resources in rescuing the Irish banks from the first wave of developer losses, the Irish state can do nothing but watch as the second wave of mortgage defaults sweeps in and drowns them.

In other words, it is starting to appear that the Irish banking system is too big to save. As mortgage losses crystallise, the Irish government's ill-conceived project of insulating bank bondholders from any losses on their investments is sliding beyond the means of its taxpayers.

The mounting losses of its banking system are facing the Irish state with a stark choice. It can attempt a NAMA II for mortgage losses that will end in a bond market strike or a sovereign default. Or it can, probably with the assistance of the International Monetary Fund (IMF) and the European Union (EU), organise a resolution that shares property losses with bank creditors through a partial debt for equity swap. It is easy for governments everywhere to forget that their states are not wholly controlled subsidiaries of their banks but separate entities; and a resolution that transfers bank losses from the Irish taxpayer to bank bondholders will leave Ireland with a low level of debt that, even after several years of deficits, it can easily afford.

The rest of this paper is as follows. The next section outlines the rise in Irish bank lending since 1997, and how this lending was funded by whole-sale markets. The following section shows how the rise in Irish house prices is almost entirely explained by increased mortgage lending. Then we explore how the rise in house prices generated a large expansion of construction activity. The following section looks at an earlier Irish bubble, in agricultural land. Then we examine the problems of bank funding and mortgages; and finally look at the causes of the Irish bubble.

Irish Bank Lending

Figure 3.2 shows deposits and lending to the private sector of Irish banks relative to GNP since the last quarter of 1992.[7] It can be seen that Irish banks were more or less completely deposit funded until 1997, with loans and deposits both around 75 per cent of GNP, and loans to the non-financial sector about 60 per cent of GNP. By comparison, loans to the non-financial private sector of UK banks were one-third higher at 80 per cent of GDP, the average level that Schularick and Taylor[8] find across twelve industrialised economies at that time.

By 2004, UK lending had risen to 95 per cent of GDP, but had been over-taken by Ireland with lending of 100 per cent. However, as Figure 3.2 shows, at this stage Irish lending accelerated rapidly.

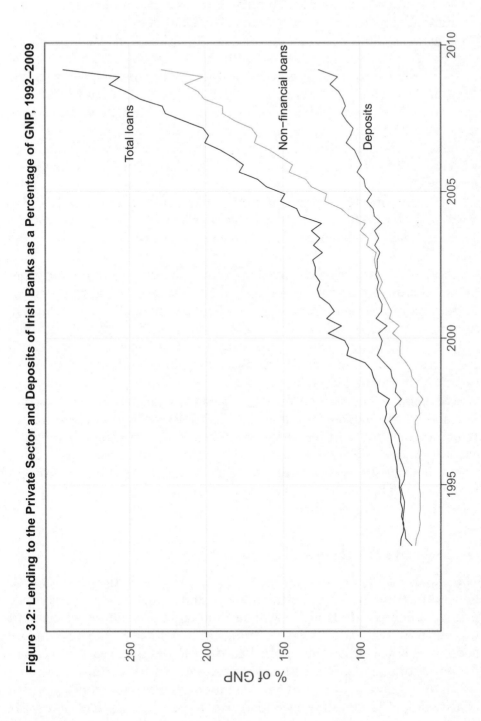

Figure 3.2: Lending to the Private Sector and Deposits of Irish Banks as a Percentage of GNP, 1992–2009

By the middle of 2008 the international credit bubble saw UK non-financial lending rise to 104 per cent of GDP, again close to the international average.[9] In Ireland however, non-financial lending had risen to 200 per cent of GNP, with total lending equal to 250 per cent of GNP, and rising to 270 per cent if securitised mortgages are added. By contrast, deposits had risen only to around 125 per cent of GNP. By the first quarter of 2009, a combination of continued increases in lending (nominal lending peaked in mid-2008 and has fallen slightly since) and falling GNP meant that non-financial lending had risen to 225 per cent of GNP and total lending to 290 per cent, rising to 320 per cent of GNP when securitised mortgages are included.[10]

It is this more than tripling of bank lending that accounts for the Irish boom since 1997. Effectively, the Irish economy segued from one driven by competitiveness in the 1990s to one driven by a credit-fuelled bubble in the 2000s.

Particularly large rises occurred in property lending, both in mortgages to households and in loans to builders and developers. As Figure 3.3 shows, at the start of the credit bubble in 1997 banks were lending €20 billion in mortgages in 2009 prices, and €10 billion to developers.[11] By 2008, the value of mortgage lending (including the quarter of mortgages that were securitised) had risen to seven times its 1997 value, while lending to developers was eleven times its 1997 value.

For comparison, during this time, thanks in large part to the construction activity generated by this lending, real GNP rose by 75 per cent. To put these numbers into further perspective, the total value of bank lending to the non-financial private sector in 2000 was around €80 billion in 2009 prices. Irish banks were therefore lending 75 per cent more in mortgages than they had been lending to everyone in Ireland eight years earlier, and 40 per cent more to developers.

Lending and Property Prices

This explosion of bank lending led to predictable rises in the prices of Irish houses and commercial property. Figure 3.4 shows that, in 1995, the average price of a house in Ireland (new or secondhand, in Dublin or elsewhere) was equal to four years' average earnings in industry.[12] At the peak in late 2006, new house prices nationally had risen to ten times earnings, while Dublin secondhand prices had risen to seventeen times earnings.

Figure 3.5 shows that the SCS-IPD index of commercial property prices, adjusted for inflation, showed similar rises to new house prices. The same

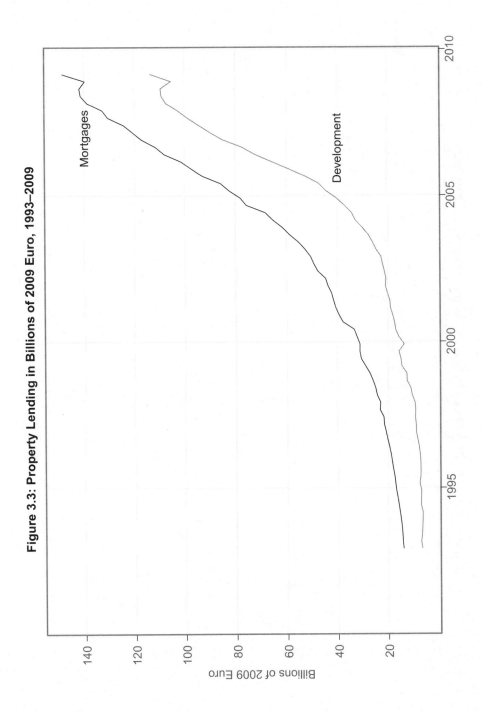

Figure 3.3: Property Lending in Billions of 2009 Euro, 1993–2009

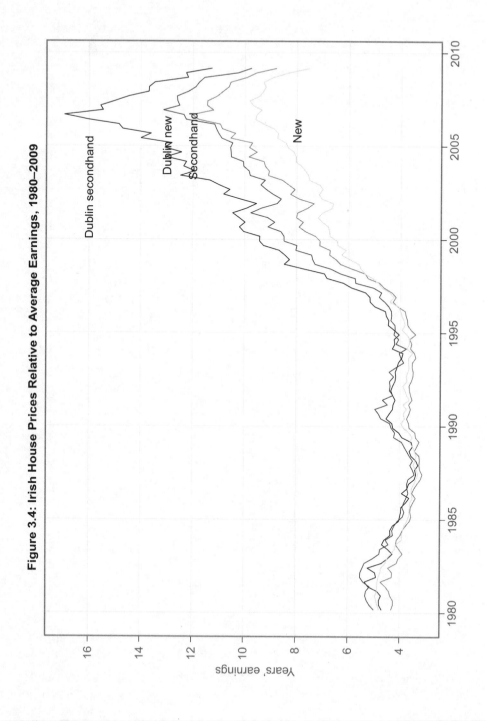

Figure 3.4: Irish House Prices Relative to Average Earnings, 1980–2009

underlying processes were driving both markets.[13] The peak in commercial prices occurred about a year after the residential peak, in late 2007.

The dearth of transactions makes the extent of subsequent falls hard to gauge. The most plausible estimates for housing are those of the estate agents Sherry FitzGerald, who estimate nominal prices nationally had fallen from their peak nationally by 37 per cent and in Dublin by 42 per cent by mid-2009.[14]

What drove the rise in property prices? The proximate cause was bank lending. In a market with rising prices, borrowers were willing to accept any loan that banks would give them so, with the property supply fixed in the short run, prices moved in proportion to the size of new loans.

The cleanest data on new lending is the Department of Environment series on mortgage approvals for first-time buyers. Figure 3.6 plots the size of mortgages to first-time buyers and new house prices, both relative to average earnings. Two things stand out. First, the two series move closely together.

Table 3.1 shows that mortgages have a strong impact on house prices, with a €1 rise in mortgages increasing house prices by €1.13. On the other hand, interest rates have a modest effect. In order to cause the ratio of price to earnings to rise by one (say, from four to five years' earnings), it takes a fall of nearly 9 percentage points in mortgage interest rates. In other words, rising house prices were driven predominantly by increases in the size of mortgages that banks were willing to give, with interest rates playing a secondary role, and population none at all.

Looking at cointegration, the first eigenvalue implies a long-run relationship between house prices, mortgages and real interest rates of

$$\frac{P}{Y} = 1.33\frac{M}{Y} - 0.17r$$

where P is the average price of a new house, Y is average industrial earnings, M is the average first-time buyer mortgage, and r is the real mortgage lending rate.[15]

The second notable thing about Figure 3.6 is that the peak of first-time buyer mortgages (in number as well as value) occurred in the third quarter of 2006, and then declined quite sharply. Mortgages for movers and residential investment borrowers follow a similar pattern.[16] While the total value of mortgages continued to rise after 2006, it did so at a much slower rate.

Just as in the United States, rapid increases in credit were accompanied by a marked deterioration in lending standards. Among first-time buyers purchasing new houses in 2006, only 24 per cent had a loan-to-value ratio

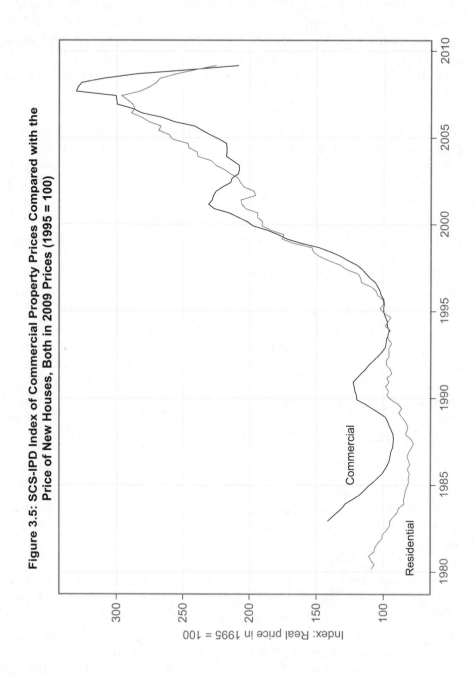

Figure 3.5: SCS-IPD Index of Commercial Property Prices Compared with the Price of New Houses, Both in 2009 Prices (1995 = 100)

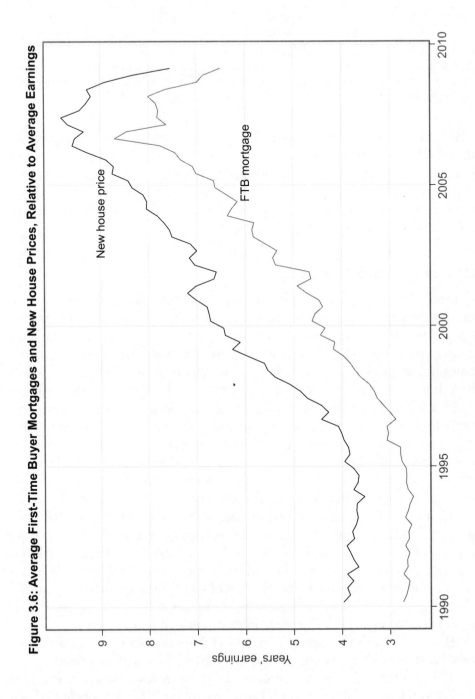

Figure 3.6: Average First-Time Buyer Mortgages and New House Prices, Relative to Average Earnings

Table 3.1: Mortgage Lending and New House Prices in Ireland 1976–2006

Intercept	Mortgage	Interest	Popn	SER	R^2	DW
7.5092	1.1259**	-0.1149**	-0.0016	0.3217	0.9676	0.5495
(4.2788)	(0.2212)	(0.0202)	(0.0014)			

OLS regression of average new house price relative to average earnings on average first-time buyer mortgage relative to average earnings, real mortgage interest rates and population. Quarterly data. Andrews HAC standard error in parentheses.

below the traditional maximum of 80 per cent (and this falls to 15 per cent in Dublin), 64 per cent had ratios above 90 per cent and 30 per cent were 100 per cent mortgages. Looking at terms of mortgages, only 17 per cent of first-time buyers of new houses took out mortgages of less than 25 years, and 58 per cent took out loans of more than 30 years, while for Dublin the corresponding figures are 9 per cent and 69 per cent.

House Prices and Construction

Q theory predicts that residential investment should rise as the price of houses rises relative to their construction cost. Because labour and material costs move with average earnings, the ratio of new house prices to earnings gives a proxy for Tobin's average q. Figure 3.7 shows how private housing completions and the ratio of new house prices to average earnings rose together until 2007. Looking at logs of the two series between 1979 and 2006, applying a Johansen procedure to a VAR (vector autoregression) with eight lags and seasonal dummies, we find a significance at 1 per cent cointegrating relationship $\ln(C) = 1.56\ln(P/Y)$ where C is private completions per quarter, and P/Y is the ratio of new house prices to average earnings. In other words, holding earnings constant, a 10 per cent rise in house prices is associated with a 15 per cent rise in completions.

Figure 3.8 shows the marked impact of house building on GNP. Until 1997, Ireland, like any other industrial economy, received from 4 to 6 per cent of its GNP from building houses. By 2006–07 this had risen to 13 per cent. By comparison, in the other major European housing boom, in Spain, housing investment peaked at 9 per cent of GDP. Adding other construction (but not roads), building was accounting for an extraordinary one-fifth of Irish national income at the peak of the bubble in 2007.[17]

If we look at the increase of Irish GNP between 2000 and 2007, 28 per cent is accounted for directly by the growth of construction output.

This construction boom created two serious distortions in the Irish economy. First, as labour demand rose, particularly for less skilled labour,

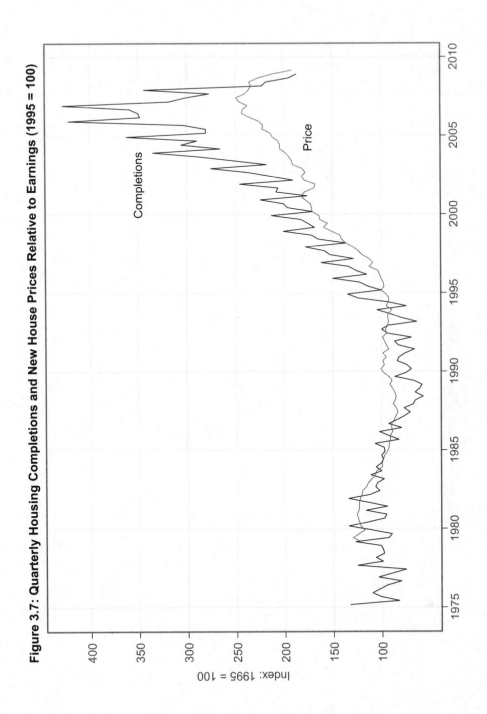

Figure 3.7: Quarterly Housing Completions and New House Prices Relative to Earnings (1995 = 100)

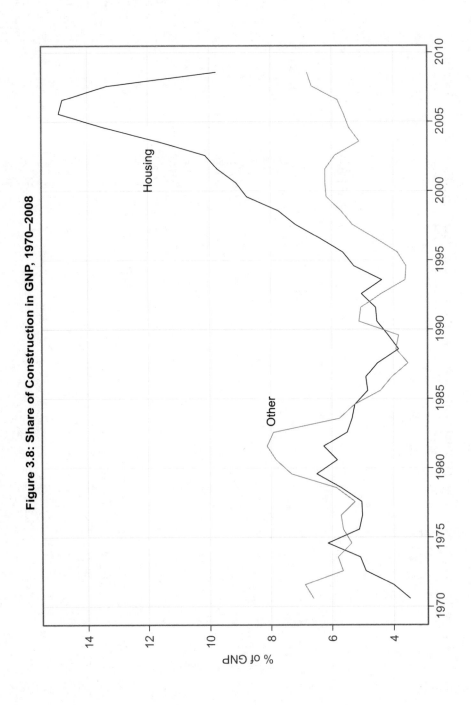

Figure 3.8: Share of Construction in GNP, 1970–2008

wage rates across the economy were driven up out of proportion to productivity growth, leading to a fall in international competitiveness. Between 2000 and 2008 hourly earnings in manufacturing relative to major trading partners rose 20 per cent.[18] The second effect of the building boom was a large rise in government revenue that funded a large rise in government expenditure, which is proving painful to reverse with the ending of the boom.

The Previous Bubble

The credit-fuelled bubble in property prices was actually the second asset bubble in Ireland in a generation. Figure 3.9 shows real land prices in the Limerick region estimated by Roche and McQuinn,[19] expressed in 1997 pounds (multiply by 1.75 to convert into 2009 euros).

After accession to the European Economic Community (EEC) in 1973, Irish banks began to lend heavily to farmers to modernise and expand. As a result, the real price of agricultural land tripled between 1975 and 1977, reaching a peak equivalent to €14,000 per acre in 2009 prices. Real Irish GNP in 1977 was 28 per cent of its 2008 level, so this price is roughly equivalent to €50,000 per acre in current purchasing power for purely agricultural land. By comparison, during the recent boom, when agricultural land prices were driven by demand for potential development, prices peaked in 2006 at an average of €21,000 per acre nationally, and €35,000 in Dublin, Kildare and Wicklow.[20]

The bubble quickly burst as farmers ran into difficulties servicing loans: between 1977 and 1980 real prices fell by around 75 per cent and remained at this level, more or less where it had started in 1973, until 1995, eighteen years after the peak. It can also be seen that, after an earlier boom at independence in 1921, it took 50 years for prices to regain their peak.

The Irish Banks After the Bubble

The collapse of the building boom left Irish banks facing large losses to builders and developers. Despite denials by the banks that they faced any difficulties, their share prices started to slide steadily after March 2007.

This decline accelerated after May 2008 as domestic banking difficulties started to merge with the deepening international financial crisis. The crisis came to a head on 29 September 2008 with a run in wholesale markets on the most aggressively expansionary of the Irish banks, Anglo Irish. Although the crisis had been building for eighteen months, the government and financial regulators appear to have been taken entirely by surprise. At

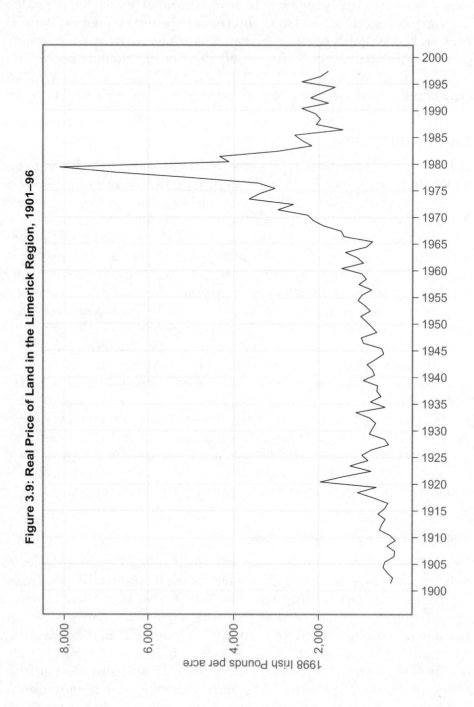

Figure 3.9: Real Price of Land in the Limerick Region, 1901–96

a late-night meeting with the banks, the Irish government committed itself to the unusual step of guaranteeing all existing senior debt of Irish banks (among European economies, only Denmark subsequently did this) as well as deposits. In addition, as well as guaranteeing the two large retail banks (AIB and Bank of Ireland) and two smaller mortgage lenders, for reasons that have never become clear the Irish government agreed to guarantee two specialist property development lenders (Anglo Irish Bank and Irish Nationwide Building Society), despite already well-known deficiencies in their corporate governance.

The most likely rationale for the Irish government's actions is that it still believed that the liquidity problems of the Irish banks merely reflected market nervousness in the wake of Lehman Brothers' collapse, and did not justify concerns about the solvency of these institutions.

Despite the liability guarantee the shares of Irish banks continued to slide, with Anglo Irish Bank being nationalised in February 2009, and the government announcing that it would establish a bad bank called NAMA to buy non-performing development loans from banks.

The idea of a bad bank is simple. Suppose that a bank has €10 billion of capital and has loans of €100 billion, including €20 billion of development loans. Suppose that they suffer 50 per cent losses on these development loans, which wipe out their capital and leave them insolvent.

If the government buys the €20 billion of non-performing loans at their face value, the banks are recapitalised and can continue lending at their previous level, although the taxpayer faces a significant loss, while the bank's shareholders and bondholders lose nothing.

This appears to be the arrangement originally envisaged by the Irish government. To mitigate adverse selection problems, every borrower of the banks associated with NAMA with more than €5 million in property loans (performing or otherwise) would have all their loans, including non-property loans, transferred to NAMA, which would then function as their bank. NAMA's portfolio would be approximately one-third development land, one-third unsold development projects, and the remaining third being so-called associated loans, the non-property loans of transferred borrowers.

Two complications intervened. First, the borrowers being transferred to NAMA included many of the largest and most profitable firms in Ireland. Predictably, a large UK bank offered to repay the loans of these firms to NAMA banks if they transferred their business to it. As a result, the Irish government has apparently agreed that Irish banks will be given a veto on the transfer of borrowers to NAMA. This means that the adverse selection problem reappears, and the portfolio of NAMA, in particular the associated loans that were supposed to generate most of its cash flow, will be worse than the government's business plan predicted.[21]

The second complication came from Europe. First, the European Commission dictated that the Irish government could pay only 70 per cent of the face value of non-performing loans. In terms of our example, this would mean that the bank receives €14 billion for its €20 billion of bad loans, leaving it with only €4 billion of capital. To maintain a minimum capital ratio of 8 per cent of loans, the bank must either raise another €4 billion of capital in the market, or halve its loan portfolio to €50 billion. For the two main Irish banks, the 30 per cent NAMA haircut on transferred loans would reduce the book value of their equity by approximately half.

For AIB, transferring €24 billion of loans to NAMA entails a haircut of €7.2 billion. Given that they have already written down these loans by €2.2 billion, their common equity will fall by €5 billion, or 49 per cent.

For Bank of Ireland, transferring €15 billion of loans to NAMA entails a haircut of €4.6 billion. Given that they have already written down these loans by €0.8 billion, their common equity will fall by €3.8 billion, or 57 per cent.[22]

However, more recently the ECB has required the Irish government to value each asset being transferred individually at market rates, rather than paying 70 per cent of their face value, sight unseen. It therefore seems likely that the amounts that banks receive, particularly for development land, could be considerably less than the 70 per cent first envisaged.

To understand if NAMA will work, we must first ask what problems the Irish banks face. There are three interrelated ones.

First, Irish banks have suffered large losses on developer loans. Secondly, to fund sharply increased lending, Irish banks borrowed heavily in wholesale markets. Thirdly, losses on other loans, in particular mortgages, are likely to be substantial.

The Irish government has, through NAMA, addressed the first problem of developer loans and, in doing so, has pushed the Irish state close to, and quite possibly beyond, the limits of its fiscal capacity. However, NAMA does not address the other two problems: on the liability side of heavy wholesale debt, and on the asset side of further possible losses on other loans. We address these problems in turn.

Bank Liabilities

The first problem that the Irish banks face is that while NAMA remedies many of the current (if not future) problems with the asset side of their balance sheet, the liability side remains difficult. As Figure 3.10 shows, the extraordinary expansion of Irish bank lending after 1997 was funded mostly in wholesale markets, both through interbank borrowing and bonds. Like other financial institutions, Irish banks were able to take advantage of the great moderation – the decade when it was believed that risk had been engineered out of financial systems – to borrow wholesale at almost central bank rates, and to lend at low rates in the Irish property market.

Figure 3.10 shows the evolution of the non-capital liabilities of Irish banks.[23] It can be seen that in 1999 public deposits were much the largest liability. By December 2007, bonds were almost as large as public deposits, while interbank deposits were considerably larger. From early 2008, the Irish banks have faced a sustained loss of bond funding, which has been replaced by interbank borrowing and borrowing from the European Central Bank. There has also been a marked decline in 'other liabilities', corresponding to swap contracts.

The positions of AIB and Bank of Ireland are particularly worrying. AIB had outstanding bonds in August 2009 of €24 billion (plus €5 billion of subordinated debt) and ECB borrowings of €34 billion. Bank of Ireland had bonds of €45 billion (plus €8 billion of subordinated debt) and ECB borrowings of €17 billion. By comparison, even if valuations go as they hope, AIB will receive only €17 billion from NAMA, while Bank of Ireland will receive €11 billion.

The problem of the size of bank debt is compounded by its short maturity. In 2010 AIB has €9.8 billion of bonds maturing, Bank of Ireland €12.2 billion and the nationalised Anglo Irish Bank €9.2 billion. In addition, the Irish state will have to borrow about €20 billion, and roll-over €7.4 billion in maturing debt. Borrowing such sums, on top of issuing €55 billion of NAMA debt to the banks, is likely to prove challenging, even if the markets do not continue to grow more nervous about the sovereign and quasi-sovereign debt of weaker Eurozone states.

The difficulties of funding Irish bank activities are likely to be aggravated by the announced withdrawal of ECB support. During the international financial crisis Irish banks were able to benefit from the ECB's policy of quantitative easing by borrowing against lower quality assets at 1 per cent interest. Now that the French and German economies have technically left recession, the ECB has announced that special lending facilities will start to be curtailed. To the extent that the ECB feels it necessary to re-establish a reputation for political independence, harsh treatment of one of the smaller, peripheral Eurozone economies could be seen as a useful way to send a signal to international markets and larger Eurozone economies that it still takes the stability pact conditions seriously.

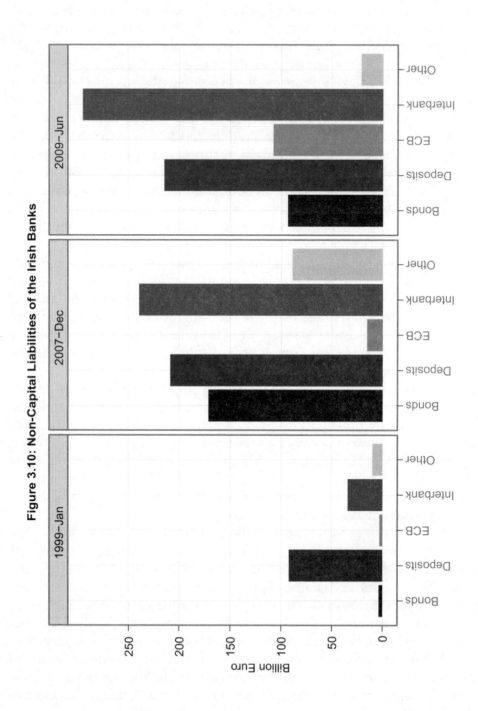

Figure 3.10: Non-Capital Liabilities of the Irish Banks

In summary then, the business model of Irish banks for the last decade of borrowing heavily in wholesale markets to lend in Irish property markets appears defunct. Irish banks now face wholesale lending rates of 5.6 per cent to fund mortgages paying 3.5 per cent interest.

Even domestic deposits are proving problematic as the Irish economy shrinks. Deposits from Irish residents have fallen by 5.5 per cent in the year to September 2009, probably as a result of dissaving by households and firms. Banks may also lose deposits as people vote with their wallets on the politically unpopular bank bailout and transfer their savings to institutions not involved with NAMA and guaranteed by more credit-worthy sovereigns.

In these circumstances, the Irish banks must shrink their balance sheets, by reducing lending and repaying debt. It seems likely that Irish credit levels will return to average international levels in the region of 100 per cent of national income. However, because €110 billion of their lending (equal to 80 per cent of GNP) is tied up in recently issued mortgages of 35 years or longer, it seems unlikely that there will be much new lending to any sector of the Irish economy for the foreseeable future.

The large mortgage book of Irish banks creates another problem for them. The interest rate on most of these mortgages is set at a fixed markup over ECB rates, so the Irish banks have a limited capacity to recapitalise themselves by widening their lending spreads, as US banks did in the early 1990s after the Savings and Loan Crisis.[24]

This sharp contraction in the supply of credit is likely to coincide with a sharp fall in demand. Irish firms and households have run up unusually large debts to fund purchases of property, which has fallen sharply in value. Just like Japan in the 1990s,[25] their overwhelming priority will be to reduce borrowings to sustainable levels.

As expanding credit caused property values to rise, so contracting credit will cause them to fall. If a return to reliance on the retail funding used until 1997 leads to a return to the lending standards of the mid-1990s, then Figures 3.5 and 3.6 would predict a fall in new house prices and commercial property prices of about two-thirds from peak levels. There is a risk, moreover, that a more or less complete cessation of lending for two or three years if banks are forced to rapidly reduce wholesale borrowings, could result in even larger falls than this in the medium term.

The return of the Irish economy to normal levels of bank lending and property prices is to be welcomed. However, it does make it inevitable that the Irish state will suffer large losses on bad loans taken over by NAMA.

The Irish government is assuming that property prices have fallen by 40 per cent from peak, and that if prices rise by 10 per cent in the next decade (in other words to 2004 levels), that NAMA can break even. However, what we have seen is that the only way that property prices can return to 2004 levels is for bank lending to grow at 2004 levels. Given the state of Irish bank balance sheets, even after NAMA, this is an impossibility.

Mortgages

As well as problems of excessive debt on the liability side, Irish banks face the prospect of further loan losses, particularly on mortgages. As we saw in Figure 3.2, mortgage lending rose to €150 billion, or over 100 per cent of late 2009 GNP, about €40 billion of which was securitised.

In the US in September 2009, over 14 per cent of mortgages were at least one payment overdue or in foreclosure, with the rate at 25 per cent in Florida. Looking at a very large sample of US mortgages, Foote et al.[26] identified two factors that overwhelmingly drive default: falls in house prices and unemployment. Among prime mortgages, they found that a 10 per cent fall in house prices increases the risk of a mortgage being in default for 90 days by 82 per cent; while a 1 percentage point increase in unemployment increases the risk by 22 per cent.[27] The level of strategic default is low even in states with non-recourse lending, and most homeowners go to considerable lengths to continue paying their mortgages even when faced with severe negative equity, viewing the prospect of losing their homes as terrifying.[28]

A notable aspect of US mortgage delinquency is the relatively high rate of self-cure: delinquent mortgages that start performing again. Adelino, Gerardi and Willen[29] find that about 30 per cent of US mortgages that are two months delinquent have started performing again within twelve months. This reflects the relative ease of finding a new job in the US. The loss of competitiveness of the Irish economy during the bubble, and the fact that many of the unemployed from the building industry have little formal education, suggests that transitions from unemployment to employment will be rarer, and the rate of self-cure correspondingly lower.

The recent falls in Irish house prices and swift rise in Irish unemployment to 12.5 per cent (compared with 10 per cent in the US) suggests that US rates of default are a strong possibility here. In addition to unemployment, Ireland has a uniquely large source of default risk in emigration. Emigration is one circumstance where strategic default becomes compellingly easy, and the possibility of walking away on a deeply underwater property loan is likely to join unemployment as a compelling reason to make a new life overseas.

Default rates for homeowners in the US start to rise sharply as the loan-to-value ratio exceeds 120 per cent.[30] How close is the average Irish borrower to this cutoff? If we look at the average first-time buyer who took out a 35-year, 90 per cent mortgage at 3.5 per cent interest three years ago at the peak of the market, it would take a fall in prices of 29 per cent to leave their outstanding loan balance (which has now been paid down by 5 per cent) 20 per cent larger than the value of their home. For the average mover, taking out a 30-year, 70 per cent loan-to-value mortgage at that time, it would take a fall of 45 per cent. Given that house price falls around 40 per cent have already occurred, it can be seen that many first-time buyers who bought around the market peak are well within the danger zone, with movers getting close to it.

In the US, banks currently recover around 57 per cent of their outstanding loan in a foreclosure.[31] In Ireland, the difficulties of evicting people from their family homes may make the losses of Irish banks from non-performing mortgages somewhat larger.

For AIB, it would take a loss of 16 per cent on its mortgage book of €33 billion to wipe out its post-NAMA book capital of €5 billion. However, it would take only a loss of 5 per cent on Bank of Ireland's much larger mortgage book of €59 billion to wipe out its post-NAMA book capital of €3 billion.

The difficulties of the Irish banks do not end with property loans. Loans to businesses account for about one-quarter of the loans of the two large Irish banks. Again, substantial losses are possible here. With construction accounting for one-fifth of national income in 2006–07, many Irish firms were heavily or entirely reliant on supplying the construction sector and have had their market effectively disappear.

The property-related borrowings of the owners of smaller Irish companies are a particular concern. By self-selection, the entrepreneurs who establish and run small and medium enterprises are more motivated than average to make money, and the surest way to make money in Ireland during the bubble decade was to borrow heavily to invest in land and property. The heavy personal debts of these business owners are now an impediment to their companies' survival and may lead to large job losses as owners are forced into bankruptcy over losses in property speculation. The destruction of the Irish entrepreneurial class may prove one of the most enduring and costly consequences of the property bubble.

Explaining the Irish Credit Bubble

Credit booms occur sufficiently often and with sufficiently alarming results to have generated a large economic literature. Financial accelerator models emphasise how, in a model of asymmetric information about project quality, rising prosperity increases the value of collateral, which stimulates lending, which further increases the value of collateral.[32] Rajan emphasises herding among banks,[33] Dell'Ariccia and Marquez show how reduced adverse selection during booms causes lending standards to be relaxed,[34] while Berger and Udell examine the loss of institutional memory among loan officers during booms.[35] In the context of the Asian crisis, Corsetti, Pesenti and Roubini argue that the existence of state guarantees of bank liabilities, explicit or implicit, encouraged moral hazard where foreign lenders extended credit to domestic banks for sub-optimal projects.[36]

Notable recent empirical studies of international bubbles include Mendoza and Terrones, who showed how rapid total factor productivity (TFP) growth and relaxed supervision precede credit booms in developed economies, while developing economy booms are associated with capital inflow.[37] Among studies of the US subprime crisis, Dell'Ariccia, Igan and Laeven find that areas with the largest credit expansions experienced the largest declines in credit standards,[38] while Mian and Sufi show that income and mortgage credit growth are negatively correlated across zip codes during the subprime boom of 2002–05, consistent with the idea that an increased supply of credit rather than improved fundamentals drove lending.[39]

All of these factors were present for Irish banks, and their impact was magnified by failures of regulation by the Central Bank and government. The rapid expansion of credit in the Irish economy and the consequent rise in property prices and construction activity represent systematic failures of control at all levels of the Irish economy.

At the first level, bank management lost awareness of the riskiness of their portfolios, extrapolating past rises in incomes and property prices to assume that prices could only go on rising or, at worst, stabilise. The financial accelerator was amplified in Ireland by the extreme narrowness of markets, especially for commercial property, so expansions of credit by a single bank could have a large impact on prices.

The mismanagement of Irish financial institutions was amplified by the presence of a genuinely rogue bank, Anglo Irish. Through aggressive property lending, this had gone from an insignificant merchant bank in the 1990s to the joint second largest bank by 2007. The two large retail banks,

AIB and Bank of Ireland, came under sustained pressure from analysts to match the profits and growth of Anglo Irish, and responded with ultimately baleful consequences.

Since the seventeenth century, financial innovation has consisted of banks finding new ways to lose money. However, while US, UK and European banks lost money in exotic derivatives, Irish banks lost money the old-fashioned way, by making bad property loans.

It is well known that banks get carried away during booms, which is why institutions called central banks exist to curb their enthusiasm. The Irish Central Bank has not had a history of independence from government and, after joining the Eurozone, contented itself with gathering statistics and issuing currency, and made no effort to control the obvious credit bubble engulfing the Irish economy. While there was no explicit relaxation of regulation as occurred in the Nordic economies prior to their credit boom in the late 1980s,[40] the mindset of the Central Bank – that Ireland was a small region of a larger economy where prices and interest rates were set exogenously so policy could have no impact – did lead to the effective disappearance of the active regulation that had been maintained when Ireland had an independent currency.

While the Irish Central Bank lost power to set interest rates, we have seen above that interest rates actually had a limited impact on property prices: the decisive effect was the increased size of loans. Had the Central Bank restricted mortgages to traditional levels of 80 per cent loan-to-value, and three to four times income, house prices would have risen in line with income and many of the distortions of the past decade would have been avoided.

The failings were even graver with respect to development loans where, in many cases, collateral was dispensed with and banks lent against so-called 'personal guarantees' that the bank would have recourse to the borrower's personal assets in the event of default. Large developers were able to borrow hundreds of millions without posting collateral on the strength of their believed equity in other highly leveraged projects they had undertaken.

In summary, the activities of the Irish banks remained extremely simple by international standards and could easily have been regulated had the will to do so been present.

Given the weak independence of the Irish Central Bank, the will to control banks derived ultimately from government. As Johnson argues, the expansion of banking activities since 1990 has seen the effective capture of governments by the financial industry, as politicians in industrialised economies came to view finance as the root of national prosperity.[41] Two factors in Ireland aggravated this tendency. The first is the small size of the country, which ensures that politicians and financiers are inevitably well known to each other: it is easy to become 'too connected to fail'.

Secondly, the unusual magnitude of the Irish credit bubble made the apparent bounty of the banks' activities appear larger here than elsewhere. In particular, the rise in employment stemming from the construction boom – particularly among low-skilled workers in rural areas without other forms of employment – generated a natural alliance of interests among politicians, developers and banks.[42]

The Irish government was therefore poorly equipped to understand the crisis when it finally occurred in late September 2008. Instead of recognising the borrowing difficulties of Irish banks as the result of well-grounded market apprehension about their solvency, the Irish government responded to the crisis as if it were a temporary problem of liquidity in the aftermath of the Lehman Brothers collapse.

Once committed to guaranteeing all senior debt as well as deposits of all six Irish banks, the Irish government found itself in the position of not being able to change direction to share losses with bank bondholders without being forced to admit that it had made a mistake in its initial guarantee.

However, the question remains of why, given that Ireland's bankers were probably no more reckless, its regulators no more spineless, and its politicians no more clueless than their counterparts elsewhere, did Ireland come to have a far larger credit boom than other wealthy economies, with the exception of Iceland? The most likely reason is that Ireland's credit boom was preceded by a decade of real, competitiveness-driven growth. Irish lenders, borrowers and regulators became accustomed to economic growth of 6–7 per cent, which disguised the magnitude of the credit bubble that followed it.

Conclusions

In the last decade, the Irish economy has experienced an unusually large credit bubble. Lending as a fraction of GNP increased from 60 per cent in 1997 to over 200 per cent in 2008, twice the level of other industrialised economies.

In the aftermath of this bubble, the Irish banking system faces three interrelated problems. The first is that it has made large losses on loans to property developers. The second is that it has large wholesale liabilities to international bondholders and, increasingly, to the European Central Bank.

The final problem is that it faces likely further large losses on mortgages and business loans.

The Irish government's policy response has been solely to address the first problem of losses on developer loans by establishing a state institution to buy these loans (NAMA). However, by ignoring the second problem of the large wholesale liabilities of the Irish banks, this project will inevitably end in expensive failure.

As Irish banks are forced to repay this wholesale borrowing and to shrink their balance sheets to normal international levels, the sharply diminished supply of credit will lead inevitably to continued sharp falls in property prices. These falls in property prices will result in severe losses for the Irish taxpayer on the ill-conceived NAMA project.

Despite having pushed the Irish state close to, and quite possibly beyond, the limits of its fiscal capacity with the NAMA scheme, the Irish banks remain as zombies whose only priority is to reduce their debt, and who face complete destruction from mortgage losses.

The issue therefore is not whether the Irish bank bailout will restore the Irish banks so that they can function as independent commercial entities: it cannot. Rather it is whether the Irish government's commitments to bank bondholders, when added to its existing spending commitments, will overwhelm the fiscal capacity of the Irish state, forcing outside entities such as the IMF and EU to intervene and impose a resolution on the Irish banking system.

4

Towards Perfect Information:
The Case of the Housing Market

Ronan Lyons

Introduction

Economic models are frequently criticised for the often heroic assumptions that underpin them. One of the most heroic is the concept of perfect information, namely that all actors in the market have the same (complete) set of information available to them. Results from theory often crucially depend on this assumption. Naturally, it will never be the case that all actors in an economy have totally perfect information. Nonetheless, moving towards perfect information can help deliver the benefits suggested by economic theory. This is the case, for example, with the Irish property market, where currently market actors are expected to make decisions without a clear picture of what is happening in the market around them.

This chapter reviews the recent history of and medium-term prospects for Ireland's property market, including its significant boom and bust and the issue of negative equity. It also aims to show that better information in the property market in Ireland will contribute to more sustainable economic growth in the future. Poor quality of information in the property market contributed in no small part to the severity of the early twenty-first century boom and bust in Ireland. The current market in Ireland lacks many of the basic features of other property markets that give all actors better information on which to base some of the most important economic decisions they will make.

87

Lessons can be learned from other core systems on which modern economies are based, which are digitising and creating new streams of information for market actors. Examples from road usage and water management are discussed. Indeed, unless better information is made available to buyers and sellers in Ireland's property market, the foundations of Ireland's property market will remain unstable and therefore so will Ireland's economic growth.

The Coincidence of the Global and Irish Recessions

2009 will be remembered as a unique year in the post-war global economy, with the vast majority of the developed economies in the Organisation for Economic Cooperation and Development (OECD) contracting. The International Monetary Fund's (IMF) October 2009 *World Economic Outlook* estimated that the global economy would shrink by 1.1 per cent in 2009 – with advanced economies driving this fall in economic activity, shrinking 3.4 per cent in the calendar year.[1] Central to the global recession has been a collapse in global trade networks. The same IMF report estimates that the volume of world trade shrank 12 per cent in 2009, with advanced economies again harder hit.[2]

At the same time, Ireland's recession has been one of the most severe, with gross domestic product (GDP) 7.6 per cent lower in 2009 than a year previous.[3] Given that Ireland is one of the most trade-dependent countries in the world, it would be easy to believe that the severity of Ireland's recession is linked to its trade openness. However, the primary driver of Ireland's economic growth from 2003 until the start of the recession was a domestic boom, rather than international competitiveness. Between 1999 and 2003, when real GDP growth averaged 7.3 per cent, net exports added an average of almost 2 percentage points to Ireland's GDP growth each year. Between 2004 and 2008, when growth averaged almost 4 per cent, the equivalent contribution of net exports was just 0.2 per cent.[4]

Quite unusually, that trend reversed in 2009, with international trade making a significant positive contribution to Irish growth at the height of the global trade collapse. Indeed, during the course of 2009, the surprisingly strong performance of net exports was a huge boost to the economy, at a time when other parts of the economy were severely contracting. It is likely that net exports added close to 3 percentage points of growth to GDP in 2009, while consumption, investment and government expenditure on their own would have led to a fall in GDP of close to 10 per cent. Figure 4.1 shows Eurostat figures by country, showing the change in exports in the first three quarters of 2009, compared to the same period for 2008. Almost every country's exports were down by at least 15 per cent – and some down by a third – compared to 2008. Ireland's exports, however, were only marginally down.

Figure 4.1: Change in Exports by EU Member State, Jan–Sept 2009 Over Same Period in 2008

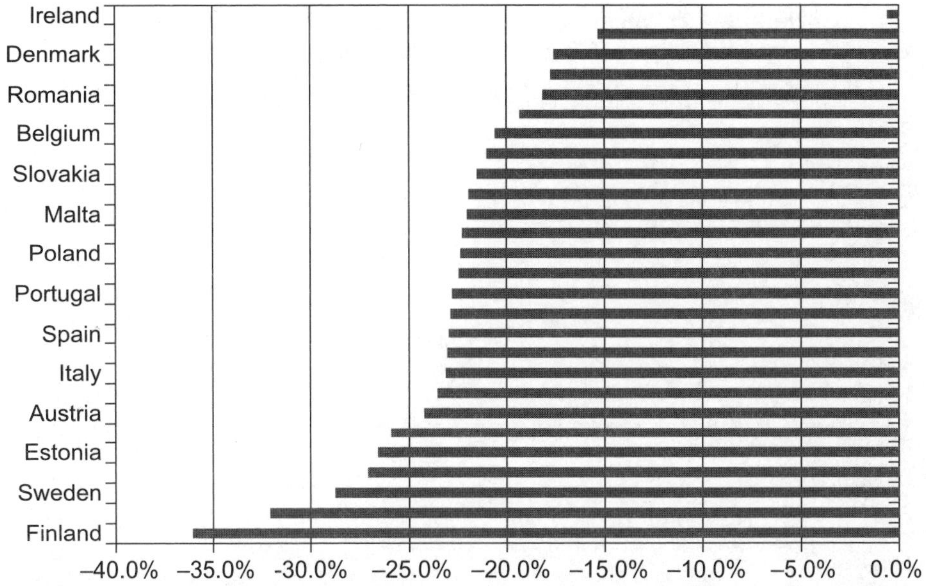

Source: Author's calculations, based on figures from Eurostat external and intra-European Union trade, No. 01/2010

Ireland's Domestic Recession

Ireland's recession, therefore, has not been driven by international factors such as the fall in global trade. The source has been domestic. In particular, it has been linked to the collapse in Ireland's construction boom and resulting falls in domestic investment and consumption. Private consumption in 2009 was almost 10 per cent below its peak in 2007, while private investment had fallen by substantially more: 40 per cent.

The result has been a sharp fall in employment, which of course brings further adverse second-round effects on consumption and investment, as well as on the Exchequer balance, through smaller tax receipts and larger social welfare spending. At the height of the boom, in mid-2007, there were over 1.75 million people in full-time employment in Ireland. By late 2009, that number had fallen almost 15 per cent to just over 1.5 million. With the numbers employed in the public sector staying largely static, the proportional fall in those employed in the private sector has been even greater.

Figure 4.2 shows the percentage fall in private sector employment from peak levels during the current recession in Ireland, compared with two major United States (US) downturns, the one starting in 2007 and the Great Depression starting in 1929.

Figure 4.2: Fall in Private Sector Employment from Peak, Ireland (from 2007) and USA (from 2007 and from 1929)

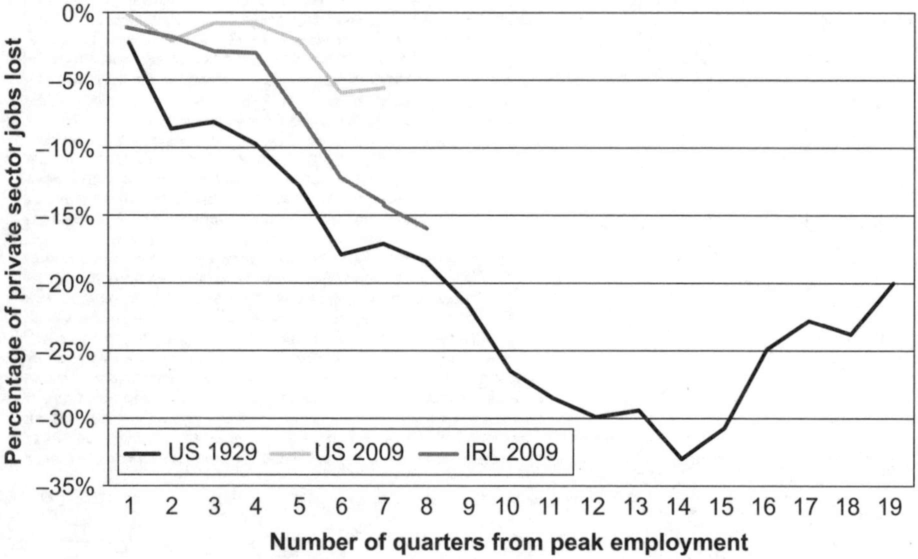

Source: Author's calculations based on CSO Quarterly National Household Survey and US Bureau of Labor Statistics CES Survey.

Understanding Ireland's Property Market Bubble

Domestically driven economic growth from 2003 on was focused around the construction industry and occurred at a time of rapidly rising house prices. House prices peaked in January 2007, having risen by almost 300 per cent in the ten years to 2007, according to the Economic and Social Research Institute (ESRI)/permanent tsb house price index (Figure 4.3).[5] The average rate of growth of over 14 per cent per annum during that decade makes Ireland's house price boom the largest among developed countries across a panel of seventeen countries surveyed by *The Economist* magazine.[6]

A range of factors was responsible for raising house prices in Ireland during that period. For a start, **average incomes rose**, with public sector wages rising by 75 per cent and industrial wages rising by 65 per cent in the

Figure 4.3: House Prices in Ireland, 1996–2009

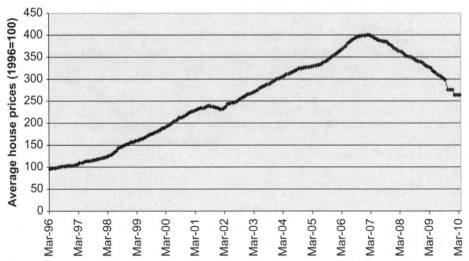

Source: Author's calculations, based on figures from ESRI/permanent tsb House Price Index.

decade to 2006.[7] An important related factor is greater participation in the labour market by women, with the **proportion of women in the labour force** growing from about 40 per cent in the late 1990s to 55 per cent in 2007.[8] Those rates of income growth and greater participation are consistent with almost a doubling of house prices. With incomes rising by a factor of 1.7, and the typical household applying with 1.55 incomes, rather than 1.4, these two factors combined would mean the typical household would be able to borrow 90 per cent more, everything else being equal.

Everything else, however, was not equal. Other factors were also changing, including the financing environment. This changed in two key respects. Firstly, **competition among banks** and a lack of specific rules about the maximum amount to be lent led to greater multiples of income being lent to prospective purchasers. Secondly, and perhaps more importantly, **interest rates fell** steadily as Ireland prepared itself for and entered into European economic and monetary union (EMU). Nominal interest rates on mortgages, which were as high as 7.4 per cent in late 1997, fell by more than half to 3.5 per cent for a prolonged period between 2003 and 2005 (Figure 4.4).[9] The real interest rate, particularly when calculated using house price inflation, rather than consumer prices, was negative every single quarter bar one, between 1997 and 2007.

Figure 4.4: Typical Mortgage Interest Rates in Ireland

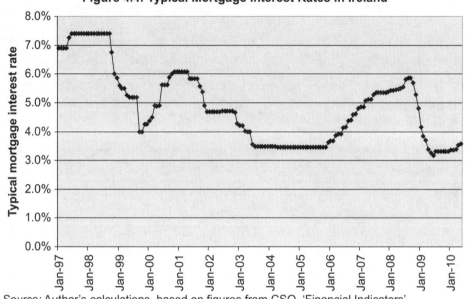

Source: Author's calculations, based on figures from CSO, 'Financial Indicators'.

A one-off downward shift in the expected medium-term nominal interest rate, from 7 per cent to 3.5 per cent, should lead to a doubling of house prices, in an environment where amounts lent are determined by the mortgage burden as a proportion of monthly disposable income. Combined with an effect of similar size from growth in incomes and participation rates as outlined above, this means that, knowing nothing else about the economy, one would expect house prices to have increased by somewhere in the region of 350 per cent over the period.

An increase of 350 per cent would have actually been greater than the best metric available on the true increase (closer to 300 per cent). It is important to bear in mind, though, that all the factors listed so far are demand-side, the financing environment being the mechanism for turning latent demand into effective demand. If, according to demand factors, house prices should have risen by 350 per cent, but instead rose by less and have since fallen substantially, what explains this?

The solution to the puzzle lies in supply-size factors, which played a huge role in Ireland's boom and bust. In 2006, Ireland's completion rate – the **number of new homes being built** per 1,000 people – was 22, compared to 6 in Finland, 3.5 in the United Kingdom (UK) and 3 in Germany.[10] That year, Ireland built more than one-fifth of the total number of properties built in the UK and Germany *combined*, while only having 3 per cent of the population. And while it did mark the peak of construction, 2006 was not a one-off. Figure 4.5 shows the total number of new homes built per 1,000 people between 2000 and 2007. Construction of new homes in Ireland was about six times the rate of the typical European country during that period. Successive years of construction well above Ireland's long-run average, fuelled by cheap credit and tax breaks, meant that the number of dwellings in Ireland increased by 60 per cent, to 1.9 million, from 1998 to 2007.[11]

Figure 4.5: Number of New Homes Built per 1,000 people, 2000–07, Various Countries (Total)

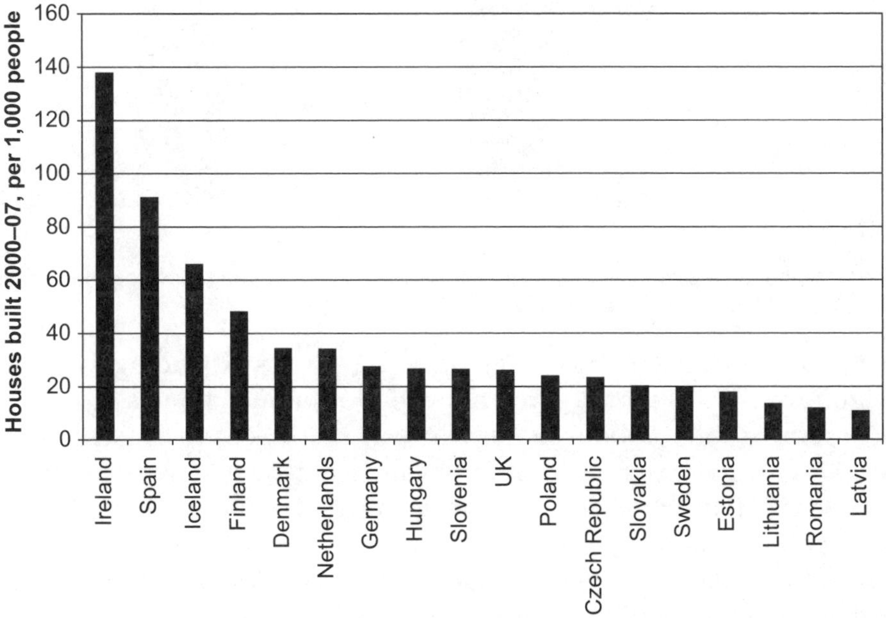

Source: Author's calculations, based on figures from European Mortgage Federation, 'Hypostat 2007'.

Some of this can certainly be attributed to population growth. But this explains perhaps only half of the increase in supply. As part of Ireland's initially export-led economic growth, the number of jobs in the economy did increase dramatically, with employment rising more than 40 per cent in the decade to 2007. However, significant unemployment in the 1990s meant that the main source of new workers was those already living in Ireland, at least until 2004. While the number of dwellings in Ireland rose 60 per cent, the number of occupied households rose by just 30 per cent over a similar period, from 1.1 million in the census of 1996 to 1.5 million in 2006, as shown in Figure 4.6.[12]

Figure 4.6: Number of Occupied Households and Dwellings, Ireland, 2002 and 2006

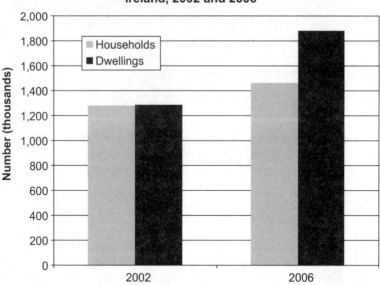

Source: Author's calculations, based on figures from the European Mortgage Federation, 'Hypostat' and CSO, 'People and Society'.

So, not only did construction keep up with Ireland's expanding workforce, it significantly overshot it. Even allowing for holiday homes, 1.9 million houses for 1.5 million households suggests that the over-construction of the 2000s has left Ireland with a significant overhang of unused properties. The rise of interest rates in 2006 and 2007 was the pin that burst the Irish property bubble.

Initially, Ireland was part of a global story, with house prices falling in most developed countries. However, by late 2009, house prices had stopped falling in 31 of 42 countries.[13] While asking prices in Ireland fell by 19 per cent during 2009, they rose in the UK by almost 6 per cent.[14] What has made Ireland's property market downturn more severe than other countries is the existence of a significant oversupply of property. Higher interest rates were the short-run trigger for falling house prices; oversupply will determine the longer-run dynamic.

Yields and the Property Market's Medium-Term Outlook

The medium-term outlook for Ireland's property market depends as much on this boom-time overconstruction as it does on other factors, such as global economic growth. In particular, the relationship between rents and house prices, commonly called the yield, will be particularly important. The yield on a property is similar to the interest rate on a savings account. At the very least, the return on holding property should exceed the cost of borrowing. The yield on an average Dublin residential property is shown in Figure 4.7, along with typical mortgage interest rates. A rate of 5 per cent is also highlighted, as this represents a likely lower bound for a feasible medium-term yield on residential property.

Figure 4.7: Interest Rates and Residential Property Yields in Dublin, 1998–2009

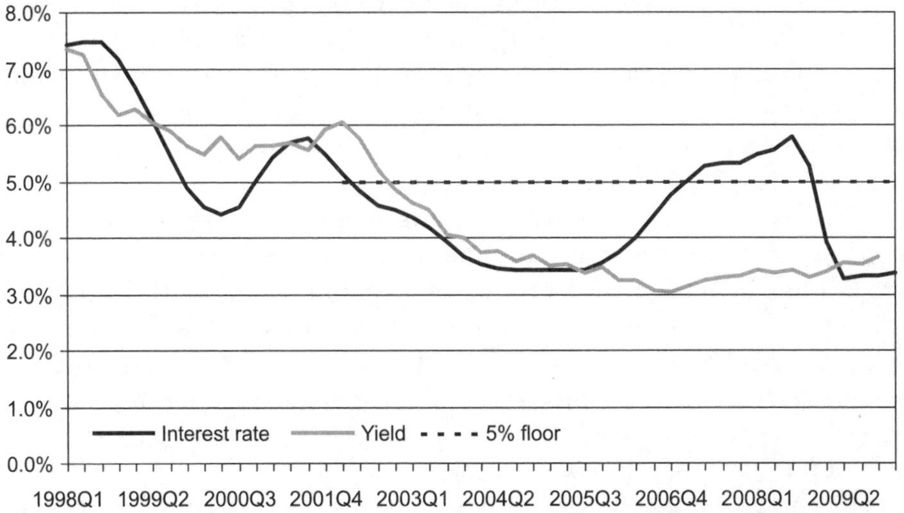

Source: Author's calculations, based on figures from CSO (interest rates) and daft.ie (rents).

Yields in Ireland have fallen substantially since 2001, as rents fell while house prices rose steadily. As the Irish economy became used to lending rates of less than 4 per cent, so were yields driven below that point. Interest rates can change much faster than yields though, and rapidly rising interest rates in 2006 were one of the key tipping points that burst the bubble in the Irish property market. In early 2007, when house prices were falling, rents were still rising, leading to a small increase in the average yield from 3 per cent to 3.4 per cent.

During 2008 and 2009, the surplus of properties that flooded both sales and lettings markets meant that house prices and rents fell steadily and at largely similar rates. Therefore, by mid-2010, yields did not improve significantly. Where rents level off, which in turn depends on the supply and demand of rental properties, will provide investors in particular – but also the property market in general – with an important signal of the return on property, which itself will help determine a floor for property prices.

The Economic Costs of Negative Equity

In one very important way, a significant fall in property costs of all kinds, from the cost of buying a home to the cost of renting office space, is very good for Ireland. It improves Ireland's international cost competitiveness. A 2006 study by the National Competitiveness Council found that, in internationally traded sectors of importance to Ireland, property costs comprised between 5 per cent and 15 per cent of costs depending on the sector and city, with Dublin particularly expensive.[15] By 2008, Dublin office rents were among the ten most expensive in the world, according to CB Richard Ellis Group.[16] By May 2010, these costs had fallen by almost 33 per cent and the city had fallen to be the twenty-fourth most expensive location.[17] In addition, falling residential property prices ease wage demands of workers, which comprise anywhere up to 75 per cent of the total costs incurred by internationally traded activities.[18]

There is an important downside, however, to falling property values. For many of those who are owner-occupiers, their home is worth less than the outstanding debt on it. Under the current system, financial institutions can refuse permission to sell a home if the debt-holders are unable to repay the entire debt following the sale of the house. Particularly for those who bought 'starter homes', or properties of a size inadequate for their needs in ten years, there is the prospect of being trapped in a property viewed at the time of purchase as a short-term move.

How prevalent will the problem of negative equity be in Ireland over the coming years? Of the 1.7 million households in the country, about 600,000 (or 35 per cent) have a mortgage. Estimates based on county-level asking prices suggest that about 150,000 homes were in negative equity by mid-2010. A further 110,000 homes were estimated to be close to negative equity, meaning that a fall in house prices from the peak of about 50–5 per cent could leave almost 260,000 homes in negative equity.[19]

Based on late 2009 prices, about 56,000 households were in severe negative equity of €50,000 or more, with a further 70,000 likely to fall into that category, should house prices halve from their peak values.[20] An important dimension to the problem is a regional one, as it is unlikely that the phenomenon of negative equity will affect all parts of the country equally, however. The proportion of homes with mortgages varies from about 30 per cent in Kerry and Donegal to 45 per cent in Meath and Kildare. Together with the uneven impact of the rise in unemployment, some counties will be particularly heavily hit by both property price falls and rising unemployment, such as Longford, Leitrim and Westmeath, while others will largely escape.

For mortgage holders who are in employment and who can continue to pay their monthly repayments, the main problem will be those trapped in properties that are too small for their needs. A more serious problem is likely to arise where households face both negative equity and unemployment. As mentioned above, about 250,000 people lost their jobs between the height of the boom and late 2009. Many of those are likely to be mortgage holders. Even assuming the rise of 'unexpected unemployment' has not been clustered in mortgage-holding cohorts, it is likely that over 20,000 households face the twin problems of unemployment, where they cannot pay back their mortgage, and negative equity, where they cannot sell their property because they cannot cover their outstanding debt. These figures broadly correspond to Financial Regulator figures published in December 2009, which showed that just over 26,000 mortgages (3.3 per cent of all mortgages) were in arrears of greater than 90 days.[21]

Solutions to Ireland's Negative Equity Crisis

There are no easy solutions to Ireland's negative equity problem. There have been calls to introduce mortgages of greater than 100 per cent loan-to-value, to allow people to essentially "double-up" their negative equity into a new mortgage. For example, consider a couple who bought a two-bedroom apartment in Dublin for €350,000 in 2005 with a 95 per cent mortgage. By 2010, with the apartment worth about €200,000, they would have paid back about 10 per cent of the principal, meaning that they would have an outstanding debt to the bank of €300,000, i.e. they would be in negative equity of about €100,000. Hoping to start a family, they would like to move to a three-bedroom house in the suburbs, now costing about €400,000. They have savings of €40,000, but now need a loan of €460,000 – or 115 per cent of the value of the house – to cover both the €100,000 in negative equity from their first property and the cost of their new home. Regardless of the potential risks of lending more than 100 per cent of the value of their home, their circumstances, including their employment situation, might not make them eligible for a loan of €460,000.

So while doubling up negative equity into a new larger loan may be a solution for some, such as those in the public sector with permanent contracts, other solutions will have to be found for the vast majority who find themselves in negative equity. One solution will inevitably be greater adaptability, both in terms of changing homes and extending and also in terms of commuting, on the part of those who have bought in one area but found employment in another. Another is likely to be a further breaking down of the boundaries between renting and buying. One of the unintended consequences of the construction boom is that it is now possible to rent, as well as buy, properties of all major types and sizes in all major regions of the country. This has blurred the traditional distinction of quality between rental and owner-occupier properties. Those who have bought one type of property which no longer suits, either due to location or size, and who are unable to sell due to negative equity, may find it easiest to let their original property and become tenants themselves in a property better suited to them. This indeed may be the most attractive option to those scarred by their first experience of buying property.

Property Market Information in Ireland

Quite how far Irish property prices have fallen from the peak since 2007 is unknown. Information about Irish property prices comes mainly from three sources. The first is the official data on house prices published by the Department of the Environment, Heritage and Local Government (DOEHLG).[22] While it is official, there are three causes for concern with the DOEHLG series. Firstly, it is based on data from mortgage lending institutions, as opposed to complete information on all transactions.[23] Secondly, the series is based on an arithmetic average, rather than a set of regressions controlling for house characteristics. Thirdly, and most problematically, the series is severely lagged. For example, data on prices in April, May and June 2009 were not published until October. By comparison, the US Department of Housing and Urban Development publishes a monthly series, with October 2009 data (on both median house price and the volume of transactions) published in November.[24]

The second source is a series published by the ESRI and permanent tsb.[25] Until 2010, it was published monthly and with a lag of about one month, overcoming some of the issues with the DOEHLG series. It also gave an eight-way breakdown by location, house type and purchaser, in addition to a national average. However, it is based on information provided by just one mortgage provider, with a market share in the region of 20 per cent. With a low level of transactions, as has been the case in the market between 2007 and 2009, the limitations of a series based on one mortgage provider become apparent. Firstly, in 2010, it became a quarterly rather than monthly series. Secondly, the various sub-indices were discontinued for periods of low activity. The sub-index for a three-bed semi-detached house was not published at any point during 2009, while all other sub-indices apart from 'Dublin' and 'Outside Dublin' were not published throughout the entire second half of 2009. A final issue is that the data are based on mortgage drawdowns, which will necessarily be lagged. To see why this might be problematic, consider a transaction off the plans, agreed in February 2007 based on prices set by the developer in December 2006. Were construction to take eighteen months, the mortgage would be drawn down in September 2008, at which point a price almost two years old would enter the ESRI/permanent tsb index. While this problem is most acute for off-the-plans purchases, a smaller version of the same lag is a more general feature.

The third source of data is the daft.ie asking price index.[26] The index is published quarterly and gives monthly data down to county level. Figures are based on hedonic price regressions across 300 regions in the country, with controls for a range of measurable attributes including bedroom number, bathroom number and house type. It is estimated that over 95 per cent of estate agents in the country are covered and the average monthly sample size in 2008 was over 12,000 properties.[27] However, while it is the most information-rich of all the measures, all figures are based on asking prices, rather than closing prices, and as such the index measures changes in sellers' expectations, as opposed to the prices themselves.

Used together, these three sources can provide some insight about how far property prices have fallen. The DOEHLG series suggests a 33 per cent average fall between 2007 and the end of 2009. Both the ESRI/permanent tsb and daft.ie indices showed a fall of greater than 40 per cent in Dublin and 30 per cent elsewhere between the peak and the first quarter of 2010. Given the nature of each of these statistics, though, it is reasonable to believe that the true fall between early 2007 and early 2010 was greater. If closing prices in early 2010 were 10 per cent below asking prices on average, that would suggest an average fall from the peak by early 2010 of about 45 per cent in Dublin and 35 per cent elsewhere. But it is impossible to know for certain.

It is precisely the lack of exact information that will delay stabilisiation and recovery in Ireland's property market, recovery here meaning a return to a normal number of transactions, and not a return to either high growth rates or indeed to peak prices. Given the role that construction plays in all economies, this means that Ireland's broader economic recovery will also be delayed. Prospective buyers and sellers of property in other countries have access to up-to-date information on property prices at a national level and typically also a local level. The US example was given above but is by no means an isolated example. In Australia, information similar to the US series is also published monthly.[28] In the UK, government published monthly figures at a local level are available free of charge through a website,

<www.landreg.gov.uk>.[29] In addition to price information, the volume of transactions is also available.

Ideally, those looking to transact in Ireland's property market would have both aggregate and individual property market information at their disposal. For aggregate information, the data are already being collected by the Revenue Commissioners, who have full data on property market transactions through stamp duty. For information on individual transactions, legislative changes would be needed, as currently the publication of individual transactions is in breach of data protection laws. Nonetheless, it is expected that this information will become available some time in the near future, as in August 2010 the Minister for Justice announced the establishment of a property price database to be managed by the Property Services Regulatory Authority.[30]

Better Information and Future Growth Prospects

The lack of up-to-date information in Ireland's property market reflects the mode of civil administration that prevailed in Ireland and internationally up to the late twentieth century. That mode reflected the line of thought that civil administrations were essentially outside the economy, particularly in the collation and dissemination of information and statistics.

Increasingly, however, governments recognise that they are an integral part of the economy. For example, the Australian Bureau of Statistics states: 'although the ABS acknowledges that the various price indexes it publishes are used by businesses and government to adjust payments and/or charges, it neither endorses nor discourages such use.'[31] In addition to wage adjustments, the importance of government provided information can be seen in finance. Markets around the world wait on particular series, such as the 'Nonfarm Payrolls' series in the US, which is released 'at 8:30am Eastern Time on the third Friday after the conclusion the week which included the 12th of the month' and has a significant impact on stock markets.[32]

Providing individuals and firms with access to timely and reliable information is now a key responsibility of governments around the world, one that extends beyond stock markets. It is a responsibility that will become central in many aspects of life over the coming generation, as more key systems that are the foundation of economic activity become digitised. Not only this, but increasingly the generation of information from digitised infrastructures is likely to be a differentiator between countries in the global economy.

For example, in Singapore, it is expected that in the next few years the current system of road pricing will be replaced by one based on global positioning system (GPS) technology. This will allow variable pricing of road usage, based on factors such as traffic levels, availability of public transport alternatives and vehicle emissions. The GPS-based system is expected to further improve the flow of traffic by better aligning social and private costs. But its implementation will also create significant amounts of data that in turn can be analysed to generate information about traffic volumes and road usage. There are significant benefits for road users from real-time information, particularly in the allocation of time. Concurrently, Singapore is likely to solidify its place as an international hub of activities in information technology-based (IT-based) road usage activities.

As the example from Singapore shows, transport infrastructure is likely to become more digitised around the world in coming years. The same is true for the other core systems on which modern economies are based, such as energy, where intelligent utility networks are being developed. In the area of water, digitisation is already underway in Ireland, as it seeks to prepare for the European Union Water Framework Directive. The SmartBay Galway project is an example of modern civil administration, based on the provision of real-time information to stakeholders.[33]

The SmartBay system comprises a network of buoys, seafloor cables, sensors and other communication technologies, which are used for real-time monitoring of Galway Bay. It creates real-time information on weather, waves and tides needed for responsibilities including those of harbourmaster and forecasting. This information is made available to the general public. Greater information at the disposal of those managing fishing boats or organising a family trip to the beach is a Pareto improvement.

The same reasoning applies across all the systems on which Ireland's economy is based, from energy to regulation and including its property market. Without a clear and timely picture of the volume and price of housing transactions in Ireland, it is likely that the market will overshoot in both upswings and downturns. While even up to twenty years ago, it could be argued that the capabilities needed for accessible real-time property prices were prohibitively expensive, the spread of IT and online technologies means that this sort of information can be provided very easily.

Conclusions

Ireland is currently undergoing a painful property market correction, following years of significant house price inflation. Over-construction of property in the boom years will take years to work through, particularly in areas of the country worst affected. The legacy will be long felt in other ways also, particularly by those facing significant amounts of negative equity.

The correction does give us the opportunity to shape the Ireland of the future. This is true, for example, in the area of public finances and the taxation of property. The Irish government has learned to its cost the huge dangers in relying on transactions-based duties. In its place, the government should look to institute a property taxation system that raises a similar amount in revenues but that neither requires transactions to occur nor discourages the incentive to invest in one's home.

Another opportunity also exists. While the property market is essentially on hold, the opportunity exists to modernise Ireland's property market and provide actors with clear and timely information that they can use to inform their decisions. As examples from other core infrastructures, such as transport and water, show, this is not only the future for governments' management of property markets but also for public services generally, as the huge potential of information technologies is tapped.

5

Fiscal Consolidation in Ireland:
Lessons from the First Time[1]

Colm McCarthy

Second Time Round for Fiscal Consolidation in Ireland

For the second time in a generation, Ireland is in a deep fiscal crisis, with double-digit borrowing, escalating debt and concerns about the country's solvency in international debt markets, reflected in the second largest adverse bond spreads of any Eurozone member. What's different this time is that the fiscal system's second crisis since the foundation of the state has coincided with the banking system's first. The banks have lost a large portion (on worst estimates, all) of their capital and survive only with a state guarantee of their liabilities and liquidity furnished, on a prodigious scale, by the European Central Bank.[2]

Parallels with the first Irish fiscal crisis in the 1980s are of limited value given the quite different circumstances. The 1987–90 consolidation did not coincide with a banking collapse, nor did it coincide with a worldwide credit crunch and a rapid world trade contraction. The next section argues that fiscal consolidation post-1987 was less daunting than is likely to be the case over the next few years, and that the role of current expenditure cuts has been exaggerated in journalistic renderings of the history of the period.

The recent deterioration in the Irish public finances has been extraordinarily rapid – even with substantial tax rate increases, revenue has fallen far more rapidly than the tax base, while spending has continued to advance, despite the widespread perception of cutbacks. The conduct of fiscal policy since 2000 is reviewed in the third section, and the prospects for a medium-term fiscal consolidation in the following section. The paper concludes with some lessons from the Irish experience for politicians – and for economists.

The 1980s Fiscal Correction and the First Bord Snip[3]

The current fiscal crisis is Ireland's second, and it is understandable that commentators should seek parallels with the first. By 1978, the debt ratio (Exchequer debt to gross national product (GNP)) had reached about 65 per cent[4] and economists had begun warning about sustainability. In January 1980, Taoiseach Charles Haughey made a famous TV broadcast in which he opined that '...we are living beyond our means'. He went on to promise an immediate fiscal austerity programme, but relented quickly. The subsequent development of Exchequer borrowing is shown in Figure 5.1.

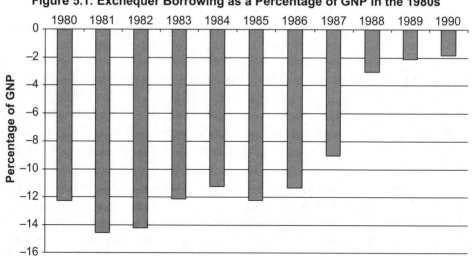

Figure 5.1: Exchequer Borrowing as a Percentage of GNP in the 1980s

Borrowing ran at double-digit rates for over a decade from the mid-1970s, and by 1988, when sustainability was re-attained, the debt-to-GNP ratio had reached 117 per cent. It is worth remembering that various fiscal programmes were prepared in the early 1980s which envisaged better macro performance than actually occurred and a more rapid return to fiscal balance. What happened in 1988 was planned to happen by 1983 or 1984.

The large deficits from 1980 onwards arose principally from a combination of revenue weakness (despite sharp increases in tax rates), expenditure growth in the early years and the build-up of debt service costs. There were three general elections in the 1981–2 period, each of which saw a change of government, and it is interesting to focus on the position in 1987 compared to 1982 under the main expenditure and revenue headings. This spans the period in office of the only long-lived government (the Fine Gael–Labour coalition which took office in December 1982) during the fiscal crisis after the penny dropped, so to speak. The figures are shown in Table 5.1.

Table 5.1: Fiscal Policy over the 1982–7 Period

	Cumulative % Change	Average Annual
Current Services	40.6	7.1
Central Fund	71.6	11.4
Total Current	47.3	8.1
Exchequer Capital	-17.9	-3.9
Total Government Spending	36.5	6.4
Total Revenue	48.7	8.3
Nominal GNP	46.3	7.9
CPI	35.4	6.3

Source: Department of Finance, Budgetary and Economic Statistics, published 25 September 2009, various tables.

Current non-interest spending rose only a little in real terms, but central fund spending (mainly debt service) rose dramatically. Exchequer capital spending actually fell, so total government spending barely exceeded consumer price index (CPI) inflation. The lesson is that, if the tax base is growing only very slowly, as evidenced by sluggish nominal GNP,[5] the build-up of debt service means that spending must actually be cut – it is not enough to just hold the line. The primary surplus never rises fast enough. The consequence was a fiscal crisis that lasted eight years from Mr Haughey's dramatic TV broadcast, and a decade from the realisation, at least in the economics profession, that this was indeed a fiscal crisis. Debt service absorbed about 30 per cent of tax revenue for ten straight years, total employment in 1991 had barely regained the level of a decade earlier and there was net outward migration in each year bar one from 1980 to 1991. In total, 221,000 people emigrated over this period, out of a population averaging about 3.5 million people, versus 4.5 million in April 2009. All of this was accompanied by external imbalance and successive devaluations within the European pegged exchange rate system of the time. Honohan and Walsh[6] provide an extended discussion of the attempts to restore fiscal balance during these years.

A minority Fianna Fail government, led by Mr Haughey and with Ray MacSharry as Minister for Finance, took over in March 1987 and proceeded to establish the first Bord Snip in May 1987. It was led by the secretary of the Department of Finance, Sean Cromien, who has recently penned an account of the episode as viewed from the civil service.[7] A surprising number of myths, none of them the handiwork of the participants, has grown up about the activities and impact of this body, of which the author was a member.

Briefly, there was no significant reduction in the real volume of current spending as a result of the first Bord Snip. There *was* a further squeeze on capital spending, a mistake in retrospect, but most of the adjustment came on the revenue side. The 'slash and burn' stories about 1987, references to the finance minister as Mac the Knife, decimation of public services and so forth are just journalistic invention. It never happened and the actual numbers are in Table 5.2.

Table 5.2: The First Irish Fiscal Correction, 1987–90

	1987	1988	1989	1990
Gross Current Expenditure	4.3	1.0	0.8	8.5
Exchequer Capital	-9.2	-23.7	-3.0	13.1
Total Government Expenditure	2.7	-1.3	0.5	7.0
CPI	3.1	2.1	4.1	3.3
Gross Exchequer Current Revenue	8.2	7.6	1.0	8.9
Exchequer Deficit as a Percentage of GNP	-9.1	-3.1	-2.2	-1.9

Debt service costs changed little over these years (interest rates had fallen, offsetting the rising debt volume), so the figures for total current spending and for non-interest spending (not shown) are similar. Current spending in real terms rose in 1987, fell a little in 1988, fell a little faster in 1989, but rose quite rapidly in 1990, by which point the real volume of current spending, however measured, was comfortably above the 1987 level. The big contributors to the adjustment were the severe cuts in capital spending and the sharp improvement in revenue. Real GNP through the 1980s developed as shown in Table 5.3.

Table 5.3: Real GNP Growth in the 1980s

1980	1981	1982	1983	1984	1985	1986	1987	1988	1989	1990
2.6	1.8	-1.3	-1.9	1.1	0.2	0.1	3.7	1.7	4.7	6.5

In 1986, the volume of GNP was about the same as it had been in 1980. It then grew 17.6 per cent to 1990, an annual average real growth rate of 4.1 per cent. A contributory factor was a well-executed devaluation in August 1986. The tax amnesty introduced in the January 1988 Budget also contributed, yielding at least 2 per cent of GNP more than expected. It was one of the most successful tax amnesties anywhere at the time, and attracted attention from policymakers internationally.[8]

The first Bord Snip contributed no doubt, but more in the sense of the old football adage that 'you make your own luck'; in other words, you get yourself into a position to get lucky. The capital cuts, in retrospect, were overdone during the 1980s, tax rates were raised to self-defeating levels and the emerging fiscal crisis could, and should, have been addressed much earlier. If it had been acknowledged in, say, 1978 and dealt with decisively, it could have been over by about 1982 or 1983.

By the end of the 1980s, the public did not need persuading that there was indeed a fiscal crisis: the topic had dominated political debate for a decade. The current position is decidedly less favourable in that regard: the deterioration has been sudden, and has coincided both with a domestically generated banking collapse and a deep international recession. Public acceptance of the need for severe spending adjustments has been weakened by a decidedly populist public spending competition through the bubble period between government and opposition, which lingers in the form of escapist proposals to somehow avoid fiscal adjustment. A further difference from 1987 is the markedly less forgiving condition of the international sovereign debt markets, in which Ireland was one of the few heavy borrowers at times during the 1980s.

On the plus side, the extraordinary pace of spending increases in the last decade means that An Bord Snip Nua has been operating in what the US Air Force would describe as a target-rich environment, which was not the case in 1987.

Fiscal Policy Since 2000

From a position of fiscal balance and a declining debt ratio that had lasted over a decade, the public finance position has, in 2010, lurched into heavy deficit, and the debt ratio has begun to rise rapidly. On the general government balance (GGB) definition, gross debt will have more than doubled as a percentage of gross domestic product (GDP) in just two years by the end of 2009. Table 5.4 shows developments in some public finance aggregates since the turn of the century.

The recent sharp deterioration in both deficit and debt ratios is of course driven in part by the unprecedented decline in GDP, as Figure 5.2 shows. On

Table 5.4: Trends in Spending, Deficit and Debt, 2000–09

	2000	2001	2002	2003	2004	2005	2006	2007	2008	2009f
Total Spend % Change*	10.4	16.1	11.0	7.7	6.2	11.1	10.6	11.5	9.8	7.1
Current - CF % Change	11.4	19.7	14.8	9.2	7.7	10.3	10.6	12.1	9.9	6.0
CPI % Change	5.6	4.9	4.6	3.5	2.2	2.5	4.0	4.9	4.1	-4.4
Total as % GNP	34.7	36.7	37.5	36.6	36.2	37.0	36.8	38.8	44.5	51.1
GGB Deficit**	4.7	0.9	-0.4	0.4	1.4	1.7	3.0	0.2	-7.7	-11.7
GGB Debt**	37.8	35.6	32.2	31.0	29.4	27.5	25.0	25.1	44.1	64.5

*Total = gross current + Exchequer capital + Central Fund (CF)
** Both as a percentage of GDP
Note: The 2009 figure is a forecasted annual figure.

any measure, spending grew rapidly from 2000 onwards, the more so when some of the measured output growth was borrowed from the future so to speak, through building a large unsold stock of houses, retail and office space, which will overhang the market for many years. Government spending relative to GNP was growing up to 2007, and even more so if the GNP growth rates and hence tax buoyancy from, say, 2002 onwards were in truth not as good as they looked, as we see in Figure 5.3. The dramatic

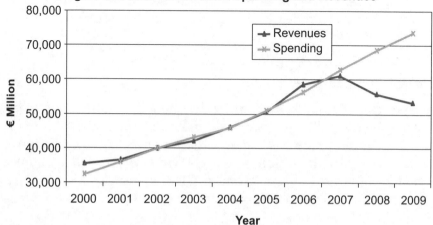

Figure 5.2: Irish Government Spending and Revenues

Source: CSO, National Accounts Database.
Note: The 2009 figure is a forecasted annual figure.

Figure 5.3: Exchequer Spending, excluding Debt Service, as a Percentage of GNP since 1983

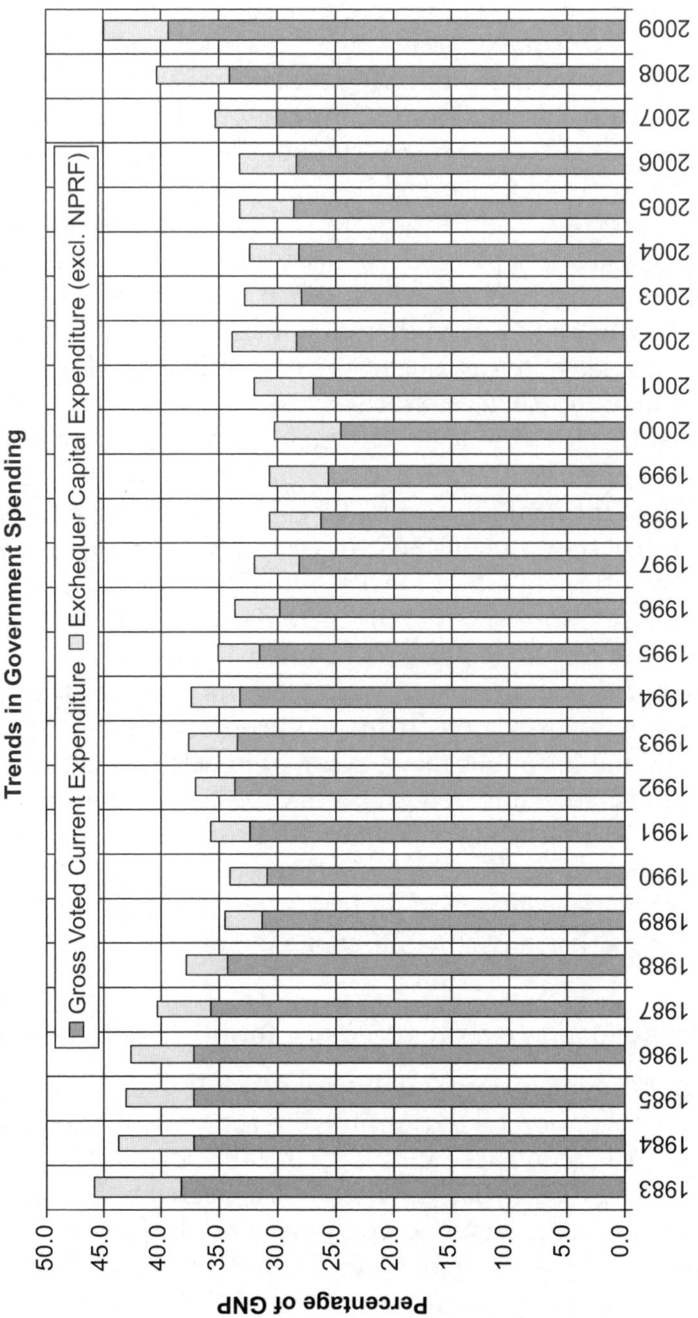

Trends in Government Spending

increase in spending ratios in the last couple of years has a large cyclical component, but it is salutary to note that the real increase in current spending in 2009, even excluding debt service, was in the double digits.

This continuing expenditure growth has been accompanied by an unprecedented collapse in tax revenue. This has exceeded by a large margin the decline in the tax base, reflecting the excessive reliance on taxing trans-actions in assets. Receipts from stamp duty, VAT on new house sales and capital gains tax (CGT) on non-residential property fell by four full GNP points from 2006 to 2009, as Figure 5.3 shows.

The recent economic history of Ireland can be divided provisionally into the fiscal consolidation phase up to the currency crisis of late 1992 and early 1993; the Celtic Tiger period, which lasted until about 2001; and then the Bubble that followed, which began to burst in mid-2007. The Irish Bubble has been, in relative terms, one of the largest in a developed country and seems destined to spawn a cottage industry for economic analysts to rival that created by the Celtic Tiger. The main domestic components were fail-ures in expenditure control and in the management, regulation and supervision of the banking system. Of course even if Irish policy had been flawless in all of these dimensions, the economy would now be experiencing a serious downturn, but it is a form of denial, and not conducive to the best policy response, to pretend that the current crisis was caused by an asteroid strike, or the unfortunate Brothers Lehman. Ireland has had a pretty spec-tacular public spending bubble, concealed from view by the transient tax revenues generated by a credit-fuelled property bubble. Spending grew dramatically, but the public finances stayed in balance until 2007. The rock-eting deficit in 2008 and 2009 reflects the simultaneous bursting of the 'double Bubble', coinciding of course with the international downturn and some more local difficulties, including the weakness of Sterling; the United Kingdom remains a key market for Irish exports and Ireland has more non-Eurozone trade than any other Eurozone member.

Fiscal Consolidation over the Medium Term

The December 2009 revised stability programme updates the commitment to fiscal consolidation targets outlined at the time of the Supplementary Budget in April 2009. These are shown in Table 5.5.

In April, the GGB deficit for 2009 was expected to be 10.75 per cent of GDP. Due mainly to tax revenue weakness, it reached 11.7 per cent. The GGB debt, shown at 59 per cent in the April Central Statistics Office (CSO) report reached 65 per cent by early 2009. The GDP decline shown for 2010 is

Table 5.5: Government's Fiscal Consolidation Programme

	2009	2010	2011	2012	2013
GGB Deficit as a % of GDP	11.7	11.6	10.0	7.2	4.9
GGB Debt as a % of GDP	65	78	83	84	83
Assumed GDP Growth	-7.5	-1.3	+3.3	+4.5	+4.3

pessimistic compared to some more recent forecasts, but the numbers pencilled in for 2011, 2012 and 2013 are ones a lot of people would settle for. The adjustment, crucially, is expected to come substantially on the revenue side. The figures also assume that spending grows very little, despite the inevitable build-up of debt service costs, implying significant real cuts in the non-interest component. These are forecasts, and debating their plausibility is pointless. What matters is the target deficit for 2014, at the Stability and Growth Pact limit of 3 per cent. The Stability and Growth Pact, adopted in 1997 to enforce fiscal discipline within EU member states, has been relaxed but not abandoned, and Eurozone members are still expected, when the dust settles, to not only (i) not breach the 3 per cent limit prescribed by the agreement to form the Pact, but also to (ii) adhere to the 0 per cent average over the cycle

The government's revised fiscal programme has been welcomed by the European Union (EU) Commission, but more importantly it has been *permitted* by the Commission, and as a concession – no other member state, so far as I am aware, has been given until 2014 to get back to 3 per cent borrowing. Thus those, such as the Irish Congress of Trade Unions, who argue for a much longer period of adjustment are in effect arguing that Ireland should go back to the Commission and re-negotiate the terms of its adherence to Eurozone rules. There can be no presumption that such a re-negotiation would succeed.

Nor is it self-evidently in Ireland's interests to spin out the adjustment to 2017 or 2018, were it to be permitted by the Commission and by the international sovereign lenders. The exit debt ratio could easily exceed 100 per cent of GDP at the end of a decade-long adjustment.[9] An important difference between the current situation and the 1980s is that worldwide sovereign debt issuance is at unprecedented levels and the markets, though improving, remain stretched. As quantitative easing programmes are withdrawn, the bond issuance which they have been supporting will also have to be trimmed, so the European Central Bank's stance will affect Ireland's options. Finally, Ireland's credit spread at ten years against the bund – a measure of the riskiness of Irish sovereign debt – was, in August 2010, around 300 basis points, the second largest adverse spread of any Eurozone member after Greece. Bluntly, this means that the markets are not convinced that Irish debt is free of risk, and countries with higher debt ratios than Ireland, and no greater liquidity, enjoy narrower spreads. Any move to delay the fiscal adjustment could see spreads widen further, adding quickly to debt service costs and thus offsetting at least in part the intended relaxation of fiscal policy. Some of those advocating stimulus or a slower adjustment are assuming an elastic supply of sovereign credit at unchanged cost, as well as low fiscal leakages, neither of which is self-evidently realistic.

Fiscal consolidation must be seen in the broader policy context. In addition to fixing the budget, Ireland needs to fix the banking system, cut wage and non-wage costs to restore competitiveness and de-leverage the national balance sheet. In a recent address to a conference in Dublin, the Central Bank Governor suggested that a reasonable medium-term target would be to re-balance the economy with revenue and expenditure shares in GNP around the levels prevailing eight or ten years ago.[10] This would mean a sharp increase in the ratio of tax revenue to GNP from current very depressed levels. Rates of tax have already been increased and there may be further increases on the way, but the tax–GNP ratio will rise anyway without rate increases. People will have to replace cars eventually, for example, and the rise in the savings ratio, which has been depressing VAT and excise yields, cannot go on forever.

But the Governor's suggestion also implies that the recent sharp increase in the ratio of public spending to GNP should be reversed. Some of it is cyclical and will reverse anyway as the economy recovers, but it must be accepted that some of the increases during the Bubble were based on a misperception of the economy's long-run taxpaying capacity. What must be avoided is any nostalgia, in any area of policy, for the unbalanced economy which emerged in the final years of the Bubble. In 2007, Ireland had full employment, easy credit and a balanced budget, but also had failing banks, excess leverage throughout the system, crowding-out of the traded sector and poor competitiveness. It felt fine, but it was not a good place to be.

A re-balanced economy will not look like 2007, unless Ireland somehow manages to persuade foreigners to finance another bubble. At its simplest, it will need to switch resources from making buildings and other non-tradables to making exports.

The 1987–90 fiscal consolidation finally took place in a more propitious environment than seems likely over the next four or five years: GNP growth rates will do well to average 4 per cent, the sovereign debt markets are more crowded and less forgiving, and Ireland cannot have another last-chance tax amnesty. Nor of course can it have a currency depreciation. But the years preceding the 1987 corrective action were ones in which current and capital spending had grown very little – this time, the fiscal correction succeeds a bubble in public spending as well as in credit expansion, and the scope for expenditure cuts is substantial.[11] The spending cuts must be sizeable given the circumstances. In a modern welfare state, spending control means control of pay and control of social transfers, as Figure 5.4 illustrates.

Figure 5.4: Distribution of Current Exchequer Spending in Ireland, 2009

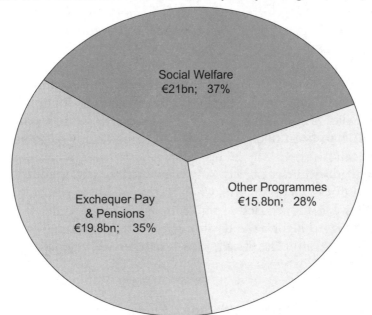

Source: CSO, National Accounts Database.

Lessons from the 1980s for Politicians (and Economists)

• The principal lesson for policymakers is that little was achieved by delaying the first Irish fiscal adjustment. Had action been taken from as late as 1980, and it would have been justified even earlier, the economy could have skipped five miserable years.
• A medium-term consolidation is more likely to underachieve the rosier the macro projection on which it is based. Better to be cautious, and be surprised on the upside!
• Even with rising tax rates, it is difficult to realise substantial increases in tax–GNP ratios in a downturn.

- With debt service building up, and pressure on social transfers, actual cuts are needed for stabilisation – it is not enough just to halt the rise in real non-interest spending.

There are some lessons for economists too. While the full dimensions of the current Irish implosion were foreseen by no one, it is simply untrue that no warnings were issued about the emerging banking and fiscal crises: whether they were loud enough is another matter, although what is heard matters more than what is said. The International Monetary Fund (IMF) reports on Ireland from the early years of the twenty-first century make interesting reading, especially on banking and credit developments. On the lack of discipline in expenditure control see Lawlor and McCarthy.[12] But it seems obvious that, after the abolition of the punt as an indepedent currency in 1999, many Irish economists began to focus more on micro-policy concerns, believing that the big macro issues, including external financial balance and budgetary policy (given the Stability and Growth Pact rules), had been taken off the list of things likely to go wrong. This was a bad call!

The legendary hurler Christy Ring was noted for taking advantage of the inattention of Cork's opponents when the referee held the ball after stop-pages in play. He was accused of gamesmanship, taking quick frees, even of swapping a soggy ball on a wet day for a crisp dry one secreted on his person. Asked about this after he retired, Ring remarked: 'Always keep your eye on the ball, especially when it's out of play.'

Appendix: Choice of Denominator for Fiscal Ratios

It is conventional internationally to express fiscal ratios (tax or total government revenue, current or total expenditure, various debt and deficit measures) as a percentage of GDP, a geographical output concept. Thus GDP answers the question, 'how much output is produced annually in China?', not how much of it accrues to Chinese economic agents, or is available for disposition by the Chinese authorities. The EU's Stability and Growth Pact explicitly employs GDP as the denominator for debt and deficit ratios, and organisations such as the IMF and Organisation for Economic Cooperation and Development (OECD) routinely make international comparisons, and do fiscal policy analysis, with GDP as the denominator.

The alternatives are GNP (gross national product), GNI (gross national income) or GNDI (gross national disposable income). They are related as follows:

- GDP plus/minus factor payments abroad = GNP
- GNP plus/minus other current payments abroad (e.g. EU taxes/subsidies) = GNI
- GNI plus/minus other international transfers (foreign aid, emigrants' remittances, net EU transfers) = GNDI

There are many countries where the differences between these aggregates are minor. A country with a small net creditor/debtor position and a small foreign sector will have GDP roughly equal to GNP, which is roughly equal to GNI, and, if it is not a big aid giver or receiver and has small migrants' remittances, GNDI will be similar too.

Ireland is not such a country. Factor payments abroad are substantial and both emigrants' remittances and outward aid flows have been rising recently. So income is less than output and the choice of denominator matters.

Some figures for the ratio of GNI to GDP for European countries are shown in Table 5.6. The Eurozone average is 99.3 per cent. Most countries are in a range of a few points either side of 100, with just 4 out of 20 below 96. Just 2, Luxembourg and Ireland, are below 90. In both cases, there are substantial annual net outflows in the form of factor payments, mainly returns on foreign capital. At least for comparative purposes across European countries, it matters which denominator is chosen in Ireland.

Table 5.6: Ratios of Gross National Income to Gross Domestic Product, 2008

Austria	98.4	Hungary	93.3	Slovenia	97.7
Belgium	100.4	**Ireland**	**85.8**	Spain	97.3
Czech Rep	92.5	Italy	98.5	Sweden	102.2
Denmark	101.8	Luxembourg	75.5	United Kingdom	102.1
Finland	99.8	Netherlands	97.4		
France	100.7	Poland (2007)	96.4	Eurozone	99.3
Germany	101.7	Portugal	96.0		
Greece	96.7	Slovakia	97.5		

Source: Statistics from OECD.org, reference series: Gross Domestic Product, available from <http://stats.oecd.org/Index.aspx>.

It also matters when looking at long time series, since the relationship between the competing denominators has been shifting. Up to the mid-1970s, GNP and GDP were roughly equal, for example, and GNP was about 90 per cent of GDP through the late 1980s and up to the mid-1990s. It has

Table 5.7: Alternative Income Measures as a Percentage of GDP, Ireland

	1995	2000	2001	2002	2003	2004	2005	2006	2007	2008
GNP	88.4	85.2	83.8	81.8	84.5	84.7	84.6	86.3	85.0	85.0
GNI	90.2	86.2	84.5	83.0	85.5	85.6	85.8	87.0	85.6	85.8
GNDI	91.1	86.1	83.9	82.4	84.8	84.9	84.8	86.0	84.5	84.4

recently fluctuated around 85 per cent. Recent trends in the income measures, as a percentage of GDP, are shown in Table 5.7.

All three ratios fell sharply from 1995 to 2000, oscillated to 2006 and have slipped again in the last couple of years.

In the context of assessing fiscal policy, and in particular of the credibility of fiscal consolidation programmes, the critical issue is taxable capacity. The best denominator for fiscal ratios, in this view, is the one closest to the tax base. Interestingly, member states pay contributions to the EU budget based on GNI, although the EU uses the output measure GDP for fiscal ratios under the Stability and Growth Pact. Thus, when it comes to levying the EU's 'tax' on members, GDP is abandoned. In supporting a contention that Irish public spending has been low compared to European averages, Karl Whelan favours GDP as the fiscal denominator. Noting that not everyone agrees, he states (in footnote 8, p. 17):

> Another argument is that GNP rather than GDP should be used for such comparisons. I disagree with these arguments because all income produced in Ireland is eligible for taxation by the Irish government. [13]

Output produced in Ireland does not translate into income available to Irish taxable entities though. A portion of GDP (corporate profits, much of which are ultimately expatriated) are nominally subject to tax at 12.5 per cent (it is not clear that all are actually taxed at this rate), but most tax revenue comes from income, payroll and expenditure taxes. These are probably best proxied by GNDI. If a choice has to be made between GNP and GDP, GNP is far closer to GNDI. Whelan's point that '... all income produced in Ireland is eligible for taxation by the Irish government' is true but not operationally significant: the excess of GDP over GNP is taxed only a little, and it is not clear that an increase in the rate of tax (on currently expatriated corporate profits) would yield extra revenue. Of course, the best way to do taxable capacity analysis is through a fully articulated model of tax revenues, and the Irish models embed a detailed revenue specification. Fiscal ratios are shorthand at best.

6

Fiscal Reductionism and the Disconnected Debate: Developing a New Fiscal Platform

Michael Taft

One of the more debilitating aspects of what was always going to be a debilitating affair – recession – is the manner in which the national discourse has became detached from the causes of that debilitating affair – the recession itself. In effect, economic issues have been isolated from the economy and subjected to an overwhelming reductionism, leading to a profound disconnect. It is not just that measures to address the recession have been sidelined. So myopic has the debate become that normally uncontroversial counter-cyclical measures are even characterised as part of the problem. Policy analysis and commentary has, thus, failed to take account of the economic impact of current deficit reduction strategies; a negative impact that, in turn, exacerbates the very problem the debate obsesses over. When historians come to analyse this period, they will not only pronounce on the decisions taken by the major actors, but on how this atomised debate influenced those decisions.

This chapter will first examine the constituent elements of this disconnect. This will be followed by an analysis of how we can reconnect the fiscal with the economic within a new macroeconomic platform.

Disconnect I: Reductionism within the Fiscal Crisis

Early in the crisis, the deteriorating fiscal situation gained prominence and, then, priority. There certainly were legitimate reasons for alarm. The deterioration in public finances was rapid. Between 1997 and 2006, Ireland experienced average annual budget surpluses of 1.8 per cent.[1] Even in 2007, with recession looming, the Exchequer appeared to be healthy, with a marginal surplus. By early 2008, however, it was clear there was something wrong, with monthly Exchequer returns signalling the scale of the sudden and unanticipated decline.[2]

In October of that year, when the Minister for Finance proposed the 2009 Budget, he faced an opening deficit of -8 per cent (compared to an estimate of -0.9 per cent in the 2008 Budget).[3] Given the scale of this decline – along with the autumn banking crisis, the worldwide financial meltdown and the collapse in global demand – it was easy to mobilise public opinion around this headline rate: people had a real and legitimate sense that Ireland was losing money as surely as it was losing jobs and businesses.

However, the general government balance, or annual deficit, is only one of two major components of public finances. The other component is the general government debt. Ireland had achieved considerable success in reducing overall debt levels from a peak of 112 per cent in 1986 to a lean 25 per cent by 2007.[4] Even with the extra borrowing necessitated by the deteriorating fiscal situation, by the time the Minister proposed the 2009 Budget Ireland still retained a healthy debt level of 41 per cent as measured under the Stability and Growth Pact (SGP) rules, compared to a Eurozone average of 66 per cent (see Figure 6.1).

Figure 6.1: General Government Debt–GDP Ratios, 2008 (%)

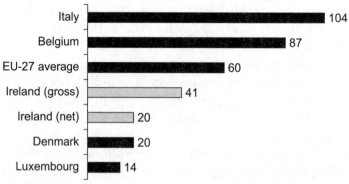

However, the SGP rules overstated Ireland's true debt level. In 2008 the National Treasury Management Agency launched a 'pre-borrowing' drive, designed to increase the Exchequer cash balance. Under SGP rules, these on-hand cash balances are counted as part of the general debt. Therefore, Ireland's net debt ratio was much lower. When the cash balances were excluded, Ireland's debt was 30.3 per cent of gross domestic product (GDP). And when Ireland's sovereign wealth fund – the National Pension Reserve Fund (NPRF) – was included, the net debt ratio fell to 20 per cent.[5]

However, though Ireland entered the recession with a relatively low-debt, asset-plenty balance sheet, this was rarely commented on. Not only was the debate in danger of being reduced to one variable, public finances, even within that variable it was in danger of being reduced to just one sub-variable.

Disconnect II: Misreading History

It is not as if the nation woke up one morning and suddenly discovered the growing mismatch between government revenue and expenditure. Nor, having discovered that deficit, did they resolve on a particular course of action over morning coffee. There were (and are) a variety of responses that could be employed to confront this crisis. To win people to a particular course, narratives have to be constructed, stories have to be told. A significant part of such storytelling is to find a similar episode from the past and discover what worked then.

Such a past example was ready at hand: the period of 1987–9 under the minority Fianna Fáil administration. By 1987, Ireland's budgetary situation was in crisis. In the preceding years, governments experienced double-digit deficits; the national debt exceeded 100 per cent of GDP while the cost of servicing the debt was running at nearly 10 per cent of national output. Within a few years, the budget balance was cut fivefold while the national debt was declining (as a proportion of GDP). Only a few years later, Ireland entered into a period of growth unprecedented since the founding of the state. Clearly, this is a period to examine closely to see what lessons might help us in our current fiscal woes.

The story told was of a government determined to 'put the public finances right' and 'make hard decisions', launching a drive to reduce government expenditure to balance the budget and set the fiscal framework for subsequent growth. There were growing references to An Bord Snip,[6] interviews with veteran board members, analysis and extrapolation – all creating an image of considerable fiscal correction that could be successfully imported into our current crisis.

Within three budgets, the government managed to reduce the deficit from -11.4 per cent to -2.2 per cent of gross national product (GNP) – a considerable feat (see Table 6.1). What accounted for this deficit reduction, from -€2.7 billion in 1986 to -€636 million in 1989?

Table 6.1: Increase in Government Expenditure and Revenue, 1986–9

	Current Expenditure	Capital Expenditure	Total Government Expenditure	Government Revenue
Nominal Increase (€ millions)	696	-443	253	1,783
Percentage Increase	5.9	-32.8	1.9	19.3

Source: Department of Finance, *Budgetary and Economic Statistics 2008*, Dublin, Department of Finance, 2008.

During that period, current expenditure actually rose in nominal terms. On the expenditure side, it was the capital programme that bore the brunt of nominal reductions. But the driving force for the fiscal adjustment was increased tax revenue, accounting for 85 per cent of the balance (see Figure 6.2).[7]

Figure 6.2: Current Expenditure Increase by Category, 1986–9 (%)

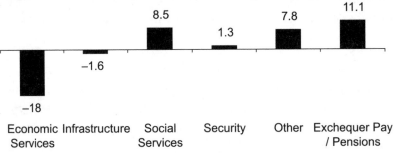

There were current expenditure 'cuts', or rather a curtailment of expenditure that resulted in prioritisations and rationalisations in several key sectors. The agriculture sector suffered the largest decline, accounting for almost all the expenditure reductions that were enacted. Other sectors still maintained growth and, when set against an average annual inflation rate of 3.1 per cent, almost maintained real growth.

If it was tax revenue that was the driving force in the fiscal turnaround, though, it was not due to increases in tax rates or new tax measures. The thrust of government policy, buttressed by the first social partnership agreement, was to reduce tax levels. This was the 'bargain' entered into with trade unions – reduced tax levels in exchange for capped wage increases. Added to this were other measures, such as the abolition of the land tax.

So if government expenditure was merely contained (as opposed to actively cut), coupled with a reduction of tax liabilities, how did the government manage to reduce the deficit so significantly? Here we have to go beyond fiscal reductionism and examine the broader economy, by way of introducing a number of sub-plotlines to the popular and, as we will see, misleading narrative.

Fiscal Correction During a Period of Growth

Unlike today, the economy was growing significantly during the late 1980s (see Figure 6.3).

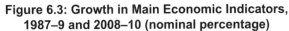

Figure 6.3: Growth in Main Economic Indicators, 1987–9 and 2008–10 (nominal percentage)

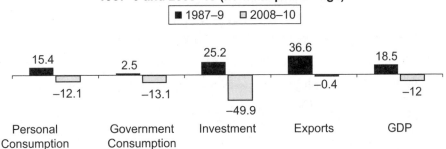

The comparison could not be starker. During the late 1980s, the economy grew by over 12 per cent, whereas in the current period GDP is expected to decline by over 11 per cent. The determinants of these trends – exports, consumer spending and investment – contrast considerably. This, in itself, should caution us when making comparisons. To compare these two periods fiscally without examining the larger economic picture is to miss the point entirely.

The source of the deficit reduction during the late 1980s now becomes more apparent. Government revenue as a proportion of GDP was, unsurprisingly, higher than today.[8] The government took between 39 and 42 per cent of GDP in revenue (the current proportion is approximately 32 per cent). Therefore, as economic activity increased through higher growth rates so did government revenue – and conversely, as GDP declines today, so does revenue.

This domestic growth was set against worldwide growth. In the late 1980s, Europe, the United States (US) and the United Kingdom (UK) experienced considerable growth rates (see Table 6.2).

Ireland's economy was participating in a general growth environment, in particular with regard to the UK, a major export market.[9] This, along with

Table 6.2: GDP at 2000 Market Prices, 1987–9 (% change)

EU-15	US	UK	Ireland
11.5	11.3	12.3	12.7

Source: European Commission, *Statistical Annex of European Economy*, Luxembourg, European Commission, Spring 2009.

the 1986 devaluation, helps explain Ireland's considerable export increase during this period.

Emigration and Employment

A second 'benefit' to the government was the massive levels of emigration that began in the mid-1980s and accelerated up to 1990. In the years 1987 to 1990, 228,000 people left Ireland, resulting in a net emigration of 132,000 (see Figure 6.4).

Figure 6.4: Unemployment and Out-Migration, 1987–90 (thousands)

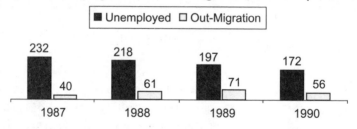

This facilitated a fall in unemployment of 60,000, or nearly one-quarter of those on the dole queues. While emigration was a major factor behind the fall in unemployment, the economy managed to start generating jobs, after a period of employment loss that stretched back to 1980. Between 1986 and 1990, employment rose on the back of rising consumer spending and export growth by 79,000 – or an average annual employment increase of 1.8 per cent.

While the comparison of this period with today is valid when it comes to emigration (the Central Statistics Office's (CSO) lagging data showed that in the year up to April 2009, emigration reached 65,000),[10] there is a clear difference between an overall increase in employment of over 7 per cent and today's decline of over 12 percent.

Stimulus

In the late 1980s, the Irish economy was the recipient of a substantial stimulus package, courtesy of the European Union (EU). During that three-year period, Ireland received over €1 billion in European Social Fund and European Regional Development (ERD) grants.[11] This three-year injection amounted to 3 per cent of the 1989 GDP. Such an injection today would be equal to €5 billion spread over the next three years. This stimulus – especially from ERD grants – would have helped make up the shortfall caused by a declining capital budget. That this situation is not comparable with today is evident; we are now on the verge of becoming a net contributor economy to the EU, having absorbed net receipts for decades.

Wages

While today there have been calls for 'real' devaluation – cuts in nominal wages – in order to reduce costs and restore competitiveness (a proposition that cannot be substantiated by reference to international wage databases), this was clearly not a factor in the late 1980s. During that period, the average industrial wage rose by over 14 per cent in the period 1986–9, or an annual average of 4.6 per cent.[12] More interestingly, the Exchequer pay bill rose by a similar level.[13] These wage increases had a twofold effect: (a) a boost to government revenue and (b) a boost to economic activity through increased private consumption.

While comparisons between different periods can be informative, we must always be careful to ensure our measurements are sensitive to the actual processes and contexts operating. For instance, depressing the rise in current expenditure may have had some impact on the fiscal turnaround of the late 1980s (the negative impact on growth would have been diluted in the general expansionary environment), but it would be wholly incorrect to suggest it was the primary contributor, as so many of today's popular commentators contend. The primary contributor was the growth environment itself, domestically and internationally. Colm McCarthy, a member of the original An Bord Snip, described the period in this way:

> Briefly, there was no significant reduction in the real volume of current spending as a result of Bord Snip I. There was a further squeeze on capital spending, a mistake in retrospect, but most of the adjustment came on the revenue side. The 'slash and burn' stories about 1987, Mac the Knife, decimation of public services and so forth are just journalistic invention. It never happened.[14]

If a debate detaches the fiscal from the economic, there is a strong likelihood that the latter's contribution will be missed or air-brushed out of view.

Disconnect III: Expansionary Fiscal Contraction

The 'story of 1987' won out, at least the one that vindicated the argument for a contractionary approach to the current fiscal crisis. This historical reading was complemented by a theoretical discourse, expansionary fiscal contraction (EFC). EFC proposes that fiscal contraction, rather than leading to a decline in output, as might be expected, will result in higher output due to its effects on private sector expectations. Consumers and investors anticipate long-run tax reductions because of cuts in expenditure, increase expenditure and so off-set the demand-side effects of the contraction, or so the theory goes. One of the more eloquent expositions of this proposition comes from Alesina, Perotti and Tavares:

> Empirical work on the effects and sustainability of fiscal adjustments has consistently reached two conclusions. First, long-lasting adjustments rely mostly (or exclusively) on spending cuts, in particular, in government wages and social security and welfare; by contrast, short-lived adjustments rely mostly on revenue increases. Second, fiscal adjustments are not always associated with reduced growth, or with deterioration in the macroeconomic environment in general.

> Fiscal adjustments that rely on cuts in government transfers and wages and are implemented in periods of fiscal stress are long lasting and not contractionary. On the demand side, the expansionary aspect of such fiscal adjustments works through an expectation effect, which is stronger the worse are initial fiscal conditions. On the supply side, the interaction of certain types of adjustment – those without tax increases but with cuts in government employment and wages – lead to wage moderation, reduced unit labor costs, and increases in profitability, business investment, and production.[15]

That Alexina et al. slightly hedge their bets ('not always associated with reduced growth') should give us pause, especially when other authors are even more hesitant.

Hogan claims that, while there is evidence that private consumption rises, it is usually not sufficient to offset the reduction in output ('fiscal contractions are not literally expansionary').[16] Prammer finds contradictions and lack of support for the general theory ('The empirical evidence surveyed ... provides no clear support for the existence of expansionary fiscal consolidations').[17] Alfonso urges care:

> [O]ne must be cautious to welcome into conventional wisdom the idea of expansionary fiscal consolidations ... it is far from clear whether one can use the positive expansionary fiscal consolidations experiences that occurred in

the past in a few countries as a rational for similar policy prescriptions in other EU countries.[18]

Resort to the theory of Ricardian equivalence is also unlikely to be of assistance. It could be argued that the emphasis on 'spending cuts' will make people feel secure that tax levels won't rise; thus, they will have greater confidence to spend and invest. Even if were to accept the abstractions that make this model work (perfect knowledge, perfect capital markets and immortality), the reality today is that no one believes that tax levels will go anywhere but up, especially as, unlike in 1987–9, the Irish economy is an ultra-low-taxed economy. In addition, keeping with this abstraction, people might believe that spending cuts will further reduce their disposable income (cuts in child income support, social protection payments, etc.), which would cancel out any anticipation of tax cuts. Reliance on abstractions is more likely to tell us how models work, rather than the economy and people's expectations.

If the term 'expansionary fiscal contraction' didn't wholly enter into the popular debate, a part of it did – fiscal contraction – the expansionary part got lost. Fiscal contraction morphed into public expenditure contraction following Alexina et al. But even on its own terms, where there might be evidence for EFC, it has traction in economies where historical public expenditure patterns might be considered high, and where economies were pushed 'close to the edge' of high debt–GDP ratios.[19] It is contestable whether Ireland fits neatly into that category (see Figure 6.5).

Figure 6.5: Current Government Expenditure as a Percentage of GDP, Ireland and the EU-15

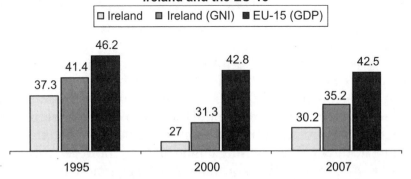

Despite the fact that Ireland consistently hovered at the bottom of the EU-15 current public expenditure league tables, whether this is measured with GDP or gross national income (GNI), this did not prevent the idea that public expenditure was a 'problem' to be solved. This argument rested on presenting nominal increases in percentage terms. The government's pre-Budget outlook (PBO) gave official confirmation to popular calculations when it showed that, for instance, social welfare increased by 90 per cent since 2003, health expenditure increased by 77 per cent, etc.[20] Once more, however, this argument detached a fiscal category from the economy. Public expenditure did rise between 2000 and 2007, but only by 3 per cent of GDP.[21] Further, this argument was divorced from the rising demand of a growing population. Whereas the EU-27 population grew by 3.5 per cent since 2000, the Irish population grew by 16.5 per cent.[22]

This 'problematising' of public expenditure gained even more force as the recession deepened. Public expenditure did increase (though the argument now veered between historical growth within the fiscal category to public expenditure as a proportion of GNP). It has been pointed out that public expenditure is 'growing':

> It [total Government expenditure] then fluctuated in a range below 40% until 2007 but reached 44% in 2008 and is expected to reach 51% in 2009.[23]

First, much of the 'increased public expenditure' was a phenomenon of collapsing output. Had output fallen at the average Eurozone rate, the increase would have been significantly less. Total government expenditure would have made up only 45.4 per cent in 2009.

Second, the increase in public expenditure was primarily due to associated costs of rising unemployment. Between 2007 and 2009, social affairs expenditure made up 73 per cent of increased public expenditure.[24]

Third, the mismatch between expenditure and revenue was almost wholly attributable to the collapse in tax revenue. In the 2009 Budget, the Minister of Finance estimated tax revenue to total €43.5 billion. The actual outturn was €32.5 billion.

To track the influence of expansionary fiscal contraction, sans expansionary, we need only go to the Minister's financial statement, delivering the 2009 Supplementary Budget. He outlined 'six steps we must take to restore and renew this economy'.[25] Oddly, for an economy in severe contraction, there was no mention of limiting the damage of the recession, or shortening its duration. Stabilising public finances, however, made up two of the steps. And to track the morphing of fiscal contraction into expenditure contraction again the government set the pace: shortly after the Minister announced that tax increases would make up nearly half of the fiscal contraction planned for 2010 he changed tack; public expenditure was now to make up almost the entire contraction.

Disconnect IV: Structural and Cyclical Deficit

Another aspect of promoting contractionary policies was the debate over the cyclical and structural components of the deficit. Such measurements are always difficult, for they rest on determining the output gap, which at times is an after-the-fact estimate. The difficulties in measuring this were highlighted by Professor John Fitz Gerald, who took issue with the European Commission's methodology, claiming that it was 'not really appropriate when applied to the Irish economy'.[26] Whereas the European Commission claimed the structural deficit was -10 per cent, Fitz Gerald said it was closer to -6 per cent.

The point here is not to resolve that debate, but rather to show how the discussion over this important issue evolved into more general contractionary demands. But first, to reinforce this point that such measurements must be extremely qualified, there is little question that Irish public finances were over-reliant on cyclical property transactions that were artificially boosted by a range of fiscal and non-fiscal polices.

One measurement of this – stamp duty and capital gains receipts – shows that their combined revenue amounted to 2 per cent of total taxation in 1997; by 2006 this proportion had risen to 12 per cent.[27] Of course, not all revenue from these sources was property-related, but a sizeable proportion was, as can be seen by the collapse of those receipts by 2009: they had fallen in nominal terms by 76 per cent.

However, this doesn't capture the full over-reliance. With employment in property-related occupations (this includes not only the construction sector but business, professional and financial sectors reliant upon rising property transactions and prices) increasing substantially, tax receipts across a range of categories – value-added tax (VAT), income tax, PRSI, etc. – were likewise inflated.

This should have been evident by 2006, the peak of the property market. The current structural deficit would have been well and truly embedded – obvious enough to measure. Except that it was missed. The European Commission not only did not identify this in 2006, it even went so far as to state that Ireland had a structural surplus.

The Organisation for Economic Co-operation and Development (OECD), in its 2006 *Economic Survey*, stated that Irish public finances were healthy and attributed rising property prices to demographic pressures only.[28] There was no mention of a structural deficit in any of the Economic and Social Research Institute (ESRI) *Quarterly Reviews* in 2006 and 2007. The government, using the European Commission's methodology, likewise did not spot the emerging structural deficit. However, by 2009, the structural deficit was suddenly prominent – but only after the fact (see Figure 6.6).

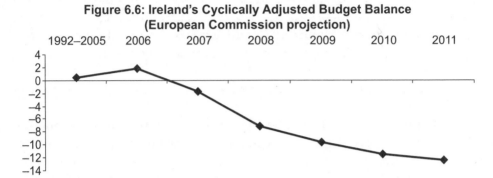

Figure 6.6: Ireland's Cyclically Adjusted Budget Balance (European Commission projection)

This is not to advance a structural-deficit-sceptic argument. However, it does suggest that we treat estimates carefully. And it certainly means that basing policy prescriptions on such a qualified measurement can overstate or understate a case.

Whatever the size of the structural deficit, it was nonetheless a useful tool in arguing the primacy of public expenditure cuts. For if it is the case that once the output gap is closed and the economy returns to near full output a structural deficit will still remain, it reinforces the argument for fiscal correction. The Special Group on Public Service Numbers and Expenditure Programmes (An Bord Snip Nua) gave that argument a programmatic and popular rallying point.

Disconnect V: The Limitations of the Household Metaphor

When a household experiences a cash-flow deficit it can either increase its income or cut its spending. If it has savings it can draw on that but if the deficit is structural resorting to savings will only postpone necessary measures. It may resort to borrowing, but unless that borrowing can be translated into a structural shift in the deficit, it will only, again, postpone necessary measures – that's if the household can even get a loan. Most people understand this household metaphor. And if revenue is optimised (and I can't convince my boss to give me more money), then at the household level people know they will have to reduce their outgoings: fewer nights out, cheaper nights in, turning off lights in empty rooms, etc. At the household level, reductions in expenditure equal equivalent savings.

It shouldn't be surprising, therefore, to find this metaphor accepted at an economic level. It's not only rational, it is experienced daily. Never mind that the household is dependent on demand for its labour, whereas governments can increase demand. Never mind that cutting back on nights out at the restaurants puts those businesses and jobs at risk. Never mind the dynamic interaction of fiscal and economic policies at different stages of the economic cycle. Cuts equal savings. Six minutes on a current affairs radio programme is not going to undermine what is a compelling experience for most people.

The Special Group propelled this household metaphor into the national debate, in a way that was detached from equally compelling economic consequences. Their conclusions quickly became part of everyday discourse. The 'savings' of €5.3 billion, the 'borrowing €400 million a week', the prolific and robust media appearances of the chairperson of the Special Group – this more than anything else ensured the primacy of public expenditure cuts. Opposition was muted even from quarters that might be expected to oppose such a course.

The consensus that developed around the central tenets of the report ignored, however, the fact that the 'savings' claimed in the Report were invented; that while there was a proposed reduction of €5.3 billion, there was no information as to how much this would actually 'save' the Exchequer (that is, reduce the deficit and borrowing requirement).

Prior to the publication of the *Special Group Report*, the ESRI ran a number of simulations to assess the economic impact of various fiscal measures.[29] One of the simulations assessed the effects of reducing public sector employment by 17,000 (or 5 per cent of the public sector workforce). This was one of the main recommendations of the *Special Group Report*. Under the ESRI simulation, this reduction was intended to reduce government expenditure by €1 billion. Figure 6.7 charts both the economic and fiscal impact in the second year.

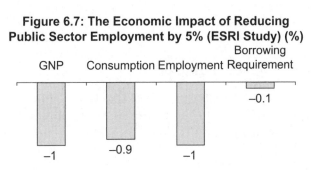

Figure 6.7: The Economic Impact of Reducing Public Sector Employment by 5% (ESRI Study) (%)

The impact would be significantly deflationary, with GNP and consumer spending falling by over €1.3 billion and €700 million respectively. Crucially, employment would fall by 18,000.

To arrive at the 'savings', all the costs associated with this deflationary impact must be deducted from the reduction in expenditure. When the ESRI did this in their simulation, they found that this measure, which would reduce public sector spending by 0.6 per cent of GDP, would only reduce the Exchequer borrowing requirement by 0.1 per cent of GDP. The actual savings to the Exchequer is substantially less than the amount cut.

This was the methodological flaw at the heart of the *Special Group Report*. It failed to present two vital and inextricably intertwined factors: (a) the impact on the economy and (b) the resulting net savings to the Exchequer. In one sense, this was understandable. If the Report contained both the impact and the net savings, if it had assessed the deflationary effects inherent in such expenditure reductions, it would have undermined its basic premise.

The Special Group failed to avail of this economic analysis – even though the ESRI had already established a model. While it may be argued this was beyond their remit, at the very least the Special Group would want to guard against perverse results, whereby a reduction in expenditure so negatively impacts on the economy that the reduction is cancelled out. In short, the *Special Group Report* offers little information relevant to deficit reduction.

In the popular debate, however, these crucial omissions meant that important questions were not raised or addressed. It is this failure to capture the dynamic effects of public expenditure cuts on output that makes the results of the Special Group's approach to deficit reduction fiscally defective. And such was the scale of the reductions proposed that they would probably exhaust the current expenditure component of even the most ambitious fiscal consolidation effort.[30] Given their potentially irrelevant impact on the deficit burden, this would have raised another provocative question: when the cuts have all been made, what is to be done now and how much deeper is the hole we're in?

Disconnect VI: Embedding the Deficit

Another play on everyday experience was the 'take the pain up front' invocation. The implication being that, if the disproportionate amount of fiscal correction could be taken at an early stage, we could *put it behind us*. This sentiment has merit in many household contexts. However, like so much of a debate that is driven by soundbites passing for informed comment, the 'pain up-front' argument lacks analytical content.

The flaw in the pain up-front argument rests on the failure to appreciate how deficit reduction measures become embedded in the economy. Again, the ESRI simulations can provide some insight (see Table 6.3).

Table 6.3: The ESRI Estimate of the Economic Impact of Two Fiscal Measures (%)

	First Year Impact	Fourth Year Impact	Seventh Year Impact
5% Reduction in Public Sector Pay			
GDP	-0.2	-0.3	-0.4
Consumption	-0.8	-1.1	-1.1
Employment	-0.1	-0.2	-0.3
Reduction in Borrowing Requirement (% of GDP)	0.3	0.2	0.2
Income Tax Increase Sufficient to Raise €1 Billion			
GDP	-0.2	-0.4	-0.5
Consumption	-0.7	-1.0	-1.1
Employment	-0.1	-0.4	-0.4
Reduction in Borrowing Requirement (% of GDP)	0.4	0.3	0.3

Source: Bergin, Conefrey, Fitz Gerald and Kearney, 'The Behaviour of the Irish Economy'.

The shocks not only continue but accelerate. Not only do the measures cause a deflationary initial impact, but this shock reverberates down the years at the very time that the economy is trying to return to full capacity. This depressing effect will effectively embed the original deficit into the economy itself.

This embedding process may manifest itself, not necessarily in high deficits (though they could remain stubbornly high enough to provoke additional contractionary measures), but rather in low growth and rising overall debt. Contributing to this will be increasing high levels of debt service, high unemployment costs and low tax revenue increases. The pursuit of fiscal contraction without reference to its impact on the economy may provoke a medium-term *low-growth, high-debt* scenario.

Disconnect VII: Turning Off the Taps

If exhortations based on precedence, good housekeeping and taking the pain up front were not enough, there was an explicit threat-based argument: if we don't correct our public finances, the international markets will stop lending to us. Public servants won't get paid, welfare recipients will do without, no funds for hospitals and schools, etc. A variant of this argument is that our economic sovereignty would end if public finances were not brought under control because the International Monetary Fund (IMF) would do it for us.[31]

The turning-off-the-taps argument gained prominence with an RTE *Prime Time* programme in late February 2009.[32] It was claimed our borrowing capacity was under threat with an imminent 'lending freeze'. This had to ignore the fact that Ireland had a relatively low-debt balance sheet (not difficult, since it didn't feature in the debate). This also had to ignore the success, only the day before, of the National Treasury Management Agency's (NTMA) €4 billion bond sale[33] or, a few weeks previous, of a €6 billion bond sale.[34] By the third week of February 2009, the NTMA had borrowed 40 per cent of its annual requirement. This was in addition to their continuing pre-borrowing programme, which had amassed 11 per cent of GDP in Exchequer cash balances.[35]

What the 'lending freeze' argument could point to was deteriorating long-term Irish debt yields. This was attributed to investor concern over the government's ability to meet its future debt obligations. However, a time-based examination[36] of this growing gap shows that it coincided with the emerging banking crisis. During the late summer and early autumn much concern – domestically and internationally – focused on the liquidity of the major Irish banks. Irish bond yields didn't so much deteriorate – between June and December 2008 the redemption yields on Irish ten-year bonds actually improved – as they failed to take advantage of increased global demand for safe investments as investors withdrew from the equity markets. This benefited other sovereign debt markets, not ours (see Figure 6.8).

The Irish debt market was to take a number of further knocks:

- First, there was a profound misunderstanding of how the bank guarantee impacted on sovereign debt, with many commentators initially proclaiming that debt was now 200 to 300 per cent of GDP.
- Second, the nationalisation of Anglo Irish Bank, with the implications it had for other banks (and for the handling of the issue by the government, which only weeks previously had announced a capitalisation of that bank), was the low point in Irish debt performance.

- Third, the misrepresentation by leading commentators of the stability of Irish debt. One commentator suggested there was a 'one-in-eight' chance that Ireland would renege on its debt[37] while another claimed that Ireland's creditworthiness was worse than Peru's.[38] Davy Stockbrokers rightly labelled such claims as 'hysterical'.[39] Still, the reputational damage was done by such unsubstantiated statements.

Figure 6.8: Irish Ten-Year Bond Bid Yields, 2008–10

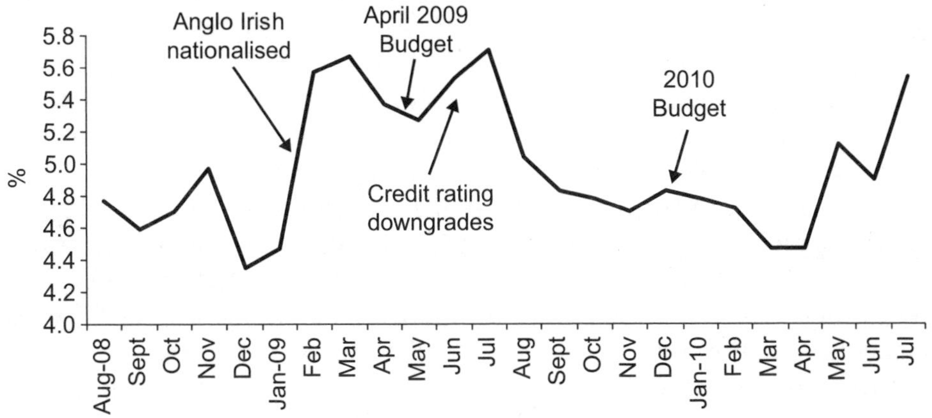

There was an unfortunate tendency to equate the robustness of Ireland's debt capacity with the speculative activity in the unregulated credit default swap markets. It was certainly the case that in early 2009 the cost of hedging against losses on Irish debt was high, peaking in February. But this neat equation ignored the speculative practice of 'shorting' the market on such swaps.[40]

Even though the credit default swap market stabilised and improved (with speculators 'moving on', as predicted by the NTMA director, Michael Somers), undue attention was again focused on the downgrading of Ireland's debt ratings by the three main rating agencies. This maintained the sense that Ireland's borrowing capacity was under threat. However, during this period of downgrading, stretching from April to June 2009, Irish bond yields continued to improve,[41] the gap with German bonds continued to narrow and the demand for Irish debt remained high. The joke in some investment circles was that if this was the result of being downgraded then maybe Ireland should request further downgrades from the rating agencies.

So, while Irish bond yields steadily improved from the low point around the Anglo Irish Bank nationalisation – and continued during the ratings downgrades – the argument that our borrowing capacity was under threat held sway.

The irony is that another pattern emerged that went largely undetected. The public were assured that 'tough measures' (usually meaning cuts in public services, wages and social transfers) would somehow appease the markets and result in lower borrowing costs. However, following each of the three deflationary interventions in 2009 – the public sector pension levy, the emergency April Budget and the 2010 Budget – there was little impact on borrowing costs. This helped explain a persistent self-denial that set in when the Greek debt crisis broke in April 2010. The public were repeatedly assured the markets didn't view Ireland in the same negative way as other peripheral economies. How could they? We had taken all the right, painful steps. Except that Irish bond yields vied with Portuguese yields to be the worst in the Eurozone, once Greece exited the market. While the markets were saying one thing, the debate was being told another, or nothing.[42]

Arguments for counter-cyclical policies based on debt financing were inevitably met with 'but, we're broke' and 'who would lend to us' objections. That we weren't 'broke', that there was a continuing high demand for Irish debt, albeit at priced-to-sell levels owing to the banking crisis, that the real concerns were the counterproductive deflationary policies pursued by the government, was rarely put forward or heard in the pro-cyclical cacophony.

The Disconnected Debate Completed

A significant aid to any consensus is an ineffectual and contradictory response; in particular from those social forces that might be expected to provide a counter-narrative. In this story, it is the social democratic and trade union forces that faltered. Their response to the crisis, rather than focusing on expansionary demands, went through various hoops only to end up acquiescing to the contractionary orthodoxy.

The Labour Party's initial response was grounded in a reflationary critique. Party leader Eamon Gilmore called for a stimulus approach,[43] emphasising the need to halt rising unemployment. This was complemented by Finance spokesperson Joan Burton calling for a 'major stimulus' programme.[44] While details were sketchy, rarely going beyond a 'bricks and mortar' programme (i.e. mostly construction projects) and never addressing the underlying macroeconomic issues of deficits, debts and borrowing, it still accorded with a traditional social democratic response.

However, by the time of the April 2009 Supplementary Budget, Labour accepted the need for fiscal contraction and published a pre-Budget submission combining a list of public expenditure savings and taxation measures.[45] When the *Special Group Report* was published, Labour opposed the cuts in social transfers to low income groups, but did not oppose the contractionary principles, even saying that reducing public sector employment was 'do-able'.[46] Labour accepted the government's target of a €4 billion contraction, even supporting their target of a €1.3 billion cut in the public sector payroll. They differed on the balance of that contraction – emphasising tax increases – and while they continued to promote the concept of 'stimulus' this was never integrated into an alternative macroeconomic framework and, there-fore, remained rhetorical.

Similarly, the Irish Congress of Trade Unions (ICTU) accepted at an early stage the need for a contraction.[47] Nonetheless, it maintained a convincing critique of deflationary policies, which made their initial acceptance of fiscal contraction somewhat contradictory. However, ICTU's analysis was never explicit on this point. They proposed a postponement of reaching the Maas-tricht guidelines to 2017[48] but were attacked over the cost, in terms of the national debt; attacks which they did not answer with their own fiscal data.

ICTU took a reasonable calculation from a collective bargaining perspec-tive – the government was going to proceed with the fiscal contraction in any event – and, by agreeing to 'staying in the tent', they hoped to divert the contraction into taxation on higher income groups, and away from public expenditure cuts. However, the government was intent on prioritising public expenditure and when it delivered its demands, first, for a pension levy and, second, for a permanent cut in public sector wages, ICTU found itself twice in abandoned negotiations.

These two events helped cement the consensus. Both Labour and ICTU emphasised 'fairness' in addressing the crisis but did not offer an alternative fiscal strategy. While there were some[49] who stepped into the breach to provide an alternative analysis, they remained, despite their best intentions, marginal to the debate. The contractionary analysis 'won out', and eventu-ally became the near-unchallenged orthodoxy. If there was a debate to help inform public policy, it was a debate of one-handed clapping.

The Fallout From the Disconnected Debate

The fallout from the disconnected debate – isolating the fiscal from the economic, ignoring the two-way feedback between the two – was the failure to model or even appreciate the impact on output. So much so that it may undermine the goals of the particular fiscal strategy itself. This may seem obvious but this 'obvious' is regrettably missing in the debate.

The recession hit Ireland particularly hard. Irish GDP has collapsed at nearly five times the rate of the Eurozone while consumer spending has fallen by more (see Figure 6.9). Investment has fallen off the scale. This has been the result of the perfect storm of financial crisis, fall in global demand, the collapse in the domestic property market and government fiscal strategy.

Figure 6.9: EU Commission Forecast, 2007–10 (Percentage Volume)

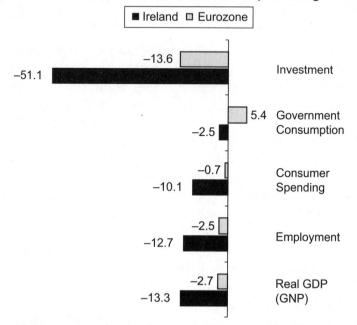

The full year extent of the measures taken in the last three Budgets, including the February 2009 announcement (i.e. the public sector pension levy) has amounted to €13 billion. Until recently, the government presented its fiscal strategy in static terms.[50] There was little evidence that account was taken of the impact of fiscal measures on economic growth or levels of public expenditure and tax revenue. An example of this was contained in the Budget 2010 Financial Statement:

> The Government over the past 18 months has made budgetary adjustments of more than €8 billion for this year. Had we not done so, the deficit would have ballooned towards 20 per cent of GDP...[51]

The Minister's calculation, even on a static basis, is questionable: the deficit would have increased to -16.6 per cent. The government has partially acknowledged these impacts. In the Supplementary Budget in April 2009, the government admitted that the fiscal adjustment would cause the GDP to fall by approximately 1 per cent.[52] In the 2010 Budget's accompanying

Stability Programme Update (SPU 2010) it was stated:

> Taking corrective action of €4 billion imposes short-term costs because taking money out of the economy (by reducing spending or raising taxes) has a dampening effect on activity and employment, all other things being equal. Quantifying the impact of these measures on economic activity is an inherently uncertain exercise and requires a combination of econometric model simulations and judgement ... the estimated loss in tax revenue [is] €897 million associated with the introduction of the budgetary package in 2010. This loss in revenue has been factored into the overall budgetary arithmetic.[53]

This is a positive step but is not sufficient. A complete fiscal multiplier would also include the impact on the expenditure side, in particular, the impact on employment.

However, we can begin to unravel the impact of these fiscal shocks and, therefore, calculate the government's substantial contribution to the recessionary slide.

Tax revenue can be seen as a function of GDP. In 2009, net tax revenue was 19.9 per cent of GDP; in 2010 this ratio fell to 19.3 per cent.[54] On this basis it can be estimated that the 2010 Budget contracted GDP by between €4.44 and €4.57 billion,[55] an implied multiplier of -1:11 (see Figure 6.10). This is supported by ESRI estimates:

> The consequences of such a further sharp correction [i.e. €4 billion] are, by our estimation, significantly deflationary. Were there to be a neutral budget in 2010, then our estimates would suggest that the recovery in GDP would occur much earlier in the year leading to positive growth in GDP for the year as a whole.[56]

Figure 6.10: GDP Decline as a Result of Budget 2010 (€ millions)

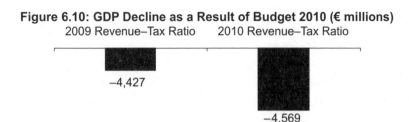

2009 Revenue–Tax Ratio   2010 Revenue–Tax Ratio

−4,427

−4,569

Unfortunately, the ESRI doesn't reveal the actual GDP growth in the absence of the deflationary 'correction'. However, the implication is that while GDP growth would be positive, GNP would still remain marginally negative. On this basis, and using the implied negative multiplier above, confirmed by

ESRI simulations, we can assess the full impact of these measures on GDP. The government's deflationary measures have reduced GDP by approximately €10.4 billion (see Figure 6.11). Though this is a tentative figure it still remains a credible indictment of government policy – to consciously and aggressively deflate the economy at a time when the economy was in a state of contraction. Government policy could have contributed well over a third to the recessionary slide.

Figure 6.11: The Effect of Fiscal Adjustments on GDP (€ millions), First Year

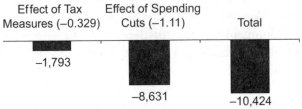

Effect of Tax   Effect of Spending
Measures (–0.329)   Cuts (–1.11)   Total

–1,793

–8,631

–10,424

Do Nothing

In the debate it is often asserted that if the government did 'nothing', the crisis would be worse. Actually, this is exactly what the government did – nothing. It failed to shore up consumer demand, limit employment falls through job retention/creation measures, and fill the widening investment gap. However, so disconnected is debate, that 'doing nothing' refers only to pro-cyclical deficit reduction (spending cuts, tax increases). It rarely, if ever, addresses the underlying causes of our fiscal deficit. By contrast, almost all other European governments have done something – but a different something; that is, some form of counter-cyclical measures appropriate to their economies.

Clearly doing nothing should not be an option, economies require intervention at all points in the economic cycle to smooth out the booms and the busts. However, a 'do nothing' scenario can provide some insight into how to 'read' the economy and the cycle, and help determine the nature and extent of the fiscal intervention. This is all the more important in the Irish case, bringing a substantial structural deficit into the recession. Based upon the above multipliers, the impact on GDP can be tentatively estimated.

Without fiscal correction, the GDP would be higher, entering into overall positive nominal growth in 2010 (see Figure 6.12). This is consistent with the ESRI's observations above. The advantages would be considerable: there would be more businesses in business, more people employed, more wages, more consumption and less emigration (thus, less loss of potentially valuable skill sets and spending power).

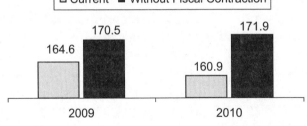

Figure 6.12: Government Projection and Estimated GDP Without Fiscal Adjustment (€ billions)

The goal of fiscal policy should be to secure the advantages of maintaining – and even boosting – output while introducing measures that can minimise the deterioration of the deficit at least cost to growth. This strategy, however, was not pursued. The government, supported by a general consensus, targeted the deficit only, not mindful of its immediate economic impact or the dangers of that deficit becoming embedded in the economy going forward.

The economy contracted by more than €10 billion as a result of the government's fiscal adjustments, or over a third of the total fall in output. This, however, probably understates the negative impact. It should be noted that the ESRI's impact assessment calculates shocks in €1 billion tranches. We may find that the accumulated impact of €5.4 billion tax measures implemented in a short time frame produces a deflationary effect beyond a static multiple of five; similarly with spending cuts. Indeed, this might help explain, along with the fall in property-related taxes, why net current revenue in 2007 was 25.2 per cent of GDP, while this ratio is projected to fall to 19.3 per cent by 2010.

Banking on Growth

Starting from 2010, the government's new fiscal adjustment projections – €6.5 billion as opposed to the €11 billion that appeared in the April 2009 Supplementary Budget – make up approximately two-thirds of the total deficit reduction by 2014. The remainder comes from growth – or the cyclical side of recovery. The government is putting considerable store in its growth projections. If these don't come right, then the government's debt/deficit strategy may come under serious pressure.

We can stress-test the government's projections by comparing them with those of other forecasters. It's not that these forecasters are prescient; rather, it's that all such projections are by their nature precarious. To provide a range of forecasts is merely to provide a wider landscape view without being pre-committed to one perspective.

For instance, the government projects real GDP growth to rise to 4 per cent by 2014. However, the NCB *Irish Economy Monitor*[57] projects growth to be less, at 2.9 per cent, while the IMF projects growth to be even less, at 2.5 per cent.[58] Already, in 2010, both the EU Commission[59] and the Irish Business and Employers' Confederation (IBEC)[60] have revised downwards GNP growth projections. This has little to do with the international environment (export projections remain high) but rather reflect domestic demand, which is being hit by the government's deflationary policies.

Low growth rates will obviously impact negatively on the fiscal deficit. Tax revenue will be undermined, employment generation will remain sluggish and, as a consequence, unemployment costs will remain high. One of the few forecasters to examine the long-term trend in deficit reduction suggests that on current policy, the government's budget will not return to Maastricht compliance (i.e. bring the deficit to below -3 per cent of GDP) until 2018 or 2019, as opposed to the government's goal of 2014.[61] Little wonder that the EU Commission has invited the Irish government to develop an alternative fiscal framework in case the 'favourable' as opposed to 'plausible' growth rates don't materialise.[62]

The government has acknowledged considerable downsides that are not factored into their projections. The PBO, for instance, states that GDP growth may not be job-rich; if it is not wage-rich or spend-rich as well, this may have a more depressing effect than otherwise projected. Other factors, some of which are mentioned in the SPU 2010, may cause future downward revisions: rising interest rates that exacerbate household deleveraging resulting in lower spending growth, oil and other commodity price increases, continued credit shortages and National Asset Management Agency (NAMA)-related costs, a weakening of demand in export markets and currency depreciation, the slowing down of live register outflows (in particular, emigration) resulting in higher than anticipated net unemployment, etc.

In other words, the risks to the government forecasts are most likely on the downside. To ensure both growth and debt control in an uncertain environment, the Irish economy needs an insurance policy – a hedge against sluggish indicators, unforeseen events and poor forecasting. It needs to avoid a low-growth, high-debt scenario. This requires reconnecting the fiscal with the economic. This requires a new macroeconomic platform.

A New Macroeconomic Platform

We are here now. Surveying past arguments is only intended to shake loose their influence over what will come.

The primary focus of fiscal policy should be to limit the impact and shorten the duration of recession. This is done to ensure that the economy continues to function above a fiscal-neutral level; that once the recession troughs and the economy is attempting to generate growth to reach full output, there are more businesses in business, more people in employment and more investment entrenched in the economy (giving it a head start as private investment comes back on stream); all this to ensure that the GDP starts its upward trajectory from a higher level. Fiscal consolidation is then introduced with, not against, the grain. It is less of a shock to the economy when wages, consumer spending, investment and employment are rising.

This is not to exclude certain contractionary measures from the start – after all, the key indicator is net expansion or net contraction. However, even here, it is necessary to ensure that such contractions initially target the least deflationary parts of the economy – the truly unproductive expenditure, the tax sources that are likely to be saved to no good output effect.

Above all, this requires a government that can 'read' an economy and engage in artful fiscal management; all the more so when trying to steer its way in a global tempest.

A new macroeconomic platform can, therefore, become a tool to ensure the economy reaches the output levels that will enable it, with the appropriate consolidation strategies, to close the fiscal gap. In Ireland, however, it must be capable of doing more – it must address the myriad of economic, social and infrastructural deficits. Merely solving the fiscal may only reinforce a low-growth future, which will be incapable of overcoming those deficits that are implied in current government strategy.

Physical Infrastructure

The government proposes a long-term real decline in capital investment. In the five years to 2014, it will decline by 23 per cent in nominal terms and 29 per cent in real terms. Colm McCarthy has reasonably argued that such a reduction can be justified on the grounds that reduced population and economic activity has taken the urgency out of capacity-enhancing projects;[63] this, along with anecdotal evidence of tender price reductions, means that cuts in the capital programme are non-harmful. These arguments are valid to a point. However, this should not blind us to the degraded state of our infrastructure.

While the World Economic Summit's Global Competitiveness Index combines objective and subjective data, the result is still concerning. The latest index ranks overall Irish infrastructure as sixty-fifth in the world – one of the worst among industrialised countries.[64] This poor infrastructural quality is confirmed by the Institute of Management Development's assessment:

> ...[S]ignificant weaknesses also emerge. These include ... a range of weak infrastructure indicators, including technological (23rd) and scientific (22nd) but in particular basic infrastructure (39th), energy infrastructure (44th) and investment in telecommunications (54th).[65]

If Ireland is serious about competing internationally, it will need to modernise its physical infrastructural base as quickly and as efficiently as possible.

Social Infrastructure

The government's strategy also envisages a decline in current non-interest expenditure of -8.3 per cent in the five years up to 2014. This will put pressure on public services to maintain output quality. The government projects current expenditure to be only slightly above 2002 levels, even though it will be carrying over three times the level of unemployment (see Figure 6.13).

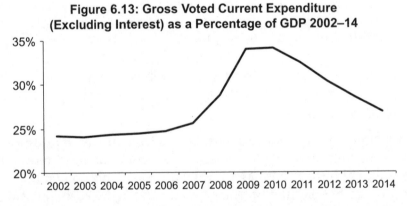

Figure 6.13: Gross Voted Current Expenditure (Excluding Interest) as a Percentage of GDP 2002–14

While some will point out that falling unemployment (assisted by emigration) will reduce costs between 2010 and 2014, the Social Affairs (now known as the Department of Social Protection) budget will remain subject to high demand. The government expects unemployment to fall from 13.2 per cent to 9.5 per cent between 2010 and 2014. There should be 80,000 fewer people unemployed. However, the growth in old age pensioners is gaining pace. In the five years to 2008, old age pension programmes experienced a rise of 65,000 recipients.[66] In addition, between 2010 and 2014 inflation will rise by 7.2 per cent, necessitating an increase in social welfare rates. Therefore, the fall in unemployment could be offset by other factors. In such a scenario, we could expect to see other programmes bearing a disproportionate amount of the real decline in current spending.

It is not a matter, though, of simply maintaining the current level of public services, many of which are European in name only. For instance, Forfás found that while 82 per cent of three-year olds in the EU-15 were in state-funded pre-primary education, only 1.7 per cent of Irish children were.[67] They further found that, whereas early education is almost entirely publicly funded in OECD countries, in Ireland it is almost entirely privately funded. This begs considerable questions regarding our future knowledge capital and current social equity. Addressing this will require increased public expenditure and a larger public sector payroll.

Social Protection

While social protection is often discussed in terms of fairness (and given that Ireland suffers one of the highest levels of relative poverty[68] and the lowest levels of income support,[69] fairness is a legitimate concern), it also needs to be discussed in terms of economic efficiency. Galbraith identified five reasons for the depth and duration of the US Depression in the 1930s.[70] First on the list was the high level of inequality ('the bad distribution of income'[71]), which meant that the people's spending power was not capable of sustaining demand. While not to the same degree (the US in the 1930s had only a minimal welfare state), Ireland, too, has suffered from weak automatic stabilisers with social welfare replacement ratios among the lowest in the EU-15. This has no doubt contributed to the collapse in consumer spending compared to the Eurozone average.

Further, the European Anti-Poverty Network has shown that for key welfare-dependent categories, there is no economic logic to take up work.[72] The lack of an integrated tax–social-welfare framework results in considerable disincentives to work (in the case of lone parents, they are financially worse off taking up full-time work on the minimum wage). To create the proper incentives, the tax and welfare systems will need to be integrated; but if this is done through a levelling down, then it will raise questions of equity and demand maintenance. Rather, this requires a levelling up and an extension of welfare state security to all low and average paid earners. This would be costly.

Indigenous Enterprise

A substantial part of Irish economic history since independence can be read as one long and only partially successful attempt to build a strong indigenous enterprise base. From protectionism in the 1930s to the introduction of foreign capital in the early 1960s through to the 'vulgar Keynesian' experiment of the late 1970s; all were launched with the intention to spur indigenous enterprise development. With the indigenous sector accounting for 10 per cent of both merchandise and service exports, with gross value-added levels not much higher, with low job creation rates in the tradable services and with poor performing research and development (R&D) and innovation, the indigenous sector's performance has been underwhelming.

The climatological school of economics[73] states that if we get the atmosphere right – low taxes, low regulation, high labour flexibility (on employers' terms) and limited public intervention – everything else should come out right. This we have had and, still, the indigenous sector flounders. That's because its problems have little to do with atmosphere: a concentration of indigenous activity in low value-added sectors, managerial deficits, small fragmented sectors, access to capital and market intelligence – especially in the export sector – chronic under-investment in product and process innovation, poor labour relations strategies, etc.

Reliance on market-led strategies is unlikely to succeed for the simple reason that the failure is endemic to the very market itself. The remedies will require a renewed investment in sectoral planning with negotiated strategies between the social partners and the financial sector taking place within, and effected through, the public realm. It will require new ways of doing business. And it will require investment.

A new macroeconomic platform will need to be capable of addressing these deficits. But in the first instance it will have to challenge the many presumptions that have driven the debate to date:

- Deflationist reading of 1989
- Selective use of international literature on fiscal contraction
- Simplistic assertion that cuts equal savings
- Highly qualified measurements of the structural deficit
- Reduction of not only the economic to the fiscal but the reduction within the fiscal whereby our low-debt profile is marginalised

This will hopefully open up a debate over more sophisticated multi-track strategies to promote economic growth and reduce debt. Stimulus should be timely and temporary. In Ireland's case, we are past that. The recession is expected to trough sometime in 2010. The current challenge is to avoid a low-growth, high-debt future, to overcome the physical and social deficits that will continue to depress growth. This won't require so much a stimulus in the conventional sense, but a sustained long-term investment programme through fiscal activism.

A New Platform: The Investment Track

One of the key informing principles of an active fiscal intervention is that those investments that are necessary to improve our productivity and competitiveness – those that would have to be made in any event – should be proceeded with. This will seek to embed investment, rather than deficit, into the economic base.

One of the more interesting proposals to date is Fine Gael's NewERA programme.[74] Building on original ICTU proposals,[75] they propose to combine the asset strength of commercial public enterprises into a single holding company with provision for establishing new public enterprises. This would carry out an €18 billion investment programme capable of creating 100,000 direct and downstream jobs. They identify key infrastructural and enterprise areas:

- Upgrade of the electricity grid, with emphasis on conservation, renewables, micro-generation and even electric cars
- An open access, high connectivity fibre-optic and wireless network to support next generation broadband services to every home and business
- Commercialisation of next generation bio-energy technologies
- Investment in early stage green energy companies and applied renewable energy research
- An expanded water infrastructure investment programme
- A National Recovery Bank to finance insulation retrofitting

A second priority is the educational infrastructure, in particular, the rolling out of an early education and childcare sector with a strong pedagogical input. Not only has Forfás shown the near non-existent state of early education, the OECD identifies Ireland as having one of the most expensive and, therefore, inaccessible childcare systems in the industrialised world.[76] The combined effect is to limit our knowledge capital, driving up public costs through educational underachievement[77] and restricting access to the labour market while squeezing consumer spending through the high costs of private childcare and early education.

Third, investment in social protection would have a twofold effect: the flattening effect of a more progressive redistribution system would ensure that domestic demand can be more effectively maintained while increased demand in low-income areas could result in multiplier effects that would arguably be higher. At the same time, the integration of the social welfare and taxation systems can not only remove barriers to the labour market but can spread benefits higher up the income deciles (e.g. free general practitioner (GP) care, housing supports, etc.), which can limit upward pressures on labour costs.

Ordinarily, Ireland's low-debt status would provide it with a strong platform to access funding on the international markets, especially for the purpose of increasing and modernising its capital assets (e.g. infrastructure). Not only is Ireland's debt level below Eurozone average (see Figure 6.14), its accumulated Exchequer cash balances (approximately 12 per cent of GDP) puts it in an even stronger net debt level.[78] However, a combination of government deflationary policies, which have created legitimate concerns over future economic performance, the cost of bank bailouts and global concerns over rising sovereign debt, many of which are misplaced, have produced a situation where future borrowing costs will be high.

Figure 6.14: Net Debt as a Percentage of GDP, 2010 (estimated)

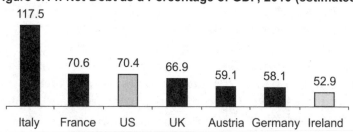

Still, the ESRI points out that Ireland will retain nearly €50 billion, or 30 per cent of GDP, in combined Exchequer cash balances and NPRF assets. The potential to access some of these resources is considerable. In addition, there are non-Exchequer sources that can be accessed. Fine Gael claims that half of their NewERA programme would be financed through borrowings by the new public enterprise holding company and loans from the European

Investment Bank. Clearly, a restructured public enterprise could provide a substantial contribution to an infrastructural and enterprise investment programme[79] and could help make up for the decline in Exchequer capital expenditure.

There are other mechanisms to access more resources:

- The government announced the launching of the National Solidarity Bond, a medium-term national savings product aimed at small investors as an additional source of funding for capital investment.
- Comhar, the Sustainable Development Council, has put forward proposals for Green Bonds to access investment into green technologies.[80]
- Proposals for revenue and general obligation municipal bonds have been advanced by Deeter and Kinsella, adding a new investment source for local and regional government.[81]

Progressive strategies for financing investment – employing a range of Exchequer and non-Exchequer instruments – can build on our low-debt status.

A New Platform: Net Fiscal Consolidation

Given the government's determination to maintain historically low levels of public spending, a new macroeconomic framework requires a fiscal consolidation strategy that can both address the structural deficit and overcome the social deficits which the government's strategy will reinforce.

It will also have to generate a debate over what new target levels for expenditure and taxation will be optimal. A critical omission in the fiscal consolidation debate is what level we want to consolidate around. The ESRI's John Fitz Gerald has offered a personal preference – 'target a level of expenditure and revenue in the medium term equivalent to 45 per cent of GDP'.[82] This is in line with pre-recession Eurozone averages, but let's not underestimate the magnitude of this eminently sensible challenge. In 2007 this would have meant an increase of 25 per cent in public expenditure – over €16 billion. While total public expenditure today stands above Professor Fitz Gerald's threshold, this is a result of collapsed output in combination with high unemployment costs. The government's current strategy is to bring that spending–GDP ratio well below the Eurozone norm, perpetuating the low-tax, low-spend model that has dominated economic and political discourse.

Tax-Based Consolidation

The ESRI's simulations clearly show that tax-based consolidation measures are far less deflationary and less harmful to employment than public-expenditure-based measures. When comparing tax increases (income, property and carbon tax) and spending cuts (public sector wages, jobs and investment) – each designed to achieve a €3 billion contraction – tax measures are far less harmful to growth and employment and achieve a higher net income (see Figure 6.15).

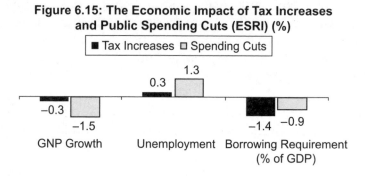

Figure 6.15: The Economic Impact of Tax Increases and Public Spending Cuts (ESRI) (%)

Historically, the Irish economy has been relatively low taxed. Breaking from this model will open up new options. To date, however, the debate over what kind of tax architecture is appropriate for the Irish economy has been limited. Unfortunately, the Commission on Taxation's report, which contained much that was worthy of further analysis and debate, was side-lined by the narrow parameters it imposed on itself.[83]

Further, there has been little debate over the timing of fiscal consolidation. As the economy emerges out of contraction, it is imperative that consolidation initially targets the least deflationary source of revenue. This would mean focusing on higher income groups with less propensity to spend. The Department of Finance's survey of the effective tax rate of high income earners[84] is helpful, as is the complementary attention being paid to the role of tax expenditures[85] that distort the efficient allocation of resources and lower Exchequer revenue. Indeed, focusing on effective tax rates – on income and capital – can shift the debate away from the marginal rate and back to the base.

The increasing discussion of property tax is another instance of shifting the impact of taxation from labour. However, the ESRI[86] has shown that a poorly designed model may lead to a lack of progressivity between middle and higher earners.[87] This is a direct result of base limitation. A comprehensive property tax would not stop with 'house property' (which makes up the primary asset of most low and middle income earners); it would not discriminate between forms of property – land, house and financial; in this respect it would take on the nature of a 'net assets' tax, levied on global assets. Goodbody Stockbrokers, working with Central Bank data, have estimated that between 2006 and 2010 household housing assets will fall in value by 34 per cent; financial assets will actually rise.[88] Therefore, a comprehensive property, or net assets, tax would have greater robustness.

In the medium term, greater attention will have to be paid to what kind of tax architecture can achieve the transition to continental European tax levels. Comparative data throws up some interesting insights.[89] Ireland is one of the most fiscally centralised tax systems. When the main 'central taxes' are observed (income, corporation, capital and indirect taxes), Ireland actually comes out as a 'high tax' system in the EU-15 (this may come as a surprise to those who contest Ireland's low tax model). Where Irish revenue levels 'underperform' are in the areas of social insurance and local government taxation (see Figure 6.16).

Figure 6.16: Taxes Received by Administrative Level (Percentage of GDP), 2007

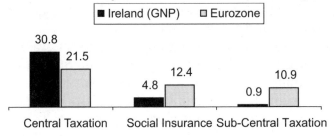

■ Ireland (GNP) □ Eurozone

	Central Taxation	Social Insurance	Sub-Central Taxation
Ireland (GNP)	30.8	4.8	0.9
Eurozone	21.5	12.4	10.9

Social Insurance

Social insurance can play a particularly helpful role. Unlike general taxation, it has the character of a contract: in exchange for x levy, you will be entitled to y goods or services. This would allow the Exchequer to re-route much of central expenditure through an enhanced social insurance fund. A health insurance levy paid for by employees, employers and the self-employed would be exchanged for greater access at lower cost to healthcare, especially primary care (GP care, prescription medicine, etc.). This has the benefit of diverting demand from expensive tertiary care. Pension tax expenditures can be diverted into a mandatory earnings-related second tier social insurance system – one which bypasses the vagaries of the equity markets and introduces a defined benefit scheme for all workers from savings socially pooled. Even the financing of higher education, a subject of considerable contention, can be partially addressed through social insurance: an education levy which would enable people to access not just higher education but continuing and lifelong education. Higher taxation levels may meet with less resistance if it comes via a social bargain, or social insurance.

Local Taxation

Currently, local governments are dependent on business rates, service charges, development levies (which have declined with the fall in the property market) and central government grant funding. Where revenue comes from flat rate payments (e.g. service charges) they become regressive, which limits the appeal of local government financing.

The decentralisation of service provision has much to offer. It can potentially be more accountable to local needs and be subject to greater local scrutiny. The goods and services which my local taxes buy can be more readily observed and consumed (e.g. parks, leisure centres, recycling centres, road repairs) – or, at more advanced decentralist models, health, education and transport provision, along with investment supports for municipal and community enterprises.

This raises critical questions regarding legal powers, scale of local provision and progressive taxation powers. While the *Special Group Report* proposed an amalgamation of several local authorities for 'savings' purposes, such an amalgamation of local authorities into regional governments which have greater scale and a potentially wider tax base is certainly worth discussing (this needn't eliminate county, city and town level councils, it would however limit their scale and administration appropriate to their subordinated levels). As to new fiscal powers, the original Commission on Taxation Report[90] showed, without recommending, that an income tax could be applied in an efficient manner with the Revenue Commissioner acting as the collecting agency.

The expansion of local government taxation along European lines, therefore, will require more than fiscal reform; it will involve large-scale institutional reform as well.

* * *

Short- and long-term fiscal consolidation is not merely a fiscal task. It will involve social provision delivery and institutional reforms. To accommodate the deficit reduction targets in the government's programme while at the same time addressing the social deficits will require a net consolidation in excess of current targets. The ability to achieve this is highly dependent on growth trajectory, the capacity of the economy (i.e. people and enterprises) to absorb higher levels of taxation and social insurance, the efficiency of new practices and structures, and the productivity of public expenditure. Most of all, it will depend on people believing they are getting a good deal.

Public-Expenditure-Based Consolidation

As seen above, public expenditure is low by European standards. The OECD declared that Ireland has one of the smallest public sectors in the industrialised world.[91] While much attention has been paid to nominal expenditure increases over time, such expenditure as a proportion of national wealth has increased only incrementally.

To date, the debate has failed to distinguish between productivity and cost. In terms of the former, one international study has found that the Irish public sector is one of the most productive in the EU-15.[92] While the National Competitiveness Council, which has highlighted this in several annual reports, is right to warn us against reading too much into such findings, as 'techniques for measuring public sector productivity are at an early stage',[93] it should also give us some international perspective.

That productivity and output are not necessarily enhanced by 'cuts' can be seen in two instances: currently, the Revenue Commissioners are experiencing a shortfall of key personnel in their investigations division due to the public sector hiring freeze.[94] This freeze has resulted in reduced public expenditure. But the effect on the agency's capacity to ensure taxpayer compliance has yet to be assessed. We shouldn't be surprised to find that the number and scale of special and routine audits will be reduced, that the tax yield will suffer and that the demonstration effect will be negative (more people escaping legal tax liabilities), never mind the morale effect on the remaining investigators. The same effect can be visible in relation to social welfare fraud investigations. In both cases, perverse results could be reached – reductions in expenditure are exceeded by increased costs (tax evasion, social welfare fraud).

Similarly with nurses, specialist skill nurses are forced to perform non-nursing tasks (administrative, telephony, janitorial, etc.), which may result in declining productivity and output. There are few advantages in employing specialist skilled labour when they are required to perform work outside their specialism. Nursing productivity may be improved if more people are employed in 'civilianisation' roles, releasing nurses to do what they are trained to do.

The public expenditure debate also needs to separate reform that can be resolved at industrial relations level from that which can only be resolved at political management level. That demarcation rigidities persist is unsurprising in organisations as large as the public sector, where dense codes of work practices developed throughout the decades; yet, there are other rigidities at institutional level that are just as profound. In the health sector, we have yet to fully model the economic cost of operating a unique two-tier health system with such a high degree of public–private interpenetration and where treatment can be dispensed on an ability to pay. There are serious issues of resource allocation, bureaucratisation to monitor the conflicting interests and private producer capture in our public system. In the primary education sector we find confessional, non-denominational and language-based schools competing for students in the same catchment areas, with separate property, administrative and operating costs. An alternative model, preserving 'choice', could see the amalgamation of such schools into one campus, sharing the costs but administering their own streams. In both instances, these public sector reforms are essentially political choices.

The debate is a long way from these concerns, narrowly focusing on gross cuts in expenditure output. But even this has its limitations. A popular recommendation of the Special Group was the rationalisation of government departments and public agencies, referred to as the 43 'quangos'. The proliferation of such agencies has come under criticism from many quarters, and not just for cost reasons: issues of democratic accountability have also been raised.[95] However, rationalisation does not suggest a high savings outcome. The Special Group estimated a headline reduction of €170 million arising from their proposals, or 3 per cent of the total 'savings' contained in their report. This does not count associated costs if such rationalisation leads to lower employment, in which case the savings become less.[96]

There are alternative ways of capturing public expenditure efficiencies and productivity. Health policy analyst Sara Burke has proposed €1 billion savings in non-deflationary expenditure proposals without affecting output or service quality.[97] One could 'pocket' that €1 billion gain in net reduction. Or it could be embedded into public expenditure without increasing net costs (or a combination of both). For instance, part of these savings could be invested into the civilianisation referred to above. This would increase employment (generating tax revenue and reducing unemployment costs) while increasing nursing productivity.

None of this is to gainsay the role that public expenditure reduction can play in fiscal consolidation. It merely suggests a more profound debate is necessary – one focused on productivity and output rather gross reduction. The issue becomes 'value for money', efficiency and delivery, not the illusory 'cuts equal savings'.

A New Platform: Temporary Stimulus Measures

Investment that embeds growth in the economic base and fiscal consolidation that works with the grain of that growth are not likely to achieve immediate results. Capital investments can take up to eighteen months before coming on stream. Similarly, expenditure-based consolidation measures involving institutional reforms or emerging from traditional collective bargaining have a lead-in time. Even tax-based consolidation measures such as a comprehensive property or net assets tax have a time lag before optimal full-year yields flow in.

Therefore, more traditional stimulus means may be necessary to promote stop-gap growth inputs. 'Shovel-ready' projects have a place in this mix – especially with the slack in the construction sector. Approved local authority projects such as urban regeneration programmes, roads programmes and other capital projects can play a key bridging role until sustainable programmes can come on stream.

There are other temporary measures that can be considered:

- Dr Jimmy Stewart puts forward a provocative proposal to issue consumer vouchers to be used for stays in hotels and approved B&Bs.[98] Not only would this assist the hospitality sector, it would result in positive multipliers in the locales (restaurants, shops, petrol stations, etc.).
- Temporary targeted cuts in VAT could follow the French example of cutting VAT on restaurants and other labour-intensive services.
- A state-guaranteed loan scheme for small to medium enterprises (SMEs): whatever about the long-term success of NAMA, in the short term it is unlikely to unlock credit for the cash-flow-starved SME sector. The urgent issue is to get credit into businesses.

A range of measures could be considered that would maintain consumer spending and assist enterprises dependent on domestic demand in the short term.

A New Fiscal Platform: Multiplying Growth

There are few subjects that create more debate than the efficacy of the multiplier effect. Old/neo Keynesians, new Keynesians, classical, fresh-water, saltwater schools combined with the myriad of syntheses – all create, refer and draw upon models that vindicate their own assumptions and cast doubt on others. Those arguments cannot be settled here except to say that any set of multipliers will be highly contested. With this caveat in mind, the following will apply the multipliers provided by Lane–Bénétrix, one of the few works on fiscal shocks in Ireland.[99] These are consistent with Michael Burke's survey of multipliers employed by the ESRI in their evaluation of government investment.[100]

Long-Term Infrastructural Investment

Using ICTU's investment model, as developed by Fine Gael's NewERA policy, this measures a €9 billion investment introduced over a four-year period.[101] There are two dimensions to measuring output:

- Demand-side or short-term impact: the benefit arising when the actual work is being done to create the product or service.
- Supply-side or long-term impact: the benefit arising when the actual good or service is being used.

The former is exhausted in the medium term, the boost having worked its way fully through the economy (see Figure 6.17). The latter is near permanent, reflecting the addition to public capital.

Figure 6.17: Demand-Side Impact of €9 Billion Infrastructural Investment

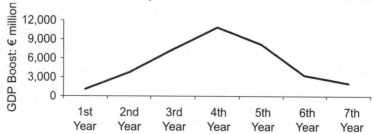

As can be seen in Figure 6.17, the boost from the demand side peaks at a little short of €11 billion in the fourth year (or a little over 5 per cent of the government's 2014 GDP projection), continuing until it has been spent by the ninth year.

Government tax revenue arising from this investment – assuming that the current revenue–GDP ratio of 33 per cent holds – will exceed €10 billion by the fifth year, thus paying off the original investment. In this respect, an investment strategy pays for itself, which shouldn't be too surprising as this is what enterprises and households experience.

However, the long-term supply side provides a boost of approximately 5 to 7 per cent[102] of the original investment when fully implemented. This implies a permanent output boost of over €500 million with a resulting permanent increase in government revenue.

There is more to an infrastructural investment programme than just a mechanical boost to output and tax revenue. To the extent that it establishes viable entities (a next generation broadband company, bio-energy and related green companies, etc.), the investment becomes embedded into indigenous enterprise, which boosts domestic sourcing, R&D, exportable home-grown innovation, new skill sets, etc. In addition, these can generate sustained productivity increases, with a resulting decline in *real wages* that can sustain nominal wage increases, thus boosting Exchequer revenue ... and so on as the virtuous cycle of investment and growth take root.

Short-Term Infrastructural Investment

This examines the effect of a traditional once-off capital investment of €2 billion that can act as a bridge until the activity from longer-term infrastructural and enterprise investments come on stream. This usually includes traditional 'shovel-ready' projects, particularly construction – the type of projects that have already been approved (contracts signed, planning permission granted, etc.). These can brought on stream quickly.

We see a similar, if smaller, impact at work (see Figure 6.18): a short-term boost to output continuing to the sixth year with resulting tax revenue exceeding the original investment by the third to fourth year. The impact could be concentrated and enlarged if such investment took place in local markets (cities and towns outside Dublin) where unemployment is higher and the multipliers would have a greater impact.

In a real sense, this is not about inventing a new wheel but getting us back to the point where we can repeat the 1987–9 experience – pursuing fiscal consolidation through growth. The key difference is that, unlike back then, we don't have the advantage of an automatic growth environment. We must 'manufacture' that growth environment, by replicating the stimulus that was available in the past (EU funding) but now supplied out of our own resources.

Figure 6.18: Demand-Side Impact of Single-Year €2 Billion Capital Investment

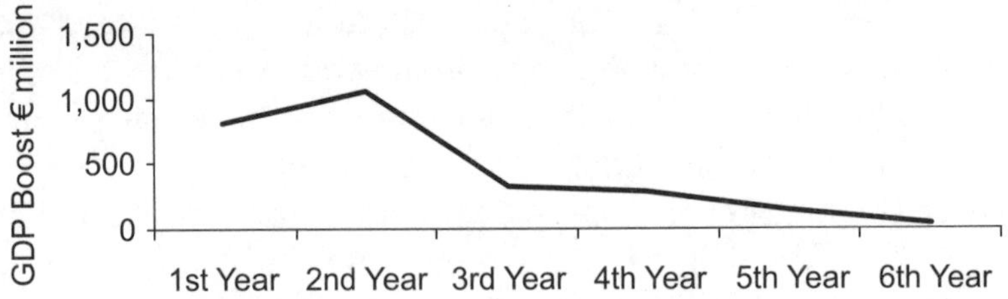

All of the above suggest a general principle – that an investment strategy at all times in the economic cycle can be self-financing. This is most effective when the output gap is large, there is considerable slack in the labour market, credit is constrained, etc.; that is, when we are in a recession. However, as the economy moves towards full output, such fiscal activism can lead to higher inflation, imported interest rates where there is a national currency and an unbalanced labour market when labour is imported. In such circumstances, investment strategies need to be more forensic and carefully calibrated to avoid these negative impacts.

Therefore, this is not a simplistic 'we can spend our way out of debt' (though there is much common sense in that simple dictum).[103] But to paraphrase Keynes, 'Look after the investment, and the budget will look after itself'.

The New Fiscal Dynamic

Platform, not framework; this is not to engage in semantics. It only points out that any fiscal policy is contingent upon a range of interpenetrative policies which, depending on their efficacy, can fulfil, undermine or neutralise the goals of the fiscal policy itself. If there is a fiscal stimulus, it matters what kind. If investment, it matters how productive (the building of a motorway or merely digging holes and refilling them). If contractionary, it matters whether it is tax-based or spending-reduction-based. If spending, it matters whether it actually cuts 'fat' or cuts 'bone'. If tax, it matters whether it reduces the propensity to spend or the propensity to save. Weaving all these together into a coherent platform requires the ultimate skill in economic management. Fiscal policy may presume; it cannot determine.

A framework implies an ability to set parameters within which all other relevant policy levers operate. It is, however, people who operate those levers and in many cases they are forced to do so in the dark where historical precedent may be instructive but not formulaic. In many cases we can't know if a policy is successful until well after the fact. In many cases we may never know – or may not want to know – if an alternative course might have been better. This is not an argument against measurement, just a caution: our instruments may not be as precise as the conclusions we draw.

That is why *fiscal platform* may be a better formulation. It conjures an image of inviting the players and policies to stand upon it and act. It is the place from which policy commences outwards towards less certain conclusions. The platform discussed here suggests a different set of policies than has been pursued or which, under current strategy, will be pursued.

There were choices. There always are. Irish policy set aside the tools by which the damage and duration of the recession could be both limited and shortened. This is not just a graph. People lose jobs, livelihoods, hope; businesses built up over years collapse in months; savings and investments for old age disappear or sour; the very inputs – the actors that generate activity, growth, prosperity – are turned into objects when they should actually be the subjects. This is the ultimate reconnection: between the fiscal, the economic and the life of society.

It's not too late to change course. There are, after all, other directions.

7

The Phillips Curve and the Wage–Inflation Process in Ireland

Anthony Leddin[1]

Introduction

National Wage Agreements (NWAs) between the social partners (government, trade unions and employer representatives) were re-introduced in Ireland in January 1988 and, while there is debate surrounding their effectiveness, they have been generally credited as being a significant factor underlining the economic prosperity of the 1990s and 2000s.[2] By 2008, there were seven successive agreements spanning a twenty-one-year period. In September 2008 a new twenty-one-month pay award was agreed but, following an eleven-month pay freeze, the government rescinded on paying the first 3.5 per cent pay instalment and this ended the partnership process. The economic downturn in 2008, due, in part, to the collapse of the building and construction sector, resulted in a significant fiscal deficit and the government had little choice but to renege on the pay agreement.

This chapter uses data derived from the wage agreements to examine the interrelationship between wages, unemployment and inflation in Ireland. Of particular concern is the role of domestic factors in the inflation process and the decline in price competitiveness over the last decade.

The outline of the chapter is as follows: in the first section, a new, monthly, nominal 'pay award index', for both the public and private sectors, based on the wage agreements, is constructed. These indexes show how a worker would have fared if his or her salary was wholly determined by the pay awards over the period. The pay award indexes are then compared to wage indexes published by the Central Statistics Office (CSO) in order to ascertain if the wage agreements acted as a constraint on pay developments in the public sector and in the wider economy.

The next section provides a brief account of the evolution of the Phillips curve theory and outlines both the New Keynesian Phillips Curve (NKPC) and the Triangle Phillips Curve (TPC) models. The NKPC model is based on forward-looking inflation expectations, whereas the TPC model emphasises inertia and persistence effects and allows for supply-side shocks. The third section contains a descriptive analysis of the interrelationship between the pay award indexes, inflation as measured by the consumer price index (CPI) and unemployment over the twenty-one-year period. What emerges is a familiar Phillips curve story of falling unemployment and unexpected inflation provoking a wage–inflation spiral. This was an important contributory factor to the significant deterioration in Ireland's price competitiveness after 2001.

We then formally investigate some of the issues raised in the previous section by estimating both the NKPC and the TPC models using the public sector pay award index as the dependent variable. The TPC model appears to out-perform the NKPC model as variables representing inertia and persistence effects and supply-side shocks are found to be important in explaining nominal wages. However, because nominal wages are locked for the duration of the pay awards, lagged real earnings was found to be an important explanatory variable. This raises the question as to whether the Phillips curve models should be generalised to accommodate wage agreement type scenarios. The penultimate section reviews briefly the experience in relation to price competitiveness and the final concluding section summarises the main findings and briefly discusses the policy implications.

The Pay Awards and Nominal Earnings

Until recently, the CSO published five series relating to average wages in building and construction, financial institutions, the public sector (excluding health), distribution and business services, and all other industries. This data was based on the *Quarterly Industrial Inquiry* (QII) but the series was discontinued after the second quarter of 2007 (Q2 2007) and has been replaced by an *Earnings, Hours and Employment Cost Survey* (EHECS). However, the EHECS data is, as yet, only available back to 2005 and is therefore insufficient to cover the period under review in this paper.

The analysis in this section is based on the QII and is confined to the period Q1 1988 to Q2 2007.

Table 7.1 shows average weekly earnings in each of the five earnings categories in Q1 1988 and Q2 2007 and also the percentage change over the period. Topping the list in Q2 2007 is the public sector on an average weekly wage of €926. Earnings in financial institutions was €886, building and construction €800, distribution and business services €708 and, at the bottom, all other industries €627. Hence, despite the apparent constraint of the pay agreements, the trade unions were able to negotiate pay awards that ensured that the public sector had the highest average weekly level of pay by mid-2007. It is evident from Table 7.1, however, that while building and construction had the lowest level of pay in Q1 1988, this sector had the largest percentage increase over the period (240 per cent compared to 177 per cent in the public sector).

Table 7.1: Average Weekly Earnings and the Percentage Change, Q1 1988 and Q2 2007

	Average Weekly Earnings (€)	Average Weekly Earnings (€)	
	Q1 1988	Q2 2007	Percentage Change
1 Public sector (excluding health)	334.7	926.6	176.9
2 Financial institutions	375.4	886.3	136.1
3 Building and construction	235.4	800.1	239.9
4 Distribution and business services	N/A	708.5	N/A
5 All other industries	244.2	627.2	156.8
	Index	Index	Percentage Change
6 Public sector pay award (including benchmarking)	100	234.0	134.0
7 Public sector pay award (excluding benchmarking)	100	214.1	114.1
8 Private sector pay award	100	206.7	106.7

Table 7.2 summarises the nominal wage awards under each agreement between January 1988 and October 2008 for the public sector.[3] It can be

Table 7.2: Nominal Wage Awards for the Public Sector Under Each Agreement between January 1988 and October 2008

National Wage Agreements / Public Sector Pay (Includes benchmarking)		1 Nominal Wage Award	2 Local Bargaining	3 Early Settler Provision	4 Inflation Compensation	5 Once-Off Payment	6 Benchmarking ***	7 Total Award
		%	%	%	%	%	%	%
1	Programme for National Recovery (PNR)							
	Jan. 1988–Dec. 1988	2.5						2.5
	Jan. 1989–Dec. 1989	2.5						2.5
	Jan. 1990–Dec. 1990	2.5						2.5
2	Programme for Economic and Social Progress (PESP)							
	Jan. 1991–Dec. 1991	4						4
	Jan. 1992–Dec. 1992	3	3					6
	Jan. 1993–Dec. 1993	3.75						3.75
3	Programme for Competitiveness and Work (PCW)							
	Jan. 1994–May 1994	Pay freeze						0
	June 1994–May 1995	2						2
	June 1995–May 1996	2						2
	June 1996–Sept. 1996	1.5						1.5
	Oct. 1996–Dec. 1996	1.5						1.5
	Jan. 1997–June 1997	1						1
4	Partnership 2000 (P2000)							
	July 1997–March 1998*	2.5						2.5
	April 1998–June 1998	2.5						2.5
	July 1998–June 1999	2.25	2					4.25
	July 1999–March 2000	1.5						1.5
	April 2000–Sept. 2000	1						1

(Continued)

Table 7.2: (Continued)

National Wage Agreements Public Sector Pay Includes benchmarking		Column						
		1 Nominal Wage Award	2 Local Bargaining	3 Early Settler Provision	4 Inflation Compensation	5 Once-Off Payment	6 Benchmarking ***	7 Total Award
		%	%	%	%	%	%	%
5	*Programme for Prosperity and Fairness (PPF)*							
	Oct. 2000–Sept. 2001	5.5		3				8.5
	Oct. 2001–Sept. 2002	5.5			2	1	2.23	10.73
	Oct. 2002–June 2003	4						4
6	*Sustaining Progress Part 1 (SP 1)*							
	July 2003–Dec. 2003	Pay freeze						0
	Jan. 2004–June 2004	3					4.45	7.45
	July 2004–Nov. 2004	2						2
	Dec. 2004–May 2005	2						2
	Sustaining Progress Part 2 (SP 2)							
	June 2005–Nov. 2005**	1.5					2.23	3.73
	Dec. 2005–May 2006	1.5						1.50
	June 2006–June 2006	2.5						2.50
7	*Towards 2016*							
	July 2006–Nov. 2006	Pay freeze						0
	Dec. 2006–May 2007	3						3
	June 2007–Feb. 2008	2						2
	March 2008–Aug. 2008	2.5						2.5
	Sept. 2008	2.5						2.5

*2.5 of first £200 of basic pay
**1.5% or 2% on €351/month or less
***Average payment under benchmarking was 8.9%:
1 Dec 2001: 25% of the recommended increase
1 Jan 2004: 50% of the recommended increase
1 June 2005: 25% of the recommended increase

seen that there were seven different pay agreements spanning a period of twenty-one years. It should be noted that there are some important differences between this table and the private sector wage awards. In particular, the public sector was awarded 'early settler' and 'benchmarking' awards and was also subjected to three pay freezes. Based on the pay awards to both sectors it is possible to construct three different 'pay award indexes': the public sector, including and excluding the benchmark awards, and the private sector.[4]

Reverting back to Table 7.1, rows 6, 7 and 8 shows the change in these three indexes over the period 1988–2007. A number of points emerge from the table. First, the 134 per cent increase in the public sector pay award (including benchmarking) (row 6) is equivalent to an average cumulative increase of 2 per cent per annum. The lowest increase was during the *Programme for Competitiveness and Work*, 1994–7 (8.25 per cent over 42 months) and the highest during the *Programme for Prosperity and Fairness*, 2000–03 (15.1 per cent over 33 months).

Second, a 27.3 percentage point gap emerges between the public (including benchmarking) and the private sector pay award index by the end of the period (rows 6 and 8). Of this difference, 20 percentage points is explained by the Public Service Benchmarking Body (PSBB) award and the remainder by local bargaining and early settlement clauses.[5]

The third issue relates to the extent that the pay awards influenced pay developments in both the public and private sectors. Trade union membership of all employees in Ireland has fallen from 62 per cent in 1980 to 31 per cent in 2007. Membership was estimated to be 70 per cent in the public sector and 25 per cent in the private sector in 2007.[6] This would suggest that the wage agreements have only a marginal influence on earnings in the private sector. However, advocates of the agreement process have argued that their influence is much more significant as the awards have been used as a benchmark for many non-unionised industries and employments.

The percentage change in the private 'pay award index' of 107 per cent (row 8) is well short of that in building and construction (240 per cent) and industry (156 per cent), but more in line with the outcome in financial institutions (136 per cent). This suggests that while the partnership agreements may have had a constraining effect on nominal earnings in the financial sector, market conditions clearly dominated in the case of building and construction and elsewhere.

In the case of the public sector, the gap between the pay awards and actual earnings is 43 percentage points (rows 1 and 6). Even allowing for the twenty-year time frame, this seems to be a significant degree of slippage between the actual pay bill and the pay awards in the public sector. This raises the question of whether the constructed pay award index is a 'purer' measure of wage developments over the period. What it shows is how a person's wages would have evolved if they were in continuous employment in the public sector from 1988 to 2008 and they received no additional wage increases. The CSO published series, on the other hand, is influenced, among other factors, by increments, promotions and/or people being hired into the public sector at higher career grades. The CSO data could be inter-preted as a combination of 'signal' plus 'noise'. The noise-to-signal ratio should be low but the data here indicate that it is quite high. It is also notice-able that the noise element is in an upward direction only.

The Phillips Curve

As has been well documented, the original, non-linear equation fitted by Phillips[7] related the rate of change of nominal wage rates (ω) to the unem-ployment rate (U):

$$\omega_t = -0.90 + 9.64 U_t^{-1.39} \tag{1}$$

Samuelson and Solow[8] replaced the nominal wage with the inflation rate, labelled the fitted non-linear curve the 'Phillips curve' and examined the policy implications of the potential trade-off between unemployment and inflation.[9] Friedman[10] and Phelps[11] introduced the natural rate of unem-ployment and an adaptive expectations measure of expected inflation.

$$p_t = \beta_1 E_t p_{t+1} - \beta_2 (U_t - U_N) + e_t \tag{2}$$

where p_t is the inflation rate in time t, $E_t p_{t+1}$ is the expected rate of inflation in time t+1 and U_t and U_N are the actual and natural rate of unemployment respectively. Lower-case letters indicate first differences of logarithms and upper-case letters indicate logarithms of levels. Later, Lucas[12] replaced adaptive expectations with rational expectations. These contributions by Friedman, Phelps and Lucas demolished the notion that a trade-off existed between inflation and unemployment and instead pointed to the long-run neutrality of monetary policy.

However, as Gordon[13] points out, a difficulty with the Friedman–Phelps–Lucas model was that, apart from the assumption of continuous market clearing:

Deviations of the current actual price level from the expected price were the *only* allowable source of business cycle movements in real GDP [gross domestic product]. The assumption of imperfect information implied that business cycles would be eliminated if we had accurate current information about the aggregate price level, and such information was available every month when the latest CPI data were released.[14]

That is, it is not plausible to suggest that only unanticipated inflation could explain the 'multi-year business cycles' observed in numerous countries.

Gordon notes that, 'since 1975 the development of PC doctrine has followed two divergent paths, called here the "left fork" and "right fork" of the road, with no sign of convergence, and indeed little sign that the two sides are paying attention to each other.'[15] These paths are the New Keynesian Phillips Curve (NKPC) and the Triangle Phillips Curve (TPC) model.

The TPC model has three main explanatory variables representing the roles of inertia, demand and supply:[16]

$$p_t = \beta_1 E_t p_{t+1} - \beta_2 (U_t - U_N) + z_t + e_t \tag{3}$$

where z_t is a variable representing supply-side shock variables. According to Gordon,[17] the inertia and persistence effect arise because of the 'transmission time' from changes in raw and intermediate good prices to the final output price and also the effect of fixed duration wage and price contracts between suppliers and producers of final goods. This effect is captured by the $E_t p_{t+1}$ variable, which is derived by using a long series of lagged inflation rates and not simply a one-year adaptive expectation measure.

Demand shocks are represented by the unemployment gap ($U_t - U_N$), but can also be proxied by an output gap or by real marginal or average cost. The introduction of the unemployment gap immediately raises the problem of how to measure the natural rate of unemployment and whether this variable moves over time.[18]

Supply shock variables are represented by the z_t term. This variable can include changes in the relative prices of food and energy and the growth rate of productivity. The inclusion of the z_t term represents a departure from earlier Phillips curve representations as supply shocks can now have a direct influence on inflation.

The New Keynesian Phillips Curve (NKPC) was developed by Kydland and Prescott[19] and Gali and Gertler.[20] This formulation specifies that the inflation rate (p_t) depends on expected future inflation ($E_t p_{t+1}$) and the unemployment (or output) gap:

$$p_t = \beta_1 E_t p_{t+1} - \beta_2 (U_t - U_N) + e_t \tag{4}$$

Gordon points out that there are two essential differences relative to the TPC model:

First, there is no explicit treatment of supply shocks; these are suppressed into the error term. Second, expectations are explicitly forward-looking in [the NKPC] whereas in [the TPC model], expectations could be either forward-looking or backward-looking, or both.[21]

Because inflation expectations are strictly forward-looking in the NKPC model, there is no role for the persistence and inertia effect.

Real Earnings and the Wage–Inflation Process

The analysis in this paper does not fit neatly into the world of workers reacting almost instantaneously to the published, monthly CPI data. Here workers are locked into a wage agreement where nominal wages are fixed for a time period of approximately three years into the future (ignoring local bargaining or inflation compensation clauses, which were, in any case, used sparingly). Given the difficulty in accurately forecasting inflation over such a period, the real wage outcome at the end of the agreement is uncertain.[22] If the real wage outcome is lower than anticipated the trade unions could be expected to be more aggressive in the next round of negotiations ('real wage catch-up'). Equally, against the backdrop of a rapidly expanding economy and falling unemployment, the trade unions could be expected to attempt to improve on the real wage outcome from one period to the next ('real wage mark-up').

To get an insight into the wage–inflation process, Figure 7.1 shows the interaction between unemployment, CPI inflation and the rate of change in the public sector 'pay award index' (including benchmarking). The latter variable is the percentage change in pay award index compiled in Table 7.2. Monthly data over the period January 1988 to August 2008 are used and each of the seven wage agreements are identified in the diagram. To facilitate the exposition, the analysis is divided into six distinct phases. These phases do not entirely coincide with the actual pay awards.[23]

Phase 1 relates to the interaction between the *Programme for National Recovery* (PNR) and the *Programme for Economic and Social Progress* (PESP) agreements. Under the PNR (1988–90), inflation completely eroded the annual nominal pay award of 2.5 per cent, leading to no change in real earnings for both public and private sector workers over the three-year

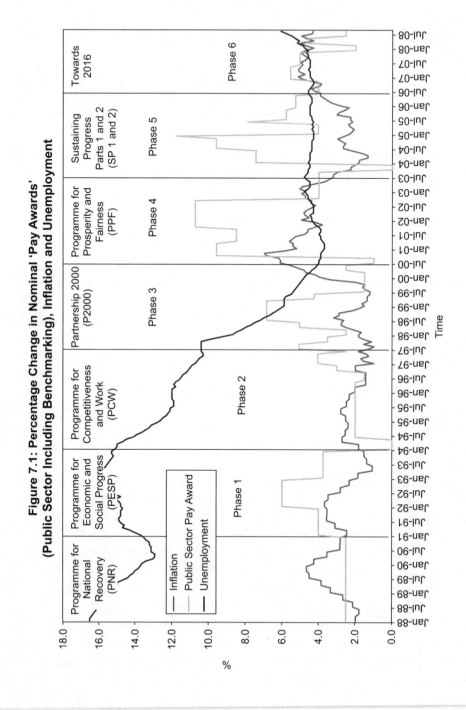

Figure 7.1: Percentage Change in Nominal 'Pay Awards'
(Public Sector Including Benchmarking), Inflation and Unemployment

period. By January 1991, the real pay award index for both private and public sectors was 100.7. In the Celtic Tiger literature, this outcome is often cited as a willingness on behalf of the trade unions to accept low real pay increases in return for the promise of tax cuts in the future. Low wages would improve cost competitiveness and thereby promote growth and employment. In turn, an expanding economy would reduce the government's budget deficit and facilitate cuts in the marginal rate of income tax. As things transpired, marginal income tax rates were cut from 35 per cent, 48 per cent and 58 per cent in 1988 to 20 per cent and 41 per cent in 2008 (to reduce income tax, the upper rate of 58 per cent was abolished, leaving just the two lower rates, which were then reduced). An alternative, more cynical, explanation is that the trade unions simply underestimated the inflation rate (it rose to 4.7 per cent in December 1989) and this is why there was no change in real earnings over the period.

Whatever the explanation, the trade unions would appear to be more aggressive under the following PESP (1991–3) programme and 'real wage catch-up' seemed to be very much on the agenda. Against a backdrop of subdued inflation, by January 1994 the real pay award index for private and public sectors had climbed to 105.1 and 103.1 respectively (the divergence is due to a pay freeze for public sector workers). Evidently, the Celtic Tiger explanation of low pay in return for lower taxes did not last very long. The trade unions clearly used the PESP programme to make up the ground lost during the PNR programme and this cynical explanation seems to be the more plausible.

Phase 2 in the analysis relates to the end of the *Programme for Competitiveness and Work* (PCW) and the onset of *Partnership 2000* (P2000). Over the first two-and-a-half years of the PCW, there was no change in real earnings for either the public or private sector workers. By September 1996 (a period of nearly nine years), the cumulative real wage index remained at 105 and 103 for the private and public sectors respectively. However, after this date and against a backdrop of rapidly falling unemployment, the trade unions succeed in increasing real wages as nominal wages moved well ahead of inflation. By July 1999, the real pay award index for the private and public sectors had climbed to 109 and 111.7 respectively.

What seems to emerge from Figure 7.1 is that there are two possible episodes of 'real wage catch-up'. The PESP was used to make up ground lost under the PNR, and P2000 to make up ground lost during the PCW. Note also how the public sector had moved ahead of the private sector by July 1999. For the public sector, the gain in real earnings in the second P2000 episode significantly exceeds that of the first PESP episode and this could be interpreted as 'real wage mark-up' (facilitated, no doubt, by the dramatic fall in unemployment in the background and a surplus in the fiscal budget).

Phase 3 contains the seminal point in the whole process as Irish inflation suddenly and unexpectedly shot up from 1.48 per cent in October 1999 to 7.03 per cent in November 2000 (the Central Bank of Ireland, for example, underestimated this acceleration in inflation). This increase can largely be explained as a combination of demand-pull inflation, cost-push inflation and external developments. Driven on by a succession of expansionary fiscal policies, six years of Celtic Tiger economic growth manifested itself in capacity constraints and demand-pull inflation ensued.[24] Unfortunately, at this time, the euro exchange rate also declined on the foreign exchanges and this resulted in higher import prices. Also, the ECB increased interest rates and this would have fed through to CPI inflation. The trade unions clearly did not anticipate the hike in inflation and by September 2000 the real wage index fell back to 108.3 and 105.2 for the private and public sectors respectively. The public sector fell behind the private sector at this point because a 5.5 per cent pay award kicked in earlier for the private sector.

The stage was now set for a typical Phillips curve type wage explosion: unemployment had fallen from 17 per cent to 4 per cent, unexpected inflation had eroded much of the previous gain in real earnings and workers' share of national income had fallen by 20 per cent.[25]

Phase 4 is very much in line with the standard Phillips curve wage–inflation spiral. Following the seemingly unanticipated inflation in 1999, inflation expectations seem to have been revised upwards and there was a dramatic upsurge in nominal pay awards. By July 2002, the real pay award index increased to 113 and 116.9 for the private and public sectors respectively. The public sector unions used the benchmarking process during this period to once again improve their position relative to the private sector.

As demand-pull inflation fed into cost-push inflation, the Irish inflation rate remained relatively high over the next three years. It took until December 2003 before inflation came down again to the ECB's upper target limit of 2 per cent. During this period, Ireland experienced the highest inflation rate in the European monetary union (EMU) and, as a result, suffered a significant loss of price competitiveness (compounded by movements of the euro exchange rate). But this moderation of the inflation rate appears to have had little or no effect on nominal wage demands. In Phase 5, under *Sustaining Progress, Parts 1 and 2*, and against a backdrop of a 4 per cent unemployment rate, nominal wages rose significantly. By July 2006, the real pay award index increased to 118.8 and 129.8 for the private and public sectors respectively. It is of interest to note the lack of symmetry at this point: the trade unions were quick to revise inflation expectations upwards but slow to move in the opposite direction.

Finally, Phase 6 relates to the programme *Towards 2016*. Inflation again increased and removed some of the gains conceded in earlier pay awards. By August 2008, the real pay award index increased to 113.6 and 127.2 for the private and public sectors respectively. Following the collapse of the building and construction sector in mid-2007, the economy moved into recession and, for the first time since the late 1980s, unemployment started to increase.

In summary, what appears to emerge is a story of 'real wage catch-up' followed by a wage–inflation spiral. The upsurge in inflation (due to demand-pull and external developments) in October 1999 seems to have been the catalyst that ignited a wage–inflation spiral, particularly in the public sector, in subsequent years. In a short period of time, and exaggerated by an appreciation of the euro exchange rate, the Irish economy suffered a sharp deterioration in price competitiveness.

Empirical Results

In this section, illustrative preliminary results of empirically estimating the New Keynesian Phillips Curve (NKPC) and the Triangle Phillips Curve (TPC) models are presented. In both models, and in line with the original Phillips curve specification but contrary to NKPC and TPC models, the dependent variable is the annual percentage change in the public sector nominal pay award index (ω).[26] This gives 247 monthly observations after making necessary lag adjustments. It should be borne in mind that the analysis relates to a situation where the nominal wages of public sector workers are constrained by the pay agreements for long periods of time and wages cannot be changed in response to published CPI data.

A central problem in estimating the NKPC model is how to measure the forward-looking inflation expectations term, $E_t p_{t+1}$. If this variable is measured using lagged inflation rates then the NKPC model loses its key feature and begins to resemble the TPC model. The approach adopted here is to use the Central Bank of Ireland's one-year ahead forecast of CPI inflation as the expected inflation rate ($E_t p_{t+1}$). These forecasts are published in the bank's *Quarterly Bulletin* and can be compiled to create a continuous monthly series. A comparison to the actual inflation outcome reveals the average forecast error was -0.04 per cent over the period. However, there were some years, 2000 and 2002 in particular, when the actual inflation rate was significantly underestimated.

The estimated NKPC model is as follows (note that relative to the earlier specification, Equation 3, the unemployment gap has been replaced by the level of unemployment (U) and the rate of change in unemployment (u)[27]):

$$\omega_t = \alpha + \beta_1 E_t p_{t+1} - \beta_2 U + \beta_3 u + e_t \tag{5}$$

As before, lower-case letters indicate first differences of logarithms and upper-case letters logarithms of levels. The results of estimating this equation over the period February 1988 to August 2008 are given in Table 7.3, columns 1 and 2. Overall, the model performs poorly. There is a low R^2 of 0.08, the expected inflation variable is incorrectly signed and there is evidence of autocorrelation in the error term. On the other hand, the level of unemployment (U) variable is correctly signed and significant. The positive sign on the (u) variable suggests that the rate of change of unemployment has a strong bearing on wage demands.

Table 7.3: New Keynesian Phillips Curve (NKPC) model

Dependent Variable: ω	February 1988–August 2008		February 1988–August 2008	
	1	2	3	4
Variable	Coefficient	t-Statistic	Coefficient	t-Statistic
C	3.78	5.07	-10.23	-1.86
$E_t p_{t+1}$	-1.10	-2.25	0.04	0.11
U	-0.72	-3.88	-1.04	-3.13
u	11.72	2.27	9.01	2.31
T			3.07	2.15
RW_{-1}			0.65	13.40
rw_{-1}			0.17	2.63
R^2	0.08		0.56	
F-statistic	6.67		50.04	
Durbin-Watson statistic	0.51		1.88	

Suppose now that the NKPC model is re-specified to include variables associated with the national wage agreements. Does this make any appreciable difference? The variables included are an income tax rate (T)[28] variable and the level and rate of change in real wages (RW and rw, both lagged one period). The latter two variables are intended to capture the 'real wage catch-up' effect mentioned above.

The re-specified NKPC is:

$$\omega_t = \alpha + \beta_1 E_t p_{t+1} - \beta_2 U + \beta_3 u + \beta_4 T + \beta_5 RW_{-1} + \beta_6 rw_{-1} + e_t \tag{6}$$

The results given in Table 7.3, columns 3 and 4 show a major improvement relative to the previous results. The R^2 climbs to 0.56, the autocorrelation is removed (D-W statistic = 1.88) and all of the explanatory variables, with the exception of the expected inflation variable, are statistically significant. The insignificance of the 'forward-looking' expected inflation variable suggests that the trade unions were more concerned with 'what went before' rather than 'what lies ahead'. As before, the level and the rate of change of unemployment appear to be critical variables underlying wage demands.[29] Also, the tax variable is correctly signed and significant, indicating the importance of income taxes in the wage process. Against a backdrop of rapidly falling unemployment, the positive and significant sign on both the level and the rate of change in real wages (RW and rw) points to an attempt by the trade unions to improve on the real wage outcome over time. This is evident from the public sector data in Figure 7. 1 when the real wage increase under 'phase 1' was surpassed by the increase under 'phase 2' and this, in turn, was surpassed by the increase under 'phase 3'.

Overall, the findings strongly suggest that the original NKPC equation does not give a good explanation of the wage determination process in Ireland over the last twenty years. In particular, a 'retrospective element' appears to be missing from the specification.

Turning now to the TPC model, the dependent variable, the nominal pay award index in the public sector (ω), remains the same. To capture the inertia, i.e. the persistence effect, expected inflation ($E_t p_{t+1}$) is now calculated as a simple, six-period moving average of CPI inflation lagged one period. The unemployment variables (U and u) remain the same. There are a number of different variables that could be used to represent the 'supply-side' shocks: energy prices, real effective exchange rate or the growth rate of productivity.[30] It was, however, decided to use the real interest rate (RI) lagged three periods as the supply-side variable.[31]

The initial TPC model is as follows:

$$\omega_t = \alpha + \beta_1 E_t p_{t+1} - \beta_2 U + \beta_3 u + \beta_4 RI_{-3} + e_t \tag{7}$$

The results of estimating this model are given in Table 7.4, columns 1 and 2. As with the NKPC model, the basic TPC model is also not very well specified. The R^2 of 0.13 is low and the Durbin-Watson statistic of 0.56 points to autocorrelation in the residuals. However, the explanatory variables are correctly signed and statistically significant. In contrast to the forward-looking measure in the NKPC, the backward-looking measure of expected inflation is highly significant and positively signed. Again, the two unemployment variables (U and u) are strongly significant and retain their negative and positive signs respectively. The real interest rate is also significant and positively signed and this suggests that higher real interest rates would provoke higher wage demands and vice versa.

Table 7.4: Triangle Phillips Curve (TPC) Model

Dependent Variable: ω	February 1988–August 2008		February 1988–August 2008	
	1	2	3	4
Variable	Coefficient	t-Statistic	Coefficient	t-Statistic
C	2.69	4.08	-6.20	-1.14
$E_t p_{t+1}$	1.30	3.96	1.07	4.70
U	-1.82	-4.39	-1.11	-2.78
u	6.07	1.17	3.46	0.91
RI_{-3}	1.38	3.77	0.55	2.14
T			1.86	1.34
RW_{-1}			0.66	14.03
rw_{-1}			0.16	2.55
R^2			0.60	
	0.13			
F-statistic	8.50		49.44	
Durbin-Watson statistic	0.56		2.01	

Note: Included observations: 247 after adjustments

Augmenting the TPC model with income tax and real wage variables gives the following representation:

$$\omega_t = \alpha + \beta_1 E_t p_{t+1} - \beta_2 U + \beta_3 u + \beta_4 RI_{-3} + \beta_5 T + \beta_6 RW_{-1} + \beta_7 rw_{-1} + e_t$$

$$(8)$$

Table 7.4, columns 3 and 4 show that the R^2 jumps to 0.60 and the Durbin-Watson statistic at 2.01 indicates no autocorrelation in the residuals. Retrospective-based expected inflation, unemployment, the real interest rate and lagged real earnings appear to be important in explaining nominal wage demands. It is interesting to note that the level and rate of change of unemployment remain statistically significant whether the NKPC or TPC models are estimated and no matter what other explanatory variables are included in the models.[32] Generally, the TPC model appears to be more relevant to the Irish situation as inertia and persistence effects are clearly important. However, it would appear that the TPC model needs to be made more generic if it is to capture the particular scenario that is the Irish social partnership arrangement.

Price Competitiveness

While the empirical findings relating to the amended TPC model do seem to accord with the descriptive analysis in pages 167–71, it is worth going one stage further by illustrating the implication for overall price competitiveness. Figure 7.2 shows the real effective exchange rate for Ireland and the real exchange rate relative to the United States (US) and United Kingdom, (UK) using monthly data, between 1991 and 2009.[33] The three indexes tend to move in tandem and show that between January 1991 and October 2000, there was a *gain* in competitiveness of 39 per cent relative to the US, 17.3 per cent relative to the UK and 15.8 per cent against a basket of 56 trading countries (the real effective exchange rate (REER)). This outcome is primarily driven by movements of the Irish pound exchange rate (including the devaluation of 10 per cent in January 1993) and more or less coincides with the Celtic Tiger boom from 1994 to 2000.

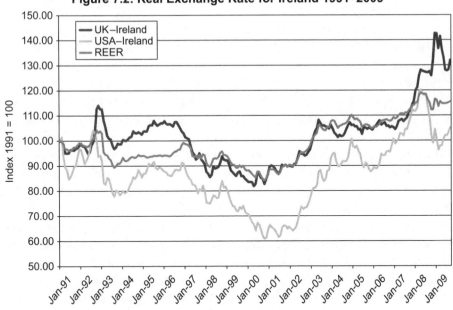

Figure 7.2: Real Exchange Rate for Ireland 1991–2009

However, driven by an appreciating euro exchange rate externally and a wage–inflation spiral domestically, between October 2000 and September 2009, a *loss* of price competitiveness of the following magnitudes was recorded: 72 per cent relative to the US, 60 per cent relative to the UK and 37 per cent overall as measured by the real effective exchange rate. As has been documented elsewhere,[34] the Celtic Tiger boom came to a halt in 2001 and was replaced (due primarily to low interest rates) by a boom in property and construction. Up until 2007 the economy continued to grow over 4 per cent per annum as the property boom compensated for the loss of price competitiveness. When the downturn finally arrived in 2007, the Irish economy was in a very vulnerable position and this has manifested itself in an unprecedented economic recession in 2009. This serves to illustrate the point that EMU membership did not deliver low inflation in the period under review and domestic variables appear to play a critical role. The logical policy conclusion must be that inflation and wage targeting are valid policy objectives.

Conclusion

This paper examined the wage–inflation process in Ireland using a new wage index, for both the public and private sectors, derived from the various national wage agreements over the period 1988–2008. These two indexes were initially compared to the wage series published by the Central Statistics Office and it was found that, with the possible exception of the financial services sector, the wage agreements did not act as a constraint in either the public or private sectors. However, against this, it is possible that the CSO series contains a good deal of 'noise' and that the newly constructed wage index series provides a purer indicator of wage trends as it is based only on 'signal'.

The analysis in this paper identified October 1999 as the seminal point in recent Irish economic history. At this time, domestic inflation increased from 1.4 per cent to over 7 per cent. This provided the catalyst for a wage–inflation spiral after this date, culminating in significant loss of price competitiveness. There were two main factors driving an upsurge in wage demands: first, between 1988 and 1999 the wage agreements resulted in only a small increase in the cumulative real earnings to both the private and public sectors and, second, a rapidly falling rate of unemployment. There was therefore a pent-up demand for real wage increases, which manifested itself after the rise in inflation in 1999.

After October 1999 a standard Phillips curve wage–inflation spiral appears to have ensued and it took nearly four years for Irish inflation to return to the ECB's upper limit of 2 per cent. With hindsight, it is difficult to believe that policymakers in Ireland allowed this process to unravel without doing anything to address the problem.[35] The combination of high relative wage and price inflation and an appreciating euro exchange rate resulted in a significant loss of price competitiveness.

The determinants of the negotiated wage awards in the public sector were empirically investigated by estimating both the New Keynesian Phillips Curve (NKPC) and the Triangle Phillips Curve (TPC) models using the public sector pay award index as the dependent variable. A TPC model, augmented to take account of the special circumstances surrounding the wage agreements, performs better than the NKPC model as backward, retrospective variables representing inertia and persistence effects are clearly important. One variable found to be significant is the lagged real wage, as the trade unions seem to have engaged in 'real wage catch-up'. However, this variable does not fit easily into either the New Keynesian or Triangle Phillips Curve models and, as such, there may be a case to generalise both models to allow for different scenarios.

Entry into EMU in 1999 may have convinced Irish policymakers that inflation would henceforth be largely externally determined by developments in the Eurozone. However, the analysis in this paper suggests that this is not the case. It follows that a key element in any 'strategy for recovery' should be the adoption of a specific policy relating to wage and inflation targeting and ultimately price competitiveness.

8

Ireland and the World: Competitiveness for the Future

Eoin Gahan[1]

Introduction and Overview

The crisis in the Irish economy has led to a dramatic decline in output and a severe increase in unemployment. In the face of major difficulties at the macroeconomic level, negative growth, major government deficits and the special problems of the banking sector, there is a risk that insufficient attention may be given to the fundamental sources of growth in the Irish economy and the need to maintain and strengthen them. Exports have held up quite well in a major world downturn in 2009. A revived world economy will bring renewed growth in Ireland, provided that we understand the dynamics of that changing world economy and provided we ensure that the structure and focus of enterprise is aligned with it. This chapter looks at the kinds of policy responses that are needed in Ireland if we are to take advantage of world trends and maintain the growth impetus that has provided dramatic increases in living standards over the last twenty years. The paper examines competitiveness issues and world trends, and there is particular focus on four key policy areas: trade diversification, energy, next-generation networks (NGNs), and systems of policy formulation and implementation.

The very grave position of the public finances has been well examined elsewhere. The need to address this is recognised by all even if there are many differences as to the focus, the sequencing and the timescale of different interventions. The need for drastic cuts in public spending in terms of current expenditures, recognised in Budget 2010, will continue to be the overwhelmingly dominant theme of the budgets for years to come. In such a context, the temptation will inevitably be to postpone any thoughts of new investment. But the response to the current crisis in government finances should not be the occasion for cutbacks in the programmes needed to allow future growth in the economy, especially those that expand and diversify our international linkages, those that improve our innovation capacities and those that enable new enterprises to emerge and to thrive in an open-world trading and investment environment.

Competitiveness in the Long Term

Long-term competitiveness is based on economic sustainability considerations, but it should also be based on global trends. For this reason, the government needs to carry out regular foresight activity, monitoring what is happening in the enterprise sector and monitoring also the emerging trends internationally and attempting to map out a strategic path. In practice, governments are often captured by short-term and reactive issues. They are affected by the pressure of public opinion and the media who demand quick solutions to problems. One of the greatest challenges for government is to balance short-term pressures and long-term objectives, both in competitiveness and in many other areas of public policy, such as ageing, health, education, urban infrastructure and the environment, which can only be addressed adequately over the long term.

In this context, Forfás carried out some analysis of future socio-economic scenarios for Ireland and explored the policy implications.[2] The framework for the study was given by a key strategic question: in the context of broader societal goals such as prosperity and full employment, social justice and equity, security, liberty and well-being, what decisions should be made to ensure a sustainable competitive enterprise sector in 2025 and 2040? The study identified four critical uncertainties, the trends and issues that have the highest degree of uncertainty and the highest impact on the key strategic question. They are factors that are outside our control. They were as follows:

- The changing nature of energy supply and security
- The consistency and complexity of regulation and response to climate change and the environment
- Who/what is driving and shaping the world economy?
- The interaction, differentiation and focus of social values and systems

The implications of these factors, and the policy requirements to meet them in all the main areas of government responsibility, were analysed in detail. As well as more detailed policy options, three higher level priorities emerged:

- Bringing more long-term thinking into today's policy analysis, decision making and implementation
- Developing institutional capacity to anticipate and prepare for future challenges, trends and opportunities in a systematic way
- Enabling the public sector to work more cohesively and collaboratively in policy formulation and implementation on the major cross-cutting priorities in areas such as competitiveness and enterprise development, labour market developments, climate change and energy policy, social inclusion and cohesion, and well-being

In the continuing process of public sector reform, it will be important to keep such priorities to the forefront.

The National Competitiveness Council has defined competitiveness as:

[A] broad concept that encompasses a diverse range of factors and policy inputs including education and training, entrepreneurship and innovation, Ireland's economic and technological infrastructure and the taxation and regulatory framework. For the National Competitiveness Council, the goal of national competitiveness is to provide Ireland's people with the opportunity to improve their living standards and quality of life. Improving living standards depends on, among other things, raising incomes (and providing employment). To raise incomes, productivity gains are necessary but in an economy with a small domestic market, this requires a healthy exporting sector to achieve economies of scale necessary for productivity gains. For a vibrant exporting sector, Ireland must maintain its national competitiveness.[3]

Since 1998 the National Competitiveness Council has been undertaking reviews of competitiveness, benchmarking Ireland against a wide range of other countries in terms of the main factors of production and so-called framework conditions. Quantitative and qualitative indicators have been used, and have helped to highlight the detailed policy areas in which change is needed, and have helped to inform the council's policy recommendations. This work is an extension of the benchmarking approach that is well established at the enterprise level. There are other components of business strategy that may also be useful to consider at a national level, and that can be critical for success either in exporting or in attracting foreign direct investment. They include the following:

- Price
- Quality
- Competition
    - competition for investment
    - competition for prestige events
    - competition for tourism
- Tourism
    - diversity and tourism
    - culture and tourism

For enterprises, pricing strategies are the most predominant of the different possible approaches to the question of competition. For countries, the exchange rate is in some cases and for some periods an instrument of competition but the more fundamental instrument is the cost base in the economy as a whole and the way in which this affects the exporting sector. Ireland's trajectory towards joining the euro was marked by a growing stability and predictability in the public finances and the macroeconomic environment, and the low inflation and low interest rate environment to which it led in a relatively smooth way was an important factor in encouraging growth in the enterprise sector. The well-known deterioration in cost competitiveness in Ireland subsequent to this has now been exposed by the collapse of the construction sector and other domestic sectors, including retailing and personal services.

Quality is also a focus of strategy for enterprises, but it can also be so for countries. It is used explicitly in a number of cases as a recognised selling point for a wide variety of goods, as in Germany for instance. But when the country has sufficiently achieved an image of quality then that can become disembodied, and the actual manufacturing outsourced, such as in the case of IKEA, where the label may say, 'Made in xxxx, Design by IKEA of Sweden'. In general, quality has become a national policy instrument or objective in most countries, and encouragement and support is provided either to industry associations to further the quality agenda or directly by bodies such as national standards bodies. And just as companies will pay attention to issues of service, innovation, image and branding, so too do individual countries as a component of their national enterprise or economic development strategies. Thus countries pursue analogous objectives to those of companies, and use analogous instruments, and thus the application of the competitiveness concept to action at national level is carried out in practice, whatever the theoretical arguments against it.

Competition for investment is another field in which nations, and within them regions and cities, compete internationally for investment projects. The kinds of issues on which focus is made, whether by the National Competitiveness Council or by the Industrial Development Agency (IDA Ireland) in its marketing, are the right kind of issues, because they are a focus in many countries: the level of prices, comparative tax rates, skills availability, levels of infrastructure, the quality of regulation, etc. This focus reflects, in turn, the kinds of issues with which international companies are concerned and, if we forget these, and if policymakers neglect the task of maintaining and improving our performance under the standard headings, we will be at a competitive disadvantage when decisions are being made as to the location of new productive capacity by multinationals.

This is not to say that there is a standard formula for success in attracting foreign direct investment and that we have only to pay attention to the same set of indicators as other countries also track. As well as this, there is a need always to develop unique selling points, special emphases which distinguish Ireland's offering from those of other countries, significant strengths that cannot be matched by others, and preferably combinations of such strengths which are less easy to be duplicated by competitors.

Competition for prestige events is another way in which countries compete. The immediate objectives may be to attract tourism and business travel expenditures. This ranges from the 'convention' business to the attraction of large and preferably repeated events, which can bring additional benefits to the local economy. Other objectives may include the encouragement of infrastructure development, such as the holding of the Olympic Games in London, which will include the regeneration of the eastern part of the city, or the Shanghai Expo, which has completely replaced a run-down industrial area near the centre of the city, and brought with it additional developments such as bridges and additional metro lines. A further objective may be the direct encouragement of business linkages, such as in trade fairs, or to improve the country's image in scientific or technological terms, such as the European City of Science role that Dublin will play in 2012.

Competition for tourism is a further focus of national strategies. Often this will be accompanied by marketing campaigns that seek first to establish the brand, and a number of countries in Asia and Eastern Europe have taken this route. Tourism as a sector has the obvious effect of increasing services exports, but it can also reinforce other trade and investment strategies through a wider dissemination of the image of the country (assuming this is on the whole positive). Holidaymakers may also be businesspeople and identify opportunities even during their vacations. The difficulty of tourism development is that it often requires a general upgrading of the economic environment including health, security and international connectivity. Associated with tourism needs is a range of other issues that in Ireland's case are particularly important. These include most immediately air links and public transport, telecommunications, retailing, hotels and restaurants. Dealing first with air links, these will be, for some years to come at least (until oil and climate change considerations become very pressing), the main means by which tourists come to Ireland. The development of Terminal Two in Dublin Airport is very welcome but it will need to be accompanied as quickly as possible by efficient public transport links.

Diversity in the retail sector is another important means by which the tourist experience can be improved. The trend towards homogenisation in the retail sector, where the centre of every Irish town is occupied by the same retail chains, presents a less attractive offering as far as tourists are concerned, since they may be in search of something different. Local authority retail strategies can therefore have important positive effects, but enterprise policy has neglected the retail sector, and the county enterprise boards explicitly exclude it.

The cultural aspects of tourism are also significant. The economic impact of the arts should be recognised as important even by those who see culture as something always to be at the bottom of the list of priorities. The arts, diffused internationally, contribute to an attractive image for the country as a destination, and sports supported by the state can also play a significant role in encouraging tourism. Tourism can also be specialised in sectors that have wider impact. Examples of this include education tourism and the increasingly important area of health tourism.

Future Trends in International Investment

In general, in recent years there have been significant changes in the pattern of world investment: it is expected to decline as a result of recent trends in the world economy and, overall, investments to developing and transition economies have grown rapidly, increasing the share of these countries in global foreign direct investment (FDI) flows to 50 per cent in 2009, partly due to a concurrent large decline in FDI flows to developed countries. A striking feature of international foreign direct investment is still the pre-eminence of the United States. It continued to lead the world in FDI inflows as well as in outflows, and also continued in the first position with regard to inward and outward FDI stock, which is the cumulative total of FDI in the country and abroad, respectively. Ireland has rejoined the top 20 host economies for FDI inflows in 2009, at position 16, and is ranked at 21st position for inward FDI stocks.[4]

The rise of China and other powers, the increased dependence on imported energy, the long-term effects of the large US government and trade deficits, and the heavy demands on the US in playing a global economic, political and military role are often pointed to as bringing about US decline in the future. Nevertheless, the continued innovation that characterises the United States may bring about a new economic model that allows for a stronger role for their SMEs internationally, a new wave of innovation induced by resource constraints and the need for energy security, and a rethinking of the role of inward foreign direct investment. More broadly, innovation may become the main determinant of competition in the future, and such a trend would certainly play to US strengths.

Profound shifts in economic power continue worldwide, and there are additional pressures on specific resources such as oil, water and food. It is likely, therefore, that international agreements on trade issues will become more difficult, especially because of the growth of regionalism and the fact that negotiation mechanisms have not kept pace with changes in the world economy.

Skills availability will also continue to be a key driver of cross-border investment, and will also be linked more closely with advances in technology. Product life cycles are continuing to shorten, and this in turn means that investment decisions are made more frequently. Old companies will decline, unless they reinvent themselves from both marketing and planning perspectives as well as from a technological one, and new companies will be more frequent, emerging alongside new products and services but having correspondingly shorter life spans.

From the point of view of national FDI strategies, the identification of the companies to be targeted becomes correspondingly more difficult. A related trend may be more positive: more complex supply chains may increase the importance of duplication of production facilities in order to provide more flexibility to changing economic conditions, including trends in regional trade agreements, thus increasing the potential number of FDI projects for decision.

Another major force in determining investment trends, linked to the skills question to some degree, is that of next-generation networks (NGNs). NGNs are high-capacity telecommunications networks that allow for the provision of advanced services, and are discussed further below. The countries that have widespread availability of NGNs will be the focus of increased investment, to take advantage of the skills they offer and the market opportunities they present. They will also be the source of increasing innovation and start-up activity. Finally, they will be more attractive as a place to live for high-skilled staff. The growth of services in world trade is likely to continue, and this will be partly fuelled by a continuing increase in the range of services marketed internationally, and also driven by the spread of NGNs.

In an NGN context, trust and security will become important issues for success. Future NGN development will heighten the need for standards, trusted third parties, secure registries, guarantees, mediation and arbitration services, repositories and the like. The degree to which governments can offer specific relevant services, or encourage their availability, will increase the attractiveness of an investment location.

In the related field of energy, a number of issues arise for FDI. The concept of 'peak oil' is becoming more widely accepted, and is discussed further below. Oil peaking will accelerate the trends towards renewables, but the adjustment period will still take many years, and for this reason all energy-related sectors will be increasingly significant. The development of fuel sources will be a significant driver, and other energy-related opportunities will arise in the areas of energy security, networking, storage and transport. Climate change is also likely to affect investment patterns.

The Need for Continued State Investment

Government investment, by contrast, is subject to a considerable degree of scepticism. The concept of investment in education for instance took a long time to be accepted. Research and development (R&D) investment was not fully recognised as a priority until the late 1990s. Moreover, the calculation of the return on government investment has raised methodological problems on a continual basis. The role of environmental concerns or constraints in determining the savings to be achieved is something that we have come to terms with, but wider concerns such as flexibility, diversification, security and international connectivity, which should be important determinants of government investment in Ireland, have yet to be fully quantified or incorporated into standard methodologies.[5] Yet, as has been emphasised, such considerations will powerfully determine the degree to which Ireland is a location for successful enterprises in the future. It is essential therefore that project appraisal for the future takes these kinds of dimensions fully into account.

It would be all too easy to accept that public finance constraints will mean a halt to significant new government investment in the years to come. Certainly, analysis of the figures is likely to point to that sort of conclusion, but there is still a lot that can be done in terms of preparation for investment, even if the main project expenditures are postponed for a year or two. In the first place, there are all the necessary regulatory processes and approval procedures to be gone through, such as thorough economic and environmental impact analysis, together with the necessary planning approvals. Secondly, large-scale capital projects typically involve extensive technical planning and procurement stages, which may nevertheless represent a relatively small part of the total cost. If an investment project is considered to be important for national competitiveness, the fact that the capital funding is not yet available for the project should not necessarily mean that the initial stages are not undertaken. By clearing the ground, both literally and figuratively, the projects themselves will be quicker and more efficiently implemented when funding is secured.

However, this preparatory stage should also be more comprehensive in its approach. The issues of future competitiveness, sustainability, security, diversification and international linkages should, as noted, be considered, but the full implications of that approach are that projects should not be considered in isolation but as far as possible as part of a package of investment that is intended to be undertaken in the planning period. This means that different kinds of infrastructure development, for instance, should be reviewed and appraised at the same time, even if the actors are different. Some infrastructure projects are undertaken by the National Roads Authority (NRA), others by the Electricity Supply Board (ESB), CIE (Córas Iompair Éireann, Ireland's semi-state transport body, in charge of the national and local bus and train services) or local authorities. The Transport 21 initiative was a first attempt to assemble a package of projects in the transport field, but the approach ideally should be multi-sectoral because, for instance, transport development will affect infrastructure requirements in other fields. This is not a call for very elaborate and unrealistically precise quantitative modelling of all possible interactions; rather it is drawing attention to the need for some kind of matrix in which such interactions between projects in different sectors will at least be assessed to some degree, and by so doing the timing and sequencing considerations will be highlighted.

Another priority will be to investigate new funding possibilities. Project finance, rather than funding from general government borrowing, should be the priority emphasis. There has been increasing use of public–private partnerships (PPPs) by the public sector. These should continue as an option, but there are also other possibilities in terms of direct funding on commercial terms. For instance, the ESB and Bord Gáis (the Irish Gas Board) have recourse to commercial bank borrowing, sometimes supplemented by European Investment Bank funding for particular projects and expansion plans, on the basis that lenders are all attracted to utility-based investments, which tend to offer a less volatile return over a number of years. Clearly, the fact that both these companies have significant shares of their respective markets and are state owned also helps their credit ratings.

Another source of funding is the bond market, and here similar considerations apply. Karl Deeter and Stephen Kinsella have drawn attention to the opportunities for local authorities to raise finance through this mechanism,[6] and it would have the added benefit of improving governance at local level if it were accompanied by some degree of local taxation.

Changes in Regulation

Sectoral regulation now presents a complex landscape. Regulatory bodies proliferate, some with primarily economic mandates, others with health and safety or consumer protection as priorities. There may be a case for mergers in this field, or at least the sharing of common services. It should be noted that the sectoral regulatory system has been created in parallel with an existing regulatory system, also known as the legal system, and this system itself should be examined with respect to the interactions with enterprise.

Too much should not be expected of competition policy on its own. For many goods and services, Ireland is a small market and is isolated from much of Europe, both physically and culturally. There is a limit to how much can be achieved by applying institutional models and legislation that may be more effective in larger markets. Instead, the active promotion of inward direct investment in sectors where there appears to be inadequate competition may also be needed.

Another priority is to deal with administrative burdens on business. At European level, a target for administrative burden reduction has been adopted, both by the European Commission with respect to legislation at European level and by member states with respect to theirs. The target is for the administrative burden on business of compliance with the relevant legislation to be reduced by 25 per cent by the year 2012. Ireland adopted this target by a government decision in March 2008, and work is under way in all government departments to identify the principal burdens on enterprise and to seek ways to reduce them. Note that the burdens in question are not those of complying with the regulation: the purpose of the regulation has to be maintained but easier ways of meeting its obligations are needed as far as business is concerned. What is in question here are often-criticised activities such as 'paperwork' and form-filling, providing the same information to different departments or agencies of government, being subjected to multiple inspections, being required to have licences of different kinds for different related activities, and the like, together with the general procedural difficulties that are often described as 'red tape'.

Reducing such burdens presents particular difficulties because Ireland is a lightly regulated country by international standards. Our performance in the field of administrative burdens is good, and this means that to identify savings that will add up to 25 per cent of the total (measured by estimating the cost of staff time needed in meeting the burden requirements) is a difficult task. In general in Ireland there will be no obvious large administrative burden ('low-hanging fruit') that can be identified and eliminated. Instead the burden reduction will have to be achieved by a large number of small steps, in which the 'information obligations' are reduced in each individual case. The difficulty with this approach is that from the perspective of a businessperson they may not get the sense that in their particular case the burden has been reduced, even if a rigorous process has been followed in which existing regulations have been comprehensively reviewed and the burden specifically quantified, in order to identify where burden reduction measures can be most effectively applied.

As well as this programme, therefore, a more comprehensive effort will be needed in the field of e-government. E-government is the use of information and communication technologies (ICT) by government to exchange information with and provide services to citizens, businesses and other departments within government, with the objective of improving the delivery of public services and processes. It therefore includes the transformation of all aspects of service delivery and the development of a 'customer' focus.

Why is e-government important? It is so for a number of reasons. It enables government departments to achieve efficiency improvements in the processing of large volumes of data and other administrative operations. Significant savings can be obtained in data collection and transmission as well as in the provision of information to the population. There is also scope for even greater efficiencies through greater sharing of information within and between government departments. E-government is also an important driver of public sector modernisation as it can ultimately lead to better quality services, more focus on the citizen, more efficient and effective work practices and improved decision making. If governments take the lead in the application of information technology (IT) to their processes and inter- actions, they can sensitise and encourage those businesses to fully employ the power of information and communication technologies in their own operations. It also improves the international credibility and reputation of the economy, and can encourage the development of firms specialised in the software and communications technologies, as well as in business process improvement and a broad range of services. Progress has been made in Ireland, but there is scope for more. From the point of view of business perceptions, the systems such as those the Revenue Commissioners provide are well regarded and widely used by business. Revenue is cooperating with a range of government departments and agencies also. But business inter- actions with other parts of government have not yet been the subject of such impactful IT development, nor are the systems within government and the information flows between government departments yet organised in an optimal way.

Four Main Policy Priorities

In considering the most urgent steps to date with respect to enterprise development of the future, it is important not to be too despondent. Some aspects have been well examined and appropriate solutions have been found. The most striking example has been that of science and technology, where major improvements have been made to public policy, our institu- tions and our enterprise base. Overall, while the innovation system will continue to need improvement, there has been a fundamental change in our approach to these questions and our capabilities have been transformed over the last twenty years. The challenge for the future is to generate R&D- based start-ups and to build scale in these as soon as possible.

Four priority areas suggest themselves where there has not been as much progress as in science and technology or in skills: trade diversification, next- generation networks, long-term energy policy, and systems of policy formulation and implementation.

Trade Diversification

The arguments for trade diversification in Ireland's case include both posi- tive and negative considerations. From the first point of view, Ireland needs to continue its export growth, and will therefore always need new markets, especially fast-growing ones, in order to achieve improved performance. The alternative is to continue with existing markets, but mature markets tend to grow more slowly and to attract more competition; it is difficult to increase market share in these conditions. The negative arguments for trade diversification relate partly to market vulnerability. Too much concentration in one market leaves us open to the full effects of a decline in that market. Again, currency fluctuations can lead to similar effects. This is shown periodically when Sterling declines against the Euro. Irish-owned manufacturing is heavily focused on the UK market, and a fall in the value of Sterling often has significant impacts on the competitiveness of their exports on this market. Calls for intervention and support often follow.

Analysis of trade intensities shows an undiversified pattern of trade.[7] Table 8.1 gives trade intensities for total manufacturing exports to the Eurozone from Ireland. Trade intensity indices are defined as the share of one country's trade with another country divided by the other country's share of world trade.[8] When the figure is greater than 1, it indicates that the two nations have a comparatively strong export (import) relationship; when the figure is greater than 2, it indicates an extremely strong export (import) relationship. A value of 1 for trade intensity indicates that the trade is more or less normal, that is, that Ireland has secured a share of that country's imports that is proportionate. Most, if not all, of the values in the Ireland row of Table 8.1 can be seen to be less than 1 in value, while exports to the UK can be seen to be at extreme values. Belgium is the exception to this pattern.

The picture with respect to imports is very similar, with the UK again dominating as a source. Again, this high share may be partly due to the fact that many products having their origins beyond the UK, whether from the Eurozone or from other parts the world, will be distributed from there to Ireland, and many agents and distributors have the UK and Ireland together as a single distribution area. But in recent years the high import share may also be related to the strong presence of UK retailers in Ireland.

Imports are also important from a policy point of view, and it can be argued that they are as important as exports, even though exports receive a great deal more attention. It is acknowledged that we export only to pay for our imports, but in fact exporting is seen as an important, almost patriotic, social contribution, for which awards are made, while importers tend to keep their heads down. In fact, the importer may make an equally important contribution if he creates downward pressure on prices, and may also contribute to technology diffusion and improvements in quality, depending on the equipment or materials that are brought into the Irish market. The

Table 8.1: Export Intensities for EU-15 Countries, 2006

	France	Belgium & Luxembourg	Netherlands	Germany	Italy	UK	Ireland	Denmark	Greece	Portugal	Spain
France	—	2.98	1.64	2.04	1.89	1.51	1.50	0.91	0.25	1.34	2.11
Belgium & Luxembourg	1.54	—	3.52	1.62	0.63	0.98	5.03	0.38	0.10	0.46	0.43
Netherlands	0.68	2.20	—	1.41	0.41	0.93	1.08	1.03	0.13	0.44	0.40
Germany	1.03	1.47	2.06	—	0.90	0.60	0.84	1.35	0.27	0.61	0.51
Italy	1.69	1.16	1.18	1.71	—	0.60	1.30	0.78	0.76	0.53	1.16
UK	1.41	1.53	1.85	1.67	1.06	—	4.98	1.76	0.36	0.81	0.94
Ireland	0.50	0.65	0.81	0.65	0.39	4.18	—	1.13	0.11	0.26	0.32
Denmark	0.63	0.83	1.36	1.85	0.71	1.11	0.98	—	0.24	0.42	0.49
Greece	3.26	2.75	3.45	3.94	7.97	1.90	2.71	3.61	—	0.99	3.11
Portugal	2.29	1.60	1.69	2.10	2.13	1.44	1.50	1.72	0.38	—	11.82
Spain	3.70	1.63	1.70	2.44	2.86	1.58	2.36	1.38	0.55	7.26	—

Source: Forfás, *Review of the European Single Market*, January 2008.

price as much as the quality of imports is therefore an appropriate focus of policy; and the diversification arguments apply to imports as much as to exports.

Pursuing the diversification route, in practice, is not easy. The multinationals may have the marketing power, but their operations in Ireland may be part of a wider production system and it is not necessarily the case that they will automatically export the goods from Ireland directly to a wide variety of other countries. For an Irish manufacturer, launching a marketing activity in unfamiliar markets can be a daunting task, even with the support of Enterprise Ireland and its representatives in the field. But it may well be that the most difficult obstacle is the psychological one: when a company is used to dealing only in the UK markets, where language and business practices are broadly the same, the difficulties of selling to continental Europe or to new markets in Asia or Latin America may be seen as too great and perhaps as greater than they are.

Ireland's globalisation strategy should start with the recognition that on a globe, any country is the centre. Past success has been mainly based on Ireland's acting as a transatlantic bridge for FDI and, more recently, R&D and innovation in goods and services, acting both as a physical bridge in providing a location for business activity but also acting to some degree as a cultural mediator between the US and EU markets. The future requires an even wider view of possibilities, in which multiple relationships are developed and in which Ireland acts as a hub between different world regions.

NGNs

Statistics show that the number of broadband connections in Ireland has been increasing rapidly and we have now reached the European average in this regard. At first sight, this appears satisfactory, but it is not, for a number of reasons. The most important one is that the definitions have changed. What we mean by broadband in Ireland is now a much less demanding service than what is provided in more advanced countries. In fact, in other parts of the world the debate has moved on to what are called next-generation networks (NGNs), because these will provide for the full integration on a common platform with a common protocol for services that at present are distinct, such as data, telephony and television. From the user point of view what is significant about next-generation networks is that they are being prepared in anticipation of much greater data volumes and services that need such volume, and the hardware involved is therefore being developed in the light of the new requirements. Thus, fibre to the home (FTTH) has received considerable support as the only really future-proof platform to deal with the services of tomorrow.

FTTH has been pioneered by Japan and the Republic of Korea in particular, but a number of European countries are now making significant advances in this field. Sweden, Norway and Denmark are notable in this respect, but the Slovak Republic now leads Europe with 28 per cent of all connections being fibre. In Ireland only 1 per cent of total connections are fibre, compared to 54 per cent in Japan, 43 per cent in the Republic of Korea and 23 per cent in Sweden. Ireland remains behind leading regions in terms of upgrading the local access network to fibre and in offering very fast connection speeds over fibre.[9] In Norway, fibre to the home is providing quadruple play services (HDTV, internet, telephone and mobile services, the latter being switched automatically to the fibre connection on entering the home). FTTH is provided on a commercial basis, and demand is strong in a country whose population is similar to ours and whose land area is enormous.

The importance of NGNs for Ireland should not be underestimated. It is not a question of providing better facilities for HDTV or online gaming only. NGNs enable the development and provision of a huge range of new services and industries, including significant opportunities in the health care, education and entertainment fields, and also facilitating major new activities in the areas of smart infrastructure and environmental monitoring. Ireland's international connectivity is good and there is significant capacity in our links to international networks. But without the right national connections, Ireland's entrepreneurs and developers will not be able to enter the new markets that are developing; they will not be able to provide the emerging services because they will not have high-speed, high-capacity and responsive support. The information content of communications is increasing all the time; screen resolutions, sound quality and speed of response will all be critical in the provision of new services. Education, healthcare and entertainment possibilities, as well as the necessary enabling framework for a wide range of other applications, will not be available in Ireland for many years if present trends continue and specific action is not taken.

The need for intervention is now clear. Other countries are moving rapidly ahead in NGNs. Ireland will be permanently disadvantaged, and its international credibility in terms of the knowledge economy seriously questioned, if action is not taken urgently. At present, the state already owns the nucleus of an NGN. The state-owned companies ESB, CIE and Bord Gais have fibre backbone networks throughout Ireland. The NRA has ducting which could also accommodate fibre. The state has also a number of metropolitan area networks (MANs) in major towns around the country. If these were combined, and fibre then built out from them, Ireland could have significant FTTH coverage in a short time. The state assets are not central to the activities of the state-owned companies in question, and they do not need them to carry out their core activities. Moreover, these disparate assets would be worth far more (because of network effects) if they were combined than when they are separate as they are at present. It can indeed be argued that the state has a fiduciary responsibility to maximise the returns from the assets that it holds.

Putting together these assets could be done by a new state-owned company, which would be perhaps owned by the existing state companies in proportion to the value of the assets that they contributed. It would raise the cost of the FTTH build-out on commercial terms, since a stable utility with the prospect of a long-term income stream would be attractive to both banks and bond markets. It would maintain a network on an equal access basis: it would not engage in service provision of its own, but simply provide a platform on which all service providers could compete on equal terms.

There is a further important consideration: changes in electricity and water metering will require house-by-house intervention, with some associated civil works for installation. It is essential that this work be undertaken in conjunction with the extension of FTTH, to ensure cost minimisation in building Ireland's NGN.

Energy Strategy

Peak oil has moved from being a crank theory to a central issue in national energy policy and company strategies. Briefly put, peak oil means that oil production increases until it reaches a peak, after which it cannot be increased further and begins to decline. This behaviour manifests itself in individual oilfields but also in aggregate in national markets. For instance, USA oil has peaked and is now in decline. Similarly, North Sea oil is also in decline. It is expected that world oil production will peak in a similar way, although there is debate about the timing of this, with some suggesting that it has already peaked, while others put the date out as far as ten or fifteen years or more.[10] The timing issue is difficult to resolve, because there is considerable uncertainty about the extent to which oilfields in Saudi Arabia have peaked, and Saudi Arabia contributes 12.6 per cent of world oil production,[11] and is considered to have 20–1 per cent of world oil reserves.[12] When oil peaking occurs, considerable volatility in price, but at a high level, is expected to follow.

Many countries have already adapted their energy policy to take account of the need for carbon reduction in order to mitigate climate change. An emphasis on renewables has followed. However, the need to reduce oil dependency has been also a strategic consideration in many cases. France's emphasis on nuclear power was a consequence of earlier oil crises. The United States' focus on bio-fuels was also given a strategic rationale. Even those who do not accept the oil peaking theory recognise that much of the world oil supplies originate in volatile and vulnerable regions and that too much dependence on oil as a fuel undermines energy security.

Ireland is one of the most oil-dependent countries in the world. In spite of progress in the use of renewables for electricity generation, there is still a huge oil dependency for private cars, freight transport and, in many cases, domestic heating. Dispersed residential patterns, exemplified by one-off housing, have reinforced and in some cases copper-fastened these trends. The major improvements in road networks have encouraged long-distance commuting and public transport has not yet developed sufficiently. Rail passenger transport has grown, and there have also been some encouraging developments in the reopening of old rail lines for commuter purposes, such as in Cork and in the Western Rail Corridor. However, the rail network is not electrified, with the exception of some of the Dublin commuter lines. High prices for oil in the years to come will in any case reduce our competitiveness. There is no substitute for oil as a source of aviation fuel, and our international connectivity will suffer as a result.

Accordingly, all possible measures should be taken to reduce our dependency on oil. These include electrification of the railway lines and encouragement of recent developments in rail freight that can help to increase it from a very low base. A rapid extension of the national grid and accelerated energy conservation measures are other necessary steps.

In general, Ireland has four sometimes competing objectives for energy policy:

- **Competitiveness:** we want to keep our energy costs as low as possible, and lower than those of our competitors.
- **Security of supply:** we want to provide against discontinuities in our energy supply in terms of a physical disruption or a price shock/price volatility,
- **Sustainability:** we want to ensure that the necessary energy resources are there in the future.

- **Climate change:** we want to reduce our contribution to global warming via our reduction in greenhouse gas emissions.

What fuel choices will meet these objectives? The answer depends on what weight we give to the four, and also on what way the world economy and resource availability evolve over the years to come. Regulatory change at a global or at least at European level will also affect the cost of different fuels. The long-term energy choices that are made will affect our competitiveness, security, sustainability and our contribution to climate change. But they will also affect the enterprise base and the opportunities for growth and innovation. There are many opportunities for Ireland in the energy-related goods and services sector, including smart grid development with software, sensors and ICT applications; energy-efficient ICT management; nanotech applications in energy-related materials and systems; electricity interconnection to support renewable generation and export excess capacity; carbon capture and storage; renewable generation, particularly wind and bio-energy; renewable heat in terms of solar thermal and geothermal; outsourced energy management and onsite heat and power generation facilities; marine energy technologies; and eco-construction-related materials, products and services. How much of these are realised depends on the fuel choices we make.

Governance

In the review of future policy requirements carried out in *Sharing Our Future*,[13] one important conclusion was on the need to review governance at all levels in Ireland. A number of factors combine to make such a review an urgent matter. In the first place, many enterprises have their competitiveness eroded through high local authority charges. A system of local taxation on a wider basis would provide more transparency and a greater awareness among communities of the consequences of their preferences. It would also encourage competitive strategies among local authorities in order to attract and sustain enterprises within their areas. The size of those areas should also be reviewed: if more and strategic decision making is to take place at sub-national level, it would be better to examine the optimal size for this activity. Also, as global warming continues, the expectations are that weather patterns will become increasingly volatile and that increased levels of flooding will take place, together with a rise in sea levels. Responses to such events, and serious preparations in anticipation of them, cannot be achieved without a much clearer delineation of responsibility between central and local government

Public Policy and Its Needs

Globalisation and the rapid pace of technological change, as well as global environmental concerns, have all combined in recent years to present many challenges to policymakers. The growth of international regulation has been evident in many areas, most notably in the role of the World Trade Organization (WTO), but also in a number of international agreements, for example with respect to climate change and ozone layer depletion. Other international organisations such as the Organisation for Economic Cooperation and Development (OECD) continue to extend their reach and undertake ambitious programmes of policy development and analysis, also seeking to develop activities with other parts of the world. The kinds of questions discussed and the policy guidelines formulated are usually highly relevant to Ireland, whether because of our existing enterprise base or our ambitions in the future. The setting of international standards is also significant for Ireland, because it affects the future products and services that we may find on world markets and the opportunities for Irish enterprises in the fields in question. Finally, and most importantly, the European Union is the most important policy framework for trade policy, science technology and innovation, ICT policy and a huge range of other issues. The debate and negotiation within it eventually leads to legislation, all of which has to be carefully scrutinised for its impact on Ireland. In addition, the consultation aspects are important. Policy debate in Ireland tends to be diffuse and exhaustive, in any case, and there are formal consultation requirements associated with regulatory impact assessment. For the policymaker, obtaining the views of what are called stakeholders is a significant task, let alone considering unsolicited views also, and finding the balance between them is consistent with government objectives.

To summarise, the questions are becoming more complicated and more frequent, and they are being posed in an increasing variety of international fora. Very often the questions arise as a result of initiatives led by countries that have devoted considerable resources to the issue in question and have arrived at a position that protects and furthers their interests. Often the issue may be abstruse, at the heart of it some chemical or commodity that may be a vital ingredient of an industrial process in one enterprise in Ireland. This means that the issue may be a vital one for Ireland but we may not be able to mobilise the necessary resources to address the issue correctly in time.

For Ireland, it is essential that sufficient resources are available to government to analyse the questions as they appear, and preferably before they do so. Here there is no substitute for human resources, and mindless reductions in civil service numbers would seriously jeopardise our economic prospects for the future. The issue relates to many government departments, and, if numbers cannot for the moment be increased, then better ways have to be found to use the existing resources. Public sector reform should explicitly consider the needs for detailed analysis at the enterprise level, so that Ireland's negotiating position internationally is as strong as possible. In general, we need to take good decisions quickly. International pressures will continue to make this more difficult and more necessary.

Understanding the issues for Ireland in the four priority areas, and taking action to address the problems identified, will go a long way towards creating a sustainable growth path for the Irish economy in the future. Some of the steps needed require investment, and if not all the funds required are available at present, a start should be made nevertheless. Other steps require regulatory change; again, legislation is an unwieldy process, but there are strong benefits to making the changes as quickly as possible. Finally, other steps simply require new ways of thinking, recognition of what is happening in the world and a determination to mobilise analytical and human resources to prepare Ireland for the challenges ahead.

9

An Employer of Last Resort Programme for Ireland[1]

Edward J. Nell[2]

Introduction

Ireland had a wonderful boom, though a little unwise; now it's paying the price in depression. The papers have been full of the problems of the banks; arguably the problems of the people are more important. Statistics tell a bleak story. Unemployment rose by more than 7.5 per cent from Q1 (Quarter 1, January–March) 2008 to Q1 2009, affecting workers at all levels of education. In some ways middle class and semi-professional or professional workers were especially hard hit. And the social consequences were severe: reports of domestic violence have increased;[3] public order offences have increased from 56,636 in 2006 to 61,829 in 2008;[4] and crimes against property have also increased.

The composition of unemployment shows us which sectors were hardest hit, and among these are construction and related services, and financial services. The age structure of unemployment does not match the labour force as a whole; the gender patterns shows young men, under 25,were hardest hit.[5] Figures also show that the more educated part of the labour force appears to have been hardest hit – though the popular press may have overemphasised this. For example, 14.4 per cent of the population is now at risk of poverty.

The ELR as a Solution[6]

So the recession has led to a disaster not only for the Irish working class, but also for a large section of the new Irish middle class. A great deal of effort (and even more talk) has gone into developing plans to save the banks and the financial system. But what are needed are jobs, at all levels.

Of course, many economists, particularly those with a conservative orientation, are worried by programmes to provide jobs. They fear that a strong effort to boost employment through new government spending could set off inflation. High employment might encourage a wage–price spiral, but low employment has large social and economic costs. There is no escaping this dilemma with current tools. New policy options are needed. Here we propose one, the creation of an Employer of Last Resort programme (ELR) – a natural extension of the idea of an automatic stabiliser. As the name implies, in an ELR the government provides the opportunity to work to anyone unable to find a job in the private sector. This, we shall see, provides automatic stabilisation in two respects: the ELR tends to stabilise employment at near the full employment level, while at the same time stabilising money wages. The following sections look at an ELR programme in the context of the United States (US) but the general concept could be a valuable addition to Irish economic policy.

Government Automatic Responses Working with the Market's Responses

When unemployment emerges or inflationary pressure begins to show itself, an immediate offsetting response is the most effective way to prevent it developing into a deep recession or full inflation. The problem is that it takes time to gather data and understand what is going on, to decide what to do, to implement the decision and for the policy to take effect. Ideally, policy should be set up to work *automatically*, with the desired outcome achieved as a by-product of individuals and organisations following market incentives. Even better, the policy response should be designed to offset both the onset of recessions and the beginning of inflation. And that, we shall argue, is precisely what an ELR can do.

It is easy to see this in the case of unemployment. In a slump laid-off workers will head for the nearest ELR office, driven by the need to maintain family income. In a boom they will head back, to earn the higher wages offered by the private sector. The ELR wage will put a floor under wages in the slump; the existence (and size) of the ELR pool of (suitably trained) labour will prevent labour shortages from developing in the boom, so wages will not be driven up.[7] The ELR then works in response to market incentives.

Replacing the Price Mechanism With the ELR

The craft economy of the nineteenth century possessed two automatic stabilisers, the price mechanism and the gold standard. The adoption of mass production methods changed the cost structure of business and, as we have seen, this ultimately altered the way markets adjusted. With the creation of a modern monetary system these stabilisers were lost. The volatile 'multiplier–accelerator' – the process of re-spending that expands or contracts gross national product (GNP) by more than an initial change in investment or government spending – has replaced the stabilising mechanism of supply and demand. Quite apart from what governments did, this opened the possibility that the economy could sink into stagnation and stay there.

The volatility of the new adjustment process was at least partially kept in check by the growth of government and the development of Keynesian 'demand management' policies, which enabled advanced countries to counter and to some extent prevent drastic unemployment – in spite of many bad judgements and costly errors. Fiscal and monetary policy, often coupled with direct controls, appeared to be able to counteract and contain the movement of the cycle, at least in part; in addition, the larger size of government provided a kind of anchor.

Yet from the beginning a problem was evident: the policies could only be expected to work properly if they were calibrated to the right level and put into operation at the right time, both of which posed political problems. Fiscal and monetary decisions affected the pocketbooks of many different groups. Achieving consensus required compromise and building compromises took time; these political necessities weakened and sometimes undermined the effectiveness of demand management policies. Governments did not have the luxury of making decisions on technical grounds alone, even when such grounds could be clearly defined. And, although the policies appeared to work, they were most successful in the period during which the inflation-adjusted rate of growth of output typically exceeded the real rate of interest. Yet even during the period when demand management seemed to work, nothing took the place of the anchor tying down the value of money that had been provided by the precious metals. In fact, it soon emerged that only *managed unemployment* seemed to provide a reliable safeguard against inflation. When inflation threatened, policy-makers engineered a rise in unemployment; when inflation was low, a boom could be encouraged to bring unemployment down. The resulting policy system – sometimes known as 'stop-go' – was a colossal waste of resources and damaging to human lives. And in the second half of the post-Second World War period the apparent inverse relationship between unemployment and inflation broke down. Unemployment and inflation frequently appeared to move together rather than inversely, and demand management has been much less successful.[8] In part this might have been due to the fact that the real rate of interest has been set and maintained at a level lying above the rate of growth of output.[9]

Consider fiscal policy: both taxes and spending are hot political issues. Fiscal programmes cannot be put into place easily or quickly, quite apart from foolish demands for budgetary rectitude. Both taxing and spending measures are passed by legislatures and carried out by executive branches for reasons that have nothing to do with demand management. Both taxes and spending have redistributive aspects, and both may be concerned with supporting or suppressing activities. (As the *Federalist Papers* noted, 'The power to tax is the power to destroy.') The rationale for a tax measure or for a spending bill will very likely bear no relation to any demand management issue. For these reasons it is difficult to adapt decisions to impose taxes and develop spending plans to the needs of demand management.

Monetary policy, while partly free of the demands of electoral politics, has its own problems. First, it essentially comes from the European Central Bank, not Dublin. A certain amount of local autonomy exists with regard to the allocation of credit, and the national government can offer support and guarantees to banks when they are in trouble. It can also use various methods of persuasion to encourage banks to do its bidding (though it may not succeed). At present, European policy is set to encourage recovery, but Ireland cannot be sure that this will always be the case. Secondly, the effectiveness of monetary policy is sometimes over-stated. A modern central bank has essentially one tool to work with: its ability to control the overnight rate of interest. But it cannot be sure what the impact of changes in the overnight rate will be on output (where some of the effect, at least, will be direct), let alone on prices, where the effects will be largely indirect. The old saying 'you can't push on a string' holds true here. Moreover, policy must be formulated in the midst of arguments over conflicting objectives, and must be based on data that experience has shown to be inaccurate – this quarter's data will generally be revised over the next two or three quarters, often substantially. Finally, changes in the overnight rate will sometimes not translate into proportional changes in other interest rates.

To avoid some of these problems it has been argued that policy makers should act on the basis of rules rather than make discretionary decisions. Simple rules, such as keep the money supply growing at a fixed rate, have proved impossible to implement. More complicated rules which rely on expected inflation rates and the gap between current and non-accelerating inflation rates of unemployment have the same problems of information as discretionary decisions.[10] Indeed, one can never do away with judgement in the assessment of what is going on and how to apply the rule. As we saw in previous chapters, central bankers often tried to 'lean into the wind', a policy suggestion that goes back to Bagehot in the nineteenth century. Indeed, it would be hard to do otherwise, but just how far should the monetary authorities lean?

Similar difficulties arise with proposed budgetary rules. Instead of trying to adjust the budget to the anticipated state of the economy, it has been suggested that the administration should simply follow the rule of balancing the budget. But in a slump, cutting spending to try to balance the budget will shrink the tax base, and lead to a decline in revenues, reproducing the deficit. A more sophisticated balanced budget rule argues that the aim should be to achieve a 'full employment' balanced budget, so that if the economy was running at less than full employment there would be a deficit, and if it was running at a higher level there would be a surplus. This allows the budget to function as an 'automatic stabiliser', since when the economy falls below full employment spending will rise and tax collections will fall, creating a simulative deficit. When demand exceeds full employment, tax revenues will rise while spending will stay the same or fall, so a surplus will emerge. Unfortunately, the political system tries to cut spending to remove deficits, and hunts for ways to 'spend the surplus'. Both are self-defeating responses.

Nevertheless, a budget balanced at full employment is desirable. Calibrating taxes and basic spending to reach a balance at full employment would enable the budget to act as an automatic stabiliser, stimulating the economy below full employment and acting as a drag on it above. But the problem with all the rules is that it is usually just as hard, and just as politically complex, to follow them as it is to craft a discretionary response. Rules need to be interpreted; they don't automatically tell you what to do. Think of the arguments over which concept of the money supply was to be controlled, or consider the arguments over how the deficit should be measured, and what counts as 'in the budget' or 'off-budget'. The same applies even to employment – 'discouraged workers' (those who have stopped looking for work) are surely unemployed by a common sense definition. How, exactly, then would we define the case of a budget with zero balance at 'full employment'? In short, conceptual and political arguments can arise over what the rules mean. Moreover, following a rule can require building a consensus almost as much as formulating a discretionary policy.

By contrast, the right approach, we have argued, is to set up automatic stabilising responses, *which work through the market*. Once upon a time the market provided automatic stabilisation; with the move to mass production that was lost. (Not too many tears should be shed for the loss – the old-time market stabilisers didn't work all that well.) Now we can replace the price mechanism with an automatic stabilising system of our own design. This will make it possible to accomplish the goals of demand management by developing government-managed *automatic* market-like institutions that will tend to stabilise *both* employment *and* prices, in effect replacing traditional markets with a system deliberately designed to achieve full employment and stable prices – and at lower cost. Government responses will work *with* the market, and also through the market, but will be designed to be stabilising. Moreover, these institutions are compatible with – and complementary to – traditional demand management policies. And – a bonus – they supplement or even replace a number of supply-side policies.

The idea is to introduce a set of institutions that guarantee a job of some sort for everyone able and willing to work. These are called 'employer of last resort' (ELR) systems. Then when private sector employment declines – lay-offs rise because of a collapse in demand – workers will migrate to the ELR, taking jobs there. As a result consumer spending will not fall, or will not fall much. (ELR wages will be the economy's minimum; private sector wages will be higher, because the private sector has to bid workers away from the ELR.) When aggregate demand rises workers will be hired back by the private sector. In the meantime, their skills will be supported and/or upgraded, and they will have maintained their work habits. Workers newly entering the labour force during the period in which the private sector is suffering from a shortage of demand will be brought into the ELR and given training and an opportunity to establish work habits and a work record. (This training can be targeted, as far as possible, towards potential labour shortages.) With a renewed expansion labour will flow out of the ELR into the higher-paying private sector jobs, allowing the expansion to proceed smoothly, without experiencing a labour shortage.

Nor need there be pressure to bid up the wages of scarce categories of skilled labour, since the ELR system can be training workers in anticipation of skills needs. In short, employment overall will be kept full; anyone who wants a job and does the work assigned to them will be employed. Hence, consumption demand will not fluctuate very much; there will not be much of a multiplier. And money wage rates need not fall in a slump, nor will they be bid up in a boom.

Potentially, this is a better stabiliser than the price mechanism ever was. First we need to consider several possible versions; then we will sketch the institutions appropriate to the US. Next we have to consider whether it would be sufficient to prevent inflation – since inflation has a number of different possible triggers. Then we will work through the market relationships in more detail.

Employer of Last Resort (ELR) Policies

There are several variations of an ELR proposal. In some the government hires the workers itself; in others the government provides subsidies to firms to hire the workers. The proposals also vary in how workers are paid. In some all workers are paid the same minimum wage regardless of the kind of work they are performing, while in others the wage rate depends upon the kind of work being done and is set at the going market rate.

An ELR policy fits well with important and widely accepted moral beliefs. It fulfils the work ethic, while providing opportunities both for work and for training to everyone. And it helps to ensure that no one who is able-bodied and competent need go without the basic necessities of life.

But *any* kind of ELR makes the opportunity for employment universally available. It is not that everyone has 'a right to a job'; if someone doesn't do the work they can be fired. If they are not qualified and are unable to learn or refuse to learn, no one has to hire them. But the state has the duty to provide an *opportunity* for a job to everyone. Nor is this a new idea. In the US it was a component of Roosevelt's economic bill of rights and it appears in the Universal Declaration of Human Rights, to which the United States and the countries of the European Union, including Ireland, are signatories. By making the opportunity for employment an entitlement this right becomes effective. It is a meeting of mutual responsibilities between the society and the individual – the former offers a job, the latter takes on the responsibilities of work. People are assured of the self-sufficiency and self-reliance that come with the dignity of a job.[11]

ELR programmes mean the state takes direct action to assure employment. Through some mechanism the government will provide jobs to those unable to find them in the private sector. These have sometimes been referred to as 'employment assurance' programmes. Such programmes differ from the US's current Structural Economic Policies under Title II of the Humphrey–Hawkins Act, where the government is called on to create jobs in recessions, in that they are automatic and comprehensive. Under current law the President of the United States is required to have available a set of programmes to provide employment during rising unemployment that can be phased out as employment increases. However, putting any such programme into effect would require an act of Congress. An ELR, however, would work like an entitlement (such as unemployment insurance): anyone meeting the programme's requirements would receive a job, upon application. It would be treated in the central government budget in the same way as other non-discretionary programmes. An ELR would differ from what the literature calls 'workfare' (and, for example, other famous American employment programmes such as Jimmy Carter's Comprehensive Employment and Training Act (CETA) and Franklin D. Roosevelt's Work Progress Administration (WPA) and Civilian Conservation Corps (CCC)) in that there could be no means test. The programme would not be restricted to the poor.

Broadly speaking, proposals for ELR programmes come in three kinds: wage subsidy programmes, market wage public employment programmes and minimum wage public employment programmes. Wage subsidy programmes provide jobs for the unemployed in the private sector. Firms are given subsidies to employ and usually train the unemployed. Sweden has a rather successful ELR that is largely of this type. Market wage public employment programmes provide jobs in the public sector at wages similar to those in private industry. This does not mean that workers are guaranteed jobs or wages similar to those they lost. The type of jobs available and the wages paid will depend upon the activities being undertaken.[12] Minimum wage public employment programmes pay the minimum wage or a wage rate adjusted to payments of unemployment insurance. (Senator Paul Simon proposed an ELR of this kind during his 1987 campaign for the Democratic nomination for President of the United States.)[13] Both of the public employment programmes would have training components. It is possible to mix either type of public employment programme with a wage subsidy programme.

The ELR should be designed to ensure that it has four effects. First, it will be an automatic stabiliser. It will tend to increase government spending in recessions, decrease it in expansions. Second, it will help to stabilise the money wage. The wage or structure of wages that the government uses for the ELR could become benchmarks for industry. Further, the absorption of labour at a given wage should slow any tendency of wages to fall in a recession. The release of labour at that wage should slow any inflationary tendencies.[14] Third, by enhancing the skills of the unemployed the training programme could reduce bottlenecks caused by shortages of skilled workers in expansions. It also should increase productivity and the life prospects of working people.[15] Fourth, by offering direct employment rather than simply compensation it should reduce some of the social dislocation caused by long-term unemployment.[16]

An Overview of the ELR

None of the three basic elements of an ELR programme – job placement, job training and public service employment – are new undertakings for most modern central governments. But the scale, organisation and characteristics would have to be different from previous programmes if it is to have the desired macroeconomic effects. Figure 9.1 shows the overall picture and each element is briefly explained below.

Figure 9.1: Components of an ELR

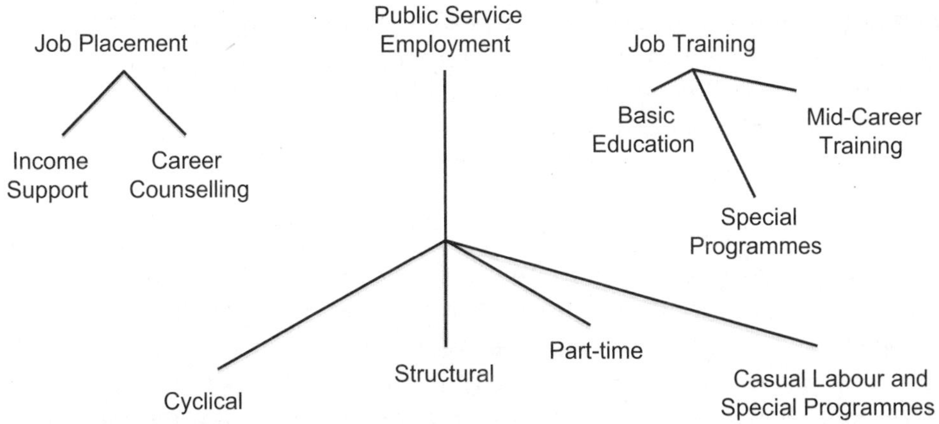

Job Placement

When someone enters the ranks of the unemployed, we can imagine them visiting a local ELR office similar to the One Stop Career Centers currently being established in the US under the Workforce Investment Act of 1998. These offices would be set up with the cooperation of local government. An intake officer would explain the services offered to the unemployed by the ELR: job placement, job training and public service employment.

Initially the unemployed will receive job placement assistance. This will consist of two services: income support and career counselling.

Income Support

Income support is provided by unemployment insurance. This helps people to maintain their consumption while searching for new employment on a full-time basis.[17] The ELR programme would provide this support on terms similar to the One Stop Career Centers. It would be available for a set period of time, say 16 weeks, for those who have been employed for a significant period of the previous year, say 36 weeks. The compensation, like that of the current programme, would be based on prior earnings. However, payroll taxes and the associated funds are both unnecessary and regressive, and can be scrapped. The income support programme can be paid for in the same way as the rest of the ELR.

Career Counselling

Career counsellors can assess the skills of applicants and attempt to match them with vacancies in the private sector. This too is a continuation of a long-running US federal programme. Such services are currently offered under the new Workforce Investment programme, but the Federal Employment Service and various state agencies have offered career counselling since the 1930s. These have not been as widely used as they might have been; for better or worse, private employment agencies have been more popular. Under the ELR programme this might well continue. Even so the ELR should provide this service. If the ELR is to prevent inflation and enhance productivity by providing workers trained in needed skills, it has to closely monitor the local labour market. A broad well-run employment service will yield an intimate knowledge of both the characteristics of a local workforce and the skill requirements of local firms. So the ELR programme should play a much larger role in career counselling than current federal programmes, especially for the non-professional and non-managerial parts of the workforce.

Job Training

The unemployed should be encouraged to improve their marketability through job training. Depending upon their needs, they can be referred to one of three types of programmes: basic education, mid-career training and special programmes for youth and those marginally connected to the jobs market. Within each there will be a range of options provided, for the most part, by outside suppliers. The options will vary in prerequisites, the career they lead to, the time they take, the financial and/or labour contribution that they require from the participants and whether or not they can be combined with public service employment.

All of these programmes will have some common features. First of all, they will be voluntary. The provision of other ELR services, unemployment insurance, job placement assistance and public service employment will not be contingent upon the acceptance of training. Secondly, individuals must have choice among training programmes. Obviously there are limitations on this. Some programmes will have prerequisites. For example, auto mechanics, licensed practical nurses and secretaries cannot be illiterate. The programmes offered would be contingent on reasonable rates of completion and reasonable rates of placement in non-ELR positions that make use of the training provided. Moreover, the training programmes must provide skills needed in local labour markets, e.g. we probably don't need to train more actors and screenwriters.

Finally, training works best when there is a commitment to it. ELR training programmes should not be seen as an easy alternative to work. In short, training should require contributions from the trainees. Some programmes will combine public service work with training, others may involve apprenticeships in the private sector or with non-ELR public agencies, and still others will require the payment of tuition, say, at a community college.

For programmes without labour requirements, individuals could be provided with 'lifetime training accounts' that they would be able to use to 'purchase' desired training at prices assigned by the ELR. These prices need not be the same as those paid by the ELR to the training supplier and can be adjusted to help direct people away from oversupplied activities and towards those in short supply. Individuals would be provided with a lifetime fund that they could use whenever they wish. Should they have depleted that fund or the cost of the training exceed what is available in the fund, the ELR will provide subsidised loans similar to those currently provided by the current federal student loan programmes in the US. Part-time public service work should be available for those undergoing training who desire it. Obviously, this contribution needs to be assessed with care. People cannot eat training and the unemployed will come to the ELR with differing resources. We wish training to be available to all of those willing and able to effectively use it.

Basic education will be for those who do not possess Leaving Certificates, allowing them to obtain a secondary school equivalency certification. It could also provide English as a Secondary Language classes for those with weak English skills. The ELR will make use of the current programmes of local school boards, perhaps providing them with funding assistance. Basic education classes may also be structured to make their extent, timing and content compatible with some types of public service employment. In general no tuition will be required of these programmes. Since this part of the workforce is likely to have the fewest resources one might even wish to treat classroom time as public service work, compensating it at the ELR wage rate as long as the work is done in a satisfactory manner.

Mid-career up-grading could well be the heart of the ELR's training programme. The programme must be designed so that it works with the market. Individuals will have choice in the training that they receive; since they are making commitments of time, labour and financial resources they have an incentive to choose well. Programmes will be diverse, provided by schools, non-profit organisations, unions and profit-making organisations. Their compensation will depend upon their ability to attract workers who wish to be ELR participants. This of course will depend upon their ability to offer something that the participants want: useful training. The ELR programme's role should be largely to provide information and monitoring. It should provide participants with good assessments of their skills and their prospects for success in any line of training. It should provide good information on training programmes, their experience in placing workers in jobs, and the expected future earnings in the various fields. It should provide tough monitoring of programmes to assure the validity of this information. It also should develop its knowledge of the local jobs market to help training providers establish new programmes, keep established ones up to date and where necessary to shut down obsolete programmes. Grants to providers should be available for these purposes.

Young people entering the jobs market, and those who have been only marginally connected to the jobs market in the past, may require special programmes, programmes that will acculturate them to the basics of the world of work. But for reasons that we will discuss below, all efforts should be made to move these people into the mainstream of the training programme as soon as possible. As a by-product of its mission the ELR programme will help those in poverty, but it is not a poverty programme.

Post-Secondary Education and Job Training

To do its job ELR training will have to be on a larger scale than current programmes. But the ELR programme will differ in other ways from current national programmes. First, we shall take a look at existing US federal training programmes and how they developed to see what lessons we can learn.

Broadly speaking, the current effort can be divided into post-secondary education programmes and job training programmes. Post-secondary education programmes provide government support both to colleges and universities and to those who attend them. We can look to the US for examples of how this has worked. In the US the federal government has supported higher education since the Morrill Act of 1862. This gave the states large grants of federal land (30,000 acres per member of Congress). These lands were to be sold and the funds used to endow colleges devoted to agriculture and the mechanical arts. Many US state universities and state agriculture and mining schools were founded in this way. But federal support moved onto an entirely new level with the GI Bill of Rights in the 1940s and continued on a high level even after that bill expired. The bulk of this funding goes to the education of the managerial and professional portion of the workforce and, by any account, has been enormously successful. A small but increasing portion of it is going to training skilled workers at community colleges and private vocational schools.

Job training programmes are directly vocational, aimed at developing skills directly applicable to current or future employment. Federal programmes are quite varied, including veterans' training, the Job Corp, subsidised apprenticeship programmes, the recent Jobs Training Partnership programme and the current Workforce Investment programme. Such training can take place in classrooms or on the job. Most programmes are short-term, generally taking less than four months. In some cases the training services are contracted out, with trade unions providing apprenticeships and various non-profit organisations conducting classroom training. In recent years the federal government has continued to provide funding but has increasingly left the choice and management of these programmes to state and local government.

The federal role in job training was almost nonexistent prior to the 1960s. Then concerns over the skills of the non-college-educated part of the American workforce led to the enactment of the first major job training programme – the Manpower Development and Training Act, 1962. The hope was that by improving workforce skills, productivity and international competitiveness could be improved. But these goals quickly became submerged in another problem, that of poverty. Job training programmes became targeted at the poor. They provided brief training to allow the young, and those marginally connected with the workforce, to become employed. As anti-poverty programmes they were modestly successful. Those involved could expect to earn more then workers with similar characteristics who did not participate in the programmes. In general, this extra earning came from more steady employment rather than higher wages.

The division among federal training and education programmes thus more or less follows the social assistance/social insurance division of the Keynesian state. And, as in most other cases, programmes intended to aid the population in general have been more successful politically and have better achieved their goals. Job training programmes have usually been underfunded and have reached only a portion of those eligible. With the exception of a few years in the early 1970s, spending on post-secondary education programmes has greatly exceeded that on job training. In recent years federal post-secondary education spending has been 2.5 times greater than federal spending on job training.

For graduates of these programmes there is another problem. Unfortunately, social assistance programmes stigmatise. Those who receive such training must have started with low skills and come from an impoverished background. This in turn suggests that they may not be well acculturated to the working world. Such stigmatising helps undo some of the good that the training achieves.

The ELR training programme should attempt to capitalise on the current programme's success and avoid its pitfalls. The key is to try to avoid the dichotomies between assistance and insurance and between programmes-for-the-poor compared to programmes-for-the-rest-of-us.

But we also have to remember the purpose of ELR training. Training is intended to enhance productivity. As long as the training results in employment in the field trained in it probably is doing this.[18] Appropriate standards of completion and placement for ELR training programmes, as discussed above, will help ensure this.

Moreover, it also is intended to help prevent inflation by reducing bottlenecks. If labour market bottlenecks can be prevented or quickly reduced one of the triggers of conflict inflation can be eliminated. This means that the ELR has to maintain close contact with the labour market, offer training in the bottlenecked skills, encourage workers to accept that training and do so in a timely fashion so as to prevent inflation from taking hold. The kind of short-term training offered by current poverty-orientated job training programmes reaches only the very bottom of the jobs market, a part not usually bottlenecked and one that has very little impact of inflation. The current post-secondary programmes, with their emphasis on getting bachelor degrees, cannot turn out trained workers in a timely fashion. Bottlenecks cannot be allowed to persist for four years. The ELR programme's focus should be on mid-career adults, already possessing skills, who with training of a year or less, can add to their skills in ways that meet labour shortages and bottlenecks. So what we might call 'lifetime training accounts' should be directed primarily to adults over the age of 25 or with at least five years' full-time work experience.

In general, the ELR should not be the place to earn a B.A. (or M.B.A., Ph.D., etc.). But ELR counsellors will have to be knowledgeable about government aid and loan programmes and should develop knowledge of local colleges and their programmes. They should be able to help those wishing for such a college degree to investigate the possibilities and then turn them over to school counsellors for additional assistance. The ELR programme might also wish to provide part-time public service employment that could be used as part of a work–study arrangement for those at colleges and universities.

Colleges and universities could be encouraged to offer more short-term college certificate programmes that could be a part of the ELR, such as in bookkeeping or catering for those with Leaving Certificates or engineering and financial services for those with a B.A. Whether or not such courses could later be used as part of an advanced or higher certificate in Food Services or an MBA would be up to the institution. The ELR should neither forbid it nor require it.

Public Service Employment

While job search and training are important, an ELR programme is about work. Providing public service jobs for all of those seeking them is the key component of the programme. We are proposing a modified minimum wage public employment programme. The wage will be set with market criteria in mind, and the private sector will have to pay more to attract labour. But the programme will *not* compete to keep labour; quite the contrary, when private demand increases, the ELR programme is meant to act as a pool from which trained and experienced workers can be drawn.

In this programme most participants would be paid the same wage, no matter what their skill or type of employment in the ELR. (In this it would be similar to the Carter Administration's Comprehensive Employment and

Training Act of the 1970s and the New Deal's Works Progress Administration under Franklin Roosevelt's administration.) However, as experience develops the programme may find it necessary or desirable to institute a wage scale, paying a premium for higher skills and greater experience. The scale, of course, must be less than the comparable levels in private industry. The exception to this would be the ELR staff, who would be regular state employees, and various supervisory personnel, who would be regular employees of national or local government and non-profit agencies that are helping to run the programme. They would be paid at the usual state employee scale for their position.

It is worth contrasting the main features of the three kinds of ELR programmes: Wage subsidy programmes provide jobs for the unemployed in the private sector. Firms are given subsidies to employ and usually train the unemployed. Market wage public employment programmes provide jobs in the public sector at wages similar to those in private industry. This does not mean that workers are guaranteed jobs or wages similar to those they lost. The type of jobs available and the wages paid will depend upon the activities being undertaken. But for macroeconomic purposes the most attractive form of ELR is the minimum wage public employment programme. This programme would pay the minimum wage or a wage scale below that of corresponding industries in the private sector. Since private (non-ELR) employment will generally have a higher productivity than the ELR we would wish people to move into private sector jobs when and if they become available. This would occur automatically if the private sector paid higher wages. In a market wage public employment programme competitive wages and greater security would make many people reluctant to shift to jobs in the private sector. Conceivably this could be a source of labour bottlenecks and inflation.[19] Public jobs programmes of this kind usual have time limits, something we seek to avoid for the ELR. Wage subsidy ELR programmes have two problems. First, they impact upon the competitive process. The pressure of costs and competition is one of the sources of technical change and transformational growth. By partially paying for some workers the ELR may delay the discovery and adoption of labour-saving devices. Second, there is the problem of 'substitution'. Firms that may be perfectly happy to hire a number of workers would be even happier to hire that number if the government pays part of the bill. This means that wage subsidy ELRs may be subsidising firms rather than creating jobs. Wage subsidies should be used with care, perhaps reserving them for training and apprenticeship programmes.

Applicants for a full-time minimum wage ELR programme are likely to have some combination of the following characteristics:

- They have exhausted the income support component of their job search benefits
- They never qualified for such benefits because they are new to the jobs market
- The condition of the local economy is such that there is no expectation of employment in a reasonable period of time
- Their current need for income makes job training impractical[20]

For all of these, the ELR programme will be the last resort.

Differences in skills and abilities in this population, combined with the extreme economic conditions they face, require that they be offered a number of different sorts of public service work. Public service employment will be most sought when unemployment in the private sector is high; that is, when there is significant cyclical unemployment. (The stabilising effects of the ELR programme will reduce but not eliminate this problem.) This will require a cyclical employment sub-programme to the ELR programme. When the economy is doing well, the programme's staff will develop a set of public service projects: things worth doing that can be undertaken when the labour is there and shut down as people return to the private sector.

Some unemployment reflects long-term economic problems. Industries die and new ones may not locate in the same place; in particular agriculture may change character and require fewer workers. Many people often are forced unwillingly to migrate to another part of the country, or to move from the countryside to towns and cities, leaving behind home, family and maybe even, in some cases, language and culture. An ELR public service employment programme would provide an attractive alternative. Such programmes can also help in some of the inner cities. ELR training could be helpful, making the unemployed economically more valuable, encouraging firms to locate so as to use their skills, and breaking down some of the social isolation.[21] Even so, for communities of this kind the ELR will have to be able to provide steady long-term employment. This will require an ELR structural employment sub-programme, one that provides employment for a prolonged period of time. As part of this programme, ELR workers would provide a regular set of public services, especially in distressed communities.

Part-time employment is also important. It helps support education and training, families with school-age children, and senior citizens. Being unable to obtain a part-time job when you need one is also unemployment.

We have already made reference to part-time public service employment in support of the training programme. A more general programme would also be well advised. In all likelihood it would require a permanent component to provide for those in training and a project-oriented component that could be expanded when unemployment rises.

There are people who are barely able to support themselves or might contribute to their own support, but who are not able to work every day. Mental illness, depression, substance abuse and family difficulties may lead to frequent absences that no regular job, including the ELR, could tolerate. But these people can still have good days when they can work. Fifty years ago there was a casual or day labour market that these people could turn to. But technical change has largely eliminated this kind of work. The ELR could institute day-to-day work programmes, which might also function as a supplement to treatment, helping to build self-esteem. Indeed, treatment is often slow and uncertain for these problems. Providing opportunities to work would help many of these people avoid homelessness.[22]

This would suggest that an ELR public service jobs programme should have four sub-programmes: cyclical, structural, part-time, and a casual labour or special problems sub-programme.

What would ELR Public Service Workers Do?

An ELR programme should not be monolithic – 'let a hundred flowers bloom'. There should be many kinds of projects and many opportunities. Large bureaucratic projects could be set up. For example, public corporations could be established to monitor and clean up the environment, to supply special support to schools, to offer after-school programmes, to provide remedial education or training to upgrade skills. The ELR programme would train and supply the labour force. Instead of setting up new large bureaucratic programmes, however, grants of trained labour could be offered to existing agencies. For example, grants could be offered to state and local governments for special projects. These grants could also be farmed out to smaller local groups. Grants could be offered to private sector corporations for special 'venture capital' projects, which will be spun off if successful. Again the ELR would train and supply the workers for projects that, although potentially profitable, also have sizeable externalities. And, of course, grants could also be offered to newly formed groups, for example, of private citizens who think they have a non-profit project which has social value – community sports, midnight basketball, music education, community theatre, art galleries, after-school activities and the like.

Many of the above projects, or very similar ones, were actually funded by the Carter Administration's CETA programme.

There are many other possible socially useful ventures, some of which might also bring in enough revenue to be self-supporting. An ELR programme might develop a 'home day care' programme, training competent people to take children into their homes for day care. Besides training, the ELR would provide teaching materials and appropriate toys and furniture. Likewise, a programme for home-based care for the elderly could be developed, setting up small social centres in suitable homes. The poor often face inadequate public transport and in areas so affected the ELR could set up and run informal taxi and bus services catering to the poor, the elderly, and children going to school or day care. The ELR could train and supply 'home handymen', who could make small but important repairs to buildings and appliances in poor neighbourhoods.

Among the Irish unemployed, 5 per cent, say, might be qualified to act as a teacher's helper; a rough estimate suggests that 2,000 or more classrooms could be improved with an assistant;[23] moreover, two kinds of tutoring could be offered: tutoring to bring backward students up to speed and tutoring to help exceptional students move ahead faster. Most construction work requires training; 15 per cent of the unemployed, however, have this and could be put to work pulling down and cleaning up unfinished buildings, and cleaning up the construction sites abandoned for lack of funding. Moreover, they could work at repairing and improving poverty area housing and slums. In addition, many of the younger unemployed might be trained to assist the police in various ways. Finally, unemployed artists could be set to work creating artwork for public buildings and in public spaces, and presenting theatre and concerts in public parks.

An Example – New Hope

A privately funded community service jobs programme, the New Hope Demonstration Project in Milwaukee, funded jobs for workers similar to those who would join our structural programme. Jobs were found with a variety of non-profit agencies. As in our programme, workers were paid the minimum wage but only for the hours for which they actually worked. If they did not show up or failed to perform satisfactorily they could be fired.[24]

For our purpose the thing of interest is the variety of occupations (see Figure 9.2).[25] While general clerical duties (office support), janitorial work (maintenance) and construction predominate, there are a variety of other activities including day care, data entry and food service (catering). The programme had no problem finding agencies willing to take their workers. The agencies were generally pleased with the workers and felt that real work was being done.[26] This is a small programme operating in a relatively strong jobs market but it gives an idea of what can be done.[27]

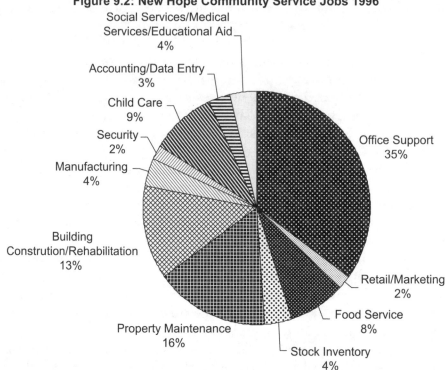

Figure 9.2: New Hope Community Service Jobs 1996

Auctioning ELR Programmes

An ongoing problem for CETA was 'fiscal substitution': local and state governments would set up CETA programmes and put them to work (in part) performing tasks normally done by full-time government employees. This would then allow them to reduce their workforce and save money on their regular budgets.

To avoid this, and also to ensure that projects are useful and well-designed, we propose awarding projects on the basis of a competition. Local and state governments will bid for ELR funding by submitting fully worked-out projects with a plan and an estimated but flexible budget. The ELR funds should be desirable, since the projects will provide work that will take people off welfare and contribute to the reduction of poverty, indirectly benefiting the local economy. These will be projects that can be expanded in recessions and contracted in booms, possibly even being largely shut down in strong booms, but capable of starting up again in a downswing.

The total ELR budget will depend on the state of the economy; ELR funds will expand with need. So the projects are not allocated by budget, they are allocated by quality. The reason for bidding by local and state authorities or agencies is that they get to manage the project and to bring the various externalities and public benefits to themselves or to their districts.

Projects submitted by state and local authorities will be examined and evaluated first by ELR 'in-house' experts, who may recommend changes and offer help in redesigning the plans. But then they will be given over to an expert panel for evaluation and ranking. The panel will 'score' the projects and develop a ranking. Then the top projects will be funded. Some of the others may be rejected outright, while still others may be sent back for further development.

Scoring will take into account:

- The social usefulness of the project
- The extent to which it does not substitute for present government programmes
- A pledge by the local government to continue its programmes in recessions
- The extent to which it helps workers upgrade and develop skills
- How long the programme is expected to last
- How well it will integrate with other projects
- Whether the local government will take on some of the workers permanently after the programme ends

Local government can not only pledge to continue to spend during recessions, the ELR can offer countercyclical loans to help them do so. These loans would be advanced during recessions but would have to be repaid during booms. Being required to repay during the boom times will prevent local and state governments from cutting taxes in boom times. Asking for such loans would add positively to the score.

Non-profit foundations can also offer projects for ELR funding, on the same basis, with a similar system of scoring.

Private profit-making firms can also bid for ELR projects, but their projects should probably be evaluated as venture capital. However, in some cases, private companies might want to offer a socially useful project, which, for example, might have externalities that would benefit their business, in which case it could be evaluated along with non-profit projects.

What happens to local areas that fail to bid successfully for ELR funding? How can the entitlement which provides anyone with a right to a job opportunity be honoured in such areas? The central government ELR programme would offer job placement services and job training programmes as it would anywhere else. Initially, ELR applicants would deal with these parts of the programme. But there would have to be 'basic' programmes that would absorb applicants, even if the programmes were not ideal. In the absence of local programmes the national ELR would have to absorb workers from the areas that had failed in the bidding process.

The national programme might run a daily work line-up: ELR job candidates would turn up and be picked for work from the line-up by representatives of companies, state and local governments, non-profits – anyone who has signed up with the ELR for workers. To sign up to pick from the line-up a company would have to show why it should get ELR workers for these activities, rather than hire on the regular jobs market. (In general, a company or institution would have to pledge to take on some number of ELR workers permanently.)

Remedial education would be a good general programme. Some workers might be taken in by a redeveloped Civilian Conservation Corps or other environmentalist programmes in the forests or along the beaches. But most would want jobs near home. For some this might involve training for parenthood, plus in-home small-scale day care, though it would surely be better if such programmes were run by local agencies. For others there might be cityscape cleanup, though this could overlap with jobs in city services.

Local government failure to win in bidding for ELR funds might create severe problems in some areas during the period in which the ELR gets established. But after it is up and running, there should be programmes everywhere. However, the bidding process will continue, since programmes will finish and new ones move in to replace them. The point of the bidding process is to prevent fiscal substitution and to ensure that the programmes are properly vetted and can be adjudged useful. It also will help support the macroeconomic goal of preventing local governments from pro-cyclical behaviour in regard to spending, i.e. spending more in a boom and less in a slump. Indeed, it should introduce a countercyclical pattern, which is what is needed.

Additional Possibilities for an ELR

In choosing what to pay ELR workers several considerations must be balanced. The ELR is a jobs programme, real work for real pay, and not a form of work relief or welfare. The programme must pay a wage per hour worked. But, while the ELR is not an anti-poverty programme, it seems reasonable that someone who works full time should not live in poverty. At the same time, we do not want ELR jobs to displace private sector and regular public sector jobs either because workers prefer ELR jobs or the government prefers ELR workers to regular employees. Over the past 40 years the minimum wage in the United States has varied between 37 and 50 per cent of the average worker's wage. The ELR wage should be somewhere in that range. A wage rate at the upper end of this range would allow a full-time worker to support a family of three above the poverty line. Most jobs in the government and the non-profit sector funded by government require steady workers with some skill. In a minimum wage ELR such workers would only stay until a better job could be found. This would make it hard to use ELR workers in the place of sanitation workers, firefighters, book-keepers or teachers. There still would be some temptation to find ways to substitute nationally funded ELR workers for employees paid from national and local taxes. Previous US federal jobs programmes have shown that appropriate regulation can minimise this fiscal substitution. A wage in this range makes the programme more expensive, but it also means that increases and decreases in the ELR will have substantial stabilising effects.

The basic ELR wage will come to be the minimum wage in the economy. This will have to be so; no one will work in the private sector for less, since they are entitled to try an ELR job. The private sector cannot attract workers unless it pays above the ELR. If the ELR basic rate is set above current poverty wages, some businesses may be forced to shut their doors. This may be a good thing. If they cannot pay a living wage they should not be in business – shape up or shut down.

Note that this is a minimum wage that enforces itself. An administered minimum wage can be evaded in various ways, but the private sector *has* to meet the challenge of the ELR wage. If they don't they won't be able to attract any workers.

However, if ELR wages are close to market levels this may slow down movement out of the buffer stock. Those who hold ELR jobs equal to or better than their previous positions are likely to be reluctant to leave for the private sector. This would be especially true where the problems are regional and relocation is required to take up a private position. Organising ELR jobs in projects that have a beginning and an end would help with this. While employment would be guaranteed, specific jobs would be available for only as long as the project runs. The project focus would also help keep a divide between the ELR and regular government activities.

It would be sensible to maintain both short-term unemployment insurance and welfare. For people with reasonable prospects for a quick return to private employment, unemployment insurance may be superior to the ELR programme. Unemployment insurance is a popular programme. It supports people while they search for work. It would be costly and disruptive to an ELR programme to have a lot of people entering and leaving shortly thereafter. People would normally enter the ELR programme because they thought their prospects of quick re-employment were low, because they desired ELR training or because they were among the long-run unemployed who had exhausted their unemployment benefits. Welfare (like the temporary assistance for needy families (TANF) programme and state programmes like New York's Home Relief) should also be maintained to provide assistance to those in disastrous situations with few other resources. With the ELR programme, welfare would be less frequently necessary and federal TANF time limits would become a lot more humane. The ELR programme would replace Workfare; this latter requires the unemployed to work at various, usually short-term, jobs in order to 'earn' unemployment or welfare benefits. It is designed to ensure that the unemployed do not end up getting 'something for nothing', as that will undermine 'incentives'. The ELR is designed to guarantee everyone an opportunity to work, to provide a universal right to a job.

Recent proposals for an expanded earned income tax credit[28] are practical and humane. Such a tax credit would benefit the working poor inside and outside the ELR programme. It also will help those for whom regular work is difficult but casual or part-time labour is possible.

There is also an important choice between a full federal and a federal–state programme. The literature is divided on this issue and one can make a case for each side. Our leaning is towards a federal–state programme so as to be able to utilise state project and training capabilities. The fiscal substitution problem would have to be managed through project selection. In either organisational scheme non-profit community organisations and local government will provide most of the training and employment opportunities.

To provide jobs for parents, especially single parents, with small children it will be necessary to provide day care.[29] This could well be one of the areas in which ELR programmes are developed. Suitable applicants could be trained, and then put to work setting up and staffing day care centres for other ELR programmes. (An incidental benefit would be to provide training for parents who lack the skills of parenting and household management.) Moreover, these services could be offered on a commercial basis to the private sector.

What Would It Cost?

This is not a simple question. To exhibit the complexities, we will provide estimates for a US programme; obviously the Irish case will be very different, but the structure of the problem of presenting costs and benefits will be the same.

In the US, for jobs programmes like CETA, Congress would provide a fixed sum designed to fund a given number of jobs at an authorised wage rate. As long as you know how many people you are going to employ estimating costs is relatively easy. But our ELR creates a new entitlement, the opportunity to work. The cost of the programme depends upon the number of people who take the government up on its offer, which depends on the number of people out of work. But the programme is also meant to help stabilise the economy. It will reduce the number of unemployed both directly by providing jobs and indirectly through the extra spending of people who now have jobs. To estimate the cost of the ELR you need to model the economy, especially the effect that the programme has on unemployment.

We have done this using Fairmodel-US, a well known macro-econometric model.[30] Getting an ELR programme going will take time, and forecasting more than a few years into the future is dicey, so we have back-cast. That is, we supposed that an ELR was enacted around the peak of the last business cycle. The programme starts up slowly in January 1989 and is fully operational five years later, in January 1994. We use the model to simulate the programme's effect through to the end of 2004.[31]

Before looking at the results, a word about reading the graphs. An economic model, even a forecasting model, is a simplified version of the world. When you evaluate a model you compare it to the real world. But in looking at a policy you begin with the model's unchanged or base predication and compare that to the model's predication about the policy. So the base in the figures below is what Fairmodel predicts without an ELR.[32]

In Figure 9.3 we can see the ELR's impact on unemployment. The effect is significant, lowering the rate of unemployment between 0.75 per cent and 2 per cent compared to the no ELR case. The ELR reduces unemployment by more than simply the number of people it puts to work. It does so by increasing employment within the private sector.

The ELR's public service employment will vary with the rate of unemployment. In our simulation ELR employment would peak at about 1.6 million during the recession of the early 1990s, gradually falling to less than

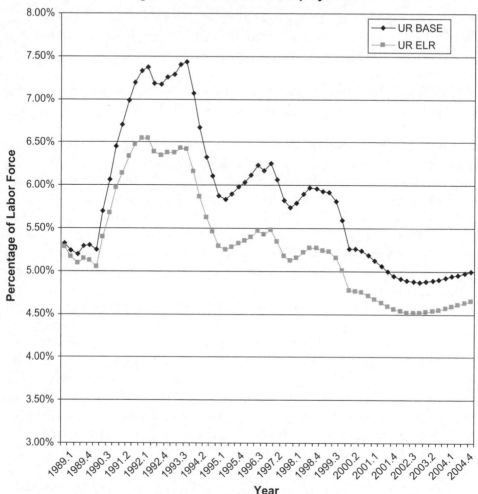

Figure 9.3: The Rate of Unemployment

Note: UR-Base is the base rate of unemployment without an ELR programme. UR-ELR is the unemployment rate with an ELR programme.

400,000 in 2002 (see Figure 9.4). In this the programme would be roughly twice the size of CETA during the 1970s.

The extra employment, both inside and outside the government sector, means that extra output is being produced. Real gross domestic product (GDP), adjusted for inflation, is higher in the ELR scenario than in the base. This is true even in years without a recession. The extra boost the ELR gives in those years also increases the economy during expansions (see Figure 9.5).

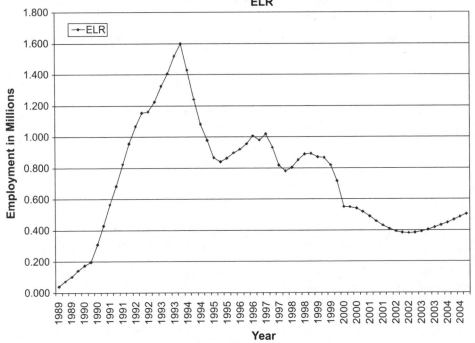

Figure 9.4: Long-Run Effects on Unemployment Rate Following Imposition of an ELR Programme, Simulated ELR

If we look at inflation we find the programme had little effect during the period simulated (see Figure 9.6). During the recessionary period of the early 1990s the rate of inflation fell less with the ELR than without. In the rest of the period annual inflation was almost identical in the two scenarios and after 1999 slightly lower with the ELR.[33]

The programme's cost can be looked at in a number of ways. The simplest is the net cost (see Figure 9.7). This is the increase in federal spending due to the programme. For the fully operational programme, spending would vary from around 0.5 per cent to 0.9 per cent of GDP. This is less than other entitlements such as social security (around 4.5 per cent of GDP) and Medicare (1.75 per cent to 2.5 per cent of GDP). But with the exception of national defence (3 per cent to 6 per cent), it is larger than discretionary programmes such as federal transportation spending (0.5 per cent) and the justice department (0.33 per cent).

Figure 9.5: Simulated GDP Growth Relative to Base GDP Growth

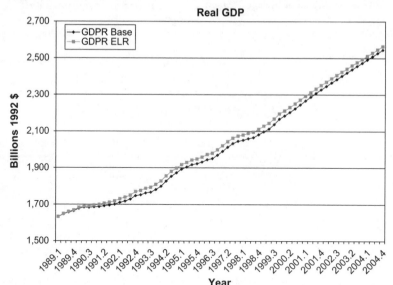

Note: GDPR Base is the base rate of GDP without an ELR programme. GDPR ELR is the rate of GDP with an ELR programme.

Figure 9.6: Price Deflators for an ELR Programme
Relative to the Base Case, Simulated

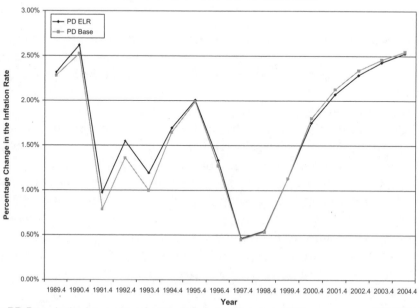

Note: PD Base is the base rate of price deflators without an ELR programme. PD ELR is the rate of price deflators with an ELR programme.

Figure 9.7: The Net Cost of the ELR

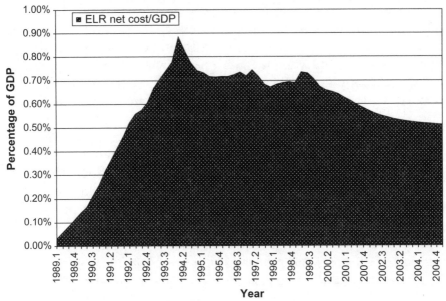

Figure 9.8: National Structural Deficits in the ELR and Base Cases, Simulated

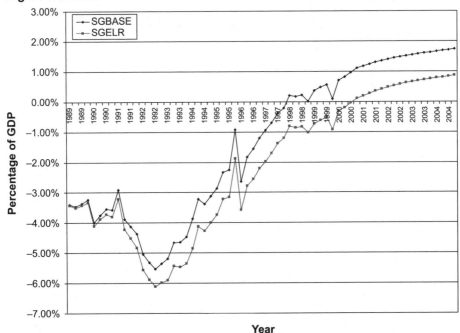

Note: SGBase is the base rate of national structural deficits without an ELR programme. SGELR is the rate of national structural deficits with an ELR programme.

This doesn't capture the whole story. Among other things, the programme also increases tax revenues, since employed people pay more taxes than the unemployed. This increase does not quite match the programme's net costs, with the result of a modest increase in the federal deficit. As we know, deficits are appropriate when there is unemployment and a surplus is good when the economy approaches full employment. With the ELR the federal budget goes into surplus during 2001 and stays there through to the end of the forecast period (see Figure 9.8).

But to fully understand the policy we need to consider its benefits as well as its costs. In terms of national income our benefit is the extra output the programme directly and indirectly generates. If we subtract the net costs from the extra output we find, correcting for inflation, that we are ahead between $4 billion and $10 billion for each quarter that the programme is fully operational (see Figure 9.9). For the period that we simulated the extra output would have exceeded cost by around $400 billion. This may not capture all of the costs and it certainly does not capture all of the benefits, even so we can confidently say that this is a programme that pays.

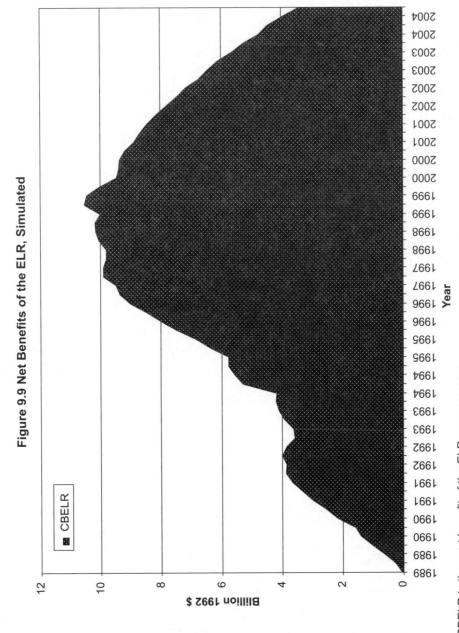

Figure 9.9 Net Benefits of the ELR, Simulated

Note: CBELR is the cost benefit of the ELR programme.

10

Credit Crisis Theory *Redux*:[1]
A Critique and a (Re)Construction

K. Vela Velupillai

Dedicated to the Memory of George Shackle[2]

> The functions of credit have been a subject of as much misunderstanding
> and as much confusion of ideas as any single topic in Political Economy ....
> Credit has a great, but not, as many people seem to suppose, a magical
> power: it cannot make something out of nothing.[3]

A Preamble

> Professor Leontief does not accept [that instability is an unrealistic hypoth-
> esis] and maintains that we may utilize *dynamical systems that are unstable
> throughout and cites capitalism as an example.*[4]

In his regular column in the *Financial Times*, on 4 January 2009, Martin
Wolf heralded the New Year, acknowledging the relevance of the 'Minsky
moment'. Apparently after taking the United States (US) off the Gold Standard, President Nixon is supposed to have paraphrased a variant of Milton
Friedman's *Time* magazine enunciation[5] as, 'I am now a Keynesian in
economics'. With friends such as these, who needs enemies, is the old
cliché!

The Friedman observation was the beginning of the end for Keynesian
economics in its *neoclassical synthesis* form and the rise of what eventually came to be *New Classical*[6] economics, although one had to traverse the

transition regimes of fix-price macroeconomics and variations of monetarism and New Keynesian economics, before capitulating to the world of
Lucasian fantasies.

If such histories repeat themselves, the spectre of what may come after
New Classical economics, when high priests of orthodoxy announce on
public pulpits the age of Minsky and the return of Keynes, boggles and
terrorises the mind of those of us who have been outliers to orthodoxy for
a quarter of a century. It may well be time, then, as one who has been an old-
fashioned Keynesian throughout the New Classical age, to take a critical
look at Minsky and the Keynesian foundations of the 'Minsky moment'.

This chapter is a first attempt at such a critical study. It is largely non-
technical, although I intend supplementing this with a companion piece
that substantiates the technical details in some detail.[7]

One of the casualties of the current crisis, whether it be a 'Minsky
moment' or not, seems to have been the Irish economy. The Irish economy's
epoch as the 'Celtic Tiger', from about 1995 until 2007,[8] could easily become
yet another example to be added as the eleventh 'bubble' in, perhaps, the
sixth edition of Kindleberger's justly famous and immensely readable narrative history of almost four centuries of financial crises, described as *Manias,
Panics and Crashes*.[9] If the post-Celtic Tiger experience – as a 'Paper Tiger',
perhaps? – evolves into consistency with the Kindleberger scheme, and
satisfies the *Panic* characteristics, then a full 'Minsky moment' would have
been experienced by a generation of the Irish population.

The Kindleberger narrative of 'the big ten financial bubbles' is an interpretation of these crises in terms of 'a model developed by Hyman Minsky'.[10]
That this one single model, assuming it is possible to encapsulate Minsky's
various variations on a theme within the framework of 'a model', developed
on the basis of the experiences of advanced capitalist economies during the
latter two-thirds of the twentieth century, could be used to make sense of
four centuries of episodes of financial *turbulence*,[11] is remarkable, and
almost beyond belief.

I have always felt Hyman Minsky's singular contribution to crisis theory,
in credit economies of the 'capitalist' type, to be in the grand tradition of
Rudolf Hilferding's classic *Das Finanzkapital* – but without the Austrian
capital theoretic foundations, nor the Marxian monetary theoretic underpinnings of that early twentieth century classic. Nor, indeed, are the policy
inferences by these two pioneers of capitalist financial crises, and their institutional underpinnings, very similar.

Orthodox interpretations of Hyman Minsky's important contributions
to crisis theory, not without considerable support from the master,[12] have

placed him squarely as someone who completed the Keynesian vision of capitalism's financial fragility, albeit with a liberal infusion of Fisherian elements. The methodological conundrum here is, of course, the fact that the Keynesian vision of a multi-equilibrium,[13] unstable, capitalist economy does not sit too comfortably with a Fisherian commitment to a uniquely stable equilibrium system, with or without credit. Moreover, Keynes's agents are *behaviourally* rational; Fisher's intertemporally optimising agents, on the other hand, provide a significant foundation for orthodoxy and its relative insensitivity to crisis theory.[14]

Here lies an unresolved – indeed, virgin territory – issue: the *behavioural* foundations for one or another of the Minsky-based models of crises. Much lip service is devoted – not least by the master himself – to 'Keynesian Uncertainty', 'Fundamental Uncertainty', 'Systemic Uncertainty', even 'Knightian Uncertainty', and so on. However, to the best of my knowledge, there is not a single Minsky-based model of crises, of a formal, mathematical kind, based on any formalisation of these ostensibly 'pregnant' concepts. That old horse, the tiresome dichotomy between 'risk' and 'uncertainty', is invoked, before the former is dismissed as irrelevant and, thus, any and all reliance on probabilistic mechanisms to formalise intertemporal dynamics is also eschewed. At least that is the official stance, although the praxis is a muddle, even by the master in some of his joint, formalised work.

Minsky-based models are said to encapsulate 'Keynesian', 'pervasive', 'Fundamental' or whatever 'uncertainty' – or is it 'systemic uncertainty' – with fashionable appeals to *The General Theory of Employment, Interest and Money (General Theory or GT)* and its much maligned Chapter 12.[15] The resulting *ad hoc* models are, then, claimed to have the capacity to replicate all kinds of patterns; worse, even to be able to be so general that their one or another specialisation – usually for parameter variations – is a realisation of every conceivable model, non-orthodox or not.

Minsky also emphasises the instability of a capitalist economy based on advanced credit mechanisms and institutions. The catchphrase, of course, is 'stability is ... destabilizing'.[16] However, other pioneers of emphasising the role of credit in the accumulation and growth processes of an advanced capitalist economy, primarily Schumpeter and Keynes, would have agreed with Leontief's trenchant observation on the pervasive instability of such an economy, *with or without credit*, i.e. with or without 'financial institutions'. Nonlinear and evolutionary endogenous growth and cycle models, both of the Schumpeterian and Keynesian variety, are a testimony to this proposition, although none of these kinds of models have been developed far enough to substantiate the full force of Leontief's interesting suggestion.[17]

Instability, multiple equilibria, multiple credit regimes and 'pervasive Keynesian uncertainty' are the methodological quartet that seem to characterise a Minsky model of crises in advanced capitalist economies with well-developed, and constantly evolving, institutions and mechanisms of credit. So far as I can see, the distinctive contribution by Minsky to the vast and noble literature on credit crisis theory, from Mill to Minsky, is the explicit tripartite characterisation of behavioural regimes in advanced, credit-based capitalist economies, in terms of *hedge, speculative* and *Ponzi* epochs, in addition to exhortations to incorporate 'Keynesian uncertainty', both at the individual and the institutional level. However, neither of these features has ever been defined with any kind of systematic formalisation, in any one integrated mathematical model, even by the faithful.

A brief, highly potted summary of the high points of crisis theory, from Mill to Minsky is discussed in the next section. The purpose is only to place in context the much vaunted 'Minsky moment' and, perhaps, also to demystify much of the present hype. In the following section a characterisation of Minsky's modelling desiderata, for understanding crises – perhaps also for taming them – are presented and discussed. I suspect the purpose of this section is to critically expose the inadequacy of any and all current attempts at encapsulating the rich vein of suggestions in Minsky's many writings, not all of them always displaying accurate doctrine historical traditions; nor even showing much historical knowledge of the exact underpinnings of Minsky's own claims and attributions.

Following that, I suggest a 'new' vision for classical behavioural economics, incorporating and conjoining Shackle's world of *bounded uncertainty* with Simon's more developed world of *bounded rationality*, as a foundation for modelling crises, whether of a Minsky type or not.

The final, brief, section outlines how and where one can go, to advance the formal suggestions of the 'new' vision.

Brief Notes on Credit Crises in Theory – From Mill to Minsky

Credit is thus *inherently unstable*.[18]

It will not be an exaggeration at all to say that Hyman Minsky's noble progenitors – leaving aside Marx and Hilferding – are Mill,[19] Wicksell,[20] Fisher,[21] Schumpeter,[22] Hawtrey,[23] Currie,[24] Keynes,[25] Lindahl[26] and Myrdal.[27] Minsky, however, acknowledges his explicit debt only to Fisher and Keynes, with an occasional nod towards Schumpeter. With hindsight at my disposal, this is not surprising. Minsky has not bothered to anchor his theories in the noble traditions of theories of credit crises. This is a pity and may be one of the reasons for the relative neglect of his work in textbooks and policy circles, till the recent resurgence of interest in the form of 'Minsky moment' incantations.

In this brief section I simply want to record the tradition, perhaps to develop it further and deeper at a later date; or, perhaps, provide hints to others who may be better equipped to pursue the necessary scholarship and make the important links and draw the necessary implications.

Even in the classic tradition noted above, there needs to be a sub-classification. There were those, like Mill, Marshall, Fisher and Hawtrey, who subscribed to a fundamental equilibrium vision of a capitalist economy, even when credit-based, and the disequilibria and instabilities were transitory, even if policy may be required to re-settle the economy on its self-adjusting, self-equilibrating path.

On the other hand, the Wicksell vision,[28] developed intensively and to great depths by Lindahl and Myrdal, was of a monetary macroeconomy that was inherently unstable and had no endogenous, self-equilibrating properties. Moreover, the benchmark monetary equilibrium in a Wicksel-lian economy, at the hands of Lindahl and Myrdal, was not reducible to the real equilibrium of a Walrasian economy.[29]

That there is no reference at all to Hawtrey,[30] or to any of Laughlin Currie's work in the 1930s, in any of Minsky's writings is more than myste-rious. In particular, it seems to be a pity that there is no attempted anchoring and links to Hawtrey's notion of '*credit deadlocks*' nor to Currie's important scheme for so-called '100% money'. The latter scheme, as elegantly argued by Roger Sandilands:

> [W]as indeed a political non-starter, but its main logic – the need to gain firm control over bank reserves for effective control of the supply of money, hence the business cycle – was the inspiration for the 1935 Banking Act that was to establish a true central bank for the United States and shift the power base of the Federal Reserve System from New York to Washington.[31]

Most importantly, of course, from the point of view of the 'Minsky moment', there is his Keynesian allegiance. To this, Minsky has paid tireless attention, although as I shall try to show, the key concept of 'Keynesian uncertainty' never rises above the proverbial 'lip service' in the constructed models – by Minsky or his acolytes. Thus, I have doubts about the repeated invoking of the message of 'Ch. 12 of the *GT*' in Minsky scholarship. To this I must add a further scepticism on the claims that the other Minsky anchoring, on 'Ch. 17 of the *GT*', which is also questionable and is discussed in the next section.

There is also the question of whether any one complete cycle of 'manias and panics' is unique in its characterising features or whether any one such episode is one of a definable 'genre', as assumed by, for example, Kindleberger. Hence the attempt by the latter to provide a coherent narrative of ten such episodes, spread over about four centuries, allegedly using the one framework of a 'Minsky model'.

Recent orthodox literature seems to have feet in both strands of thought. For example, Tirole seems to 'believe' in an interpretation of financial crises that will allow him to sit comfortably on the fence:

> No two crises are identical. At best we can identify a set of features common to most if not all episodes.[32]

But scholars more knowledgeable in the historical literature are more nuanced in their attitude to this issue.[33]

Just for the record, I should also mention the hardcore orthodox approach to an analysis of financial crises as 'bubbles', rational or not, with or without rational expectations. I don't think Minsky was even remotely influenced by this technical literature, nor do I think his technical repertoire was adequate to make sense of this seemingly sophisticated approach. However, I hasten to add that I myself do not think this literature is either mathematically sophisticated or even technically interesting, let alone conceptually or empirically meaningful.

It may, however, be useful to mention that work by, for example, Shiller,[34] has inspired some interest in trying to provide *behavioural* economic foundations for macroeconomic financial crises. This is a satisfactory development, at least from my point of view of trying to fill one important missing link in Minsky's attempt to anchor his vision in 'Keynesian uncertainty', with Shackle's notion of *boundedly uncertain* decisions in the face of '*potential surprises*'.

Even a cursory doctrine-historical point of view, in reading and trying to understand Minsky's kaleidoscopic visions of crises, may suggest that somewhere between Wicksell – as interpreted by Lindahl and Myrdal – Keynes and Shackle/Simon, there lies a fruitful combination and compounding of analytical, conceptual and technical building blocks that may, yet, launch a rigorous, behaviourally and institutionally founded theory of crises that will do justice to Minsky's attempted theorising.

Minsky's Precepts for Modelling Endogenous Crises: A Critique

> Keynes' *General Theory* viewed the progress of the economy as a cyclical process; his theory allowed for transitory states of moderate unemployment

and minor inflations as well as serious inflations and deep depressions .... In a footnote Keynes noted that 'it is in the transition that we actually have our being'. This remark succinctly catches the inherently dynamic characteristics of the economy being studied.[35]

I shall assume that Minsky's study and modelling of 'the inherently dynamic characteristics' of a credit-based capitalist economy is one that is always in 'transitory states of being', never 'becoming' stable or unstable, but always tending to the one or the other. Technically, from the point of view of dynamical systems theory, this means that the tripartite Minsky regimes (see below) are always in one or another 'basin of attraction' of a dynamical system, without ever reaching (or ever 'being' at) the system's attractors.

The conceptual underpinnings of Minsky's desiderata for modelling crises in credit-based capitalist economies seem to have been culled out of selected contributions by Irving Fisher, Maynard Keynes, Michael Kalecki[36] and Dudley Dillard,[37] although there are also some stray Schumpeterian elements dotting the Minsky vistas.

Papadimitriou and Randall Wray have provided an admirably succinct encapsulation of the vast canvas that was constructed by Minsky to understand the unstable macroeconomic dynamics of credit-based capitalist economies:

> Minsky borrowed his 'investment theory of the cycle' from John Maynard Keynes. Minsky's cycle theory derived from combining two things: the famous exposition found in Keynes's Chapter 12 of the *General Theory*, which focuses on the inherent instability of investment decisions as they are made in conditions of fundamental uncertainty, and the approach taken in Chapter 17 to valuation of financial and capital assets .... While Minsky credited Keynes for pointing the way toward analyzing the process of *financing* investment, he found it necessary to go much further. Thus Minsky's contribution was to add the 'financial theory of investment' to Keynes's 'investment theory of the cycle' .... Since financing investment is the most important source of the *instability* found in our economy, it must also be the main topic of analysis if one wants to *stabilize the unstable economy*.[38]

In answering the question 'Why does investment fluctuate?',[39] Minsky postulates his famous 'three types of financial postures': *hedge finance, speculative finance* and *'Ponzi' finance*. The 'path dependence' – i.e. history dependence – of any current state of the economy, in transition, is characterised by the evolving mix of these three types of financial postures.

The transition from one or another of these ideal types to another is when 'Keynesian uncertainty' kicks into action, although it is not clear, in Minsky's voluminous writings – nor in any of those by Minsky scholars – how this is played out by the interaction between individual and systemic reactions. In other words, how an individual's or an institution's decision processes leave the domain of pure risk analysis – and, hence, perhaps in the world of orthodoxy, expected utility maximisation (EUM) and the efficient market hypothesis (EMH) – and enter the domain of 'Keynesian uncertainty'. Neither the transition from one pure regime to another, nor the evolution of the dynamics in the speculative or Ponzi regimes, underpinned by behaviour (of individuals and institutions) based on 'Keynesian uncertainty' has, to the best of my knowledge, ever been formalised.

Now, the economic reason for the transition 'from an initial financial tautness', say in the hedge finance regime, is that financial flows signal a tightness in the intertemporal flows of the income generating process. This signal of a tautness 'is transformed into a financial crisis'[40] and the transition to the next regime is initiated. At this point Minsky's interpretation of the Kaleckian macroeconomic pricing process plays its crucial role.

But long before Kalecki, Wicksell's immediate Swedish followers – particularly Lindahl and Myrdal[41] – had devised a similar scheme, under the much-maligned forces of 'Keynesian uncertainty', to generate unstable, disequilibrium monetary economic trajectories. More importantly, it was this development that inspired George Shackle's pioneering work on non-probabilistic decision theory in the face of incompleteness of knowledge, a situation far more coherent and amenable to precise formalisation with the tools of modern, non-orthodox mathematical analysis. I shall return to these issues in the next section.

Finally, to the tripartite financial regimes and the Kalecki-type pricing rule, was added the methodological precept of 'stability ... is destabilizing', in every transition regime. It is understood that every economy is always in a transition regime, and every transition regime is a mix of the pure regimes, even when the Ponzi financial regime rules.

Five critical caveats need to be mentioned, at least cursorily, at this point. Firstly, there is the question of nonlinear dynamics in Minsky's work and in the attempts by many of his followers and admirers to model 'Minsky crises' nonlinearly. Secondly, there is the question of policy for 'stabilising an unstable economy'. Thirdly, there is the thorny issue of 'equilibrium'. Fourthly, there is the crucial question of the correct domain and range for the economic variables in any version of Minsky-type models. Finally,

Minsky's understanding of 'orthodox' theories, whether macroeconomics or microeconomics, at their frontiers.

There is no evidence whatsoever, at least to this writer, that Minsky ever understood the mathematics of the nonlinear macrodynamic models that emerged from what is generally acknowledged to be the pioneering works of Kaldor,[42] Hicks[43] and Goodwin.[44] At a most banal level, there is the repeated reference to the 'ceiling-floor' models of Hicks and Goodwin and the absurd claim that the Hicksian trade cycle model is 'linear'. There are no *exogenous* 'ceilings' and 'floors' in any of Goodwin's many nonlinear macrodynamic models. Hicks has two regimes, one with entirely endogenously determined, unstable equilibrium, and another, also an unstable equilibrium, in which only one of the exogenous constraints is, in fact, active; the second one, usually the 'ceiling', is endogenous. All the way from Minsky in 1957 and 1959[45] to Minsky in 1965,[46] Ferri–Minsky[47] and Delli Gatti et al.,[48] there is a series of misrepresentations of the structure, mathematics and economics of the pioneering nonlinear macrodynamic models.[49]

Thus he – and his followers – were, unfortunately, unable to realise that the identical endogenous mechanisms generating the unstable, disequilibrium, nonlinear dynamics could have been harnessed to model, endogenously and nonlinearly, a complete Minsky model of a three-regime crisis, with the Kaleckian pricing rule and transition regimes that encapsulate the idea of 'stability ... is destabilizing'.

Where such models remain inadequate is where every formal attempt – again, to the best of my knowledge – to model *Minsky Crises* as formal (*ad hoc*, nonlinear) dynamical systems has failed to endogenise 'Keynesian uncertainty'. Not even the admirably concise, nonlinear attempt by Taylor and O'Connell[50] or its more pedagogical and clearer version in Taylor,[51] escape the *ad hockery* of enlightened curve shifting.

Secondly, on policy for 'stabilising an unstable economy', there was the noble 'Swedish tradition', emanating from Wicksell, but most comprehensively developed by Lindahl and Myrdal. Apart from a curiously unerudite, passing footnote, in Ferri–Minsky,[52] there is no evidence at all that Minsky took the trouble to familiarise himself with the classic framework of an unstable credit economy that Wicksell developed and Lindahl and Myrdal completed in the form of a dynamic, disequilibrium macroeconomy with an unstable monetary equilibrium that is in no way related to the real equilibrium of orthodox theory.

Thirdly, there is the issue of *equilibrium*. Minsky's economies are in their transition configurations, within the 'basin of attraction' of some attractor, whether they are stable or not does not matter. Thus, when approached from the point of view of global, endogenous capitalist dynamics, a Minsky model must naturally encapsulate multiple equilibria. Are the destabilising financial forces generated during the transition to a stable equilibrium – i.e. the genesis of a pure speculative regime in an endogenously evolving dynamic process during the time the economy is in the basin of attraction of the hedge regime. This is formally impossible within the framework of dynamical systems theory, without a plethora of unattractive *ad hockeries*.[53] Why not simply give up on 'equilibrium'? My conjecture is that Minsky's reading of Chapter 17 of the *General Theory* was heavily indebted to Dillard's interesting, but incomplete, interpretation. Minsky, therefore, was not able to discern the Sraffian point in that important chapter: that *every configuration of the economy is some equilibrium*, making the notion vacuous.[54] If every configuration of the economy is an equilibrium,[55] there are no transition paths, nor is there any sense in the distinction between stable and unstable equilibria!

I now come to an issue that may have the air of an exotic 'objection': the relevance of real variables and real analysis in formalising the dynamics implicit, say, in a balance sheet constructed for an abstract Minsky-type economy, say as in Table 9.3 in Taylor.[56] The numbers that enter such balance sheets can, at best, be rational values (both positive and negative). But the dynamical system that is supposed to reflect the evolution of the economy represented in the balance sheet – say, as depicted in Figure 9.8 of Taylor[57] – 'resides' in the unrestricted two-dimensional Euclidean space. Any facile response that the answer to this conundrum is to work with difference equations, or a discrete dynamical system, misses the point. Of course, this is an objection to all 'unrestricted' dynamical system modelling in economics. I'll return to this theme in the next section.

Finally, Minsky's understanding of the frontiers of orthodoxy, whether it be macroeconomics or microeconomics, had entered a time warp at a point around the time when the neo-classical synthesis, fix-price macroeconomics, Friedmanite monetarism, and all kinds of revived New Keynesian bastardisation of old Keynes had all been properly buried and their deaths officially proclaimed by the New Classicals. Minsky was fighting old wars and lost battles and banging against frail and irrelevant walls, invoking Hahn's pathetic irrelevancies against claims by any and every kind of macroeconomist who was trying to found the subject on general equilibrium theory.

Indeed, the new orthodoxies that were defining the new frontiers could even claim to encapsulate two of the Minsky finance regimes[58] – *hedge finance* and *speculative finance* – quite comfortably, so long as neither

Minsky nor his acolytes provided a formal mechanism in which to frame 'Keynesian uncertainty', a fact which seemed to have escaped the attention of many of the 'Minsky moment' enthusiasts.

Unless and until a proper formalisation of 'Keynesian uncertainty', at the level of the individual and the institution, is not forthcoming from the Minsky corners, orthodoxy will not take too seriously the other three pillars of the Minsky edifice: multiple equilibria, Kalecki-type pricing and 'stability ... is destabilizing'.

Bounded *Underlined Uncertainty* Meets *Bounded Rationality* – Towards a *Behavioural* Rejuvenation of Crisis Theory

> [The] solution of the problem of reconciling uncertainty and imaginative experience ... I have ... called the focus-hypothesis solution .... Creative decision, ... if real, .. is performed in the face of uncertainty .... It is only *bounded* uncertainty that will permit him to act creatively ... [and] Probability must be abandoned in favour of *possibility* ....[59]

Shackle introduced his concept of *potential surprise* first in his seminal *Economic Journal* paper of 1939 and made his intentions clear at the very outset:

> My concept of 'potential surprise' is *something very different from that of mathematical probability for which I wish to substitute it*. It is purely subjective.[60]

I have long conjectured that the origins of Shackle's concept of *potential surprise* came about as a result of his deep and enthusiastic studies of Myrdal's *monetary equilibrium*, of which he wrote:

> [*Monetary equilibrium* is] perhaps the most undervalued work of economic theory ever written .... To me having no German, Myrdal's ideas became known only through a lecture course given by Mr Brinley Thomas in 1935 [at the London School of Economics] .... I emerged [from the lectures] with only an inkling of what Myrdal had said, but the idea of *ex ante* and *ex post*, of the vital role of expectation, had struck fire in my thoughts.[61]

It was, however, only after a recent serendipitous encounter with Shackle's *Expectation and Liquidity*[62] that I was able to substantiate my conjecture in a reasonable way. Shackle,[63] refers to Myrdal's discussion of 'investment gains and investment losses', where the latter states:

> For gains and losses in *revenues and costs must actually occur at some time*, and since they contain an element of **surprise**, in so far as they have not

been anticipated with full certainty, gains and losses arise in the *ex post* calculations regardless of how short the periods into which the process is divided.[64]

My purpose here is to try to make the case, however thin the reed on which I hang my conjecture, that Shackle was motivated to devise a scheme of rational decisions under *incomplete knowledge* without relying on the probability calculus.

Bounded uncertainty,[65] underpinning *creative decisions* by a rational agent facing *incomplete* knowledge, gives rise to *potential surprise*. I think this one sentence characterises the most important aspect of Shackle's theory of rational decision in the face of incomplete knowledge, not just *imperfect* knowledge, which will turn out to be a special case of the former.

Four remarks and observations are in order, before proceeding to the coupling of boundedly uncertain agents with Simon's boundedly rational ones.

First of all, Shackle[66] distinguishes between *listable* and non-*listable* 'distinct sequences of events' that are 'ordered' by a boundedly uncertain (rational) agent. I interpret this distinction to be equivalent to that between a *recursive* and *recursively enumerable* sequence, as in computability theory. Thus data – real and conjectured – form recursively enumerable sequences that are not recursive. This is sufficient to induce potential surprise in a formal sense.

Secondly, the definition of bounded uncertainty is preceded by noting that:

> [A] world where there are constraints upon the ways in which events can follow each other, yet where even a complete and perfect knowledge of these constraints would leave us ignorant of 'what will happen next' ....[67]

Bounded uncertainty, then, is precisely this situation that a rational agent who has to make a decision faces.

Thirdly, decisions in the face of bounded uncertainty in Shackle's world are exactly as in Simon's world of boundedly rational agents (and institutions): they are *decision problems* in the precise sense of *metamathematics*.[68]

Finally, Shackle is remarkably perceptive in making it clear that the sequence space and the decision space are defined on a lattice, by 'saw-tooth-like' functions – i.e. the domain and range of economic variables are rational valued. However, his lack of mathematical expertise in dealing with such a space forces him to work with real variables and classical analysis:

> We can treat each of G ['face value; or pure desiredness-undesiredness] and
> y [the possibility] as a stepping-stone variable consisting of discrete values,
> so that these variables together form a lattice whose points will be expecta-
> tion elements as defined in the foregoing.[69]

I shall not need to fudge the issue by having to deal with illegitimate real analysis and shall retain the original assumption of discrete (in fact, rational) values for all relevant variables (again, as in Simon's world of boundedly rational agents).

The next step is to embed Shackle's agents within the behavioural, boundedly rational, satisficing agent solving decision problems. In my *Computable Foundations for Economics*[70] I have given a complete charac-, terisation of the dynamics implicit in Simon's boundedly rational, satisfying agent solving decision problems. In it I have also shown the equivalence between such an agent and a formal dynamical system capable of *computation universality*. Moreover, an equaivalence between such a dynamical system and a Turing Machine is also formally demonstrated. Invoking these results I can say that – formally – an institution can be represented by a system of coupled Turing Machines and an economy by a system of coupled institutions. They can be represented on a (to be sure a vast) lattice, as Shackle would have desired.

This is, formally again, no different from a vast table reflecting the balance sheet of an economy, except that the dynamics are not implicit, but (more than) explicit: it is possible to implement the lattice as a dynamical system and observe its evolution.

What was missing in my earlier Simonian constructions were the crucial elements considered by Shackle: the *boundedly uncertain, creative decision-maker* facing *incomplete* knowledge, giving rise to *potential surprise*. However, Simon, when considering *models of discovery*,[71] formalised as boundedly rational agents solving problems – i.e. as *human problem solvers*[72] – encapsulated the equivalent of Shackle-type considerations of both 'bounded uncertainty' and 'potential surprise' in his scheme. This is most clearly explicated in Kulkarni and Simon.[73] In *Computable Foundations for Economics*[74] I have formalised Simon's models of discovery, with boundedly rational agents, also as (coupled) Turing Machines.

Therefore, it is easy – again, formally speaking – to incorporate the Shackle elements within the mechanism that formalises the boundedly uncertain rational agent, satisficing in the solving of decision problems in which potential surprise is a possible element to which the computation universal dynamical system – or the Turing Machine in its computation path – must react, and proceed on its dynamic evolution.

Finally, it is easy to show that halting machines, for example finite automata, are those that correspond to agents, or a system of agents, forming an institution or a macroeconomy, depict a Minskyan economy in the hedge finance regime. Next, the pure speculative finance regime will be equivalent to finite automata or Turing Machines facing recursively enumerable sets of sequences of economic data to process that are also recursive. Finally, the case of an agent or a system of coupled agents in a mixed hedge–speculative finance regime would have to solve decision problems satisfactorily by processing sequences of economic data that are recursively enumerable but not recursive.

Concluding Reflections

> We do not know why a great speculative orgy occurred in 1928 and 1929. *The long accepted explanation that credit was easy and so people were impelled to borrow money to buy common stocks on margin is obviously nonsense.* On numerous occasions before and since credit has been easy, and there has been no speculation whatever.[75]

What has been suggested, in the constructive part of this paper, which means, essentially, the previous section, is that the agents who populate an economy, or the institutions in which they 'reside', or even the whole macro-economy, be viewed algorithmically. This was a natural implication of the Shackle–Simon vision I tried to suggest in the previous section, hopefully providing the missing link of 'Keynesian uncertainty' for Minsky-type modelling of credit-based capitalist dynamics. In the implied formalisation of the Shackle–Simon agent, institution or economy, there is the possibility of interpreting their algorithmic implementation as a dynamical system capable of what is called computation universality.

However, the natural algorithmic domain and range for the variables, parameters and constants are the constructive or computable numbers. This fact meshes comfortably with the other important fact that economic variables, parameters and constants are, at best, algebraic numbers, although in practice they are simply rational numbers. This means the dynamical system equivalent of a Turing Machine has to be a discrete dynamical system acting on rational numbers (or the natural numbers).

Even if such is possible – i.e. constructing a discrete dynamical system acting on rational numbers – the further requirement, for the kind of crisis theory Minsky seems to have had in mind, such a dynamical system must be capable of encapsulating three additional properties:

1. The dynamical system should possess a relatively simple global attractor.
2. It should be capable of meaningfully and measurably long – and extremely long – transients.
3. It should possess not just ordinary sensitivity dependence on initial conditions (SDIC) that characterise 'complex' dynamical systems that generate strange attractors. It should, in fact, possess super sensitive dependence on initial conditions (SSDIC). This means that the dynamical system *appears* to possess the property that distances between neighbouring trajectories diverge too fast to be encapsulated by even partial recursive functions.

Is it possible to construct such rational valued dynamical systems or, equivalently, algorithms that imply such dynamical systems?

The answer, mercifully, is yes. In a forthcoming article,[76] I have discussed how, for a Clower–Howitt 'Monetary Economy',[77] with rational valued, sawtooth-like monetary variables, it is possible to use the *Takagi function* to model its dynamics, while preserving its algorithmic nature. But in this case, it is necessary to work with computable – or recursive – analysis. It would be more desirable to remain within classical algorithmic formalisations and, hence, working with rational- or integer-valued dynamical systems that have a clear algorithmic underpinning.

It is a pleasure to end this paper of many speculations (sic!) with a positive conjecture: I believe Goodstein's algorithm[78] could be the paradigmatic example for modelling rational- or integer-valued dynamics[79] of a credit-based capitalist economy.

Even more satisfactorily, if we are to take the Minsky vision of the dynamics of credit-based capitalist economic dynamics seriously, and try to solve its policy dilemmas, then it seems to me that the best analogy – as pointed out in endnote 52 – is the policymaker as poor Hercules and the *hedge-speculative-Ponzi* being as Hydra.[80] In other words, every time Hercules slays one of the heads of the Hydra, two more sprout from the source of the slain one. Is this to be a Sisyphean task for the poor policymaker – or can she emulate Hercules and find the equivalent of Iolaus to conquer, once and for all, the seemingly eternal repetition of 'manias and panics' in credit-based capitalist economic dynamics?

Formally at least – and actually, of course, in Greek mythology – there is a solution to the problem of Hercules vs. Hydra, meaning by this there may well be a policy resolution to the eternal dilemma of recurrent manias and panics.[81]

But I shall end with a more down-to-earth tone, invoking the ever-wise and sobering reflections of John Kenneth Galbraith, from his masterly study of the Great Crash:

> [T]he collapse in the stock market in the autumn of 1929 was implicit in the speculation that went before. The only question concerning that speculation was how long it would last. Sometime, sooner or later, *confidence* in the short-run reality of increasing common stock values would weaken. When this happened, *some people* would sell, and *this would destroy the reality of increasing values*. Holding for an increase would now become meaningless; the new reality would be falling prices. There would be a rush, pell-mell, to unload. This was the way past speculative orgies had ended. It was the way the end came in 1929. It is the way speculation will end in the future.[82]

Amen!

Cycles, Crises and Uncertainty

Stephen Kinsella[1]

Introduction

In the 2008–10 period Ireland experienced a cumulative deflation – a fall in the general price level of goods and services – of around 7–8 per cent. The cost of living in Ireland has fallen at the fastest rate since the Great Depression. The appearance of a deflation during a period of unprecedented indebtedness by Irish households, firms, banks and the state is cause for concern.

The purpose of this chapter is to examine the likely effects on the recovery of the Irish economy from the interaction of an increased cost of debt, combined with a sustained but relatively mild domestic deflation of a country within a monetary union with a large and growing unemployed population. Ireland's macroeconomic situation is relatively unique, and deserves study for that reason. We first describe the evolution of Irish household, national and commercial debt levels, moving on to a description of a simple model of debt deflation that may help us understand the effects of over-weaning debt on small open economies, and close by considering the prospects for recovery of the Irish economy in the medium term, and suggest that one way to decrease uncertainty regarding Irish banks would be to introduce asset-based reserve requirements, which would mitigate the effects of another asset inflation, when one arises.

What Is the Nature of the Problem?

Ireland is one of the most indebted economies in the developed world. In 1995, the ratio of household debt to gross domestic product (GDP) stood at 48 per cent. In 2004, this figure had risen to 113 per cent, and it had grown to 176 per cent by 2009.[2] Total gross indebtedness by the state, the banks and the non-financial personal and corporate sector stood at €1,671 billion (€1.6 trillion) at the end of 2008,[3] more than doubling over a six-year period.[4]

Ireland is currently experiencing an 'ugly' type of deflation.[5] 'Ugly' deflations coincide with periods of steeply declining prices associated with severe recessions. By any standard, as previous chapters in this volume have outlined, Ireland's current economic downturn is severe. Figure 11.1 plots the deterioration in Ireland's GDP over the last six years, as well as conservative forecasts for a return to growth in 2011 and 2012.[6] The optimism Figure 11.1 shows in assuming a return to sluggish growth by the end of 2010 may be unfounded. Indeed, though a 'statistical' end to the recession may be in sight, a rebounding of domestic economic activity capable of absorbing the large numbers of newly unemployed may take considerably longer. Two external factors may also serve to dampen Ireland's recovery, and perhaps hasten the contraction of some domestic sectors of the economy.

Figure 11.1: Ireland's Real Gross Domestic Product, Actual and Predicted

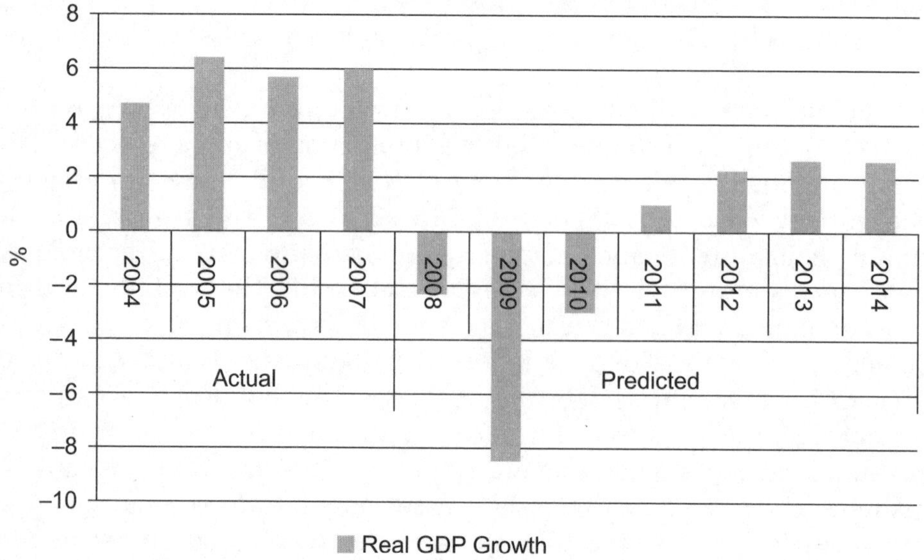

Source: IMF, 'Staff Report for the 2009 Article IV Consultation'.

First, our nearest neighbour, and significant trading partner, the United Kingdom (UK), is pursuing a policy of quantitative easing. In theory, quantitative easing is not 'printing money', but rather a creation of more funds on banks' balance sheets, which are used to buy private banks' assets and government bonds. Quantitative easing pumps money into a demand-deficient economy with the hope of increasing economic output. Quantitative easing also makes UK exports more competitive, and has the effect of reducing Ireland's export competitiveness. Almost 18 per cent of Ireland's exports went to the UK in 2008, and 33 per cent of Ireland's imports came from the UK.[7]

Second, our European Union (EU) membership, and mandated (long-term) adherence to the EU's Stability and Growth Pact, together with the lack of an independent monetary policy, constrains our wages and price levels to fall, and fall quickly, while on the fiscal front the government must rein in expenditure to cope with a much reduced tax take and resultant budget deficits. All adjustments must take place through the wage and credit channels in the absence of an independent monetary policy, which makes Ireland's current experience unique among developed countries. The Irish government and its people, over the year 2009, accepted the need for a reduction in wages and price reductions, and a fiscal contraction.

Once one accepts the need for fiscal contraction, solutions are simple but difficult and contentious to execute: reduce public service provision and public sector pay; reduce social welfare payments and government transfers of many kinds; increase the tax take by increasing taxes and broadening the tax base; and bring about fiscal balance in a short space of time, with a credible commitment to maintaining that fiscal balance going forward. As a result of this policy mix, wages and disposable income for households will, perforce, fall, and with them will fall the price level. Debt levels, however, will remain, and in the presence of deflation, the real cost of debt repayment will rise.

Debt Deflation Theory

Debt deflation occurs when a fall in the price level raises the real value of nominal debt.[8] This phenomenon can exacerbate the costs of deflation: households that find themselves heavily in debt do not continue to consume more at the margin, but rather refrain from investing and consuming out of discretionary income in order to pay down loans more quickly. Domestic consumption and non-autonomous investment in productive capacity, as well as import and export demand, all suffer. The economy contracts as a result of the de-leveraging activities of firms and households, which further deepens the crisis. Combined with increases in government expenditure from automatic stabilising mechanisms like social welfare payments, the increase in debt-servicing costs can be punitive for small open economies like Ireland, unable to stimulate their economies in a textbook Keynesian (or new-Keynesian) manner.

Tobin describes the problem in stark terms:

> When nominal prices and wages are deflated, debt service is a higher proportion of debtors' incomes, and the reduction or elimination of their margins of equity disqualifies them from further access to credit. Bankruptcies and defaults do likewise, and transmit the distress of debtors to their creditors, threatening the solvency and liquidity of individual lenders and financial institutions.[9]

The issue of stability arises because the relationship runs both ways: deflation causes financial distress, and financial distress in turn exacerbates deflation. Negative aggregate price shocks had a significantly negative impact on financial conditions during the Great Depression.

The link from financial distress to deflation (and back again) takes place through several channels. Different authors have, naturally, focused on different channels.

Fisher,[10] who originated the modern theory of debt deflation, argued that borrowers attempting to reduce their burden of debt engage in *distress selling*, where owners sell equity in a hurry, without regard to the equity's underlying value, to raise money for repaying debt. But repayment in aggregate causes a contraction in the money supply, and price level deflation. Fisher's finding was echoed by Kindleberger,[11] who expanded Fisher's analysis to other crises in economic history. Keynes[12] argued that a downward spiral of prices (and especially nominal wages) in an economy suffering from substantial unemployment would increase the real interest rate and the burden of servicing debts, and would discourage businesses from beginning new investments, making the liquidity constraint facing the economy worse.[13] Keynes held that nominal wage cuts could not bring about a fall in the real wage, because nominal wages are a large part of the costs of production. As nominal wages fall in the economy, all producers find their costs lowered, and competition will force them to lower the prices of goods and services bought by workers in proportion. This movement keeps the real wage constant, and leaves the economy with involuntary unemployment. A downward spiral of money wages and money prices is the last thing an economy suffering from substantial unemployment needs.

A modern Keynesian story for a small open economy like Ireland in a highly globalised international financial system runs like this: Periods of persistent consumption growth can foster investment booms and output expansion, which in turn reinforces optimistic outlooks for permanent income and further stimulate consumption demand. So a mild consumption expansion triggered by optimism may turn into prolonged periods of over-expansion and, via a simple multiplier–accelerator process, the economy becomes destabilised. When borrowers have strong incentives to accumulate assets and lenders are willing to supply credit elastically, endogenous boom–bust cycles can emerge, and such cycles result in excessive investment and over-accumulation of capital during the boom and under-investment in the slump.[14]

Minsky elaborated and extended Fisher's original concept to incorporate deflation in the asset market.[15] Minsky recognised that distress selling reduces asset prices, causing losses to agents with maturing debts and, importantly, to highly leveraged agents with new debts. This reinforces distress selling, and reduces consumption and investment spending, which deepens deflation. Bernanke argued that debt deflation involves widespread bankruptcy, impairing the process of credit intermediation.[16] The resulting credit contraction depresses aggregate demand, thus exacerbating the crisis.

Woodford has argued that macroeconomic outcomes are largely independent of the performance of the financial system, and, in a bubble, simple wage-cost deflation towards trend is in fact desirable.[17] This projection is borne out in Irish policymaking and policy advice in 2009.[18] Von Peter has emphasised the need for a removal of equilibrium constraints in modelling the current crisis.[19]

For an economy with an independent monetary policy, unlike Ireland, the standard policy prescription is for the central bank to credibly commit to being expansionary for a considerable period of time, by keeping interest rates near zero even after the economy has emerged from deflation.[20] The notion of unstable debt deflation ultimately relies on reasons why agents try to contain or reduce their indebtedness. Margin requirements can be one such reason. A credit crunch, which interferes with the accommodation necessary for stability, can be another.[21]

The 'modern' debt deflation process therefore encompasses falling asset prices, debt repayment difficulties, a reluctance to lend, a financial crisis, the impact on the banks and the inter-dependency of the financial system. Recent debt deflations have been aborted by lender-of-last-resort intervention and government support of the financial system during a crisis.

There is a limit to the amount of 'first pass deflation' Ireland can experience, because it is part of the Eurozone. 'First pass' deflation is a repeated fall in the general price level, as the United States (US) experienced during the Great Depression. Ireland is a member of a currency union. Because Ireland's currency is not fluctuating at the same time as our price level, there is a natural limit to national level deflation, even though the correction prices must take to reach EU averages of inflation may take several years. So long as the European Central Bank (ECB) avoids deflation at the Eurozone level, a 'first pass' deflationary spiral for Ireland in the Fisherian sense is impossible. Many commentators have compared Ireland to Japan because of its high debt levels and falling price levels. Surface comparisons between the two countries are not appropriate. Japanese-style deflation is not possible for an individual member of a monetary union. Declines in the price level are ultimately self-correcting through a competitiveness gain from the cumulative real depreciation in the price level.

However, the secondary and tertiary effects of overarching debt on credit provision, residential and commercial deleveraging, and domestic consumption as a result of this deflation – 'second pass' deflation – can have knock-on and feedback effects through other channels, which may destabilise the economy further. This type of lingering deflation, which robs the economy of the momentum required to escape recession, is certainly possible. Ireland's price level, tied as it is to the EU average, requires that the contraction in economic activity takes place through the wage and asset price channels, with corresponding contractions in domestic consumption. Wage-led deflation can only be 'self-correcting' in the sense that after a bubble bursts, wages and prices return to trend. Growth requires that the competitiveness effect from the wage–price reduction must outweigh the real interest rate/increased real debt effects. This relationship may not necessarily hold, given the levels of Ireland's indebtedness

Effects of Deflation during a Crisis on Households, Firms and the Macroeconomy

Analogies abound between the current international downturn and the Great Depression of the 1930s. Deflation was a serious threat during the Great Depression. DeLong writes that 'almost every analyst placed general deflation, and the bankruptcies it caused, at or near the heart of the worst macroeconomic disaster the world had ever seen'.[22]

One reason a prolonged deflation might be considered a macroeconomic disaster is because deflation increases the real value of debt. With a deflation of 7 per cent, say, a one-year loan of €100 today will cost €107 when it is repaid, plus whatever interest is levied on the principal.[23]

On the debit side of the balance sheet, deflation decreases the purchasing power of the debtor at a time when the economy requires increased levels of consumption and investment, which deepens the downturn and exacerbates the crisis. The two depressions of the last 150 years – in the 1890s and the 1930s – had substantial deflations. Prices fell at a rate of up to 15 per cent per annum in the 1890s in the United States. Prices fell over 10 per cent per annum for two years during the Great Depression.[24] In a deflation, even a relatively low nominal rate of interest becomes a larger real interest rate, forcing a contraction in economic activity. In Ireland in 2010, real interest rates are around 9–10 per cent for a business loan. To place that figure in context, in 1986, at the height of Ireland's last economic crisis, a business loan was 10–14 per cent in real terms.

On the credit side, deflation increases the value of creditors' assets. However, with a large percentage of Irish firms and households over-indebted – unable to service their debts and meet recurring expenses – the increase in uncertainty associated with an increased likelihood of large-scale default (and consequent bad debt write down by public and private banks) outweighs the potential increase in creditors' funds from the deflation.

A higher level of debt finance imposes obligatory interest and principal repayments on firms[25] and households. High personal debt also inhibits the formation of new businesses and the expansion of existing small enterprises, since the balance sheet of owners is an important determinant of the ability of a firm to obtain credit. A common defensive reaction of firms that have suffered an adverse income shock is to reduce discretionary expenses, for example investment, employment, wages and/or dividend payments. A highly indebted set of firms can more easily fail or go into liquidation under the weight of debt service costs that cannot be met out of current income or cash reserves, increasing unemployment.

At the macro level, modern monetary systems require relatively stable price levels. Financial institutions and contracts are based on the prescription of reasonable price level stability.[26] They cannot operate efficiently with large price changes. Unexpected changes in price levels change the terms of contracts, since fully price-contingent contracts are too complicated to design. Price flexibility of the kind demanded by some commentators would damage the basic contracting structure of the economy.[27] In terms of fiscal policy, the failure to foresee the 2008 and 2009 falls in prices meant that the inflation rates underlying the Budgets for 2009 were much too high, leading to a divergence between government expenditure and receipts. The lack of competitiveness of the economy, and the consequent increase in uncertainty arising from the fact that there could be a further deflationary surprise next year, needs to be kept in mind when formulating fiscal policy for 2011 and 2012.

Where Did the Debt Come From?

The property sector accounted for much of the borrowing that took place in Ireland since 1999.[28] Irish borrowing on mortgages in 2002 stood at 34 per cent of GDP, and by 2007 it stood at 75.3 per cent, an increase of 121 per cent. Table 11.1 shows wide disparities internationally when mortgage debt is computed as a percentage of GDP. In terms of percentage increases, Ireland's steep ramp-up of mortgage debt in such a short space of time underscores the inflationary effects of an asset price bubble, but these figures do little to inform us of the distributional effects of the bursting of the bubble.

Due care must be taken when interpreting these figures. First, because they are aggregated, these figures are not very useful for informing us about median debt burden. Second, these data do not tell us the fraction of households close to financial distress – the over-indebted households, those most likely to default on loans. The size of the potential bad debt pool these households represent is one source of the uncertainty which we discuss below. Data on these households are not available at the time of writing. Third, Irish households both saved from income and borrowed through the banking system to acquire assets in Ireland and abroad now worth substantially less than when bought.

There is, of course, another side to the balance sheet. In the case of mortgage debt, the asset secured on the loan is usually a property. In addition to a deterioration in credit availability, the decline in the net worth of these properties due to an oversupply of comparable assets, and a collapse in investor and consumer confidence in these assets as recorded in the Economic and Social Research Institute (ESRI) consumer confidence measures shown in Figure 11.2, means the economy as a whole must support a smaller national balance sheet, all with the expectation of that balance sheet shrinking further. This deleveraging is evident in Ireland's balance of payments deterioration since 2007, and in the decline of money and credit aggregates. While nominal savings did not decrease in Ireland over the 2000–09 period, the extent of the over borrowing on now-devalued property implies that, in real terms, little saving has taken place. The Irish

Table 11.1: Mortgage Debt–GDP Ratios in Percentages for Selected EU Countries, 2002–07

	2002	2003	2004	2005	2006	2007
Austria	16.3	17.6	20.4	22	23.6	24.1
Belgium	23.8	26.1	27.8	31.7	34.2	36.8
Bulgaria	0.7	1.2	2.6	4.7	—	9.9
Cyprus	7.9	10	12	16	0	44.8
Czech Republic	4.4	5.9	7.8	9.7	12	15.3
Denmark	82.2	81	85.4	92.1	98.1	92.8
France	22.5	24.1	26	28.8	32.9	34.9
Finland	21.5	24.7	27.3	30.9	32.4	34.3
Germany	43	43.4	43	42.9	42.3	47.7
Greece	14.7	16.9	19.6	23.7	26.8	30.2
Hungary	0	7.7	9.4	10.2	11.9	12.4
Iceland	88	86.3	88.8	102.1	—	121
Ireland	**34**	**39.6**	**50**	**58.8**	**63.4**	**75.3**
Italy	10.2	11.6	15.3	15.3	16.6	19.8
Latvia	0	7.3	11.8	19.3	28.9	33.7
Luxembourg	29.3	32.4	34.6	36	36.4	38.5
Malta	19.7	23.9	27.5	31.7	34.8	37.6
Netherlands	60.8	63.4	67.7	72.9	72.6	100
Norway	48	52.5	54.1	55.1	53.4	53.3
Poland	3.4	4.5	4.3	5.4	7.5	11.7
Portugal	48	48	49.3	5.4	59.2	62.1
Slovakia	3.9	4.8	6.7	1.8	10.4	11.9
Slovenia	0.8	1.1	3.1	8.2	6.6	8
Spain	32.4	35.5	40	49.5	56.1	61.6
Sweden	31.4	31.2	34.8	37.3	41.3	57
Switzerland	0	112.6	115.5	119	132.3	131
UK	63.9	69.3	73.9	78.2	82.8	86.3

Sources: European Mortgage Federation, European Central Bank, Swiss National Bank, International Monetary Fund, Eurostat, Bank of England.

economy would seem to be poorly placed to de-leverage without a run of defaults.

With all caveats in place, however, it is clear that Ireland's mortgage debt build-up in this period is substantial, putting Ireland in the same class as Switzerland, Denmark and Iceland in terms of debt roll-up, and the highest in the group studied in terms of percentage change over the five-year period.

In addition to the build-up of debt, of which mortgage debt was only one part, Ireland experienced an increase in inflation followed by a steep turnaround in that inflation in late 2008 and 2009. The EU harmonised index of consumer prices (HICP) does not take mortgage interest into account, and so is a better measure of the across-the-board deflation taking place in the Irish economy, subtracting the contraction in sectors of the economy dependent on construction. The Central Statistics Office (CSO) national consumer price index shows the deflation running at 6.9 per cent in the year to October 2009. Figure 11.2 plots the drop in the price level (on the right-hand axis) against the increase in mortgage debt as a percentage of GDP and the ESRI index of consumer expectations, which also suffered a drop over the 2007–09 period. Other measures of consumer and investor confidence show the same broad trends.

Figure 11.2: Consumer Sentiment and Mortgage Debt, 2001–09

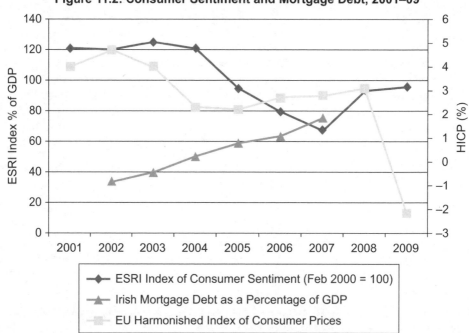

Sources: Economic and Social Research Institute, European Mortgage Federation, European Central Bank, Swiss National Bank, International Monetary Fund, Eurostat, Bank of England, Eurostat.

Does a Debt Deflation Story Fit Ireland?

Minsky's financial instability hypothesis argues that a capitalist economy with sophisticated financial institutions could fall into a depression, as an excessive build-up of private debt occurs over a number of financially driven business cycles. The key Minskyian insight is that decision-making units are constrained by their inherited financial positions.[29] There are five stages in Minsky's model of the credit cycle: displacement, boom, euphoria, profit-taking and panic. A displacement occurs when investors get excited about an event – an invention, such as the internet, or a war, or an abrupt change of economic policy – something which favours an upswing in investment. The current cycle can be dated from 2002, with the decision of US monetary authorities to reduce short-term interest rates to 1 per cent, and an unexpected influx of foreign money, particularly Chinese money, into US Treasury bonds. With the cost of borrowing, and mortgage rates, in particular, at historic lows, a speculative real estate boom quickly developed, which was much bigger, in terms of overall valuation, than the previous bubble in technology stocks which had burst in 2000. Ireland was caught in the same perfect storm of cheap credit, buoyant domestic demand for new housing, an increasing population (many brought to Ireland by the promise of building these houses), rising real wages and property price appreciation. Displacement, boom and euphoria can be dated from 2003 to 2007.

As a boom leads to euphoria, banks and other commercial lenders extend credit to ever more dubious borrowers, often creating new financial instruments to do the job. During the 1980s, junk bonds played that role. More recently, it was the securitisation of mortgages, which enabled banks to provide home loans and create unsecured debt instruments. At the top of the market (in this case, mid-2006), some smart traders started to cash in their profits, but most rolled any gains made back into the markets in the expectation of making more profits in the next cycle.

The onset of panic is usually heralded by a dramatic change, as we can see from monthly figures released by the Central Bank of Ireland in December 2008: the percentage of private credit on issue in Ireland from 2005 to 2008 had fallen from a growth rate of 30 per cent in 2005 to a rate of 3 per cent by the end of 2008. Relative to the peak of the housing bubble, mortgage lending has practically disappeared, and new house starts are at a fifteen-year low.

There are several routes to a deflation, and several types of deflation. In Ireland's case, our exchange rate is fixed. The sticky nominal variable that explains how changes in the real economy are translating into downward pressure on prices is the nominal exchange rate. Changes in the economy's external environment mandate a depreciated real exchange rate, which can only occur through a reduction in the price level and via nominal wage reductions.

Ireland has had several deflationary experiences since independence. An examination of Ireland's 1952 Budget shows it contributed to a deflation in an already depressed economy,[30] and in fact Ireland experienced a deflation in 1958. Within the macroeconomic slump of the early 1950s, the Budget reduced domestic demand severely by discouraging investment in industry and manufacturing and inhibiting export development. Similarly, the fiscal correction of the mid- to late 1980s was also mildly deflationary in the public sector as the economy deleveraged from a debt–GDP ratio of 183 per cent in 1988 to a debt–GDP ratio of 145 per cent in 1994.[31]

A Minsky Story for Ireland

The algebraic core of Minsky's theory was extracted by Taylor and O'Connell[32] and built upon by Palley,[33] and Minsky's insights are now gaining currency in economic thought with the work of Fostel and Geanakoplos.[34] The dynamics implied by Minsky's description of each 'type' of decision-making unit at different points in the credit cycle described above can be easily modelled (see Figure 11.3).

Minsky distinguishes between 'hedge' and 'non-hedge' financial units. Hedge units are further subdivided into 'speculative' and 'Ponzi'.[35] Hedge financial units are characterised by realised financial outflows not exceeding realised financial inflows, and therefore do not have liquidity problems in the current period; they expect that this will also happen in each of the future periods within the decision time horizon.

Speculative and Ponzi financial units, on the other hand, have problems of liquidity in the current period, as their financial outflows exceed their financial inflows. Speculative financial units expect that these liquidity problems will characterise only the early periods of their decision time horizon, while they expect a surplus of inflows in subsequent periods, assuring their solvency.

Ponzi decision units expect instead that their liquidity problems will last longer, so that only a huge expected surplus in the final period of their time horizon will ensure, at some point, their solvency. The Ponzi units are also characterised by a second criterion: while the speculative units expect to be always able to pay the interest due, this is not true of Ponzi units, which have a much more urgent need to rollover their debt.

Let L_{it} be an index of liquidity measurement for one economic unit i at time t. We can think of 'economic units' here as households, banks or governments, in that all that is required is a capacity for consumption and debt, and an expectation over future periods. Liquidity at any t is the difference between unit i's inflows, In_{it}, and outflows, OUT_{it}. Let L_{it}^* be the expected solvency of unit i between point t and a later point $t + m$. The funding ratio at any moment is given by $L_{it} = IN_{it}/OUT_{it}$.

Long-term financial sustainability requires that $L_{it}^* < 1$. Assume a liquidity threshold, μ, which each unit holds. μ is a maximum value of the solvency ratio sufficiently lower than 1 for the unit to continue operating, and we can consider μ set by a central bank or regulatory authority, analogous to a reserve ratio in more traditional models.

Figure 11.3: Minsky Regimes

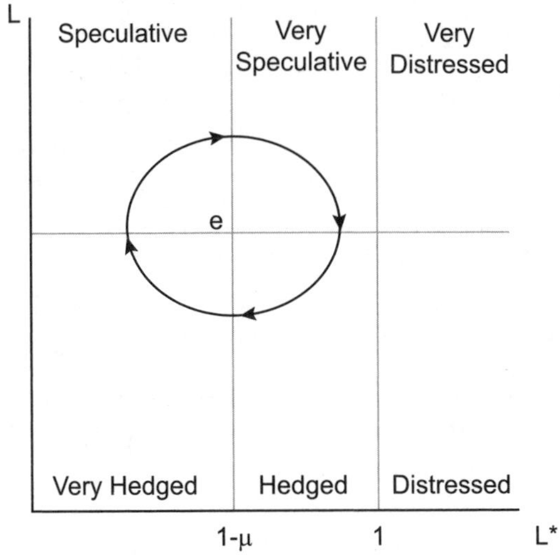

As soon as a unit perceives itself to be beyond the safety margin $1 - \mu_i$, it reacts by reducing its current illiquidity margin $1 - L_{it}$ with a resulting decrease of L_{it}^*. Whenever a unit is within the safe zone $L_{it}^* < 1 - \mu_i$, the unit is pushed by competition to increase the financial outflows more than its inflows, and thus its L_{it}, in order to increase utility or returns. An increase of L_{it} beyond the liquidity line (where $L_{it} > 1$), in principle, deteriorates L_{it}^*, by increasing debt while worsening expectations, and vice versa. The feedback between L_{it} and L_{it}^* may be represented by a very simple continuous-time model of the form:

$$\dot{L}_{it}/L_{it} = -\alpha_i[L_{it}^* - (1 - \mu_i)] \tag{1}$$

and

$$\dot{L}_{it}^*/L_{it}^* = \beta_i(k_{it} - 1) \tag{2}$$

Here α and β are simple speeds of adjustment of each economic unit over time. This Lotka-Voltera structure is well studied,[36] and its equilibrium, e_i, represents the difference between the flows of IN_{it} and OUT_{it} to induce a shock and perturb each agent at a particular time. We can think about financial fragility as the smallest shock to IN_{it} and/or OUT_{it} that produces insolvency.

We can see the effects of Minsky's cycle theory by examining Irish banks' leverage ratios. The loan-to-deposit ratio is the value of a financial institution's loans in comparison with the level of customer deposits. The International Monetary Fund (IMF) suggests that a loan-to-deposit ratio of less than 100 per cent is optimal for financial institutions. A ratio of 100 per cent or more suggests the bank is dependent on the wholesale credit market to preserve liquidity. On average, EU banks in 2009 have had loan-to-deposit ratios of over 120 per cent, while the top 1,000 international banks had an average of 104 per cent. For Ireland's largest banks, leverage ratios were above 200 per cent. Finally, Figure 11.4 shows the ratio of total assets to shareholder equity of Ireland's four main banks. On average, US banks have a ratio of around 20:1, while the European average is around 35:1.

Figure 11.4: Irish Banking Institutions' Leverage (Total Assets/Shareholder Equity)

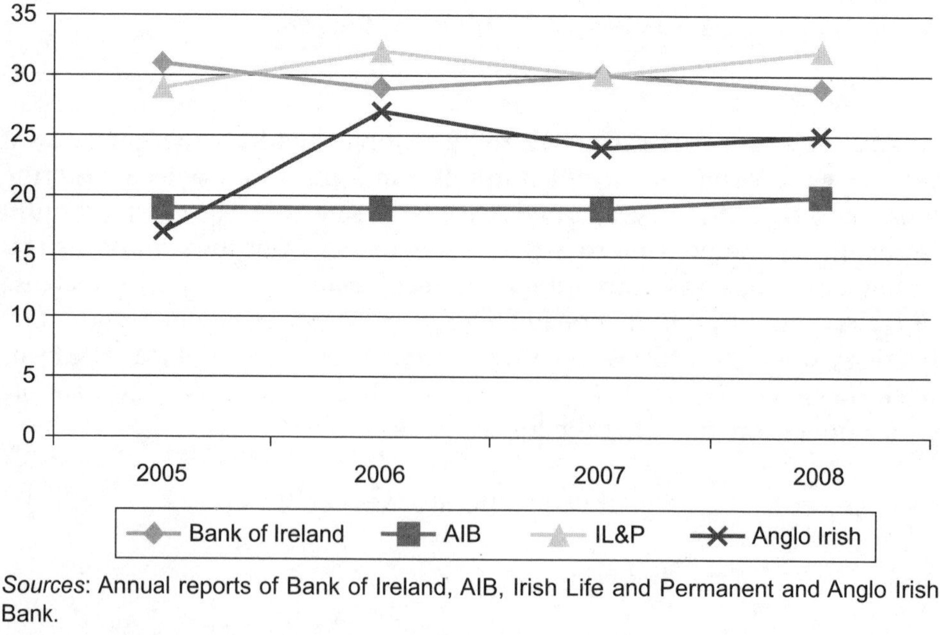

Sources: Annual reports of Bank of Ireland, AIB, Irish Life and Permanent and Anglo Irish Bank.

Figure 11.4 shows that Ireland's banks are in the upper tail of the EU average. Highly leveraged financial institutions can experience large profits during an upswing, but clearly market downturns can render them insolvent and requiring injections of capital to cover actual and expected losses. Clearly, Ireland's banks have moved from the very speculative to distressed quadrants of Figure 11.3, with a balance-sheet clean-out from the National Asset Management Agency (NAMA) following a government guarantee required to keep Ireland's banks solvent.

We have argued that Ireland does in fact fit a debt deflation story that may hinder a return to robust growth, not via the Fisherian debt deflation, but rather through a second-pass deflation that hampers credit growth through distressed lending agencies, with the resultant restriction on the level of lending into the real economy.

Conclusion: Imagining a Way Forward – Reduce Uncertainty

Despite the presence of 'second pass' debt deflation, the problem remains: how do we tame an asset price bubble within a monetary union? Is there a way forward to curb the excesses of the next credit bubble for small open economies?

One solution is asset-based reserve requirements.[37] We assume the generation of finance is relatively endogenous, leading to the types of instability described by Minsky and others. The existence of this instability means the balance sheets of large banks require regulation. An asset-based reserve requirement has several distinct features to increase the level of regulation and to encourage better risk management among for-profit banks. Asset-based reserve requirements have the following features:

- Financial institutions are mandated to hold reserves against all assets, but some categories can get zero-rated.
- Asset requirement ratios are set by the European Central Bank.
- Asset requirements hold across all financial institutions in the EU.

There are several advantages of an asset-based reserve requirement system. The reserve measure is not liability-based, as traditional (and current) measures are. In traditional reserve requirements, the composition of liabilities determines the level of required holdings. Risk-based, and debt equity, measures are similarly liability-based,[38] where the level of debt held determines the minimum level of equity holding. The asset-based reserve requirement alternative instead focuses on asset regulation, with the composition of assets determining the reserve holdings of individual economic units. Each bank would be required to hold liabilities of their central bank as reserves also. Having the reserve requirement vary by asset category allows a monetary authority to change the relative costs of holding different assets by changing reserve requirements[39] – this can be achieved without recourse to interest rate changes, leaving the interest rate free to combat inflation. In principle the monetary authority gains $n - 1$ policy instruments, where n is the number of asset classes.

Asset-based reserve requirements can be used as an alternative to tax breaks to secure socially beneficial investments. For example, the monetary authority can lower the reserve requirement for community development loans relative to other comparable asset classes, and direct flows of funds to these assets by increasing their relative return.

Asset-based reserve requirements have good countercyclical properties. One of the ongoing issues within Irish fiscal policy is the pro-cyclicality of Ireland's fiscal mix.[40] Under an asset-based regime, when asset prices and bank lending increase during booms, this increases the demand for reserves, automatically engaging monetary tightening. The converse applies when asset prices (and lending) fall during a slump: reserves get released and so contribute to monetary expansion. This automatic stabiliser is a balance-sheet property, which is important, because most credit booms are in fact expansions of balance-sheet activities. Asset-based reserve requirements can also give seigniorage to the monetary authority by increasing demand for liabilities from the central bank, and, crucially, can be implemented by a national central bank under the supervision of the European Central Bank.

Finally, when balance sheets of national central banks and by extension private banks are constrained by asset reserve requirements, Ponzi finance becomes much harder to achieve with traditional financial products. Of course new financial 'innovations' may be introduced, but an effective regulatory regime would be best placed to reduce the likely impact of a suite of highly risky new financial products. The reduction in uncertainty such requirements would bring would more than compensate for potentially reduced profits as a result of these measures being introduced.

The corresponding reduction in uncertainty would imply an easing of credit into the real economy, even in the presence of substantial deleveraging by Ireland's banks.

12

Demography and Irish Economic Growth: Past and Future[1]

Brendan Walsh

Introduction

Ireland has long been a demographic outlier. In the decades after the end of the Napoleonic Wars in the early nineteenth century, its spurt of rapid population growth – on the back of a very shaky economy – attracted attention, while the collapse of the population after the mid-1840s due to the ravages of famine, leading to excess mortality and emigration, singled the country out from even the poorest regions of continental Europe.

The population of the twenty-six counties that now form the Republic of Ireland fell below three million in the 1930s from a peak of over six and a half million in the 1840s. Population growth did not resume until the 1960s, and then only at a very modest pace. But the country was once again exceptional in the high rate of population growth recorded during the boom years of the Celtic Tiger. In the first eight years of the twentieth-first century the population grew at an annual average rate of just short of 2 per cent. This was not only the highest among the Organisation for Economic Coopera- tion and Development (OECD) countries, but also exceeded the rates recorded in the fastest growing regions of the United States and Europe. By 2004 the four million mark was passed and the estimated population in 2009 (4.5 million) is above the level recorded in the census of 1861. However, the economic crisis that began in 2007 is likely to herald a new phase in Ireland's population history in which exceptional demographic expansion is replaced by more modest growth or perhaps even a return to population decline.

This chapter explores the relationship between Ireland's demographic and economic development, first from a historical perspective and then with a focus on the likely impact of demographic factors on the country's economic recovery.

Ireland's Demographic Exceptionalism

For the best part of the past two centuries, Ireland has been exceptional by European and perhaps even world standards on most demographic dimensions. Most basically, the Republic of Ireland is the only sizeable country or region whose population today is significantly lower than it was towards the middle of the nineteenth century.[2] Ireland as a whole, but especially the twenty-six counties that subsequently became the Republic, partook to a minimal extent in the great surge in urbanisation and industrialisation that characterised the nineteenth century in most European and New World countries. Figure 12.1 shows the population of Ireland since 1841. This demonstrates how Ireland's population declined between 1841 and 1891 and again during periods of the twentieth century. Figure 12.2 shows the annual average rate of population growth in the Republic since the foundation of the new state in 1921. This highlights another unusual feature of independent Ireland's demographic history, namely an exceptionally volatile rate of population change, which varied from +1.9 per cent a year in 2001–06 to -0.7 per cent a year in 1956–61.

These wide fluctuations in the rate of population change were accompanied by a very significant regional redistribution. The nineteenth century demographic collapse was due above all else to the weakness of the rural economy and the failure of an urban–industrial economy to develop, which meant that the urbanisation of the Irish population occurred mainly in British and American cities. While the urban population of Europe and the New World was growing at breakneck speed, the urban population of Ireland declined by 15 per cent between 1841 and 1891. Urbanisation proceeded faster after independence. Between 1926 and 1971 the urban population rose from 943,000 to 1.6 million, while the population of the Dublin metropolitan area increased by 86 per cent. Yet, despite the massive exodus of people from the rural areas, it was not until the 1970s that the urban population overtook the rural.[3]

The exceptionalism was also evident in other demographic dimensions – a relatively high death rate well into the twentieth century, while high

Figure 12.1: Population of the Republic of Ireland, 1841–2006

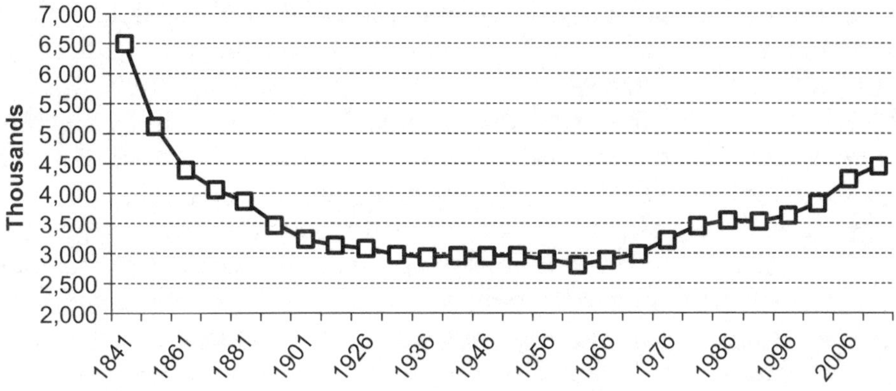

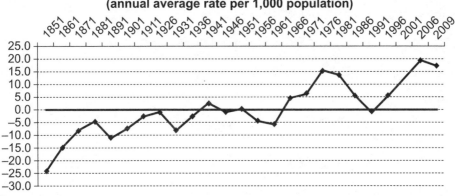

Source: CSO data.

marital fertility remained high long after the transition to small families in most of Europe. Moreover, the 'prudential check' of a low marriage rate played an unusually important role in dampening the impact of large families on the birth rate.

**Figure 12.2: Population Growth, 1851–2009
(annual average rate per 1,000 population)**

Source: CSO data.

Demographic–Economic Interactions

Of the two components of demographic change in Ireland – natural increase and net migration – the latter has tended to receive more attention. But we can see (Figure 12.3) that Ireland's rate of natural increase (the excess of births over deaths) displayed significant variation from the middle of the nineteenth century to recent times. The gradualness of the fall in the birth rate and the persistence of relatively high mortality held the rate of natural increase in check at about 0.5 per cent of the population until the middle of the twentieth century. But the combination of improving mortality rates and a modest baby boom after the Second World War led to a significant rise in this rate, which had reached 1 per cent of the population by the 1960s. Then there was a further rise in the 1970s as the traditional Irish reluctance to marry gave way to more normal European patterns, but marital fertility remained high, with the result that the birth rate rose markedly. By the late 1970s the Irish rate of natural increase had reached 1.2 per cent at a time when in many of the larger European countries the death rate was rising and the birth rate falling to the point where the rate of natural increase was close to zero. But despite these not-insignificant variations in the rate of natural increase, the main source of variation in the rate of population growth was the net migration rate (Figure 12.4). A comparison of fluctuations in the rates of natural increase and net migration clearly reveals the greater impact of the latter on the rate of population growth (see Figures 12.5a and 12.5b). Thus, the exceptional variability of Ireland's population growth over the decades since the Great Famine was mainly due to the impact of the net migration rate and its variability over time.[4] The correlation between the net migration rate and rate of population growth over the years 1871–2007 is +0.97, whereas the correlation between the rate of natural increase and population growth is only +0.48.

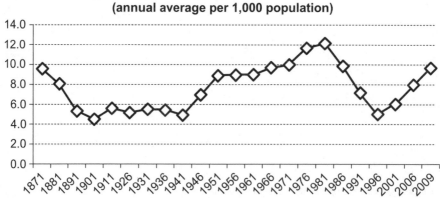

**Figure 12.3: Rate of Natural Increase, 1871–2009
(annual average per 1,000 population)**

Source: CSO data.

Ireland's belated transition to lower fertility during the 1980s was rapid. The total period fertility rate[5] fell from 3.23 in 1980 to a low of 1.85 in 1995. Although this was still somewhat above the European average, the rapid fall in fertility marked the end of Ireland's long-standing exceptionalism in

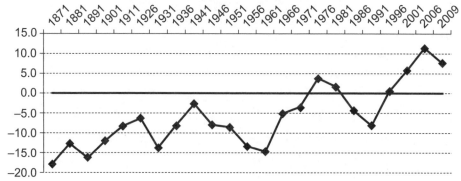

Figure 12.4: Net Migration Rate, 1871–2009
(annual average per 1,000 population)

Source: CSO data.

terms of family size. The fall in fertility more than offset continued improve-ments in mortality over these years, with the result that the rate of natural increase fell from 1.2 per cent in 1981 to 0.5 per cent in 1996.

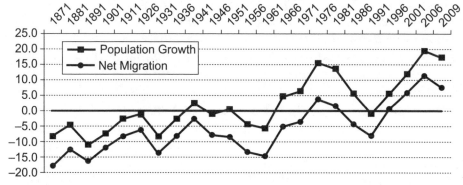

Figure 12.5a: Population Growth and Net Migration, 1871–2009
(annual average rates per 1,000 population)

Source: CSO data.

The Demography of the Celtic Tiger

When the unemployment rate (lagged three quarters to allow for the time difference between conception and birth) is plotted against the number of births registered, there is an uncannily close correlation between the onset of the prolonged economic crisis of the 1980s and the plunge in fertility. Whether it is reasonable to infer from the close correlation between the two-series causality, running from higher unemployment to lower fertility, is an open question, but the coincidence in the turning points in the series

Figure 12.5b: Population Growth and Natural Increase, 1871–2009 (annual average rates per 1,000 population)

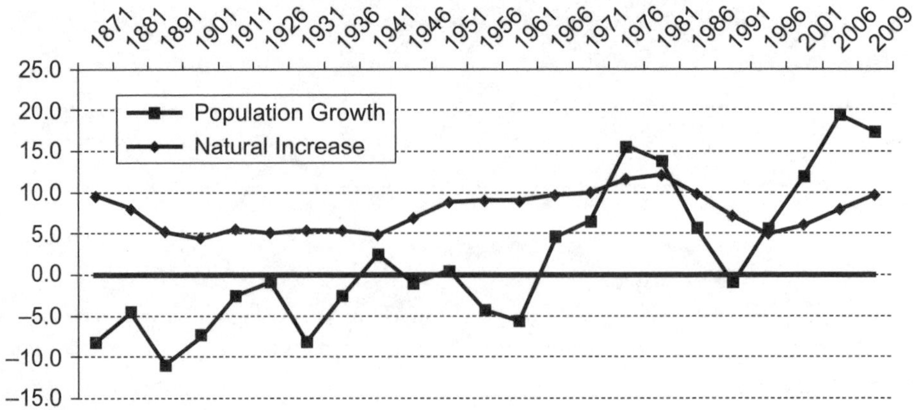

Source: CSO data.

is striking. If, in fact, the economic crisis of the 1980s triggered Ireland's sudden fertility decline, we should regard the birth rate, and hence the rate of natural increase, as endogenously determined by economic forces in the third quarter of the twentieth century.

This interpretation is rather different to the hypothesis advanced by Bloom and Canning,[6] who believe that the dramatic fall in Irish fertility after the 1980s is evidence that the link runs from population change to economic growth. Using cross-country estimates, they claim that fertility decline is a powerful determinant of income growth, operating mainly via the beneficial effects of changes in the population's age structure. They use Ireland as a case study, suggesting that the legalisation of contraception in 1980 resulted in a sharp decline in fertility and a sizeable increase in the share of the working-age population in the total population. They even claim that 'this demographic shift, operating in conjunction with a favourable policy environment, can explain in large measure the birth of the Celtic Tiger.'[7]

Whatever about the possible role of the fall in the fertility rate, and the resultant lessening of the burden of child dependency, in triggering the Celtic Tiger, there was a surprising reversal of these developments as the boom intensified during the first decade of the twenty-first century. The Irish fertility rate rose sharply from the low point reached in the mid-1990s and, by 2007, the total period fertility rate was once again above 2.0 – among the highest in the OECD. Just as the collapse of the labour market in the early 1980s appears to have triggered the transition to lower fertility, there seems to have been feedback from the economic boom to demographic behaviour in the early twenty-first century. A newly prosperous Ireland enjoyed some of its increased wealth in the form of a modest baby boom.

While the potential impact of natural increase on population growth has not been trivial, in the absence of economic growth it had little actual impact on the subsequent rate of population growth. This was most clearly seen in the 1980s, when what was frequently referred to as our 'young and rapidly growing population' – a consequence of the rapid rise in the birth rate in the 1970s – was used by some commentators and politicians to account for the upsurge in unemployment and, eventually, emigration. Until the period of rapid employment growth in the second half of the 1990s, much of the population growth that was recorded was confined to the population aged under sixteen years and other non-employed categories.

In view of the obvious and readily understood link between net migration and Ireland's rate of population growth, and between the performance of the economy and the rate of net migration, it is surprising to note how, during the heady years of the Celtic Tiger boom, the direction of causation came to be reversed in many commentaries on the Irish economy. Our 'young and rapidly growing population' was no longer viewed as an excuse for rising unemployment and emigration but rather as part of the country's attraction for inward foreign investment and an important contributor to the boom. Instead of being seen as a consequence of the Ireland's economic success, whose explanation lies elsewhere, rapid population growth – which in the new century was increasingly due to an unprecedented net immigration rate – came to be seen as an engine of economic growth, fuelling aggregate demand and, in particular, justifying the exceptional rate of residential housing construction, the pace of which had few parallels in the developed world.

It would be wrong to dismiss out of hand a belief in positive feedback from demographic momentum to economic growth. It is the mirror image of the perspective prevalent in the 1950s that emigration and a declining (and ageing) population contributed to economic stagnation by creating an environment in which enterprise and investment would not thrive. However, just as the vicious circle of population decline and economic stagnation was eventually broken by increased competitiveness and favourable external conditions, the virtuous cycle of rapid population growth and entrepreneurial animal spirits proved easy prey to the crisis in world financial markets and domestic recession after 2007.

At the peak of the boom, Ireland's rate of population growth soared to almost 2 per cent a year, fuelled by an exceptional rate of net immigration, which peaked at over 1.5 per cent of the population in 2006 and 2007. Our population grew by 14 per cent between 2002 and 2008, when the population of the EU15 managed only a 4 per cent increase. As the economic boom gathered momentum, the share of the construction industry in the economy increased apace. There were many warnings that the rate of house building far exceeded the underlying or sustainable growth in demand. For example, in its *Quarterly Economic Commentary* of January 2005, the Economic and Social Research Institute (ESRI) warned that we were building more than twice as many dwellings as were required to meet the 'underlying demographic demand for housing' – proportionately seven times as many as in Britain – and hence our boom had become extraordinarily dependent on an abnormal level of house building. However, other segments of opinion – especially those allied one way or another to the construction industry – continued to argue that our 'demographic fundamentals' (basically the rapid rate of population growth) justified this exceptional level of activity.

The determinants of net migration in a small open economy like Ireland are fairly obvious. While the relative importance of the 'push' factors of poor domestic economic opportunities and the 'pull' factors of access to large and rapidly growing labour markets in Britain and the New World may be debated,[8] the combination of a stagnant domestic economy and easy access to the English-speaking world sustained large-scale emigration from Ireland over much of the period from the 1840s to the 1990s. Conversely, Ireland's extraordinary economic boom in the late years of the Celtic Tiger, which coincided with the opening up of our labour market to the new EU Accession States, triggered a very significant net inflow of workers. When this boom ended in a hard landing, the demographic momentum wound down rapidly, as we shall document more fully below.

Demography and the Current Economic Crisis

The magnitude of our housing boom was extraordinary relative to our economy and population. Between the mid-1990s and 2006, the number of people employed in the construction sector rose two-and-a-half-fold and the proportion of total employment in this sector rose from 7.5 to 16.0 per cent. Construction accounted for 20 per cent of gross domestic product (GDP) in 2006, compared with just under 10 per cent in 1995, whilst the share of other forms of capital formation remained static at about 12 per cent. Well over half of the outlay on construction was on residential dwellings. Despite an urgent need to alleviate transport bottlenecks, the outlay on new housing units was almost ten times as much as the invest-ment in roads in 2004. At the peak of the boom in 2006, housing completions reached over 90,000 units. This was three times the average level of the early 1990s and almost four times that of the depressed 1980s. For a population of a little over 4 million people, with about 1.5 million households, it represented an extraordinary rate of addition to the housing stock. By comparison, at the height of the US housing boom in 2005 completions reached about 2.1 million for a population of over 300 million with over 110 million households. The rate of housing construction in Ireland was over three times that of the US.

A recent commentary on the housing boom and bust in the United States noted that:

> Housing booms are usually triggered by demographics. The suburbaniza-tion shift of the 1950s reflected deep-rooted changes in family dynamics, as if Americans collectively decided to compensate for the low birth rates of the 1930s and 1940s. A quarter-century later, their grown-up children, and America's vast internal migration toward the Southeast and Southwest, drove the real estate boom of the 1970s and 1980s. But the demographics of the 1990s were pretty dull [and there was no national housing boom].[9]

The author goes on to note that 'the 2000s real estate bubble may be one of those rare beasts conjured into the world solely by financiers, which is confirmed by the fact that housing bubbles also occurred in ... other coun-tries where residential lending became unusually loose'.[10]

In Ireland, the low rate of house building during the 1980s and early 1990s reflected depressed economic conditions, high real interest rates, and near zero population growth. These were replaced in the second half of the 1990s and into the new century by rapidly rising incomes, falling real interest rates and record rates of population increase. Add to these changes the pent-up demand for better housing – as well as a controversial prefer-ence by many for living in 'one-off' houses well outside the older urban centres – and the upsurge in the demand for housing can be readily under-stood. Demographic factors may be said to have contributed to the boom because the expansion of employment led to a concomitant expansion of population in the prime household-formation years. Later on, the acceler-ating housing boom provided positive feedback to the housing market by drawing in unprecedented numbers of migrants.

During the second half of the 1990s, the supply of new housing units could not keep pace with the demand. As house price inflation took off, the affordability of housing to first-time buyers became a salient political issue.

Various culprits were identified, including an over-restrictive planning regime and excessive taxation on property transactions. However, the availability of easier credit and low interest rates, especially after 2002, fuelled an increasingly speculative boom. There was much discussion about whether this boom would end in a hard or soft landing. We know now that the landing was as hard as they come, comprising a collapse in house prices followed by the virtual cessation of new housing construction after 2007. Indeed, by 2010, the level of unoccupied housing units was estimated to stand at 300,000, representing about 15 per cent of the total housing stock (excluding holiday homes).[11]

But we should not forget what was achieved during the housing boom. Not only was the Irish landscape – both urban and rural – transformed (for better and for worse), but there was also an impressive upgrade of the housing stock. By the end of the first decade of the twenty-first century, a larger population was vastly better housed than had been the case at any other time in Irish history. According to the 2006 Census of Population, 17 per cent of private households were living in dwelling units built within the previous five years and 28 per cent in units built within the previous ten years. The proportion of households with central heating rose from 44 per cent in 1991 to 84 per cent in 2002 and 88 per cent in 2006.[12]

The role of population growth in fuelling the demand for housing during these years was seized on by those who believed the boom could last well into the future. Our 'demographic fundamentals' were invoked to justify an exceptional rate of new housing construction. It was believed this momentum would be maintained. The population projections published by the Central Statistics Office (CSO) in December 2004 envisaged the population rising from 3.9 million in 2002 to between 4.6 million and 4.9 million by 2016. A particularly optimistic view was taken in a report published in March 2006, which saw the population rising to between 4.8 million and 6.5 million by 2015, and the labour force growing by 2.2 per cent a year over the period 2005–15, sustained by continued high immigration and rising participation rates.[13] In much of the prevalent commentary there was a clear tendency to believe that immigration was an exogenous driver of Irish economic growth rather than an endogenous response to the economy's performance. The error of this view is now clear as the crisis has transformed an exceptionally high net immigration rate into a significant net outflow of population and 'brain drain' concerns have surfaced again, now including the possibility that the less employable of our recent immigrants will prefer to remain dependent on Irish social welfare rather than returning to their countries of origin.

The rate of natural increase – and the birth rate in particular – seems to have followed a more autonomous trajectory, although the collapse of fertility in the 1980s and its rebound in the new century could be interpreted as a response to the performance of the economy. In particular, the upsurge in births in the recent past is both striking and surprising (see Figure 12.6). The total number of births recorded in 2008 was just over 75,000 – 54 per cent more than the total for 1994. The rise has been due to an increase in both first and later births, with the average age of mothers at birth continuing to rise. It could represent compensation for the unusually low fertility of the second half of the 1990s. If so, the fertility rates over the reproductive lifetime of successive generations will be more stable than the rate measured over successive years. However, it would take great optimism to believe that this surge in the birth rate – which is already manifest in the burgeoning school-going population – will in due course be translated into a corresponding surge in the number of people in the household-formation age group that will quickly mop up the excess supply of housing left in the wake of the housing bust. For this to happen, the increased outflow from the educational system some fifteen years from now would have to be converted into an increase in employment. Whether this happens depends more on the medium-term performance of the economy than on any stimulus from the recent increase in the birth rate.

Figure 12.6: Number of Births, 1990–2008

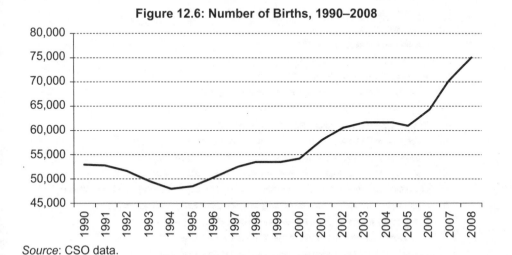

Source: CSO data.

The best available indication of the likely development of the demographic factors underpinning the housing market is the population projections published by the CSO. In April 2008 the CSO published population projections for 2011–41 using the results of the 2006 Census as the starting point. The range of migration assumptions used varied upwards from zero net migration. (This allows for some net inflows and outflows within individual age groups that sum to zero for the whole population.) The gravity of the recession that was already underway did not impinge on the exercise sufficiently to include net emigration among the core scenarios. The population and migration estimates published in September 2009 contained evidence of a resumption of net emigration between April 2008 and April 2009. Given the sharp deterioration of the labour market in the course of 2008 and 2009, with the unemployment rate rising from 4.5 to 12 per cent in little over a year, this resumption of emigration is likely to be a harbinger of much higher net outflows over the short to medium term.

The main value of population projections is to tease out the implications of the age structure of the initial population for the size and structure of the future population. Figure 12.7 shows the distribution of the Irish population in 2006 by five-year age groups. The salient feature is the bulge in the population aged 25–9 years. This reflects the boom in births recorded in the second half of the 1970s before the fall in the fertility rate during the 1980s. An important achievement of the years of the Celtic Tiger was the

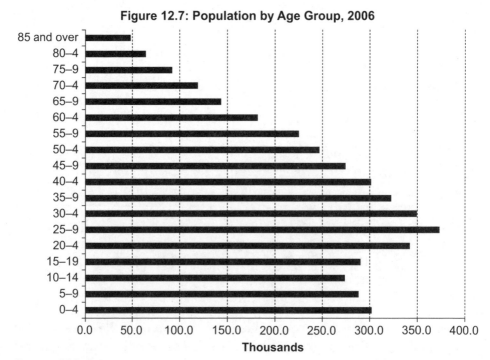

Figure 12.7: Population by Age Group, 2006

Source: CSO data.

absorption of much of this surge in births into employment. This cohort filled the new jobs created during the boom and fuelled the buoyant demand for housing during the 1990s that became part of a positive feedback loop during the new century.

The key demographic fundamental that will impact on the housing market in the short to medium term is the baby bust of the 1980s. The age groups below 25–9 years in 2006 become progressively smaller. For every 100 people in the population aged 25–9, there were only 92 aged 20–4, 78 aged 15–19 and 73 aged 10–14. The population aged 10–24 was 13 per cent smaller than that aged 25–39. The impact on the housing market of the bulge due to the baby boom of the 1970s is now weakening and, even in the absence of net emigration, the cohorts entering the first-time house buyers' market for the next fifteen years will be significantly smaller than those that entered from the mid-1990s to the present. The surge in the birth rate after 2000 will not affect the potential demand for housing until some fifteen to twenty years from now and it will not do so then unless this section of the population is retained in Ireland by an adequate supply of employment opportunities. The population projections for 2011–41 published by the CSO in 2008 are the best available basis for preparing an estimate of the likely evolution of the number of households in the country, which, in turn, can provide a basis for showing the medium-term demographic influences on the housing market. In view of the increasing uncertainty as one looks further into the future, attention is confined to the years 2011–21. The zero net migration assumption (M0) seems a reasonable compromise between assuming that there will be an upsurge in emigration on the basis of the recent (2009) evidence that emigration has resumed and the CSO's alternative net immigration scenarios.[14]

Applying the 2006 household headship rates by ten five-year age groups (male and female) to the projected 2011, 2016 and 2021 populations yields projections of the number of households on the assumption of no change in average household size within each demographic group. This makes no allowance for the probable continuing trend towards smaller households, especially at older ages. The projection of the number of households is entirely driven by the underlying population projection.

The results obtained from applying this methodology are shown in Figure 12.8. The actual change in the number of households over the four-year period 2002–06 is also shown. All figures are annualised for comparative purposes.

The projections show the growth in the number of households halving from 45,000 a year between 2002 and 2006 to a fairly steady 20,000+

Figure 12.8: Annual Change in Total Number of Households, 2002–21

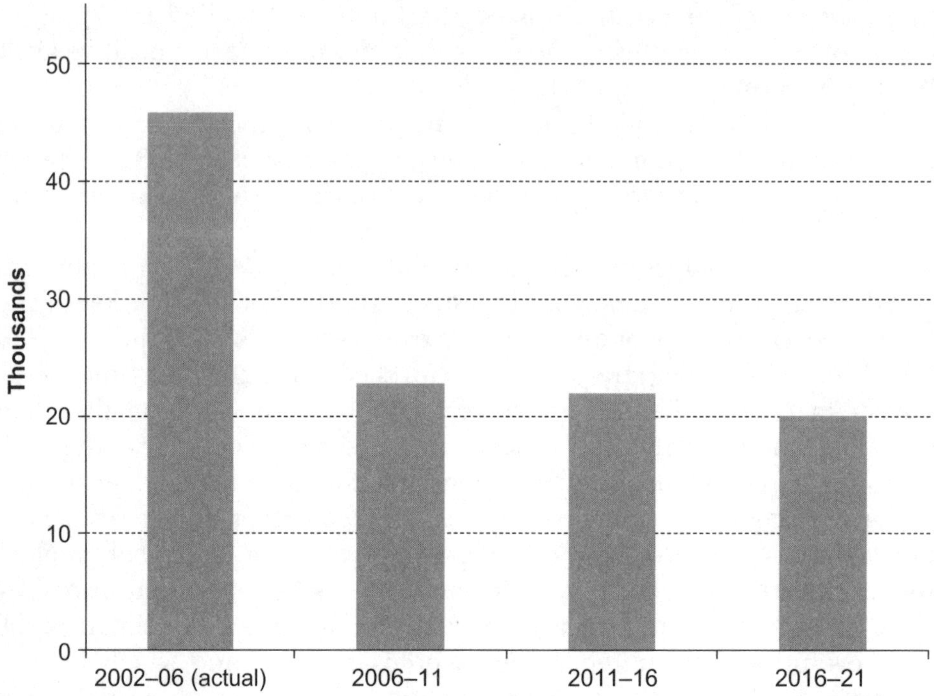

Source: CSO data.

between 2006 and 2021. This reflects the replacement of exceptionally high net immigration between 2002 and 2006 with the assumption of zero net migration after 2006 as well as the impact of the fall in the birth rate in the 1980s on the number entering the 25–44 age group after 2006.

Optimists might take comfort from the projection of a continued net increase of between 20,000 and 25,000 a year in the number of households after 2006. Even if this is less than a quarter of the rate at which dwelling units were being constructed at the height of the housing boom, it represents a need for a 1.5 per cent annual increase in the housing stock. However, this should be related to the overhang of unsold or unoccupied housing in the country, which, as we saw above, is estimated to be in the region of 15 per cent of the total stock.[15] But, more importantly, if we dig deeper and look at the projected change in the number of households by age of the person who used to be called 'head of household' and is now known as the 'reference person', the underlying demand for new housing is weaker than appears from the global increase in the number of households. Figure 12.9 shows that the change in the number of households headed by individuals aged under 45 years collapses from 24,000 a year in 2002–06 to *minus* 6,000 in 2016–21. The number of households headed by individuals aged 45–64 drops from 16,000 a year but remains fairly stable at around 11,000 a year after 2006, while the number of households headed by an individual aged 65 or over trebles from 5,000 to 15,000 a year.

Figure 12.9: Annual Change in Number of Households, by Age of 'Reference Person', 2002–21

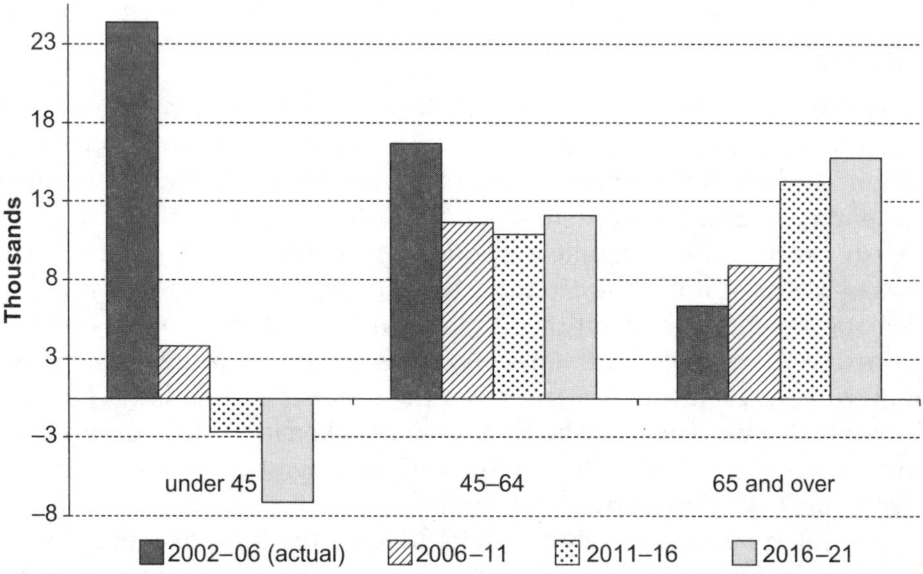

Source: CSO data.

Growth in the number of households driven by increasing numbers entering the household-formation age groups (first-time buyers or first-time renters) implies increased demand for housing units. On the other hand, growth in the number of households headed by older individuals – reflecting the ageing of existing heads of household – does not translate into a demand for net additional housing units, although it has important implications for the appropriate size and location of the required units. The salient demographic influence on the Irish housing market over the next decade is therefore the consequence of the ageing of the population, which implies that the number of households headed by someone aged 20–45 will stabilise and then decline, while the number headed by someone aged 45–64 will grow at a steady rate and the number headed by people aged 65 and over will grow at an accelerating pace.

In short, the present age structure of the population, and in particular the ageing of the relatively large cohort in the key household formation age groups, implies that the demographic underpinning of the housing market

– which was so striking a feature of the early years of this century – is weakening even in the absence of net emigration. Should net emigration resume on a significant scale as a response to a recession that is more prolonged in Ireland than in other developed countries, then the housing market would face a protracted period when both the demographic and economic determinants of demand would be very weak.

Conclusion

In the nineteenth century and for most of the twentieth century, Ireland's exceptional demographic experience can be readily understood as that of a region in a larger economic entity, namely, the Atlantic economy to which our population had for the most part ready access. Since the early nineteenth century, Irish people responded to employment opportunities abroad when the domestic economy failed to generate them at home. This led to persistent net emigration on a scale with few, if any, parallels in other countries. More recently, boom conditions generated more employment opportunities than could be met from the resident population. This drew former Irish emigrants back home and then sucked in workers from abroad on an exceptional scale. The volatility of the migration flows resulted in exceptionally volatile population numbers.

The safety valve of emigration defused the economic crises of the 1950s and 1980s, although possibly at a cost in terms of undermining the country's longer-term economic dynamism. The closest parallel with the present situation is that which prevailed in the 1980s, when Ireland's recession proved much longer and deeper than that experienced in the rest of the developed world. In the first half of the decade, this resulted in an alarming growth in unemployment as the population grew while the number at work fell. The first easing of the unemployment crisis occurred when the resumption of economic growth in the UK stimulated an outflow of population from Ireland.

In 2002, the links between Irish and UK unemployment were summarised as follows:

> The elasticity of international migration has long been a hallmark of the Irish labour market and indeed the rate of unemployment is loosely anchored by that in the UK. Net emigration has long seemed to place a ceiling on the gap between Irish and UK unemployment. Even if there had been no employment boom in Ireland, the fall in UK unemployment in the late 1990s would have exerted its traditional downward pressure on the Irish rate, but through the usual outflow of emigrants and the stagnation of non-

agricultural employment.[16]

A similar mechanism could begin to operate in 2010 and beyond. This time, however, the situation is complicated by the fact that the sharp rise in unemployment since the onset of recession in 2007 has been concentrated among recent immigrants to Ireland. Whereas the overall unemployment rate reached 12.7 per cent in the third quarter of 2009 (on the International Labour Organisation's (ILO) definitions), the unemployment rate among Irish nationals was 'only' 11.9 per cent, while that among non-Irish nationals was 17.2 per cent. Among nationals of the new EU countries (EU15 to EU27) the unemployment rate was 19.5 per cent. There are some indications that this group has a high propensity to emigrate from Ireland in the face of a deteriorating economic situation and this may ease the unemployment problem in the short to medium term, leading to a concomitant decline in the labour force and population.

During the heady years of Ireland's economic boom, a view gained ground in some quarters that the demographic impetus of our 'young and rapidly growing population' – reinforced by the unprecedented population inflow from abroad – would help prolong the boom by underpinning the exceptional rate of new house construction that was an important contributor to the boom. We have seen that this view was a mirage. In the first place, the inflow of population was induced by the boom and, once the boom imploded, no exogenous impetus persisted from this source. Second, the lagged impact of the dramatic fall in the birth rate during the 1980s – at least in part induced by the economic crisis of that decade – is now weakening the indigenous sources of demand for housing. The surge in numbers entering the prime household formation age groups that was a feature of the first decade of this century is being replaced by a contraction in the numbers in these age groups over the coming decade, even in the absence of renewed net emigration.

Nor is it plausible to look to another demographic transition to rekindle growth in line with the model proposed by Bloom and Canning[17] to explain the Celtic Tiger boom. The variations in the fertility rate since the 1990s have been relatively small by comparison with the transition to low fertility that occurred in the 1980s. The immediate impact of the recent surge in the birth rate is to place strains on public expenditure through a surprise increase in the population of school-going age. Rather than constituting a beneficial supply-side shock to the economy, the eventual impact on the labour market of the outflow of this cohort from the educational system will depend on the performance of the economy in fifteen to twenty years' time.

The longer-term implications of the surge in population due to the inflow of immigrants in the first decade of the twenty-first century are still not clear. Recent evidence on migration flow suggests that the new arrivals from the EU Accession States have displayed a fairly strong propensity to leave Ireland as economic conditions deteriorated. We do not know if they are returning to their countries of origin or moving on to other locations that have been less affected by the 'Great Recession'. Either way, the implication is that, once again, the size of the population of Ireland is strongly influenced by the country's relative economic performance.

We can conclude, not surprisingly, that Irish demographic dynamics will offer little by way of stimulus to help the economy out of its current economic crisis.

Conclusion

The objectives of this book are twofold: first, to identify what caused the current economic crisis and, second, to identify or determine what policies can be pursued to promote recovery. Hence, the title of the book: *Understanding Ireland's Economic Crisis: Prospects for Recovery*. Each contributor to this book has addressed the two main issues by focusing on a particular sector or a particular aspect to the problem and presents a set of recommendations as to what should be done to prevent the Irish economy remaining in a long-lasting economic recession.

Fundamentally, most of our contributors agree, in one form or another, on the causes of Ireland's current economic crisis. At the heart of the problem lies Ireland's membership of economic and monetary union (EMU). As the export-led boom of the 1990s dissipated in 2001 it was replaced by a property and construction bubble. This was facilitated by cuts in EMU interest rates and by easy access for Irish banks to cheap, no-exchange-rate-risk finance on the European interbank market. Outside of EMU, the Irish Central Bank would most likely have raised interest rates in or around 2003 and lending by domestic banks would have been constrained by their ability to attract deposits. In the background the appreciation of the Euro on foreign exchanges and a domestic wage–inflation spiral resulted in a significant loss of price competitiveness. Unfortunately, the boom in property and construction hid the effect of the loss of price competitiveness on domestic exports and import-competing firms and, up until 2007, the overall Irish economy posted impressive scores for economic growth and unemployment.

When the property bubble eventually burst in 2007 it unfortunately coincided with the worldwide economic and financial crisis. In a short time the Irish economy imploded. Economic 'growth' in 2009 is estimated to have been -11.3 per cent; we also faced deflation, rising unemployment, a virtual collapse of the banking system, a significant rise in both the fiscal balance and in national debt, and a huge increase in the balance of payments deficit. Clearly, finding a way to solve, move past, absorb or get around these problems is a mammoth task and given the constraints of EMU membership there are no easy, short-term solutions. Our recommendations are:

Restore competitiveness: One key problem is that Ireland's membership of EMU ensures that there is no effective 'automatic adjustment mechanism' that would quickly return the economy to its long-run growth path. Price deflation combined with a weakening of the Euro exchange rate in 2010 has already improved price competitiveness. However, deflation has also increased the real interest rate and this is acting to curtail economic expansion. In effect, there are conflicting and offsetting economic pressures emanating from the foreign exchange and money markets. This places a great deal of the 'adjustment burden' on the labour market and on wages and productivity in particular.

The debate on the pros and cons of EMU membership back in the mid-1990s emphasised the critical role of wage and price flexibility in adjusting to economic shocks. It is probably fair to say that successive Irish policymakers did not fully understand the rules of the 'EMU game', much less implement them. A good example is the pro-cyclical expansionary fiscal policy pursued by successive governments during the boom years. The key lesson of reliance on wage and price flexibility has now manifested itself with a vengeance following the 2007 downturn. Given EMU membership, all of the key automatic adjustment mechanisms – the interest rate, the exchange rate, even elements of fiscal policy – are now outside of our policymakers' control and the burden of adjustment falls almost entirely on the labour market. However, the labour market cannot provide the level of flexibility to cope with the adjustments necessary to restore the economy to its optimum growth path. The volatility in the foreign exchange market, the forthcoming general election and the fact that any further cuts in public sector salaries will be fiercely resisted imply a lack of labour market flexibility in the medium term.

To compound matters, the downturn has created a large budget deficit and the government has been forced to introduce a pro-cyclical deflationary fiscal policy. The net result is that domestic demand cannot be relied upon to compensate for external developments and facilitate economic recovery. All of these considerations add up to the prospect of a prolonged recession.

Restore employment levels: There is a pressing need to tackle Ireland's growing unemployment problem. To date, there have been few large-scale initiatives of note. Employer of last resort policies, as we have seen in this book, can help alleviate unemployment, and can direct labour towards socially and environmentally beneficial projects and problems. If we are to avoid Ireland's traditional employment safety valve – emigration – and prevent the loss of the young, enterprising and energetic from Ireland, we need creative thinking to maximise domestic employment opportunities.

Attract foreign direct investment: Ireland already possesses the necessary characteristics to be attractive to foreign investors: our low corporation tax, our intellectual property licensing and research and development laws, our location, our well-educated English-speaking workforce and our flexible working practices. The introduction of a new central bank and regulatory regime can only strengthen and lead to a more efficient institutional structure, making Ireland a more attractive destination for overseas fixed and capital investment. The restoration of confidence in the Irish financial system via prudential regulation and oversight should see an expansion in economical, productive foreign direct investment and in capital markets.

Resolve the banking crisis: The resolution of the banking crisis and the return of normal banking activity must be achieved. Normal banking activity implies traditional deposit banking, which, even in 2008, was highly profitable for Ireland's big banks. The cost of the resolution of the banking crisis cannot be estimated at the time of writing. Anglo Irish Bank's nationalisation, for example, is effectively a bill for some €30 to €40 billion that has to be paid by Ireland's taxpayers.

All authors in this book agree that the banking crisis must be resolved. Solutions range from debt equity swaps and government lending to nationalisation and asset-based reserve requirements. The first part of the government's proposed solution, the National Asset Management Agency (NAMA), has begun its work as this book goes to press. Whether NAMA succeeds in healing the Irish banking system's problems is another matter entirely. Whatever the outcome, any solution to the banking crisis must be built and regulated to withstand a likely resurgence in interbank-funded cheap credit and risky lending. The banking wind-ups and macro-prudential regulation approaches suggested in several chapters in this book will be useful in addressing Ireland's banking crisis.

We hope that this book will go some way toward stimulating thinking on these differing (and sometimes conflicting) areas of economic and social life in Ireland.

Notes and References

Introduction

1. With the economy already fairly close to full employment, much of the labour employed in the construction boom came from the new EU member states in Eastern Europe, and the inward migration further fuelled demand for housing. By 2007, construction accounted for 13.3 per cent of all employment, the highest share in the OECD (J. Fitz Gerald et al., *Medium-Term Review: 2008–2015*, No. 11, Dublin, Economic and Social Research Institute, 2008).

Chapter 1

1. Author of *Ireland and the Global Question* (Cork University Press, 2006).
2. Data comes from the late Professor Angus Maddison's (University of Groningen) database, see <http://www.ggdc.net/maddison/>.
3. See <www.cso.ie/statistics/nationalacc.htm>, accessed 24 August 2009.
4. Michael O'Sullivan, 'Was John Law Irish?', forthcoming in *Economie en Irlande*, Groupe de recherches en etudes irlandaises, Caen, Universite de Caen.
5. C. MacKay, *Extraordinary Popular Delusions and the Madness of Crowds*, Philadelphia, PA, Templeton Foundation Press, [1841] 1989.
6. Such as B. Bernanke and M. Gertler, 'Should Central Banks Respond to Movements in Asset Prices?', *American Economic Review*, Vol. 91, No. 2, 2001, pp. 253–7.
7. Shares in the Mississippi Company traded at 490 livres in May 1719, then pushed higher to 3,500 by August as expectations rose of the mineral treasures that lay buried in Mississippi. The shares rose to 5,000 livres by September and rocketed to close to 10,000 livres by December 1719.
8. MacKay, *Extraordinary Popular Delusions and the Madness of Crowds*, p. 1.
9. P. Garber, *Famous First Bubbles: The Fundamentals of Early Manias*, Cambridge, MA, MIT Press, 2000.
10. F. Velde, 'Government Equity and Money: John Law's System in 1720 France', Federal Reserve Bank of Chicago working paper WP – 2003-31, November 2003.
11. Ibid, p. 1.

12. DuTot, quoted in A. Murphy, 'Corporate Ownership in France: The Importance of History', in R.K. Morck (ed.), *A History of Corporate Governance Round the World: Family Business Groups to Professional Managers*, Chicago, IL, University of Chicago Press, 2005, p. 195.

13. Olivier Blanchard, quoted in P. Honohan and B. Walsh, 'Catching Up with the Leaders: The Irish Hare', *Brookings Papers on Economic Activity*, Vol. 33, No. 1, 2002, pp. 1–78, p. 61.

14. A. Murphy, *John Law: Economic Theorist and Policy-Maker*, Oxford, Clarendon Press, 1997.

15. Ibid, p. 6: 'gambler and murderer are peculiar items to find in the curriculum vitae of an economic theorist and policymaker'.

16. J. Gleeson (1999), *Millionaire: The Philanderer, Gambler, and Duelist Who Invented Modern Finance*, New York, Simon & Schuster, 1999, p. 69.

17. MacKay, *Extraordinary Popular Delusions and the Madness of Crowds*, p. 1.

18. Murphy, *John Law*, p. 3.

19. Gleeson, *Millionaire*, p. 6.

20. K. Marx and F. Engels, *Ireland and the Irish Question*, Moscow, Progress Publishers, 1986, p. 372.

21. Gleeson, *Millionaire*, p. 144.

22. Ibid, p. 30.

23. Velde, 'Government Equity and Money'.

24. A. Landier and K. Ueda, 'The Economics of Bank Restructuring: Understanding the Options', IMF staff position note 09/12, 2009.

25. A.J. Alletzhauser, *The House of Nomura: The Inside Story of the Legendary Japanese Financial Dynasty*, New York, Arcade, 1997.

26. IMF, 'When Bubbles Burst', in *IMF World Economic Outlook*, April 2003.

27. Data from <www.bloomberg.com>.

28. J.M. Keynes, *The General Theory of Employment, Interest and Money*, New York, Prometheus Books, 1997, p. 155.

29. C. Reinhart and K. Rogoff, *This Time Is Different: Eight Centuries of Financial Folly*, Princeton, NJ, Princeton University Press, 2009.

30. J.K. Galbraith, *The Great Crash 1929*, London, Penguin, 1992, p. 29.

31. Stated during a speech given at the Conference of the Irish Congress of Trade Unions in Bundoran, Co. Donegal on 4 July 2007.

32. MacKay, *Extraordinary Popular Delusions and the Madness of Crowds*, p. 28.

33. Ibid, p. 17.

34. C. Kindleberger and R. Aliber, *Manias, Panics and Crashes*, Basingstoke, Palgrave, 2005, p. 16.

35. Quoted in Gleeson, *Millionaire*, p. 207.

36. MacKay, *Extraordinary Popular Delusions and the Madness of Crowds*, p. 24.

37. A. Shleifer and L. Summers, 'The Noise Trader Approach to Finance', *Journal of Economic Perspectives*, Vol. 4, No. 2, 1990, pp. 19–33.

38. Kindleberger and Aliber, *Manias, Panics and Crashes*, p. 92.
39. M. O'Sullivan and R. Miller (eds.), *What Did We Do Right? Global Perspectives on Ireland's Economic 'Miracle'*, Dublin, Blackhall Publishing, 2010.
40. Credit Suisse Research Institute (2008), 'Intangible Infrastructure', Report, November 2008.
41. Ibid, p. 3.
42. From a lecture given by Adam Smith in 1755, available from: <http://www.adamsmith.org/think-piece/justice-%26-civil-liberties/wealth-depends-on-the-rule-of-law/>.
43. EU Lisbon Agenda, <http://portal.cor.europa.eu/europe2020/Pages/welcome.aspx>.
44. A. Kose, S. Claessens and M. Terrones, 'What Happens During Recessions, Crunches and Busts', IMF working paper 08/274, 2009.
45. M. O'Sullivan, 'We Need a Political System that Encourages Strategic Thinking', *Irish Times*, 14 April 2009.
46. P. Pettit, *Republicanism: A Theory of Freedom and Government*, Oxford, Oxford University Press, 1997, p. 5.
47. J.J. Lee, *Ireland 1912–1985: Politics and Society*, Cambridge, Cambridge University Press, 1989, p. 631.

Chapter 2

1. Such as P. Honohan, 'Resolving Ireland's Banking Crisis', *Economic and Social Review*, Vol. 40, No. 2, 2009, pp. 207–31.
2. Irish Financial Services Regulatory Authority (IFSRA), *Protecting Consumers Through Effective Regulation: Annual Report of the Financial Regulator 2005*, Dublin, IFSRA, 2006, p. 9.
3. R. Levine, *The Corporate Governance of the Banks: A Concise Discussion of Concepts and Evidence*, Washington, DC, World Bank, 2004.
4. C. Reinhart and K. Rogoff, 'The Aftermath of Financial Crises', *American Economic Review*, Vol. 99, No. 2, 2009, pp. 466–72.
5. K.P.V. O'Sullivan and T. Kennedy, 'Supervision of the Irish Banking System: A Critical Perspective', CESifo DICE Report 3/2008, 2008.
6. This role was undertaken by Bank of Ireland until 31 December 1971 when the Central Bank was reconstituted as the banker to the government.
7. From 1975 to 1985, the loan-to-deposit ratio of Irish banks remained relatively stable (see Figure 2.3).
8. DKM, *The Control of Banking in the Republic of Ireland*, Dublin, DKM Economic Consultants, 1984.
9. K.P.V. O'Sullivan and T. Kennedy, 'A Model for Regulatory Intervention in Irish Banking', *Journal of Banking Regulation*, Vol. 8, No. 2, 2007, pp. 113–30.
10. Ibid.

11. Such as stringent liquidity requirements or explicit sectoral guidelines on credit.
12. High Level Group on Regulation, *Report to the Government of the High Level Group on Regulation for 2001/02*, Dublin, Department of the Taoiseach, 2002, p. 3.
13. OECD, *Regulatory Reform in Ireland*, Paris, OECD, 2001.
14. J. Westrup, 'Ireland', in D. Masciandaro (ed.), *The Handbook of Central Banking and Financial Authorities in Europe*, Cheltenham, Edward Elgar, 2005, p. 355.
15. M. McDowell, *Report of the Implementation Advisory Group on a Single Regulatory Authority for Financial Services*, known as the *McDowell Report*, Dublin, Department of Finance, 1999, Chapter 6.
16. Ibid.
17. See Westrup, 'Ireland'.
18. O'Sullivan and Kennedy, 'Supervision of the Irish Banking System'.
19. J. Black, 'Forms and Paradoxes of Principles-Based Regulation', *Capital Markets Law Journal*, Vol. 3, No. 4, 2008, pp. 425–57.
20. IFSRA, *Protecting Consumers Through Effective Regulation*.
21. IFSRA, *Strategic Plan 2006*, Dublin, IFSRA, 2005, p. 12.
22. J. Black, 'Critical Reflections on Regulation', *Australian Journal of Legal Philosophy*, Vol. 27, 2002, pp. 1–35, p.1.
23. IFSRA, *Strategic Plan 2007–2009*, Dublin, Irish Financial Services Regulatory Authority, 2006, p. 9.
24. Black, 'Forms and Paradoxes of Principles-Based Regulation'.
25. Speech by Hector Sants, Chief Executive, FSA at the Reuters Newsmakers event, 12 March 2009, available at <http://www.fsa.gov.uk/pages/Library/Communication/Speeches/2009/0312_hs.shtml>, accessed 10 January 2010.
26. See Basel Committee on Banking Supervision, *International Convergence of Capital Measurement and Capital Standards: A Revised Framework Comprehensive Version*, Basel, Bank for International Settlements, 2006.
27. IFSRA, *Strategic Plan 2007–2009*.
28. Ibid, p. 11.
29. IFSRA, *Strategic Plan 2007–2009*.
30. For example, between 2004 and 2006, €118 million was overcharged by banking institutions in Ireland related to foreign exchange transactions, story available at <http://www.rte.ie/news/2006/0725/finance.html>.
31. IFSRA, *Strategic Plan 2007–2009*.
32. OECD, 'The Corporate Governance Lessons from the Financial Crisis', *OECD Journal: Financial Market Trends*, Vol. 1, No. 96, 2009, pp. 52–81.
33. European Commission, *Study on Monitoring and Enforcement Practices in Corporate Governance in the Member States*, Brussels, European Commission, 2009.
34. Ibid.

35. OECD, *Corporate Governance: A Survey of OECD Countries 2004*, Paris, OECD, 2004.

36. Principles-based regulation encourages new entrants into the marketplace and increases competition, which in turn improves levels of service provision (see IFSRA, *Annual Report of the Financial Regulator 2008*, Dublin, IFSRA, 2009).

37. For further information, see the Department of the Environment, Heritage and Local Government's statistical database on housing, available at: <http://www.environ.ie/en/Publications/StatisticsandRegularPublications/HousingStatistics/>.

38. While the Central Bank mentioned the increase in private sector indebtedness as being an area of concern in its 2007 *Stability Report*, it was not overly concerned about the size of Irish banks' property-exposed loan books.

39. IMF, *Ireland: Staff Report for the 2006 Article IV Consultation*, IMF Country Report No. 06/293, Washington, DC, IMF, 2006.

40. *The Economist* (2004), 'Why Worry' in 'The Luck of the Irish: A Survey of Ireland', *The Economist*, 16 October 2004, pp. 6–8.

41. *Prime Time* (RTE) interview with Patrick Neary, 2 October 2008, available from: <http://www.rte.ie/news/2008/1002/primetime.html>, accessed 10 January 2010.

42. From an interview with Sean FitzPatrick on *The Marian Finucane Show*, RTE Radio One, 4 October 2008, available from: <http://dynamic.rte.ie/quick-axs/209-rte-marianfinucane-2008-10-04.smil>.

43. G. Caprio Jr. and D. Klingebiel, 'Banking Insolvency: Bad Luck, Bad Policy, or Bad Banking?', in *Proceedings of the World Bank Annual Conference on Development Economics, 1996*, Supplement to the *World Bank Economic Review* and the *World Bank Research Observer*, 1997, pp. 79–104.

44. Honohan, 'Resolving Ireland's Banking Crisis'.

45. Economic and Social Research Institute (ESRI), *Negative Equity in the Irish Housing Market*, Dublin, ESRI, 2009.

46. Consumer Panel of IFSRA, *Perspective of the Consumer Panel on the Current Financial Regulatory Framework*, Dublin, Irish Financial Services Regulatory Authority, 2009, p. 3.

47. Ibid.

48. N. Rose, *Powers of Freedom: Reframing Political Thought*, Cambridge, Cambridge University Press, 1999.

49. Financial Regulator, *Consumer Protection Code*, August 2006, available from: <http://www.financialregulator.ie/press-area/press-releases/documents/consumer%20protection%20code%20-%20august%202006.pdf>, accessed 10 January 2010.

50. With Anglo Irish Bank one could also refer to the circular loan transactions with Irish Life and Permanent or the loan share purchase scheme with the 'golden circle'.

51. Department of Finance, 'Statement of the Minister for Finance, Brian Lenihan TD, on the Publication of Anglo Irish Bank Accounts for the Year ended 30th September 2008', Dublin, Department of Finance, 20 February 2009.

52. Joint Committee on Economic Regulatory Affairs, 'Anglo Irish Bank: Discussion with Financial Regulator', 13 January 2009, Dublin, Houses of the Oireachtas, p. 4.

53. See Anglo Irish Bank's 2007 Annual Report under the Directors' corporate governance statement, pp. 33–7.

54. The Financial Services Authority indicated that the internal audit department is 'an integral part of a firm's corporate governance framework'; see Financial Services Authority, *Principles Based Regulation: Focusing on the Outcomes that Matter*, London, Financial Services Authority, April 2007, p. 7.

55. Joint Committee on Economic Regulatory Affairs, 'Internal Audit Function: Discussion with Anglo Irish Bank', 3 February 2009, Dublin, Houses of the Oireachtas.

56. Ibid, p. 2.

57. Ibid, p. 3.

58. The credit risk department at Anglo Irish Bank is independent of the lending teams and reports to a separate committee of the board. It is comprised of members of the credit risk department and some board members.

59. This is surprising as Mr FitzPatrick's loans were secured by the bank and not the individual.

60. The composition of the credit committee varies from time to time and depends on the individual specifications (such as size) of the loan. It usually is made up of members from the independent credit risk department and some board members.

61. Joint Committee on Economic Regulatory Affairs, 'Internal Audit Function: Discussion with Anglo Irish Bank', p. 4.

62. Ibid, p. 3.

63. The government is in the process of redesigning corporate governance provisions in the banking system either through regulatory requirements, as proposed in the Corporate Governance Consultation Paper, or through legislation, as outlined in the Central Bank Reform Bill.

64. See Financial Reporting Council, *Consultation on the Revised UK Corporate Governance Code*, London, Financial Reporting Council, 2009. Tellingly, both Citibank and UBS, following their prospective crises, have announced boardroom departures to make way for new directors with financial and investment expertise.

65. In accordance with international best practice, all non-executive directors, whether with financial experience or not, should be subjected to a sectoral specific and risk management weighted 'fit and proper' test in the future. These tests should be vetted by an outside, independent agency and not by the Regulator itself, as is the current approach. Moreover, a training mecha-

nism should be introduced to ensure that board members' skills are constantly refreshed. Finally, non-executive directors should be required to publish a breakdown of the work they have carried out, and the time spent doing so, in the bank's annual report.

66. Westrup, 'Ireland'.
67. 'Sub-Committee on Certain Revenue Matters: Parliamentary Inquiry into Deposit Interest Retention Tax', available from: <http://www.gov.ie/commit-tees-99/c-publicaccounts/sub-rep/default.htm>, accessed 10 January 2010.
68. Westrup, 'Ireland'.
69. Central Bank and Financial Services Authority of Ireland, *Financial Stability Report 2007*, Dublin, Central Bank and Financial Services Authority of Ireland, 2007, p. 5.
70. IFSRA, *Annual Report of the Financial Regulator 2008*, p. 5.
71. IFSRA, *Annual Report of the Financial Regulator 2008*.
72. P. Honohan, 'Financial Regulation in Ireland: Past, Present and Future', speech to the Financial Services Ireland Annual Dinner, 1 December 2009, Dublin, p. 2.
73. IFSRA, *Annual Report of the Financial Regulator 2008*.
74. Honohan, 'Financial Regulation in Ireland: Past, Present and Future', p. 3.
75. For example, new liquidity requirements with cash flows assigned to relevant time bands rather than the previous stock approach. This meant that banks had to incorporate higher capital requirements for speculative land development proposals, amend their loan to value mortgage thresholds and stress-test at 2.75 per cent above European Central Bank (ECB) rates.
76. IFSRA, *Annual Report of the Financial Regulator 2008*, p. 16.
77. Ibid, p. 4.
78. Ibid.
79. M. Dorf and C. Sabel, 'A Constitution of Democratic Experimentalism', *Columbia Law Review*, Vol. 98, No. 2, 1998, pp. 267–473; J. Freeman, 'The Private Role in Public Governance', *New York University Law Review*, Vol. 75, No. 101, 2000, pp. 543–651; R. Lipschutz, *Governmentality and Global Politics: Regulation for the Rest of Us?*, Abingdon, Routledge, 2005.
80. C. Parker, *The Open Corporation: Effective Self-Regulation and Democracy*, Melbourne, Cambridge University Press, 2002, p. 245.
81. U. Beck, *Risk Society: Towards a New Modernity*, Newbury Park, CA, Sage, 1992; E. Fisher, *Risk, Regulation and Administrative Constitutionalism*, Oxford, Hart Publishing, 2007.
82. Fisher, *Risk, Regulation and Administrative Constitutionalism*; Rose, *Powers of Freedom*.
83. B. Morgan, 'The Economization of Politics: Meta-Regulation as a Form of Non-judicial Legality', *Social & Legal Studies*, Vol. 12, No. 4, 2003, pp. 489–523, p. 490.
84. N. Gunningham, 'Environment Law, Regulation and Governance: Shifting Architectures', *Journal of Environmental Law*, Vol. 21, No. 2, 2009, pp. 179–212.

85. J. Humphrey, 'A Scientific Approach to Politics? On the Trail of the Audit Commission', *Critical Perspectives on Accounting*, Vol. 13, No. 1, 2002, pp. 39–62.

86. B. Morgan and K. Yeung, *An Introduction to Law and Regulation*, Cambridge, Cambridge University Press, 2007.

87. Gunningham, 'Environment Law, Regulation and Governance', p. 191.

88. Parker, *The Open Corporation*.

89. Black, 'Critical Reflections on Regulation', p. 1.

90. J. Braithwaite, 'Meta Risk Management and Responsive Regulation for Tax System Integrity', *Law & Policy*, Vol. 25, No. 1, 2003, pp. 1–16.

91. D. Levi-Faur, 'The Political Economy of Legal Globalization: Juridification, Adversarial Legalism, and Responsive Regulation – A Comment', *International Organization*, Vol. 59, No. 2, 2005, pp. 451–62.

92. M. Moran, *The British Regulatory State: High Modernism and Hyper-Innovation*, New York, Oxford University Press, 2003.

93. D. McBarnet, *Crime, Compliance and Control*, Oxford, Oxford University Press, 1994; Parker, *The Open Corporation*.

94. C. Scott, 'Speaking Softly Without Big Sticks: Meta-Regulation and Public Sector Audit', *Law & Policy*, Vol. 25, No. 3, 2003, pp. 203–19, p. 213.

95. J. Rees, *Hostages of Each Other: The Transformation of Nuclear Safety Since Three Mile Island*, Chicago, IL, University of Chicago Press, 1994.

96. Braithwaite, 'Meta Risk Management and Responsive Regulation for Tax System Integrity', p. 2.

97. J. Braithwaite, '2004 Chief Health Officer Seminar Series – Seminar One: Health System Regulation and Governance', Chief Health Officer Seminar Series, 23 June 2004, Australian National University, Canberra, available from: <http://healthstewardship.anu.edu.au/_documents/Chief_Health_Officer_Seminar_Series/2004/Braithwaite_trans.pdf>, accessed 10 January 2010, p. 4.

98. J. Gray and J. Hamilton, *Implementing Financial Regulation: Theory and Practice*, London, Wiley, 2006.

99. A similar solution to address failures of corporate governance in the global financial system is recommended by the OECD, available from: <www.oecd.org/dataoecd/32/1/42229620.pdf>.

100. OECD, 'The Corporate Governance Lessons from the Financial Crisis', p. 11.

101. The current arrangements are that a specific committee composed of non-executive directors must prepare a compliance statement which is then reviewed by the external auditors. However, the Irish banking crisis has proven that non-executives (in the main) are not capable of performing such functions given the limited time they can dedicate to the task and the complexity of the issues involved.

102. Independent from the bank and its financial auditors.

103. Parker, *The Open Corporation*.

104. For example at Société Générale and UBS (Union Bank of Switzerland), lower management levels were aware of risks inherent in their business operations.

However this knowledge wasn't transferred to senior management. It is important, therefore, that the Regulator's evaluation of risk management systems gathers information from a *bottom-up* perspective.

105. R. Dale, *Risk and Regulation in Global Securities Markets*, New York, Wiley, 1996.

106. J. Braithwaite, 'The New Regulatory State and the Transformation of Criminology', *British Journal of Criminology*, Vol. 40, 2000, pp. 222–38, p. 228.

107. For further information see <http://php.sys-con.com/node/1205911> and <http://www.securityfocus.com/news/11566>.

108. N. Gunningham and P. Grabosky, *Smart Regulation: Designing Environmental Policy*, Oxford, Oxford University Press, 1998.

Chapter 3

1. See P. Honohan and B. Walsh, 'Catching Up with the Leaders: The Irish Hare', *Brookings Papers on Economic Activity*, Vol. 33, No. 1, 2002, pp. 1–78, especially their Figure 5.

2. Schularick and Taylor find similar figures across a wider set of industrialised economies. In this chapter we adopt the usual convention of expressing Irish figures as a fraction of gross national product (GNP), and international numbers as a fraction of gross domestic product (GDP). See M. Schularick and A.M. Taylor, 'Credit Booms Gone Bust: Monetary Policy, Leverage Cycles and Financial Crises, 1870–2008', National Bureau of Economic Research working paper no. 15512, November 2009.

3. Data in Figure 3.1 on bank lending for the United Kingdom (UK) from Bank of England, for Eurozone economies from the European Central Bank (ECB): 'Aggregated balance sheet of euro area monetary financial institutions, excluding the Eurosystem', available from: <http://www.ecb.int/stats/money/aggregates/bsheets/html/outstanding_amounts_index.en.html>. Data for private sector lending before 2003 includes insurance companies, pension funds and other non-monetary financial intermediaries. We remove them in 1997 by assuming that they are the same proportion of lending in each economy as 2008.

4. Cited by R. Pozen, *Too Big to Save? How to Fix the US Financial System*, New York, Wiley & Sons, 2009, p. 165.

5. The annual yield on a five-year bond issued by AIB on 5 November 2009, 285 basis points over the mid-five-year swap rate: 'AIB Sells 750m Five-Year Bond After Ratings Downgrade', *Irish Independent*, 6 November 2009.

6. Mortgage Bankers Association, *National Delinquency Survey*, 19 November 2009, available from: <http://www.mbaa.org/NewsandMedia/PressCenter/71112.htm>, accessed 1 July 2010.

7. Numbers are from Table C3, column 1 and Table C8 of the Irish Central Bank *Quarterly Bulletin*.

8. Schularick and Taylor, 'Credit Booms Gone Bust'.

9. As reported by Ibid.

10. The growth of Irish credit does appear sedate however when compared with Iceland, where lending to firms and households went from 1.8 times GDP in 1999 to 5 times in 2008. See <http://www.sedlabanki.is/?pageid=194> and <http://www.statice.is/Statistics/National-accounts-and-public-fin>.

11. Classified in Table C8 of the Irish Central Bank *Quarterly Bulletin* as 'Construction and Real Estate Activities'.

12. Department of Environment data. The ESRI index is similar.

13. A Jorgensen procedure finds a cointegrating relationship between the two series until 2006 significant at 1 per cent of $P=0.97C$ where P, C are real price of new houses and commercial property with value in 1995 Q1 set to 100.

14. See <http://www.sherryfitz.ie/aboutus/NewsItem.aspx? ID=515>. One anecdotal data point comes from the Commercial Court, which is hearing a large volume of cases brought against property developers by their creditors. Mr Justice Peter Kelly has stated that he is dealing 'on a daily basis' with cases with valuations of commercial property showing falls in value of 70–80 per cent: 'Judge Says Cases Showing Falls in Property Values of up to 80 per cent', *Irish Times*, 20 October 2009.

15. Using a two-lag VAR, a Johansen procedure identified cointegration relationships significant at 5 per cent: (1, -1.31, 0.16), (1, -0.70, 0.20), with eigenvalues of 0.20, 0.14. Including observations after the market peak in 2006 caused the relationship to disappear, consistent with the idea that the post-bubble housing market is qualitatively different from the bubble one, with falling supply and demand for credit, large stocks of unsold houses, and uncertainty about the magnitude of future price falls.

16. See <http://www.ibf.ie/pdfs/IBFPwCMortgageMarketProfileQ407.pdf>.

17. These data somewhat overstate the contribution of construction to Irish GNP to the extent that they include imported inputs. However the bulky nature of building materials ensures that most are produced domestically.

18. Central Bank of Ireland, *Quarterly Bulletin*, Table B4.

19. M.J. Roche and K. McQuinn, 'Speculation in Agricultural Land', Economics, Finance and Accounting Department working paper no. 1010700, October 2000, Department of Economics, Finance and Accounting, National University of Ireland, Maynooth.

20. See <http://www.knightfrank.ie/documents/Farms%20Market%20-%2009. pdf>.

21. See <http://www.ibf.ie/pdfs/IBFPwCMortgageMarketProfileQ407.pdf>.

22. Figures based on 'Supplementary Documentation, National Asset Management Agency', 16 September 2009: <www.nama.ie/Publications/2009/ Supplementary_Documentation.pdf> and H. Calenti, 'Irish Banks: Vegetative State Reducing to Underperform', RBC Capital Markets research note, 13 August 2009.

23. Figures are total liabilities of Irish banks to Irish and foreign residents from Central Bank *Quarterly Bulletin* Table C3 minus liability totals from Table C6 for credit institutions with mostly foreign operations. The interbank deposit figure excludes lending of Irish banks to each other by subtracting loans to Irish resident financial intermediaries. 1999 figures have been multiplied by 1.4 to express them in 2009 prices.

24. R. Koo, *The Holy Grail of Macroeconomics: Lessons from Japan's Great Recession*, New York, Wiley & Sons, 2008, p. 10.

25. Ibid, pp. 1–37.

26. C. Foote, K. Gerardi, L. Goette and P. Willen, 'Reducing Foreclosures: No Easy Answers', National Bureau of Economic Research working paper no. 15063, June 2009.

27. Ibid, Table 5.

28. White argues that the levels of default are irrationally low for homeowners, reflecting their shame and fear at defaulting on loans, and suggests that a higher level of default would be a socially efficient means of giving more bargaining power to households in negotiating with banks over sharing the losses from falling house prices. See B.T. White, 'Underwater and Not Walking Away: Shame, Fear, and the Social Management of the Housing Crisis', Arizona Legal Studies discussion paper 09-35, University of Arizona, October 2009.

29. M. Adelino, K. Gerardi and P.S. Willen, 'Why Don't Lenders Renegotiate More Home Mortgages? Redefaults, Self-Cures, and Securitization', Federal Reserve Bank of Atlanta working paper no. 2009-17, August 2009.

30. First American CoreLogic, *Negative Equity Report 2009 Q3*, 24 November 2009, Figure 4, available from: <http://www.calculatedriskblog.com/2009/11/negative-equity-report-for-q3.html>, accessed 14 August 2010.

31. Foote et al., 'Reducing Foreclosures'.

32. N. Kiyotaki and J. Moore, 'Credit Cycles', *Journal of Political Economy*, Vol. 105, No. 2, 1997, pp. 211–48; K. Matsuyama, 'Credit Traps and Credit Cycles', *American Economic Review*, Vol. 97, No. 1, 2007, pp. 503–16.

33. R.G. Rajan, 'Why Bank Credit Policies Fluctuate: A Theory and Some Evidence', *The Quarterly Journal of Economics*, Vol. 109, No. 2, 1994, pp. 399–441.

34. G. Dell'Ariccia and R. Marquez, 'Lending Booms and Lending Standards', *Journal of Finance*, Vol. 61, No. 5, 2006, pp. 2511–46.

35. A.N. Berger and G.F. Udell, 'The Institutional Memory Hypothesis and the Procyclicality of Bank Lending Behavior', *Journal of Financial Intermediation*, Vol. 13, No. 4, 2004, pp. 458–95.

36. G. Corsetti, P. Pesenti and N. Roubini, 'Paper Tigers? A Model of the Asian Crisis', *European Economic Review*, Vol. 43, No. 7, 1999, pp. 1211–36.

37. E.G. Mendoza and M.E. Terrones, 'An Anatomy of Credit Booms: Evidence from Macro Aggregates and Micro Data', National Bureau of Economic Research working paper no. 14049, May 2008.

38. G. Dell'Ariccia, D. Igan and L. Laeven, 'Credit Booms and Lending Standards: Evidence from the Subprime Mortgage Market', Centre for Economic Policy Research discussion paper no. 6683, February 2008.

39. A. Mian and A. Sufi, 'The Consequences of Mortgage Credit Expansion: Evidence from the 2007 Mortgage Default Crisis', National Bureau of Economic Research working paper no. 13936, April 2008.

40. P. Englund, 'The Swedish Banking Crisis: Roots and Consequences', *Oxford Review of Economic Policy*, Vol. 15, No. 3, 1999, pp. 80–97.

41. S. Johnson and J. Kwak, *13 Bankers: The Wall Street Takeover and the Next Financial Meltdown*, New York, Pantheon, 2010.

42. This is not to deny that Irish banks may have exerted more direct means to control the political process but, until Irish members of parliament (TDs and Senators) have to declare their liabilities as well as their assets, it is not possible to establish how many leading politicians received large, interest-free loans from the banks.

Chapter 4

1. IMF, *IMF World Economic Outlook*, October 2009, available from: <http://www.imf.org/external/pubs/ft/weo/2009/02/index.htm>, accessed 9 July 2010.

2. Ibid.

3. CSO, 'Quarterly National Accounts, Quarter 4 2009', available from: <http://www.cso.ie/releasespublications/documents/economy/2009/qna_q42009.pdf>, accessed 9 July 2010.

4. Author's calculations based on CSO, 'Expenditure on Gross National Product (chain linked annually referenced to 2007) by Quarter, Statistic and Expenditure Item', available from <http://www.cso.ie/px/pxeirestat/database/eirestat/eirestat.asp>, accessed 9 July 2010.

5. Economic and Social Research Institute, 'Latest permanent tsb/ESRI House Price Index', 30 April 2010, available from: <http://www.esri.ie/irish_economy/permanent_tsbesri_house_p/>, accessed 9 July 2010.

6. *The Economist*, 'Safe as Houses: Compare Countries' House-Price Data Over Time', 8 July 2010, available from: <http://www.economist.com/businessfinance/displaystory.cfm?story_id=14438245>, accessed 9 July 2010.

7. CSO, 'Labour Market and Earnings', 2009, available from: <http://www.cso.ie/px/pxeirestat/database/eirestat/eirestat.asp>, accessed 9 July 2010.

8. Ibid.

9. CSO, 'Economy', 2009, available from: <http://www.cso.ie/px/pxeirestat/database/eirestat/eirestat.asp>, accessed 9 July 2010.

10. European Mortgage Federation, 'Hypostat 2007', 2008, available from: <http://www.hypo.org/Content/default.asp?PageID=524>, accessed 9 July 2010.

11. Ibid.

12. CSO, 'People And Society', 2009, available from: <http://www.cso.ie/px/pxeire-stat/database/eirestat/eirestat.asp>, accessed 9 July 2010.

13. Knight Frank, 'Knight Frank Global House Price Index', 9 December 2009, available from: <http://www.knightfrank.com/news/Knight-Frank-Global-House-Price-Index-082.aspx>, accessed 9 July 2010.

14. Halifax, 'Halifax House Price Index', December 2009, available from: <http://www.lloydsbankinggroup.com/media1/research/halifax_hpi.asp>, accessed 9 July 2010.

15. National Competiveness Council, 'Costs of Doing Business in Ireland' Dublin, National Competiveness Council, 2006.

16. CB Richard Ellis Group, 'Global Office Rents Survey', November 2008, Los Angeles, CA, CB Richard Ellis Group.

17. CB Richard Ellis Group, 'Global Office Rents Survey', May 2010, Los Angeles, CA, CB Richard Ellis Group.

18. National Competiveness Council, 'Costs of Doing Business in Ireland'.

19. Author's calculations based on CSO, Department of Environment, Heritage and Local Government (DOEHLG) and daft.ie statistics.

20. Author's calculations based on CSO, DOEHLG, daft.ie and Irish Banking Federation statistics.

21. Financial Regulator, 'New Data on Residential Mortgage Arrears and Repossessions Published', press release, 22 December 2009.

22. See <http://www.environ.ie/en/Publications/StatisticsandRegularPublications/HousingStatistics/>.

23. It is also not clear whether the institutions supplying the data are only those that are members of the Irish Banking Federation, who account for most but not all of the Irish mortgage market.

24. US Department of Housing and Urban Development, 'New Residential Sales in October 2009', 25 November 2009, available from: <http://www.census.gov/const/newressales_200910.pdf>, accessed 9 July 2010.

25. ESRI, 'Latest permanent tsb/ESRI House Price Index', 2009.

26. See <http://daft.ie/report>.

27. Daft.ie, 'The Daft.ie House Price Report, Quarter 3, 2009', October 2009, available from: <http://www.daft.ie/report/Daft-House-Price-Report-Q3-2009.pdf>, accessed 9 July 2010.

28. See <http://www.abs.gov.au/AUSSTATS/abs@.nsf/mf/6416.0>.

29. See <http://www1.landregistry.gov.uk/houseprices> for the house price index.

30. 'Database to be Established to Monitor House Prices and Market Trends', *Irish Times*, 11 August 2010.

31. Australian Bureau of Statistics, 'Price Indexes and Contract Price Indexation', 2010, available from: <http://www.abs.gov.au/ausstats/abs@.nsf/Latest products/6401.0Main%20Features4Mar%202010?opendocument&tabname =Summary&prodno=6401.0&issue=Mar%202010&num=&view=>, accessed 9 July 2010.

32. See Bureau of Labor Statistics, 'Current Employment Statistics – CES (National)', available from: <http://www.bls.gov/ces/>, accessed 9 July 2010.
33. See 'SmartBay', available from: <http://www.marine.ie/home/services/operational/SmartBay/>, accessed 9 July 2010.

Chapter 5

1. An earlier version of this chapter was read to the conference of the Dublin Economics Workshop, Kenmare, Co. Kerry, 18 October 2009, and to the CentreForum conference in London on 12 November 2009. The author would like to thank conference participants for comments, Marie Hyland for research assistance and FBD Trust for financial support.
2. An account of the Irish banking collapse can be found in P. Honohan, 'Resolving Ireland's Banking Crisis', *The Economic and Social Review*, Vol. 40, No. 2, 2009, pp. 207–31.
3. Irish State agencies are often called 'An Bord Xxxx', meaning the Electricity Board or the Gas Board, for example. In both the 1980s and during the current crisis, the public spending reviews have been dubbed 'An Bord Snip' by the media. Officials tend to give committees titles like 'The Special Group on Public Service Numbers and Expenditure Programmes', the official title for the current review, so the media can perhaps be excused.
4. This is a backward extrapolation on the revised basis adopted from 1982 onwards.
5. Gross domestic product (GDP) and gross national product (GNP) are little different in most European countries, but GDP is considerably bigger in Ireland. There are reasons to prefer GNP to GDP for fiscal ratios – see appendix.
6. P. Honohan and B. Walsh, 'Catching Up with the Leaders: The Irish Hare', *Brookings Papers on Economic Activity*, Vol. 33, No. 1, 2002, pp. 1–78.
7. S. Cromien, 'An Céad Bord Snip', Contemporary Irish History Seminar, Trinity College Dublin, 4 March 2009, mimeo.
8. E. Uchitelle, 'The Effectiveness of Tax Amnesty Programs in Selected Countries', *Federal Reserve Board of New York Quarterly Review*, Autumn 1989, pp. 48–53, available from: <http://www.newyorkfed.org/research/quarterly_review/1989v14/v14n3article5.pdf>, accessed 05 August 2010.
9. The net debt has recently been about 20 GDP points below the gross figure (the state has financial assets, mainly cash arising from pre-funding by the debt management office and the securities held by the National Pension Reserve Fund). But the gross debt figure contains no provision for any Exchequer costs which might emerge from the bank rescue, which works the other way.
10. P. Honohan, Opening address to the ESRI/Foundation for Fiscal Studies Conference, Dublin, 13 October 2009.
11. The reports of the 'Bord Snip' 2009 spending review are downloadable from <www.finance.gov.ie>.

12. J. Lawlor and C. McCarthy, 'Browsing Onwards: Irish Public Spending in Perspective', *Irish Banking Review*, Autumn 2003, pp. 2–17.

13. K. Whelan, 'Policy Lessons from Ireland's Latest Depression', paper presented at the MacGill Summer School, Glenties, Co. Donegal, 20 July 2009, mimeo.

Chapter 6

1. European Commission, *Statistical Annex of European Economy, Spring 2009*, ECFIN/REP/51795/2009, European Commission.

2. Exchequer statement for the period ended 29 February 2008, Dublin, Department of Finance

3. Department of Finance, *Summary of Budget Measures, Budget 2008*, Dublin, Department of Finance, 2007.

4. National Treasury Management Agency, 'Preliminary Results for the Year 2008', Dublin, NTMA, 31 December 2008.

5. Ibid.

6. An Bord Snip was a government-appointed committee to examine public expenditure and propose reductions.

7. The receipts from the tax amnesty (in 1988) played a role in increasing tax revenue, estimated to have been €629 million in 1988. However, we should be careful in treating this. It can't be assumed that some of these receipts would not have flowed into the Exchequer subsequently through tax investigations and audits or taxpayers simply settling their affairs. In this respect, some of this merely represented a bringing forward of revenue that would have accrued in any event. Nonetheless, excluding the receipts from the 1988 tax take would have only meant a 2 per cent difference in the deficit–GDP ratio. That the deficit continued to be reduced in subsequent years suggests that the tax amnesty played a contributory, but not a primary, role in the medium-term rebalancing of public finances.

8. The non-exporting corporate sector had a 40 per cent tax rate, while capital gains and inheritances were also taxed at a much higher rate. The standard tax rate was 35 per cent whereas the higher tax rate was in excess of 50 per cent.

9. CSO Database Direct: in 1989, 33 per cent of merchandise exports went to the UK. See: <http://www.cso.ie/px/pxeirestat/database/eirestat/eirestat.asp>, accessed 26 July 2010.

10. CSO, *Population and Migration Estimates*, Dublin, CSO, 2009.

11. Department of Finance, *Budgetary and Economic Statistics, September 2008*, Dublin, Department of Finance, 2008.

12. Ibid.

13. Department of Finance, *Budget 1990*, Dublin, Department of Finance, December 1989.

14. C. McCarthy, 'Ireland's Second Fiscal Consolidation: Lessons from the Last Time', UCD Centre for Economic Research working paper WP09/17, October 2009, available from: <http://www.ucd.ie/t4cms/wp09.17.pdf>, p. 5.

15. A. Alesina, R. Perotti and J. Tavares, 'The Political Economy of Fiscal Adjustments', *Brookings Papers on Economic Activity*, Spring 1998, pp. 197–266, p. 199.

16. V. Hogan (2004), 'Expansionary Fiscal Contractions? Evidence from Panel Data', UCD Centre for Economic Research working paper WP03/03, January 2003, p. 3.

17. D. Prammer, 'Expansionary Fiscal Consolidations? An Appraisal of the Literature on Non-Keynesian Effects of Fiscal Policy and a Case Study for Austria', *Monetary Policy & the Economy*, Q3/04, 2003, available from: <http://www.oenb.at/en/img/mop_20043_analyses3_tcm16-21309.pdf>, p. 50.

18. A. Alfonso, 'Expansionary Fiscal Consolidations in Europe: New Evidence', European Central Bank, working paper series no. 675, September 2006, p. 31.

19. Hogan, 'Expansionary Fiscal Contractions?', p. 3.

20. Department of Finance, *Pre-Budget Outlook*, Dublin, Department of Finance, November 2009.

21. European Commission, *Statistical Annex of European Economy, Spring 2009*.

22. Eurostat, 'Population, 2009', Luxembourg, European Commission, available from: <http://epp.eurostat.ec.europa.eu/tgm/table.do?tab=table&language=en&pcode=tps00001&tableSelection=1&footnotes=yes&labeling=labels&plugin=1>.

23. Department of Finance, *Report of the Special Group on Public Service Numbers and Expenditure Programmes*, (An Bord Snip Nua), Dublin, Department of Finance, 2009, p. 2.

24. Department of Finance, *Budget 2009*, Dublin, Department of Finance, December 2008; Department of Finance, *Budget 2010*, Dublin, Department of Finance, December 2009.

25. Department of Finance, 'Financial Statement of the Minister for Finance', 7 April 2009, Dublin, Department of Finance.

26. J. Fitz Gerald, 'Fiscal Policy for Recovery', ESRI working paper no. 326, October 2009, p. 9.

27. CSO Database Direct: Details on Taxation by Item and Year, see <http://www.cso.ie/px/pxeirestat/Database/Eirestat/Eirestat.asp>, accessed 26 July 2010.

28. OECD, *Economic Survey of Ireland 2006*, Paris, OECD, 2006.

29. A. Bergin, T. Conefrey, J. Fitz Gerald and I. Kearney, 'The Behaviour of the Irish Economy: Insights from the HERMES Macro-Economic Model', ESRI working paper no. 287, April 2009.

30. Though there would still be the issue of public sector pay.

31. H. McGee, 'IMF to Have Role if Cuts Are Not Made, says Harney', *Irish Times*, 17 October 2009.

32. 'Fight for Financial Survival', *Prime Time*, 26 February 2009, available from: <http://www.rte.ie/news/2009/0226/primetime.html>, accessed 30 June 2010.

33. NTMA, 'Ireland Launches 3-Year €4 Billion 3.9% Bond', 25 February 2009, Dublin, NTMA.

34. NTMA, 'Ireland Successfully Launches New €6 Billion 4% Bond', 8 January 2009, Dublin, NTMA. The demand for Irish debt was so high that the NTMA originally intended to offer €3 billion, but they received bids of over twice that amount.

35. NTMA, 'Preliminary Results for the Year 2008', 31 December 2008, Dublin, NTMA.

36. Goodbody Stockbrokers, 'Irish Economic Commentary: Recovery in Sight', 15 October 2009, Dublin, Goodbody Stockbrokers.

37. B. O'Mahony, '15% Chance We'll Default on Debts', *Irish Examiner*, 16 May 2009.

38. *Irish Times*, 'Warning that No Vote Will Deter Future Investment', *Irish Times*, 15 September 2009.

39. Davy Stockbrokers, 'Research Report: Irish Economy', 29 September 2009, Dublin, Davy Stockbrokers.

40. D. Doyle, 'Irish Bonds "Great Bargain", Debt Chief Somers Says', *Bloomberg*, 27 March 2009, available from: <http://www.bloomberg.com/apps/news?pid=newsarchive&sid=asadtlDx3UnA&refer=worldwide>, accessed 26 July 2010.

41. Irish Stock Exchange, ISEQ® Bond Index Series, see <http://www.ise.ie/app/bondDailyIndex.asp>.

42. See M. Taft, 'What the Markets are Telling Us (and What our Commentators are Not)', *Notes on the Front*, 16 May 2010, available from: <http://noteson-thefront.typepad.com/politicaleconomy/2010/05/what-are-the-markets-really -trying-to-tell-us——we-are-not-spain-we-are-not-italy-we-are-not-portugal-repeat-we-are-n.html>, accessed 26 July 2010.

43. E. Gilmore, 'A New Deal for Ireland', speech delivered 29 November 2008, available from: <http://www.labour.ie/press/listing/1227990873132673.html>, accessed 26 July 2010.

44. J. Burton, 'Ireland Urgently Needs Fiscal Stimulus Package to Kick-Start Economy', 2 December 2008, available from: <http://www.joanburton.ie/?postid=1009>, accessed 26 July 2010.

45. Labour Party, 'Building a New, Better Fairer Future: Labour's Priorities for the Emergency Budget', 2 April 2009, available from: <http://www.labour.ie/download/pdf/building_a_new_better_and_brighter_future.pdf>, accessed 27 July 2010.

46. D. de Bréadún and M. O'Halloran, 'Big Job Cuts in Public Service Are "Doable" – Gilmore', *Irish Times*, 18 July 2009.

47. ICTU, 'Draft Framework for a Pact for Stabilisation, Social Solidarity and Economic Renewal', 28 January 2009, available from: <http://www.ictu.ie/

download/pdf/draft_framework_for_a_pact_28_jan_09.pdf>, accessed 27 July 2010.

48. ICTU, 'Congress 10 Point Plan for a Better, Fairer Way', November 2009, available from: <http://www.ictu.ie/download/pdf/congress_10_point_plan.pdf>, accessed 27 July 2010.

49. Sinn Féin, smaller left-wing parties, bloggers and individual economists and commentators – many of whom who grouped around Progressive-economy.ie.

50. Department of Finance, *Pre-Budget Outlook 2010*, Dublin, Department of Finance, 2009.

51. Department of Finance, 'Financial Statement of the Minister for Finance', 9 December 2009, Dublin, Department of Finance.

52. Department of Finance, *Macroeconomic and Fiscal Framework 2009–2013*, April 2009, Dublin, Department of Finance.

53. Department of Finance, *Stability Programme Update 2010*, 9 December 2009, Dublin, Department of Finance.

54. This does not include social insurance contributions or local authority revenue.

55. This is worked out by: Revenue Loss ÷ Revenue – GDP Ratio = GDP Loss.

56. ESRI, *Quarterly Economic Commentary*, Autumn 2009, Dublin, ESRI, p. 29.

57. NCB, *Irish Economy Monitor*, 6 July 2010, Dublin, NCB.

58. IMF, *World Economic Outlook*, April 2010, Washington, DC, IMF.

59. European Commission, *European Economic Forecast*, Spring 2010, Brussels, European Commission.

60. IBEC, *Quarterly Review: Economic Trends*, June 2010, Dublin, IBEC.

61. Ernst & Young, *Economic Eye Summer Forecast*, Summer 2010, Lisburn, Ernst & Young/Oxford Economics.

62. European Commission, *Recommendation for a Council Opinion on the Updated Stability Programme of Ireland, 2009–2014*, Brussels, European Commission, 2010.

63. C. McCarthy, 'Fiscal Adjustment and Re-Balancing the Irish Economy', paper presented to the Statistical and Social Inquiry Society of Ireland, 26 November 2009.

64. World Economic Forum, *Global Competitiveness Report 2009–2010*, Geneva, World Economic Summit, 2009.

65. Forfás and the National Competitiveness Council, *Review of International Assessments of Ireland's Competitiveness*, 20 December 2007, Dublin, Forfás and the National Competitiveness Council, p. 13.

66. Department of Social and Family Affairs, *Statistical Information on Social Welfare Services 2008*, Dublin, Department of Social and Family Affairs, 2009.

67. Forfás and the National Competitiveness Council, *Statement on Education and Training*, February 2008, Dublin, Forfás and the National Competitiveness Council.

68. CSO, 'Survey on Income and Living Conditions, 2008', November 2009, Dublin, CSO.

69. European Anti-Poverty Network, 'Social Welfare: How Ireland Compares in Europe', September 2009, Dublin, European Anti-Poverty Network.

70. J.K. Galbraith, *The Great Crash 1929*, New York, Penguin, 1954.

71. Ibid, p. 194.

72. European Anti-Poverty Network, *Out of the Traps: Ending Poverty Traps and Making Work Pay for People in Poverty*, Dublin, EAPN, 2007.

73. '[T]he tenets of the climatological school of economics argues that our purpose is to create an economic climate. From this economic climate investment will come and from the investment jobs will bloom, and from the blooming jobs there will be such a scent that poverty will be impossible. That is how the theory goes' – Michael D. Higgins, TD, Dáil Eireann, 26 January 1989.

74. Fine Gael, *NewERA*, November 2009, available from: <http://www.finegael.org/upload/NewERA.pdf>, accessed 27 July 2010.

75. ICTU, *Governance for State Companies*, Dublin, ICTU, 2005.

76. OECD, *Benefits and Wages Database 2007*, Paris, OECD, 2007. Irish childcare costs rank the highest in the OECD.

77. E. Smyth and S. McCoy, 'Investing in Education: Combating Educational Disadvantage', ESRI research series 006, 13 June 2009.

78. IMF, 'Total Government Net Debt (National Currency) Data for All Countries', *EconomyWatch*, available from: <http://www.economywatch.com/economic-statistics/economic-indicators/General_Government_Net_Debt_National_Currency/>, and Department of Finance, *Stability Programme Update 2010*, Dublin, Department of Finance, 2010.

79. Davy Stockbrokers, 'Research Report: Irish Economy'.

80. Comhar, the Sustainable Development Council, 'Towards a Green New Deal for Ireland', October 2009, Dublin, Comhar, SDC.

81. K. Deeter and S. Kinsella, 'Municipal Bonds Could Be the Solution to Many Problems', *Sunday Business Post*, 15 November 2009.

82. Fitz Gerald, 'Fiscal Policy for Recovery'. p. 15.

83. One commission member refused to sign the report because of its insistence that the net tax rate – as a percentage of GDP – should not be increased. This was not necessitated by the terms of reference.

84. Department of Finance, 'Analysis of High Income Individuals' Restriction 2007', 2009, available from: <http://www.finance.gov.ie/documents/publications/reports/2009/analytaxrestrict09.pdf>, accessed 27 July 2010.

85. Think Tank for Action on Social Change (TASC), 'TASC Calls for the Government to Cut Tax Breaks, Not Social Welfare', *TASC 2010 Pre-Budget Submission*, 3 December 2009, Dublin, TASC.

86. T. Callan (ed.), 'Budget Perspectives, 2010', ESRI research series no. 12, October 2009.

87. Indeed, without exemption limits, those in the third lowest decile will pay a higher percentage of income than any other decile.

88. Goodbody Stockbrokers, 'Irish Economic Commentary: Recovery in Sight'.

89. Eurostat, 'Taxation Trends in the European Union', Luxembourg, Eurostat, 2008.

90. Commission on Taxation, *Fourth Report of the Commission on Taxation, Special Taxation*, May 1985, Dublin, Commission on Taxation.

91. OECD, *OECD Public Management Reviews – Ireland: Towards an Integrated Public Service*, Paris, OECD, 2008.

92. Social and Cultural Planning Office of the Netherlands in association with the OECD, *Public Sector Performance: An International Comparison of Education, Health Care, Law and Order and Public Administration*, September 2004, The Hague, Social and Cultural Planning Office of the Netherlands in association with the OECD.

93. National Competitiveness Council, *Annual Competitiveness Report 2009*, August 2009, Dublin, National Competitiveness Council.

94. Vacancies are at 30 per cent at Principal Officer, 18 per cent at Assistant Principal and 15 per cent at Higher Executive Officer levels – Private communication with the Office of the Revenue Commissioners.

95. D. Ó Broin and E. Waters, *Governing Below the Centre: Local Governance in Ireland*, Dublin, New Island and TASC, 2007.

96. Indeed, while the popular, sometimes superficial, reading of the *Special Group Report* assumed the savings came from 'waste' elimination, alternative readings suggested that the *Report* was unable to find much waste in the public sector and that most of the proposals concerned reducing transfers to low income groups, enterprises and community groups. See M. Taft, 'Shock! Horror! McCarthy Vindicates Public Sector Efficiency!', *Notes on the Front*, 20 July 2009, available from: <http://notesonthefront.typepad.com/politicaleconomy/2009/07/shock-horror-mccarthy-vindicates-public-sector-efficiency——-noel-whelan-wants-you-to-read-the-report-he-wants-you-to.html>, accessed 1 July 2010.

97. S. Burke, 'My Fantasy Health Budget', SaraBurke.com, 19 November 2009, available from: <http://saraburke.wordpress.com/?s=My+Fantasy+Health+Budget>, accessed 1 July 2010.

98. J. Stewart, 'Current Policies Set to Exacerbate Economic Crisis', *ProgressiveEconomy.ie*, 12 May 2009, available from: <http://www.progressive-economy.ie/2009/05/current-policies-set-to-exacerbate.html>, accessed 27 July 2010.

99. A.S. Bénétrix and P.R. Lane, 'The Impact of Fiscal Shocks on the Irish Economy', Institute for International Integration Studies discussion paper no. iisdp281, February 2009.

100. M. Burke, 'A Genuine Economic Recovery – The Case for Fiscal Stimulus', paper presented to FEPS/TASC seminar on 'Stimulating Recovery', 10 June 2010.

101. For illustrative purposes, the timing of bringing the investment on stream is taken from Fine Gael's NewERA document.

102. E. Morgenroth and J. Fitz Gerald (eds.), 'Ex-Ante Evaluation of the Investment Priorities for the National Development Plan (2007–2013)', October 2006, Dublin, ESRI.
103. Green New Deal Group, 'The Cuts Won't Work, Second Report of the Green New Deal Group', London, New Economics Foundation, 2010.

Chapter 7

1. Contact: Anthony.leddin@ul.ie or telephone: 061 202088. The author is grateful to Vani Borooah and Brendan Walsh for comments on an earlier draft of the chapter. All errors or omissions are the author's responsibility.
2. F. Barry, 'Social Partnership, Competitiveness and Exit from Fiscal Crisis', *The Economic and Social Review*, Vol. 40, No. 1, Spring 2009, pp. 1–12; J. Fitz Gerald, 'Wage Formation and the Labour Market', in F. Barry (ed.), *Understanding Ireland's Economic Growth*, London, Macmillan Press and New York, St Martin's Press, 1999; J. O'Leary, 'Social Partnership and the Celtic Tiger', paper presented to Dublin Economic Workshop, Kenmare, October 2006.
3. The NWAs have been credited with improving the industrial relations climate, reducing days lost in strikes, curtailing the variability of labour costs and minimising the climate of uncertainty. On the cost side, due to differences in labour productivity from sector to sector, 'one wage does not fit all' and this can result in an inefficient allocation of labour resources. Furthermore, the wage agreement process is generally regarded as being both undemocratic and lacking in transparency. Negotiations are conducted behind closed doors by a very small number of government, trade union and employer representatives who are not elected by a wide franchise. The main 'players' in the Partnership talks include the director general of the employers' group IBEC, the president and general secretary of the Irish Congress of Trade Unions (ICTU), the president of SIPTU, the president of the Construction Federation and the secretary general to the Department of the Taoiseach. In the early Partnership agreements, the leaders of the main unions affiliated to the ICTU negotiated and then decided whether to enter into a particular agreement. More recently, the main trade unions balloted members at branch and national level before deciding to enter into Partnership. It should be noted that the Partnership or National Wage Agreements are not just concerned with the pay issue. The agreements also take into account a whole range of issues including legislation underlying employment standards, modernisation, industrial and workplace relations, minimum wages and migrant workers. This paper is only concerned with the pay issue. Additionally, the NWA pay awards take no account of the value of non-contributory pensions in the public sector or annual bonuses and other benefits in the private sector. Also, between January 1994 and March 1997 the construction industry received a different set of pay awards.

4. For example, starting with 100 in the base period, a pay award of 2.5 per cent in 1988 would move the index to 102.5. A further award of 2.5 per cent in the next year would move the index to 105.06 and so on for all other pay awards right to the end of the period in August 2008.

5. *Report of the Public Service Benchmarking Body*, 30 June 2002, Dublin, Stationary Office. The PSBB was established in July 2000 and reported in June 2002. Officially, the purpose of the benchmarking awards was to improve productivity in the public sector and end internal wage relativities and switch instead to private–public sector wage relativities. A major criticism of the Benchmarking Report was that, unlike the Buckley Review Group (which covered the highest levels of the public sector hierarchy) the basis underlying the various pay awards was not published and the proposed increases in productivity were not spelled out. No attempt was made in the *PSBB Report* to justify or explain the differential pay awards, and this has been a source of much criticism in the media. It was also argued that low wages in the public sector had made it difficult to recruit and motivate staff and this had adverse implications for labour productivity. The *PSBB Report* covered 145,000 public sector employees (60 per cent of total) and awarded pay increases ranging from 3 per cent to 25 per cent. The average pay award across all sectors was 8.9 per cent and this is the figure used in Tables 7.1 and 7.2 to derive the index labelled 'public sector (including benchmarking)'.

6. F. Walsh and E. Strobl, 'Recent Trends in Trade Union Membership in Ireland', *The Economic and Social Review*, Vol. 40, No. 1, Spring 2009, pp. 117–38; T. Hastings (ed.), *The State of the Unions: Challenges Facing Organised Labour in Ireland*, Dublin, Liffey Press, 2009.

7. A.W. Phillips, 'The Relation between Unemployment and the Rate of Change of Money Wage Rates in the United Kingdom, 1861–1957', *Economica*, Vol. 25, No. 100, 1958, pp. 283–99.

8. P.A. Samuelson and R.M. Solow, 'Analytical Aspects of Anti-Inflation Policy', *American Economic Review Papers and Proceedings*, Vol. 50, No. 2, 1960, pp. 177–94.

9. The usual assumption that inflation is equal to nominal wage changes minus productivity growth assumes a fixed value of labour's share in national income. However, this may not be the case as wages' share of gross domestic product (GDP) fell dramatically in Ireland in the 1990s.

10. M. Friedman, 'The Role of Monetary Policy', *American Economic Review*, Vol. 58, No. 1, March 1968, pp. 1–17.

11. E.S. Phelps, 'Phillips Curves, Expectations of Inflation and Optimal Unemployment over Time', *Economica*, Vol. 34, August 1967; E.S. Phelps, 'Money-Wage Dynamics and Labor Market Equilibrium', *Journal of Political Economy*, Vol. 76, No. 4, Part II, 1968, pp. 678–711.

12. R.E. Lucas, Jr., 'Expectations and the Neutrality of Money', *Journal of Economic Theory*, Vol. 4, No. 2, 1972, pp. 103–24; R.E. Lucas, Jr., 'Some International Evi-

dence on Output-Inflation Tradeoffs', *American Economic Review*, Vol. 63, No. 3, 1973, pp. 326–34.

13. R.J. Gordon, 'The History of the Phillips Curve: An American Perspective', Australasian Meetings of the Econometric Society A.W.H. Phillips Invited Lecture, Wellington, New Zealand, 9 July 2008.

14. Ibid, p. 12.

15. Ibid, p. 14.

16. R.J. Gordon, 'The Theory of Domestic Inflation', *American Economic Review Papers and Proceedings*, Vol. 67, No. 1, February 1977, pp. 128–34; R.J. Gordon, 'Price Inertia and Policy Ineffectiveness in the United States, 1890–1980', *Journal of Political Economy*, Vol. 90, No. 6, December 1982, pp. 1087–117.

17. Gordon, 'The History of the Phillips Curve'.

18. D. Staiger, J.H. Stock and M.W. Watson, 'Prices, Wages, and the U.S. NAIRU in the 1990s', in A.B. Krueger and R.M. Solow (eds.), *The Roaring Nineties: Can Full Employment Be Sustained?*, New York, The Russell Sage Foundation and the Century Foundation Press, 2001, pp. 3–60; R.J. Gordon, 'The Time-Varying NAIRU and its Implications for Economic Policy', *Journal of Economic Perspectives*, Vol. 11, No. 1, 1997, pp. 11–32.

19. F.E. Kydland and E.C. Prescott, 'Rules Rather than Discretion: The Inconsistency of Optimal Plans', *Journal of Political Economy*, Vol. 85, No. 3, 1977, pp. 473–91.

20. J. Gali and M. Gertler, 'Inflation Dynamics: A Structural Econometric Analysis', *Journal of Monetary Economics*, Vol. 44, No. 2, 1999, pp. 195–222.

21. Gordon, 'The History of the Phillips Curve', p. 25.

22. An anti-inflation group was established under *Sustaining Progress* to monitor unanticipated inflation. This group continued under *Towards 2016*.

23. Keeney identifies three distinct historical phases: 1980–94, 1994–2001 and 2001–05. However, the analysis is more to do with changes in the structural rate of unemployment and its impact on wage inflation. (M.J. Keeney, 'Wage Inflation and Structural Unemployment in Ireland', Central Bank of Ireland research technical paper no. 7/RT/08, October 2008 and *Journal of the Statistical and Social Inquiry Society of Ireland*, Vol. 37, 2007/08, pp. 270–90, read before the society on 29 May 2008.)

24. P. Honohan and P.R. Lane, 'Divergent Inflation Rates in EMU', *Economic Policy*, Vol. 18, No. 37, 2003, pp. 357–94; P. Honohan and P.R. Lane, 'Exchange Rates and Inflation under EMU: An Update', Centre for Economic Policy Research discussion paper no. 4583, August 2004.

25. If productivity was taken into account, the relative share would be considerably lower. It is also worth noting that wages' share of GDP at current factor cost (<http://ec.europa.eu/economy_finance/publications/publication15050_en.pdf>, Table 32, page 92) fell much more significantly in Ireland. Between 1988 and 2000, the wage share index fell by 19.7 per cent in Ireland, 2.3 per cent in the EU15, 0.14 per cent in the US and 0.13 per cent in the UK. This

substantiates the point of a rapidly expanding Irish economy and wages declining as a percentage of GDP.

26. As explained in the first section, the pay awards over the 1988–2008 period were used to compile a nominal wage index and this index was then used to derive the annual percentage change in nominal earnings.

27. The unemployment rate, seasonally unadjusted (U), was obtained from the Central Statistics Office. The unemployment gap is defined as the difference between actual unemployment (U) and the natural rate of unemployment (Un). This raises the problem of how to measure the natural rate of unemployment. Keeney, in 'Wage Inflation and Structural Unemployment in Ireland', addresses this question and discusses the various techniques that have been used in the literature. These techniques involve either estimating a full structural model, a reduced form model, univariate estimation, which decomposes unemployment into its stationary (the non-accelerating inflation rate of unemployment (NAIRU)) and non-stationary elements, or a multivariate filtering approach, which combines 'economic information' and filtering to derive a time-varying NAIRU (TV-NAIRU).

The initial approach adopted here was the use of the univariate estimation technique. This involves applying the Hodrick-Prescott filter to the unemployment data to derive the permanent or stationary component of unemployment. This stationary component is a weighted moving average of leads and lags. The degree of smoothing has to be decided in advance using a lambda operator. The standard lambda operator of 1600, for example, would remove the cyclical element in unemployment between two and eight years. However, the filtered unemployment series (NAIRU) is effectively a moving average and, as such, the unemployment gap is very small, even at high levels of unemployment. For example, in 1993 when the unemployment rate was 16 per cent, the unemployment gap was virtually non-existent. Keeney does estimate an unemployment gap using a 'semi-structural model' to obtain 'endogenously-determined Kalman estimates' of the NAIRU. A 'meaningful' unemployment gap is estimated and this shows that actual unemployment was greater than the NAIRU from 1980 to 1997 and thereafter below it. This, in turn, raises the question of what is 'natural' about a natural rate of unemployment of 16 per cent. In any case, a small and variable unemployment gap does not capture the essence of the analysis in this paper. The key point is that the very rapid fall in unemployment, in part, triggered an upsurge in wage demands and this eventually led to a wage–inflation spiral. It is not possible to capture this effect by using a filter-based unemployment gap. It was decided, therefore, to replace the unemployment gap with both the level of unemployment (U) and the rate of change in unemployment (u).

28. Income tax rates fell rapidly between 1988 and 2008 and this is frequently cited (mistakenly or not) as having an important bearing on negotiated earnings. This is because what matters to the workers is real, post-tax, wages. After a

limited amount of experimentation, the tax variable was derived by applying arbitrary weights of 0.4, 0.4 and 0.2 to the three income tax bands over the 1988–92 period and weights of 0.5 and 0.5 to the two bands over the 1992–2008 period.

29. It is possible to attempt to improve the specification by including dummy variables to capture a wage freeze from January to May 1994, October to December 2003 and July to November 2006. Other dummy variables could be included to represent the local bargaining clause in 1992 and between July 1998 and June 1999. In addition, there was also the early settler provision from October 2000 to September 2001. Most important is the first phase of the benchmarking agreement between October 2001 and September 2002 and the second phase between January and June 2004. Furthermore, a dummy variable may also account for an 'inflation compensation' award and a 'once-off payment' award made between October 2001 and September 2002. In the reported results, and in an effort to remain as close to the NKPC and TPC specifications as possible, no attempt has been made to identify the importance of these clauses.

30. For a variety of reasons, changes in productivity are likely to have a bearing on wage inflation. For example, increases in productivity are likely to reduce the time-varying NAIRU and, secondly, increase company profits and, therefore, higher wage demands in the future. Keeney, in 'Wage Inflation and Structural Unemployment in Ireland', presents empirical evidence of the importance of productivity and the sterling exchange rate in determining wage inflation in Ireland.

31. While interest rates are normally associated with the demand side of the economy, events in Ireland from about 1994 onwards ensured interest rates had an important bearing on the supply side. Nominal interest rates were externally determined from about 1994 onwards as Ireland prepared for entry into EMU and the introduction of the single currency in 1999. Critically, in 2001, as the economy was cooling down after seven years of rapid export-led growth, the ECB cut nominal interest rates when an independent Central Bank of Ireland would probably have raised rates. Given the relatively high Irish inflation rate, the real interest rate was negative for long periods of time and this was undoubtedly a critical factor underlying the property bubble in Ireland. Other studies, Keeney, 'Wage Inflation and Structural Unemployment in Ireland', for example, use the sterling exchange rate as this could reflect external trading conditions. The sterling exchange rate may also act as a proxy for the difference between the UK and Irish unemployment gaps and this, in turn, may have a strong bearing on migration.

32. This is also borne out by the findings of Keeney in 'Wage Inflation and Structural Unemployment in Ireland': 'We can say that up to 40 per cent of the estimated unemployment gap could "explain" the variation in wage inflation immediately' (p. 18).

33. The real effective exchange rate figure was derived using IMF data from January 1991 to December 1994 and Central Bank of Ireland's real harmonised competitiveness indicator from January 1995 to August 2009. The real exchange rate relative to the UK and the US were derived using consumer prices (CPI) and the Irish pound exchange rate. Due to the unavailability of earlier data the start point is January 1991.

34. P. Honohan and A. Leddin, 'Ireland in EMU: More Shocks, Less Insulation?', *Economic and Social Review*, Vol. 37, No. 2, Summer/Autumn 2006, pp. 263–94.

35. Perhaps this is partly due to the lack of economic expertise in the Department of Finance: Parliamentary Debates (Official Report – Unrevised) Dail Eireann Wednesday, 17 December 2008 – 'Deputy Joan Burton asked the Minister for Finance Q. [T]he number of people working in his Department: the number of qualified economists, having a masters degrees in economics, PhDs in economics ... and if he will make a statement on the matter. Minister for Finance (Deputy Brian Lenihan): There are currently 614 people (whole time equivalents) employed in my Department. There are currently 57 officers who hold degrees in Economics and related disciplines, 44 who hold a Masters qualification in Economics and related disciplines, and 1 officer who holds a PhD. Some officers will, of course, be included in more than 1 of these categories.'

Chapter 8

1. Head of Regulation, Trade and Policy Foresight, Forfás. Views expressed are not necessarily those of Forfás.

2. Forfás, *Sharing Our Future: Ireland 2025 – Strategic Policy Requirements for Enterprise Development*, Dublin, Forfás, 2009, available from: <http://www.forfas.ie/media/forfas090713_sharing_our_future.pdf>, accessed 10 June 2010.

3. National Competitiveness Council, see <http://www.competitiveness.ie/aboutus/ourwork/>, accessed 10 June 2010.

4. United Nations Conference on Trade and Development, *World Investment Report 2010: Investing in a Low-Carbon Economy*, UNCTAD, 2010, available from: <http://www.unctad.org/en/docs/wir2010_en.pdf>, accessed 23 August 2010.

5. Department of Finance, *Guidelines for the Appraisal and Management of Capital Expenditure Proposals in the Public Sector*, Dublin, Department of Finance, 1994, available from: <http://www.finance.gov.ie/viewdoc.asp?DocID=1216&CatID=16&StartDate=01+January+1994&m=>, accessed 10 June 2010.

6. Karl Deeter and Stephen Kinsella (2009), 'Municipal Bonds Could Be the Solution to Many Problems', *Sunday Business Post*, 15 November 2009, available from: <http://www.thepost.ie/themarket/municipal-bonds-could-be-the-solution-to-many-problems-45601.html>, accessed 10 June 2010.

7. Forfás, *Review of the European Single Market*, Dublin, Forfás, 2008, available from: <http://www.forfas.ie/media/forfas080214_european_single_market.pdf>, accessed 10 June 2010.

8. The formula for trade intensities is given by the following: Export intensity: $IEXij = (Xij/Xi)/(Mj/(Mw-Mj))$, Import intensity: $IIMij = (Mij/Mi)/(Xj/(Xw-Xi))$, where Xi = total exports from country I, Xij = exports from country i to country j, Mj = total imports of country j, Mij = imports of country i from country j, Xw = total world exports, Mw = total world imports.

9. OECD, 'Percentage of Fibre Connections in Total Broadband, December 2009', updated, available from: <http://www.oecd.org/dataoecd/21/58/39574845.xls>, accessed 10 June 2010.

10. Forfás, *A Baseline Assessment of Ireland's Oil Dependence: Key Policy Considerations*, Dublin, Forfás, April 2006, available from: <http://www.forfas.ie/media/forfas060404_irelands_oil_dependence.pdf>, accessed 10 June 2010.

11. US Department of Energy, Energy Information Administration, 'Annual Energy Review, 2008', 26 June 2009, Table 11.5, available from: <http://www.eia.doe.gov/emeu/aer/txt/ptb1105.html>, accessed 10 June 2010.

12. US Department of Energy, Energy Information Administration, 'World Proved Reserves of Oil and Natural Gas, Most Recent Estimates', 3 March 2009, available from: <http://www.eia.doe.gov/emeu/international/reserves.html>, accessed 10 June 2010.

13. Forfás, *Sharing Our Future*.

Chapter 9

1. This is an adaptation of a paper prepared jointly by Edward Nell and Raymond Majewski as part of a larger project on *Maintaining Full Employment*.

2. New School for Social Research.

3. Women's Aid, *Annual Statistics 2009*, available from: <http://www.women-said.ie/download/pdf/annual_statistics_report_2009.pdf>, accessed 9 August 2010, pp. 8–12.

4. CSO, *Crime and Justice Report 2009*, spring report, available from: <http://www.cso.ie/statistics/CrimeandJustice.htm>, accessed 9 August 2010.

5. CSO, *Live Register Additional Tables, December 2009*, available from: <http://www.cso.ie/releasespublications/documents/labour_market/2009/lrege0_dec2009.pdf>, accessed 9 August 2010, p. 3.

6. This paper sketches out an Employer of Last Resort (ELR) programme. Further details, a study of the macroeconomics of an ELR and additional simulations will be found in a forthcoming Edward Elgar book by Edward Nell and Raymond Majewski, *Maintaining Full Employment*, and in a series of papers, for example, E.J. Nell, 'The Simple Theory of Unemployment', in A.W. Warner, M. Forstater, S.M. Rosen and W.S. Vickrey (eds.), *Commitment to Full Employ-*

ment: The Economics and Social Policy of William S. Vickrey (Columbia University Seminar Series), New York, M.E. Sharpe, 2000, pp. 69–88.

7. Of course, this abstracts from all the difficulties; in practice it would not work so smoothly. Training programmes may prepare workers for jobs that are disappearing and could easily fail to anticipate the new needs of business; workers could settle into comfortable but low-paying ELR jobs and be reluctant to move.

8. This relationship, known as the Phillips Curve, has a long and largely unsuccessful history in policy analysis. It was never truly reliable. Early studies of the alleged relationship were developed by A.W. Phillips and R. Lipsey; the econometrics used – especially the procedures for identification – would not be acceptable today. See N.J. Wulwick, 'History and Methodology of Econometrics', *Oxford Economic Papers*, New Series, Vol. 41, No. 1, January 1989, pp. 170–88. It has never been clear whether money wages or prices were at issue; if the mark-up was constant it would not matter, but (marginal productivity theory being unrealistic) why should the mark-up be constant? Many different shapes and positions have been proposed; by now it seems clear that while there is certainly some sort of broad inverse relationship between unemployment and inflation, no precisely defined function can be fitted to data stretching over the business cycle (see E.J. Nell, *The General Theory of Transformational Growth, Keynes after Sraffa*, Cambridge, Cambridge University Press, 1998, Chapter 11).

9. When the inflation rate is greater than the rate of economic growth, the burden of debt is growing, forcing firms to crack down on costs; it also tends to imply that the financial sector will be growing faster than industry, weakening the growth of productivity. Growth will be sluggish even in a boom, so labour will be weak and unable to maintain enough pressure to keep wages rising with the cost of living. Therefore, inflationary spirals will tend to peter out. Also high real interest rates tend to support the exchange rate – and to weaken those of primary producers.

10. An example is a Taylor Rule, where the Central Bank would set the overnight rate equal to 1 per cent + 0.5*(percentage deviation of GDP from target) + 1.5*(rate of inflation) (J.B. Taylor, 'Discretion versus Policy Rules in Practice', *Carnegie Rochester Conference Series on Public Policy*, Vol. 39, 1993, pp. 195–214. There are of course other reasons to favour policy rules. Among other things they make it easier to anticipate government policy and help make the reasoning behind decisions easier to understand.

11. R.M. Solow, 'Lecture I: Guess Who Likes Workfare', in A. Gutmann (ed.), *Work and Welfare*, Princeton, NJ, Princeton University Press, 1998; and R.M. Solow, 'Lecture II: Guess Who Pays for Workfare', in A. Gutmann (ed.), *Work and Welfare*, 1998.

12. T.R. Marmor, J.L. Mashaw and P.L. Harvey, *America's Misunderstood Welfare State: Persistent Myths, Enduring Realities*, London, Basic Books, 1992.

13. Most American ELR proposals are of this kind, including those described in H.P. Minsky, *Stabilising an Unstable Economy*, New York, McGraw-Hill, 1986; W. Mosler, 'Full Employment and Price Stability', *Journal of Post Keynesian Economics*, Vol. 20, No. 2, Winter 1997-8, pp. 167-82; L.R. Wray, 'Government Deficits, Investment, Saving, and Growth', *Journal of Economic Issues*, Vol. 23, No. 4, December 1989, pp. 977-1002.

14. A given size of the ELR can be used as a target for monetary and fiscal policy similar to the non-accelerating inflation rate of unemployment (NAIRU).

15. M. Forstater, 'Functional Finance and Full Employment: Lessons from Lerner for Today', *Journal of Economic Issues*, Vol. 33, No. 1, 1999, pp. 1-17.

16. Senator Paul Simon's proposals in *Let's Put America Back to Work: Guaranteed Job Opportunities for Everyone Who Wants to Work* (New York, Basic Books, 1988) emphasises this. Simon is particularly interested in the problem of structural unemployment.

17. It has some (but not all) of the positive macroeconomic effects of the ELR.

18. The idea is that employers will prefer these trained workers over others if the training enhances their skills. Of course the employers could be wrong, or be hiring these workers for reasons other than their skills. A more serious problem is that the ELR programme may simply replace training that the employers or workers would have provided without government assistance. In this case it would not increase productivity, but simply shift the cost from employers and/or workers in the industry to the federal government. As we shall see, substitution of this kind is a general problem of the ELR for which there is no simple answer.

19. The problem is one of degree. It is unlikely that a market wage ELR programme would be able to provide people with the same type of job they lost. In general people in the ELR would be underemployed. So while they receive a market wage most people would be paid less than they would make in a private job if one were available. They thus would be willing to move.

20. Many people undergoing training will make use of part-time public service employment to help maintain themselves during the training. This will be a somewhat different population to full-time workers.

21. It may also be possible to coordinate structural public service employment programmes with venture capital programmes such as the Small Business Administration's New Markets programme. This programme provides venture capital and technical support to new businesses locating in economically depressed areas. In addition to venture capital the ELR programme would provide employees subsidised for a period by the programme on the condition that a percentage of the subsidised workforce is retained after the subsidy expires.

22. Solow, in *Work and Welfare*, has suggested public service work and an increase in our current earned income tax credit to aid the most vulnerable parts of our population. The increase in the earned income tax credit is an

excellent idea that will help all of the working poor whether in the ELR programme or not.

23. Department of Education and Science, *Key Statistics 2008–2009*, available
    from: <http://www.education.ie/servlet/blobservlet/stat_key_stats_2008_
    2009.pdf>, accessed 6 August 2010.

24. New Hope provided childcare, health coverage and an Earn Income Tax Credit-
    like supplement to workers' wages, benefits that they also provided to workers
    with private sector jobs in the area the programme served that met their
    income requirement. Each community service job lasted six months and the
    programme could employ a worker for no more than one year.

25. Data for Figure 9.2 and the rest of the discussion of New Hope's community
    service jobs are from S.M. Poglinco, J. Brash and R.C. Granger, 'An Early Look
    at Community Service Jobs in the New Hope Demonstration', Manpower
    Demonstration Research Corporation, evaluation paper, July 1998.

26. Ibid.

27. Minimum wage community service jobs (CSJ) had to be accessible by public
    transit from the inner city sites that New Hope served. Significant parts of
    metropolitan Milwaukee were inaccessible.

28. Solow, 'Lecture II: Guess Who Pays for Workfare'.

29. Day care does pose a problem for the employment part of our programme.
    Because of this benefit many parents with small children will prefer the ELR
    to private employment, slowing their movement into the private sector when
    jobs become available. This may cause some employers to offer day care ben-
    efits, but the scale of this effect is uncertain. A comprehensive national day
    care policy would avoid this problem.

30. Fairmodel-US has been amply documented and insightfully discussed in R.
    Fair, *Testing Macroeconometric Models*, Cambridge, MA, Harvard Univeristy
    Press, 1998.

31. As with all such simulations a number of assumptions have been made. They
    are discussed in detail in R. Majewski and E.J. Nell, 'Maintaining Full Employ-
    ment: Simulating an Employer of Last Resort Program', Center for Full
    Employment and Price Stability seminar paper no. 6, October 2000; and E.J.
    Nell and M. Forstater (eds.), *Reinventing Functional Finance: Transformational
    Growth and Full Employment*, Northampton, Edward Elgar, 2003. In the ver-
    sion presented, ELR programme stimulated employment (PSE) workers are
    paid half the average hourly earnings in Fairmodel's firm sector, there is one
    supervisor for twenty ELR PSE workers, the frictional rate of unemployment
    – the time period between jobs when a worker moves from one job to another
    – is 4 per cent and 50 per cent of the unemployed above the frictional rate join
    the ELR PSE. In addition, the spending on the Federal Employment Service
    has been doubled and a broadly expanded job training programme enacted.
    For estimates under alternative assumptions see Nell and Majewski, 'Main-
    taining Full Employment'.

32. The sharp-eyed will note that Fairmodel did not do very well in predicting the low unemployment rates of the late 1990s. These rates do not fit in with the way the economy was behaving in the late 1980s and early 1990s. If the back-cast period was shortened, say by looking at 1997–2004, the model would do much better.

33. The anti-inflation effect of the ELR's job training component was not simulated because of difficulties in estimating the size of its effect.

Chapter 10

1. A good friend, and former colleague from my 'Mexican period', Felipe Bello, a gentleman and scholar of exquisite sensitivity, whose passions for Minsky are inferior to none, sowed the seeds of my interest in Minsky many years ago. Despite the confidence and admiration shown by good friends for the works of Minsky, and in spite of current enthusiasms for the 'Minsky moment', I remain sceptical. Part of this scepticism – but an important part – is due to the education, instruction and scholarship of my critical friend and colleague, Stefano Zambelli, who – alas – remains irresponsible and does not agree to take the blame for the remaining infelicities.

2. On the occasion of two important anniversaries of the introduction of the innovative concept of *potential surprise*, with which he tried to formalise *incomplete* – not *imperfect* – knowledge, without reliance on the worn-out concepts of official probability theories, to encapsulate the distinction between risk and uncertainty (see G.L.S. Shackle, 'Expectations and Employment', *The Economic Journal*, Vol. 49, No. 195, 1939, pp. 442–52; and *Expectations in Economics*, Cambridge, Cambridge University Press, 1949). That post-Keynesians, who have relentlessly emphasised so-called '*Keynesian uncertainty*', '*systemic uncertainty*', and so on, and unreservedly asserted that this cannot be formalised by any notion of probability – even including Keynes's own 'logical' theory espoused in a *Treatise on Probability* (J.M. Keynes, London, Macmillan and Co., Ltd., 1921) – never consider the possibility of using Shackle's fertile framework remains a mystery to me. Not even 'Modern' Behavioural Economists have found it useful to envision the 'kaleidoscopic world' of George Shackle as providing a lens through which officially non-rational behaviour can be formalised. Somewhere between Shackle's *bounded uncertainty* (Shackle, *The Nature of Economic Thought: Selected Papers 1955–1964*, Cambridge, Cambridge University Press, 1966, pp. 74–5) and Simon's *bounded rationality* (H.A. Simon, 'A Behavioral Model of Rational Choice', *The Quarterly Journal of Economics*, Vol. LXIX, No. 1, February 1955, pp. 99–118), there is the rich world of *Algorithmic Behavioural Economics*, spawning *incompleteness*, *unknowability* and *indeterminism*, that could provide decision theoretic foundations for an *empirically based macroeconomic crisis theory*.

3. J.S. Mill, *Principles of Political Economy*, people's edition, London, New York and Bombay, Longmans, Green, and Co., 1898, p. 309.

4. R.M. Goodwin, 'Static and Dynamic Linear General Equilibrium Models', in *Input–Output Relations, Proceedings of a Conference on Inter-Industrial Relations held at Driebergen, Holland*, Leiden, H.E. Stenfert Kroese N.V., 1953, p. 68; italics added.

5. 'In one sense, we are all Keynesians now; in another, nobody is any longer a Keynesian', *Time*, 31 December 1965.

6. I am never sure whether to refer to this school as New Classical, Newclassical, new classical or newclassical; my 'unsureness' may well be reflected in a usage that flips from one form to another, in one and the same essay. Ditto for New Keynesian economics!

7. I should also add that the paper is a critique of a particular theoretical vision and its possible reconstruction. Despite the passing allusion to the 'Celtic Tiger' and its vicissitudes, the paper is not meant to be taken literally as a contribution to, or an attempt at, providing a framework for interpreting the facts of the current crises.

8. One of the editors of this book, Dr Stephen Kinsella, informs me that there is now an *ex post* revision of the half-life of the Celtic Tiger that has halved this period; my statement is an *ex ante* vision, as if it was made before the crisis was even on the horizon.

9. *Manias, Panics and Crashes: A History of Financial Crises*, published in August 2010. 'The big ten financial bubbles', from the 'Tulip Mania' of 1636 to the 'stock price bubble' during the final years of the twentieth century in the US, are listed succinctly on page 8 of the fifth edition, See C.P. Kindleberger and R. Aliber (2005), *Manias, Panics and Crashes: A History of Financial Crises*, fifth edition, Hoboken, NJ, John Wiley & Sons, Inc., 2005. I suspect the recent Irish dilemmas have a great deal in common with items 6, 7 and 8 in the Kindleberger list. My own study of the bubble in real estate and stocks in two of the Scandinavian countries – and why it did not happen in the third – and in Finland suggests that this is the closest parallel to the experience of the short-lived Celtic Tiger's glory years.

10. Kindleberger and Aliber, *Manias, Panics and Crashes*, fifth edition, p. 21.

11. Benoit Mandelbrot has suggested that Osborne Reynolds was inspired to use the word '*turbulent*' in his pioneering papers on fluid motion, in the period 1872–94, from a reading of Macaulay's *History of England* where, referring to a report in the *London Gazette* of 12 February 1684/5, he writes: 'In the City of London, lately so *turbulent*, scarcely a murmur was heard.' (Chapter IV, Pt. I of Macaulay). However, my own study of the Reynolds papers of the period has not succeeded in substantiating Mandelbrot's conjecture.

12. By 'the master', I am referring to Minsky himself.

13. As a matter of fact, after considerable instruction from my friend, Stefano Zambelli, I have come to interpret the analytical core of Chapter 17 of the *GT*

(Keynes's *General Theory of Employment, Interest and Money*) as advocating a *non-equilibrium* monetary production economy, not least due to the Sraffian nature of that chapter.

14. Except in so far as they can be interpreted as *rational* bubbles, of one sort or another!

15. I shall simply use the phrase 'Keynesian uncertainty', assuming the reader will give it the appropriate context, in the rest of this paper. See J.M. Keynes, *The General Theory of Employment, Interest and Money*, London, Macmillan and Co., Ltd., 1936.

16. 'Stability – or tranquillity – in a world with a cyclical past and capitalist financial institutions is destabilizing' (H.P. Minsky (1978), 'The Financial Instability Hypothesis: A Restatement', reprinted in H.P. Minsky, *Can "It" Happen Again?: Essays on Instability and Finance*, Chapter 5 ; Armonk, NY, M.E. Sharpe, Inc., 1982, p. 101). Encapsulating this idea dynamically is quite simple – even using the 'forced' version of Goodwin's pioneering non-linear business cycle model (R.M. Goodwin, 'The Nonlinear Accelerator and the Persistence of Business Cycles', *Econometrica*, Vol. 19, No. 1, 1951, pp. 1–17, particularly using equation (5e), p. 12) – via *homoclinic loops* and their *bifurcation*. Again, to the best of my knowledge, no one has attempted this kind of complete endogenous modelling of a 'Minsky Crisis' to give formal content to the catchphrase. The attempt by the master (see D. Delli Gatti, M. Gallegati and H. Minsky, 'Financial Institutions, Economic Policy and the Dynamic Behavior of the Economy', paper prepared for the International J.A. Schumpeter Society Fifth Conference, Münster, Germany, 17–20 August 1994), is completely *ad hoc*, as is the Ferri–Minsky (see P. Ferri and H. Minsky, 'Market Processes and Thwarting Systems', *Structural Change and Economic Dynamics*, Vol. 3, No. 1, 1992, pp. 79–91) attempt. Indeed, both of these contributions comprehensively misrepresent the non-linear macrodynamic literature, even of the 1950s, let alone anything that came later.

17. In my own current work, I have been able to construct a dynamical system 'unstable everywhere', to be interpreted as an endogenous model of the business cycle.

18. R.G. Hawtrey, *Trade Depression and the Way Out*, London, Longmans, Green and Co., 1931, p. 10; italics in original.

19. Mill, *Principles of Political Economy*, especially Book III, Chapter XI.

20. Knut Wicksell, *Geldzins und Güterpreise: Eine Studie über die den Tauschwert des Geldes bestimmenden ursachen*, Jena, Gustav Fischer Verlag, 1898.

21. I. Fisher, *The Purchasing Power of Money: Its Determination and Relation to Credit, Interest and Crises*, assisted by Harry G. Brown, New York, The Macmillan Company, 1911, especially Chapter 4. Although the consensus, amply encouraged by Minsky himself, seems to be that the significant progenitor is I. Fisher, 'The Debt-Deflation Theory of Great Depressions', *Econometrica*, Vol. 1, No. 3, 1933, pp. 337–57.

22. J.A. Schumpeter, *The Theory of Economic Development: An Inquiry into Profits, Capital, Credit, Interest, and the Business Cycle*, translated by Redvers Opie, Cambridge, MA, Harvard University Press, [1911], 1934, especially Chapter 3.
23. Hawtrey, *Trade Depression and the Way Out*.
24. L. Currie, 'Treatment of Credit in Contemporary Monetary Theory', *Journal of Political Economy*, Vol. 41, No. 1, 1933, pp. 58–79.
25. Keynes, *The General Theory of Employment, Interest and Money*.
26. E. Lindahl, *Studies in the Theory of Money and Capital*, London, George Allen & Unwin Ltd., [1929], 1939.
27. G. Myrdal, *Monetary Equilibrium*, London: William Hodge & Company, Ltd., [1931], 1939.
28. Despite Patinkin (see D. Patinkin, 'Wicksell's "Cumulative Process"', *The Economic Journal*, Vol. 62, No. 248, 1952, pp. 835–47), there is no evidence whatsoever in Wicksell (*Geldzins und Güterpreise*) or, more especially, in Lindahl (*Studies in the Theory of Money and Capital*) or Myrdal (*Monetary Equilibrium*), that the cumulative process was intrinsically stable. Moreover, Wicksell may have been a neoclassical economist in value theory – albeit underpinned by a deep grounding in Austrian capital theory – but he was, despite assertions to the contrary, first mythologized by Ohlin (B. Ohlin, 'Introduction' to the English translation of *Geldzins und Güterpreise* by Knut Wicksell, translated by R.F. Kahn as *Interest and Prices*, London, Macmillan, 1936), no quantity theorist. As for Ohlin's understanding of 'Swedish' monetary theory, as it was developed by Wicksell, Davidson and their immediate successors and followers in Sweden – primarily Lindahl, Myrdal, Hammarskjöld and Lundberg – at that time, the interchanges between Hamamrskjöld, Lindahl and Lundberg are most revealing. These private letters between the three are deposited in the 'Lindahl archives', with which I worked intensively in 1986. Some of the relevant – caustic – exchanges, pertaining to Ohlin, and the opinions of Hammarskjöld, Lindahl and Lundberg, on Ohlin's mastery of monetary theory, are reported in K. Velupillai, 'Some Swedish Stepping Stones to Modern Macroeconomics', *Eastern Economic Journal*, Vol. XIV, No. 1, January–March 1988, pp. 87–98.
29. See, in particular, Myrdal, *Monetary* Equilibrium, pp. 35–6.
30. Hawtrey, *Trade Depression and the Way Out*.
31. R.J. Sandilands, 'Hawtreyan "Credit Deadlock" or Keynesian "Liquidity Trap"? Lessons for Japan from the Great Depression', paper presented at the David Laidler 'Festschrift' Conference, University of Western Ontario, 18–20 August 2006, p.2.
32. J. Tirole, *Financial Crises, Liquidity and the International Monetary System*, Princeton, NJ, Princeton University Press, 2002, p. 1.
33. See, for example, E.N. White, 'Are There any Lessons from History', in E.N. White (ed.), *Crashes and Panics – The Lessons from History*, Homewood, IL, Business One Irwin, 1990.

34. R.J. Shiller [1981], 'Do Stock Prices Move Too Much to be Justified by Subsequent Changes in Dividends?', reprinted as Chapter 4 of R.H. Thaler (ed.), *Advances in Behavioral Finance*, New York, Russell Sage Foundation, 1993.

35. Minsky, *The Financial Instability Hypothesis: A Restatement*, p. 97.

36. M. Kalecki, 'A Theory of Profits', *The Economic Journal*, Vol. 52, Nos. 206–207, 1942, pp. 258–67.

37. D. Dillard, 'The Theory of a Monetary Economy', in K.K. Kurihara (ed.), *Post-Keynesian Economics*, London, George Allen and Unwin Ltd., 1955.

38. D.B. Papadimitriou and L. Randall Wray, 'Minsky's Stabilizing An Unstable Economy: Two Decades Later', in H.P. Minsky, *Stabilizing an Unstable Economy*, New York, McGraw-Hill, 2008, p. xii; italics in the original.

39. H.P. Minsky, *Can "It" Happen Again? Essays on Instability and Finance*, Armonk, NY, M.E. Sharpe, Inc., 1982, pp. 105–6.

40. Ibid, p. 105.

41. Lindahl, *Studies in the Theory of Money and Capital*; Myrdal, *Monetary Equilibrium*.

42. N. Kaldor, 'A Model of the Trade Cycle', *Economic Journal*, Vol. 50, No. 1, March 1940, pp. 78–92.

43. J.R. Hicks, *A Contribution to the Theory of the Trade Cycle*, Oxford, Clarendon Press, 1950.

44. Goodwin, 'The Nonlinear Accelerator and the Persistence of Business Cycles'.

45. H.P. Minsky, 'Monetary Systems and Accelerator Models', *American Economic Review*, Vol. XLVII, No. 6, 1957, pp. 860–83; H.P. Minsky, 'A Linear Model of Cyclical Growth', *The Review of Economics and Statistics*, Vol. 41, No. 2, Part 1, 1959, pp. 133–45.

46. H.P. Minsky, 'The Integration of Simple Growth and Cycle Models', in M.J. Brennan (ed.), *Patterns of Market Behavior: Essays in Honour of Philip Taft*, Providence, RI, Brown University Press, 1965, reprinted as Chapter 12 of Minsky, *Can "It" Happen Again?: Essays on Instability and Finance*.

47. Ferri and Minsky, 'Market Processes and Thwarting Systems'.

48. Delli Gatti, Gallegati and Minsky, 'Financial Institutions, Economic Policy and the Dynamic Behavior of the Economy'.

49. There is the preposterous assertion, in Minsky, 'The Integration of Simple Growth and Cycle Models', p. 258, that: 'Various ceiling models of cycles or cyclical growth have appeared. In all except one, Kurihara's model, the rate of growth of the ceiling is exogenous.' So far as I can see, this is just a blind paraphrasing of the incorrect claim – incorrect as to technical accuracy – in K. Kurihara, 'An Endogenous Model of Cyclical Growth', *Oxford Economic Papers – New Series*, Vol. 12, No. 3, 1960, pp. 243–8, p. 8 and footnote 5 on the same page. Had they understood the difference between an autonomous planar nonlinear differential equation and its forced version, it would have been impossible for Kurihara, and, hence, Minsky to make such absurd claims. It is a pity – at least for someone like me, who is fundamentally in

sympathy with a Minskyan vision of credit-based capitalist economic dynamics.

50. L. Taylor and S.A. O'Connell, 'A Minsky Crisis', *Quarterly Journal of Economics*, Vol. 100 (Supplement), No. 5, 1985, pp. 871–85.

51. L. Taylor, *Reconstructing Macroeconomics: Structuralist Proposals and Critiques of the Mainstream*, Cambridge, MA, Harvard University Press, 2004, Chapter 9, Section 7, pp. 298–305.

52. 'Sweden, which had a particularly sophisticated group of economists in the 1930s and a knowledgeable political leadership in their Social Democratic Party, may have knowingly introduced the welfare state', Ferri and Minsky, 'Market Processes and Thwarting Systems', footnote 23, p. 89. Surely, one would have expected a sustained advocate of active policy to 'stabilize an unstable (monetary) economy' to be more scholarly in studying the one actual example of theory and policy meshing admirably in the precise sense of Minsky?

53. The most imaginative metaphor I can think of, for this situation, is the second of the twelve labours of Hercules, the one against the Lernaen Hydra. It will not do to simply cut off head after head, when the Hydra sprouts two new heads for each one cut off. Hercules had to devise an innovative strategy, of the kind that Lindahl and Myrdal devised, disciplined by the theory of economic policy, to maintain an inherently unstable monetary economy in place.

54. Keynes, *The General Theory of Employment, Interest and Money*, especially p. 242. Minsky's indebtedness to Dillard's reading of Chapter 17 of the *GT* is most clearly expressed in H. Minsky, 'The Legacy of Keynes', *Journal of Economic Education*, Vol. 16, No. 1, 1985, pp. 5–15, especially pp. 7–8. No reading of Chapter 17 of the *GT* can be complete without placing it in the context of Sraffa's masterly critique of Hayek, where the concept of the 'own rate of interest' was first developed (P. Sraffa, 'Dr Hayek on Money and Capital', *The Economic Journal*, Vol. 42, No. 165, 1932, pp. 42–53). It is this notion that formed the fulcrum around which the whole of the argument of Chapter 17 was formed. No wonder, then, that distinguished Keynes scholars, from Dillard and Lerner (for example, A.P. Lerner, 'The Essential Properties of Interest and Money', *Quarterly Journal of Economics*, Vol. 66, No. 2, 1952, pp. 172–93), to Patinkin and Leijonhufvud, have not made much sense of this important chapter. None of these Keynes scholars have ever taken the time and trouble to understand Austrian capital theory and its deep critique by Sraffa ('Dr Hayek on Money and Capital') and, therefore, missed the essential monetary point in Chapter 17. I am eternally grateful to Stefano Zambelli for drilling this crucial point into my obdurate mind.

55. It was in the famous footnote in Chapter 17 of the *GT*, which Minsky lays stress on as the one where Keynes stressed the importance of transition regimes, that Keynes made the reference to Hume as the progenitor of the equilibrium concept in economics (p. 343, footnote 3; italics added): '[H]ume began the

practice amongst economists of stressing the importance of *the equilibrium position* as compared with the ever-shifting transition towards it, though he was still enough of a mercantilist not to overlook the fact *that it is in the transition that we actually have our being ...'*.

56. Taylor, *Reconstructing Macroeconomics*, p. 299.
57. Ibid, p. 302.
58. Orthodox theory, *even in its non-monetary growth versions*, banishes '*Ponzi schemes*' by decree, at the very basic level of the rational agent's intertemporal budget constraint (see D. Romer, *Advanced Macroeconomics*, third edition, New York, McGraw-Hill/Irwin, 2006, pp. 53–4, especially Equations 2.6 and 2.10).
59. Shackle, *The Nature of Economic Thought*, pp. 82–90; italics in the original.
60. Shackle, 'Expectations and Employment', p. 443; italics added.
61. In G.L.S. Shackle, *Expectations, Investment and Income*, second edition, Oxford, Clarendon Press, 1968, pp. xv, xvii.
62. G.L.S. Shackle, 'Expectation and Liquidity', Chapter 2 in M.J. Bowman (ed.), *Expectations, Uncertainty, and Business Behavior*, New York, Social Science Research Council, 1958. I am, once again, indebted to my good friend Stefano Zambelli for facilitating this particular serendipity. He had Georgescu-Roegen's copy of the book in which Shackle's article was published and gave it to me as I was searching in my own library for my 'Shackle books', when I was preparing my lectures on Behavioural Economics in autumn 2009. I was, at first, attracted simply by the title of Shackle's article, thinking it might have something to do with the notion of liquidity in 'The Two Triads Lectures' by J.R. Hicks (*Critical Essays in Monetary Theory*, Oxford, Clarendon Press, 1967), although the dates did not mesh. But, no! Shackle's direct inspiration was Myrdal, *Monetary Equilibrium*, where I finally found the 'missing' connection with Shackle's potential surprise and Myrdal's notion of surprise in 'investment gains and losses'!
63. Shackle, 'Expectation and Liquidity'.
64. Myrdal, *Monetary Equilibrium*, pp. 61–2; bold italics added.
65. Shackle, *The Nature of Economic Thought*, pp. 74–5.
66. Ibid, p. 75.
67. Ibid, p. 74.
68. See K.Vela Velupillai, *Computable Foundations for Economics*, London, Routledge, 2010, Chapters 11 and 12.
69. Ibid, p. 91.
70. Velupillai, *Computable Foundations for Economics*.
71. H.A. Simon, *Models of Discovery – and Other Topics in the Methods of Science*, Dordrecht, D. Reidel Publishing Company, 1977.
72. See A. Newell and H.A. Simon, *Human Problem Solving*, Englewood Cliffs, NJ, Prentice Hall, Inc., 1972.
73. D. Kulkarni and H.A. Simon (1988), 'The Processes of Scientific Discovery: The Strategy of Experimentation', reprinted as Chapter 5.3 in H.A. Simon,

Models of Thought – Volume II, New Haven, CT and London, Yale University Press, 1989, especially pp. 366–7.

74. Velupillai, *Computable Foundations for Economics*, Appendix 2 to Part IV.

75. J.K. Galbraith, *The Great Crash 1929*, Boston, MA and New York, Haughton Mifflin Company, 1954, p. 169; italics added.

76. K.Vela Velupillai (forthcoming 2010), 'Reflections on Mathematical Economics in the Algorithmic Mode', in *New Mathematics and Natural Computation*, Vol. 6.

77. See R.W. Clower and P.W. Howitt, 'The Transaction Theory of the Demand for Money: A Reconsideration', *Journal of Political Economy*, Vol. 86, No. 3, 1978, pp. 449–66.

78. See R.L. Goodstein, 'On the Restricted Ordinal Theorem', *Journal of Symbolic Logic*, Vol. 9, No. 2, 1944, pp. 33–41.

79. J. Paris and R. Tavakol, 'Goodstein Algorithm as a Super-Transient Dynamical System', *Physics Letters A*, Vol. 180, Nos. 1–2, 1993, pp. 83–6.

80. It must, of course, be remembered that the Hydra had 'only' *one immortal head*. Somewhere in the recesses of the core of the true characteristics of a credit-based capitalist economy there must be 'an immortal head'. Many prophets, not least Marx and Schumpeter, have in the past been confident they had discovered it, only to be proved false prophets within a generation or two. Minsky is only one in this long list of great prophets.

81. L. Kirby and J. Paris, 'Accessible Independence Results for Peano Arithmetic', *Bulletin of the London Mathematical Society*, Vol. 14, 1982, pp. 285–93.

82. Galbraith, *The Great Crash 1929*, p. 169; italics added.

Chapter 11

1. Department of Economics, Kemmy Business School, University of Limerick. stephen.kinsella@ul.ie. I thank David Duffy of the ESRI for the Consumer Expectations dataset.

2. Law Reform Commission, 'Personal Debt Management and Debt Enforcement', Consultation Paper LRC Cp 56, Dublin, Law Reform Commission, 2009.

3. IMF, 'Staff Report for the 2009 Article IV Consultation', IMF Country Report 09/195, June 2009.

4. As a debtor, Ireland has benefited from historically low interest rates over the period from 2000 to 2008. However, Ireland is poised to experience a further contraction in economic activity as the cost of servicing this debt rises with positive international interest rate movements once interest rates begin return to their warranted levels, following economic recovery in the Eurozone.

5. As described by M. Bordo and A. Filardo, 'Deflation and Monetary Policy in a Historical Perspective: Remembering the Past or Being Condemned to Repeat It?,' *Economic Policy*, Vol. 20, No. 44, 2005, pp. 799–844.

6. IMF, 'Staff Report for the 2009 Article IV Consultation'.

7. CSO, 'External Trade', Provisional Report, Q4 2009.

8. I. Fisher, 'The Debt-Deflation Theory of Great Depressions', *Econometrica*, Vol. 1, No. 4, 1933, pp. 337–57.

9. J. Tobin, 'Real Balance Effects Reconsidered', in J. Tobin (ed.), *Asset Accumulation and Economic Activity*, Chicago, IL, University of Chicago Press, 1980, pp. 10–11.

10. Fisher, 'The Debt-Deflation Theory of Great Depressions'.

11. C. Kindleberger, *Manias, Panics and Crashes: A History of Financial Crises*, London, John Wiley & Sons, 1996.

12. J.M. Keynes, *The General Theory of Employment, Interest, and Money*, Cambridge, Cambridge University Press, 1936.

13. Keynes also argued that a fall in nominal (he used the term 'money') prices and wages would indirectly increase liquidity in the economy if the central bank maintained the nominal quantity of money, since, when prices and wages are lower, the same nominal quantity of money represents relatively more purchasing power, relaxing the liquidity constraint on households and firms. Keynes argued that this roundabout way is the most painful way to create more liquidity in the economy, since the central bank could achieve the same thing by simply increasing the nominal money supply.

14. Within a dynamic general equilibrium framework, boom–bust cycles are created by a multiplier–accelerator mechanism, which translates a one-time positive technology shock into large and highly persistent movements in aggregate spending and output, as in N. Kiyotaki and J. Moore, 'Credit Cycles', *Journal of Political Economy*, Vol. 105, No. 2, 1997, pp. 211–48.

15. See H.P. Minsky, *Stabilising an Unstable Economy*, New York, McGraw-Hill, 1986. A concise statement of his financial instability hypothesis is in H.P. Minsky, 'The Financial Instability Hypothesis', working paper 74, The Jerome Levy Economics Institute of Bard College, May 1992.

16. B. Bernanke, 'Non-Monetary Effects of the Financial Crisis in Propagation of the Great Depression', *American Economic Review*, Vol. 73, No. 3, 1983, pp. 257–76.

17. M. Woodford, *Interest and Prices: Foundations of a Theory of Monetary Policy*, New York, Princeton University Press, 2003.

18. For example, J. Fitz Gerald, 'Fiscal Policy for Recovery', ESRI working paper no. 326, October 2009; P. Honohan, 'Resolving Ireland's Banking Crisis', *The Economic and Social Review*, Vol. 40, No. 2, 2009, pp. 207–31.

19. G. von Peter, 'Asset Prices and Banking Distress: A Macroeonomic Approach', working paper no. 167, Bank of International Settlements, December 2004.

20. G.B. Eggertsson and M. Woodford, 'The Zero Bound on Interest Rates and Optimal Monetary Policy', *Brookings Papers on Economic Activity*, Vol. 1, 2003, pp. 139–233.

21. M. King, 'Debt Deflation: Theory and Evidence', *European Economic Review*, Vol. 38, Nos. 3–4, 1994, pp. 419–45.

22. J.B. DeLong, 'Should We Fear Deflation?', *Brookings Papers on Economic Activity*, Vol. 1, No. 1, 1999, pp. 225–52, p. 231.
23. Loans of longer duration are of course subject to compounding.
24. DeLong, 'Should We Fear Deflation?'
25. At the firm level, if a firm buys assets with borrowed money, then under extreme market conditions it may owe more money than it has and, with reduced cash flow, its expectation of paying off its loans goes down, and the firm defaults. If this happens on a sufficiently wide scale, then it can severely stress creditors and cause them to fail.
26. There are asymmetric effects of variations in the price level. Unexpected jumps in inflation, say, can in principle provide a temporary stimulus, as wealth is redistributed from creditors to debtors – who include most entrepreneurs. Deflation does the opposite, and in fact undermines the financial stability of many businesses, which undermines the institutional structures upon which successful economies are built – see E.J. Nell and M. Forstater, *Reinventing Functional Finance*, London, Edward Elgar, 2003.
27. The argument runs that wage rates are above their equilibrium levels, therefore a reduction in nominal wages across both private and public sectors will achieve a lagged reduction in the price level to equilibrium levels (Fitz Gerald, 'Fiscal Policy for Recovery'). Because Ireland exports 75 per cent of its output, Ireland's international 'competitiveness' – narrowly defined as a price differential between comparable products and services – is seen as key to an economic recovery. To achieve the necessary improvement in the 'competitiveness' of the economy, it has been argued that Ireland needs a further cut in wage rates across the board, public and private, of at least 5 per cent.
28. D. Miles and V. Pillonca, 'Financial Innovation and European Housing and Mortgage Markets', *Oxford Review of Economic Policy*, Vol. 24, No. 1, 2008, pp. 145–75.
29. L. Taylor, *Reconstructing Macroeconomics: Structuralist Critiques of the Mainstream*, Boston, MA, Harvard University Press, 2004, p. 261.
30. K.A. Kennedy and B.R. Dowling, *Economic Growth in Ireland: The Experience Since 1947*, Dublin, Gill and Macmillan, 1975, p. 216; J.J. Lee, *Ireland 1912–1985: Politics and Society*, Cambridge, Cambridge University Press, 1989, pp. 324–5.
31. However, the Irish Budget deficit fell from over 10 per cent of GDP in 1985 to 2 per cent of GDP in 1994.
32. L. Taylor and S. O'Connell, 'A Minsky Crisis', *Quarterly Journal of Economics*, Vol. 100, Supplement, 1985, pp. 871–85.
33. T. Palley, *Post-Keynesian Economics: Debt, Distribution, and the Macro Economy*, Oxford, Macmillan, 1996. Minksy's approach is not without its critics. Several authors, including Godley and Lavoie (W. Godley and M. Lavoie, *Monetary Economics: An Integrated Approach to Credit, Money, Income, Production and Wealth*, London, Palgrave-Macmillan, 2006) have pointed out that leverage ratios need not be cyclical, and that, mathematically, Minsky's

description of cycles is not appropriate for higher dimensional dynamic systems. See Chapter 10 in this volume for details.

34. A. Fostel and J. Geanakoplos, 'Leverage Cycles and the Anxious Economy', *American Economic Review*, Vol. 98, No. 4, 2008, pp. 1211–44.

35. Many apparently successful financial institutions operate a 'Ponzi' scheme – an investment operation that pays returns to separate investors from their own money or money paid by subsequent investors, rather than from any actual profit earned. In this way shareholders have the illusion of profits. Named after the Italian-American fraudster Charles Ponzi who perfected the scam in the 1920s, Ponzi schemes arise because banks exploit what seems a minor but is in fact a major accounting flaw.

36. The classic study is R.M. Goodwin, 'The Nonlinear Accelerator and the Persistence of Business Cycles', *Econometrica*, Vol. 19, No. 1, 1951, pp. 1–17. A more modern version of the story may be found in Taylor, *Reconstructing Macroeconomics*, Chapters 8 and 9.

37. Palley, *Post-Keynesian Economics*; P. Arestis and M. Sawyer, *A Handbook of Alternative Monetary Economics*, Cheltenham, Edward Elgar, 2006.

38. In that they map liability holdings of, say, deposits to asset holdings of reserves in the case of collateral and margin requirements, or debt liabilities to equity liabilities in the case of risk-based capital standards.

39. For example, if a monetary authority wants to rein in what it perceives as excessive mortgage lending, it can increase reserve requirements of equity holdings.

40. P.R. Lane, 'Disinflation, Switching Nominal Anchors and Twin Crises: The Irish Experience', *Journal of Policy Reform*, Vol. 3, No. 2, 2000, pp. 301–26; P.R. Lane, 'International Diversification and the Irish Economy', *The Economic and Social Review*, Vol. 31, No. 1, 2000, pp. 37–54.

Chapter 12

1. Thanks are due to Cormac O Gráda for his helpful comments on this chapter.

2. Estimates of the population of Ireland in the early nineteenth century are unreliable (see J.J. Lee, 'On the Accuracy of the Pre-Famine Irish Censuses', in J.M. Goldstrom and L.A. Clarkson (eds), *Irish Population, Economy and Society: Essays in honour of the Late K.H. Connell*, Oxford, Oxford University Press, pp. 37–56), but the present 4.4 million population of the Republic is a third lower than the first reliable estimate of 6.5 million in 1841.

3. See Brendan M. Walsh, 'Urbanization and the Regional Distribution of Population in Post-Famine Ireland', *Journal of European Economic History*, Vol. 29, No. 1, Spring 2000, pp. 109–27.

4. The greater impact of the net migration rate on population growth follows from its much wider range – from *minus* 17 per 1,000 head of population to *plus* 11 per 1,000 head of population. The rate of natural increase, on the other

hand, ranged only between +5 per 1,000 head of population and + 12 per 1,000 head of population.

5. That is, the average number of children that would be born to a woman over her lifetime if she were to experience the current age-specific fertility rates through to the end of her reproductive life.

6. David E. Bloom and David Canning, 'Contraception and the Celtic Tiger', *Economic and Social Review*, Vol. 34, No. 3, Winter 2003, pp. 229–47.

7. Bloom has also claimed that the 'demographic dividend' accounted for a third of East Asian growth in 1965–90: *The Economist*, 29 October 2009.

8. See my 'Expectations, Information and Migration: Specifying an Econometric Model of Irish Migration to Britain', *Journal of Regional Science*, Vol. 14, 1974, pp. 107–20.

9. Charles R. Morris, *The Two Trillion Dollar Meltdown: Easy Money, High Rollers, and the Great Credit Crash*, New York, Public Affairs, 2008, pp. 66–7.

10. Ibid, p. 67.

11. See <http://irelandafternama.wordpress.com/2010/01/18/an-estimate-of-vacant-housing-in-ireland/>, accessed January 2010.

12. CSO, 2007, Table 38c. The earlier figure for central heating was supplied by John Fitz Gerald.

13. NCB Stockbrokers, 2020 *Vision: Ireland's Demographic Dividend*, March 2006, Dublin, NCB Stockbrokers.

14. At the time of writing, the population projection for 2011 was already looking shaky in light of the CSO's estimates of the 2009 population. The 'zero net migration' population aged 20 and over projected for 2011 was 3,232.5 thousand, while the estimated 2009 population was 3,243.4 thousand. The discrepancy of 10.7 thousand or 0.3 per cent is trivial but, when the numbers in individual age groups are compared, bigger discrepancies come to light. In particular, the large fall in the projected population aged 20–9 does not seem to be happening on cue. The estimated 2009 numbers in the 20–4 and 25–9 age groups were 12 and 18 per cent ahead of the projected 2011 numbers, while the estimated numbers aged 30 and over in 2009 were 3.3 per cent below the projection. This highlights the uncertainty surrounding any Irish population projections even over short time horizons.

15. There is a separate issue about the match between the stock of unsold housing and the demand for new units that may emerge over the medium term.

16. Patrick Honohan and Brendan Walsh, 'Catching Up with the Leaders: The Irish Hare', *Brookings Papers on Economic Activity*, Vol. 33, No. 1, 2002, pp. 1–78, p. 45.

17. David E. Bloom and David Canning, 'Contraception and the Celtic Tiger'.

Further Reading

Official Reports, Policy Papers and Working Papers

Adelino, M., Gerardi, K. and Willen, P.S., 'Why Don't Lenders Renegotiate More Home Mortgages? Redefaults, Self-Cures, and Securitization', Federal Reserve Bank of Atlanta working paper no. 200917, August 2009.

Alfonso, A., 'Expansionary Fiscal Consolidations in Europe: New Evidence', European Central Bank working paper series no. 675, September 2006.

Australian Bureau of Statistics, *Price Indexes and Contract Price Indexation*, 2010, available from: <http://www.abs.gov.au/ausstats/abs@.nsf/mf/6401.0>, accessed 9 July 2010.

Basel Committee on Banking Supervision, *International Convergence of Capital Measurement and Capital Standards: A Revised Framework – Comprehensive Version*, Basel, Bank for International Settlements, 2006.

Bénétrix, A.S. and Lane, P.R., 'The Impact of Fiscal Shocks on the Irish Economy', Dublin, Institute for International Integration Studies, February 2009.

Bergin, A., Conefrey, T., Fitz Gerald, J. and Kearney, I., 'The Behaviour of the Irish Economy: Insights from the HERMES Macro-Economic Model', ESRI working paper no. 287, April 2009.

Braithwaite, J., '2004 Chief Health Officer Seminar Series – Seminar One: Health System Regulation and Governance', Chief Health Officer Seminar

Series, 23 June 2004, Australian National University, Canberra, 2004, available from: <http://healthstewardship.anu.edu.au/_documents/Chief_Health_Officer_Seminar_Series/2004/Braithwaite_trans.pdf>, accessed 10 January 2010.

Burke, M., 'A Genuine Economic Recovery: The Case for Fiscal Stimulus', paper presented to FEPS/TASC seminar on 'Stimulating Recovery', 10 June 2010.

Calenti, H., 'Irish Banks: Vegetative State Reducing to Underperform', RBC Capital Markets research note, 13 August 2009.

Callan, T. (ed.), 'Budget Perspectives, 2010', ESRI research series no. 12, October 2009.

Caprio Jr., G. and Klingebiel, D., 'Banking Insolvency: Bad Luck, Bad Policy, or Bad Banking?', in *Proceedings of the World Bank Annual Conference on Development Economics, 1996*, Supplement to the *World Bank Economic Review* and the *World Bank Research Observer*, 1997, pp. 79–104.

CB Richard Ellis Group, *Global Office Rents Survey*, Los Angeles, CA, CB Richard Ellis Group, May 2010.

CB Richard Ellis Group, *Global Office Rents Survey*, Los Angeles, CA, CB Richard Ellis Group, November 2008.

Central Bank and Financial Services Authority of Ireland, *Financial Stability Report 2007*, Dublin, Central Bank and Financial Services Authority of Ireland, 2007.

Central Statistics Office, *External Trade*, Provisional Report, Q4 2009, CSO, 2009.

Central Statistics Office, *Crime and Justice Report 2009*, spring report, CSO, 2009, available from: <http://www.cso.ie/statistics/CrimeandJustice.htm>, accessed 9 August 2010.

Central Statistics Office, *Live Register Additional Tables, December 2009*, CSO.

Central Statistics Office, *Population and Migration Estimates*, Dublin, CSO, 2009.

Central Statistics Office, *Quarterly National Accounts, Quarter 4 2009*, CSO, 2009, available from: <http://www.cso.ie/releasespublications/documents/economy/2009/qna_q42009.pdf>, accessed 9 July 2010.

Central Statistics Office, *Survey on Income and Living Conditions, 2008*, Dublin, CSO, November 2009.

Comhar, the Sustainable Development Council, *Towards a Green New Deal for Ireland*, Dublin, Comhar, SDC, October 2009.

Commission on Taxation, *Fourth Report of the Commission on Taxation, Special Taxation*, Dublin, Commission on Taxation, May 1985.

Consumer Panel of IFSRA, *Perspective of the Consumer Panel on the Current Financial Regulatory Framework*, Dublin, IFSRA, 2009.

Credit Suisse, *Intangible Infrastructure*, Credit Suisse Research Institute report, November 2008.

Cromien, S., 'An Céad Bord Snip', Contemporary Irish History Seminar, Trinity College Dublin, 4 March 2009, mimeo.

Daft.ie, *The Daft.ie House Price Report, Quarter 3, 2009*, October 2009, available from: <http://www.daft.ie/report/Daft-House-Price-Report-Q3-2009.pdf>, accessed 9 July 2010.

Davy Stockbrokers, 'Research Report: Irish Economy', 29 September 2009, Dublin, Davy Stockbrokers.

Dell'Ariccia, G., Igan, D. and Laeven, L., 'Credit Booms and Lending Standards: Evidence from the Subprime Mortgage Market', Centre for Economic Policy Research discussion paper no. 6683, February 2008.

Delli Gatti, D., Gallegati, M. and Minsky, H., 'Financial Institutions, Economic Policy and the Dynamic Behavior of the Economy', paper prepared for the International J.A. Schumpeter Society Fifth Conference, Münster, Germany, 17–20 August 1994.

Department of Finance, *Financial Statement of the Minister for Finance*, Dublin, Department of Finance, 9 December 2009.

Department of Finance, *Stability Programme Update 2010*, Dublin, Department of Finance, 9 December 2009.

Department of Finance, *Budget 2010*, Dublin, Department of Finance, December 2009.

Department of Finance, *Pre-Budget Outlook 2010*, Dublin, Department of Finance, November 2009.

Department of Finance, *Financial Statement of the Minister for Finance*, Dublin, Department of Finance, 7 April 2009.

Department of Finance, *Macroeconomic and Fiscal Framework 2009–2013*, Dublin, Department of Finance, April 2009.

Department of Finance, *Statement of the Minister for Finance, Brian Lenihan TD, on the Publication of Anglo Irish Bank Accounts for the Year Ended 30th September 2008*, Dublin, Department of Finance, 20 February 2009.

Department of Finance, *Report of the Special Group on Public Service Numbers and Expenditure Programmes*, Dublin, Department of Finance, 2009.

Department of Finance, *Analysis of High Income Individuals' Restriction 2007*, Dublin, Department of Finance, 2009, available from: <http://www.finance.gov.ie/documents/publications/reports/2009/analytax restrict09.pdf>, accessed 27 July 2010.

Department of Finance, *Budget 2009*, Dublin, Department of Finance, December 2008.

Department of Finance, *Budgetary and Economic Statistics, September 2008*, Dublin, Department of Finance, 2008.

Department of Finance, *Summary of Budget Measures, Budget 2008*, Dublin, Department of Finance, 2007.

Department of Finance, *Guidelines for the Appraisal and Management of Capital Expenditure Proposals in the Public Sector*, Department of Finance, Dublin, 1994, available from: <http://www.finance.gov.ie/viewdoc.asp?DocID=1216&CatID=16&StartDate=01+January+1994&m=>, accessed 10 June 2010.

Department of Finance, *Budget 1990*, Dublin, Department of Finance, December 1989.

Department of Social and Family Affairs, *Statistical Information on Social Welfare Services 2008*, Dublin, Department of Social and Family Affairs, 2009.

DKM, *The Control of Banking in the Republic of Ireland*, Dublin, DKM Economic Consultants, 1984.

Economic and Social Research Institute, *Latest permanent tsb/ESRI House Price Index*, 30 April 2010, ESRI, available from: <http://www.esri.ie/irish_economy/permanent_tsbesri_house_p/>, accessed 9 July 2010.

Further Reading

Economic and Social Research Institute, *Negative Equity in the Irish Housing Market*, Dublin, ESRI, 2009.

Economic and Social Research Institute, *The Quarterly Economic Commentary, Autumn 2009*, Dublin, ESRI, 2009.

Ernst & Young, *Economic Eye Summer Forecast*, Lisburn, Ernst & Young/Oxford Economics, Summer 2010.

European AntiPoverty Network, *Social Welfare: How Ireland Compares in Europe*, Dublin, EAPN, September 2009.

European AntiPoverty Network, *Out of the Traps: Ending Poverty Traps and Making Work Pay for People in Poverty*, Dublin, EAPN, 2007.

European Commission, *European Economic Forecast*, Brussels, European Commission, Spring 2010.

European Commission, *Recommendation for a Council Opinion on the Updated Stability Programme of Ireland, 2009–2014*, Brussels, European Commission, 2010.

European Commission, *Statistical Annex of European Economy, Spring 2009*, ECFIN/REP/51795/2009, European Commission, 2009.

European Commission, *Study on Monitoring and Enforcement Practices in Corporate Governance in the Member States*, Brussels, European Commission, 2009.

European Mortgage Federation, *Hypostat 2007*, EMF, 2008, available from: <http://www.hypo.org/Content/default.asp?PageID=524>, accessed 9 July 2010.

Eurostat, *Population, 2009*, Luxembourg, European Commission, available from: <http://epp.eurostat.ec.europa.eu/tgm/table.do?tab=table&language=en&pcode=tps00001&tableSelection=1&footnotes=yes&labeling=labels&plugin=1>, accessed 30 August 2010.

Eurostat, *Taxation Trends in the European Union*, Luxembourg, Eurostat, 2008.

Financial Regulator, *Consumer Protection Code*, Dublin, IFSRA, 2006, available from: <http://www.financialregulator.ie/press-area/press-releases/documents/consumer%20protection%20code%20-%20august%202006.pdf>, accessed 10 January 2010.

Financial Reporting Council, *Consultation on the Revised UK Corporate Governance Code*, London, Financial Reporting Council, 2009.

333

Financial Services Authority, *Principles Based Regulation: Focusing on the Outcomes that Matter*, London, Financial Services Authority, April 2007.

First American CoreLogic, *Negative Equity Report 2009 Q3*, 24 November 2009, available from: <http://www.calculatedriskblog.com/2009/11/negative-equity-report-for-q3.html>, accessed 30 August 2010.

Fitz Gerald, J., 'Fiscal Policy for Recovery', ESRI working paper no. 326, October 2009.

Fitz Gerald, J. et al., 'Medium Term Review: 2008– 2015, No. 11', Dublin, ESRI, 2008.

Foote, C., Gerardi, K., Goette, L. and Willen, P., 'Reducing Foreclosures: No Easy Answers', National Bureau of Economic Research working paper no. 15063, June 2009.

Forfás, *Sharing Our Future: Ireland 2025 – Strategic Policy Requirements for Enterprise Development*, Dublin, Forfás, 2009, available from: <http://www.forfas.ie/media/forfas090713_sharing_our_future.pdf>, accessed 10 June 2010.

Forfás, *Review of the European Single Market*, Dublin, Forfás, 2008, available from: <http://www.forfas.ie/media/forfas080214_european_single_market.pdf>, accessed 10 June 2010.

Forfás, *A Baseline Assessment of Ireland's Oil Dependence: Key Policy Considerations*, Dublin, Forfás, April 2006, available from: <http://www.forfas.ie/media/forfas060404_irelands_oil_dependence.pdf>, accessed 10 June 2010.

Forfás and the National Competitiveness Council, *Statement on Education and Training*, Dublin, Forfás and the NCC, February 2008.

Forfás and the National Competitiveness Council, *Review of International Assessments of Ireland's Competitiveness*, Dublin, Forfás and the NCC, 20 December 2007.

Goodbody Stockbrokers, *Irish Economic Commentary: Recovery in Sight*, Dublin, Goodbody Stockbrokers, 15 October 2009.

Goodwin, R.M., 'Static and Dynamic Linear General Equilibrium Models', in *Input–Output Relations, Proceedings of a Conference on Inter-Industrial Relations held at Driebergen, Holland*, Leiden, H.E. Stenfert Kroese N.V., 1953.

Gordon, R.J., 'The History of the Phillips Curve: An American Perspective', Australasian Meetings of the Econometric Society A.W.H. Phillips Invited Lecture, Wellington, New Zealand, 9 July 2008.

Green New Deal Group, *The Cuts Won't Work, Second Report of the Green New Deal Group*, London, New Economics Foundation, 2010.

High Level Group on Regulation, *Report to the Government of the High Level Group on Regulation for 2001/02*, Dublin, Department of the Taoiseach, 2002.

Hogan, V., 'Expansionary Fiscal Contractions? Evidence from Panel Data', UCD Centre for Economic Research working paper WP03/03, January 2003.

Honohan, P. and Lane, P.R., 'Exchange Rates and Inflation under EMU: An Update', Centre for Economic Policy Research discussion paper no. 4583, August 2004.

International Monetary Fund, *Total Government Net Debt (National Currency) Data for All Countries*, EconomyWatch, 2010, available from: <http://www.economywatch.com/economicstatistics/economicindicators/General_Government_Net_Debt_National_Currency/>.

International Monetary Fund, *IMF World Economic Outlook, Sustaining the Recovery*, IMF, October 2009, available from: <http://www.imf.org/external/pubs/ft/weo/2009/02/index.htm>, accessed 9 July 2010.

International Monetary Fund, *World Economic Outlook*, Washington, DC, IMF, April 2010.

International Monetary Fund, *Staff Report for the 2009 Article IV Consultation*, IMF Country Report 09/195, Washington, DC, IMF, June 2009.

International Monetary Fund, *Ireland: Staff Report for the 2006 Article IV Consultation*, IMF Country Report No. 06/293, Washington, DC, IMF, 2006.

International Monetary Fund, *When Bubbles Burst*, in IMF World Economic Outlook, April 2003.

Irish Business and Employers Confederation, *Quarterly Review: Economic Trends*, Dublin, IBEC, June 2010.

Irish Congress of Trade Unions, *Congress 10 Point Plan for a Better, Fairer Way*, ICTU, November 2009, available from: <http://www.ictu.ie/download/pdf/congress_10_point_plan.pdf>, accessed 27 July 2010.

Irish Congress of Trade Unions, *Draft Framework for a Pact for Stabilisation, Social Solidarity and Economic Renewal*, ICTU, 28 January 2009, available from: <http://www.ictu.ie/download/pdf/draft_framework_for_a_pact_28_jan_09.pdf>, accessed 27 July 2010.

Irish Congress of Trade Unions, *Governance for State Companies*, Dublin, ICTU, 2005.

Irish Financial Services Regulatory Authority, *Annual Report of the Financial Regulator 2008*, Dublin, IFSRA, 2009.

Irish Financial Services Regulatory Authority, *Protecting Consumers Through Effective Regulation: Annual Report of the Financial Regulator 2005*, Dublin, IFSRA, 2006.

Irish Financial Services Regulatory Authority, *Strategic Plan 2007–2009*, Dublin, IFSRA, 2006.

Irish Financial Services Regulatory Authority, *Strategic Plan 2006*, Dublin, IFSRA, 2005.

Joint Committee on Economic Regulatory Affairs, *Internal Audit Function: Discussion with Anglo Irish Bank*, 3 February 2009, Dublin, Houses of the Oireachtas, 2009.

Joint Committee on Economic Regulatory Affairs, *Anglo Irish Bank: Discussion with Financial Regulator*, 13 January 2009, Dublin, Houses of the Oireachtas, 2009.

Keeney, M.J., 'Wage Inflation and Structural Unemployment in Ireland', Central Bank of Ireland research technical paper no. 7/RT/08, October 2008.

Kose, A., Claessens, S. and Terrones, M., 'What Happens During Recessions, Crunches and Busts', IMF working paper 08/274, 2009.

Landier, A. and Ueda, K., 'The Economics of Bank Restructuring: Understanding the Options', IMF staff position note 09/12, 2009.

Law Reform Commission, 'Personal Debt Management and Debt Enforcement', LRC consultation paper LRC Cp 56, Dublin, 2009.

Levine, R., 'The Corporate Governance of the Banks: A Concise Discussion of Concepts and Evidence', Washington, DC, World Bank, 2004.

Majewski, R. and Nell, E.J., 'Maintaining Full Employment: Simulating an Employer of Last Resort Program', Center for Full Employment and Price Stability seminar paper no. 6, October 2000.

McCarthy, C., 'Fiscal Adjustment and Re-Balancing the Irish Economy', paper presented to the Statistical and Social Inquiry Society of Ireland, 26 November 2009.

McCarthy, C., 'Ireland's Second Fiscal Consolidation: Lessons from the Last Time', UCD Centre for Economic Research working paper WP09/17, October 2009.

McDowell, M., *Report of the Implementation Advisory Group on a Single Regulatory Authority for Financial Services*, known as the *McDowell Report*, Dublin, Department of Finance, 1999.

Mendoza, E.G. and Terrones, M.E., 'An Anatomy of Credit Booms: Evidence from Macro Aggregates and Micro Data', National Bureau of Economic Research working paper no. 14049, May 2008.

Mian., A. and Sufi, A., 'The Consequences of Mortgage Credit Expansion: Evidence from the 2007 Mortgage Default Crisis', National Bureau of Economic Research working paper no. 13936, April 2008.

Mortgage Bankers Association, *National Delinquency Survey*, 19 November 2009, available from: <http://www.mbaa.org/NewsandMedia/Press-Center/71112.htm>, accessed 1 July 2010.

National Competitiveness Council, *Annual Competitiveness Report 2009*, Dublin, NCC, August 2009.

National Competiveness Council, *Costs of Doing Business in Ireland*, Dublin, NCC, 2006.

National Treasury Management Agency, *Ireland Launches 3Year €4 Billion 3.9% Bond*, Dublin, NTMA, 25 February 2009.

National Treasury Management Agency, *Ireland Successfully Launches New €6 Billion 4% Bond*, Dublin, NTMA, 8 January 2009.

National Treasury Management Agency, *Preliminary Results for the Year 2008*, Dublin, NTMA, 31 December 2008.

NCB, *Irish Economy Monitor*, Dublin, NCB Stockbrokers, 6 July 2010.

NCB Stockbrokers, *2020 Vision: Ireland's Demographic Dividend*, Dublin, NCB Stockbrokers, March 2006.

O'Leary, J., 'Social Partnership and the Celtic Tiger', paper presented to the Dublin Economic Workshop, Kenmare, October 2006.

Organisation for Economic Cooperation and Development, *Percentage of Fibre Connections in Total Broadband*, December 2009, available from: <http://www.oecd.org/dataoecd/21/58/39574845.xls>, accessed 10 June 2010.

Organisation for Economic Cooperation and Development, *OECD Public Management Reviews – Ireland: Towards an Integrated Public Service*, Paris, OECD, 2008.

Organisation for Economic Cooperation and Development, *Benefits and Wages Database 2007*, Paris, OECD, 2007.

Organisation for Economic Cooperation and Development, *Economic Survey of Ireland 2006*, Paris, OECD, 2006.

Organisation for Economic Cooperation and Development, *Corporate Governance: A Survey of OECD Countries 2004*, Paris, OECD, 2004.

Organisation for Economic Cooperation and Development, *Regulatory Reform in Ireland*, Paris, OECD, 2001.

O'Sullivan, K.P.V. and Kennedy, T., 'Supervision of the Irish Banking System: A Critical Perspective', CESifo DICE Report 3/2008, 2008.

Poglinco, S.M., Brash, J. and Granger, R.C., 'An Early Look at Community Service Jobs in the New Hope Demonstration', evaluation paper, Manpower Demonstration Research Corporation, July 1998.

Roche, M.J. and McQuinn, K., 'Speculation in Agricultural Land', Economics, Finance and Accounting Department working paper no. 1010700, October 2000, Department of Economics, Finance and Accounting, National University of Ireland, Maynooth, October 2000.

Sandilands, R.J., 'Hawtreyan "Credit Deadlock" or Keynesian "Liquidity Trap"? Lessons for Japan from the Great Depression', paper presented at the David Laidler 'Festschrift' Conference, University of Western Ontario, 18–20 August 2006.

Schularick, M. and Taylor, A.M., 'Credit Booms Gone Bust: Monetary Policy, Leverage Cycles and Financial Crises, 1870–2008', National Bureau of Economic Research working paper no. 15512, November 2009.

Smyth, E. and McCoy, S., 'Investing in Education: Combating Educational Disadvantage', ESRI research series 006, 13 June 2009.

Social and Cultural Planning Office of the Netherlands in association with the OECD, *Public Sector Performance: An International Comparison of*

Education, Health Care, Law and Order and Public Administration, The Hague, Social and Cultural Planning Office of the Netherlands in association with the OECD, September 2004.

Think Tank for Action on Social Change, *TASC Calls for the Government to Cut Tax Breaks, Not Social Welfare*, TASC 2010 PreBudget Submission, Dublin, TASC, 3 December 2009.

United Nations Conference on Trade and Development, *World Investment Report 2010: Investing in a Low-Carbon Economy*, UNCTAD, 2010.

US Department of Energy, Energy Information Administration, *Annual Energy Review*, 2008, 26 June 2009, available from: <http://www.eia. doe.gov/emeu/aer/txt/ptb1105.html>, accessed 10 June 2010.

US Department of Energy, Energy Information Administration, *World Proved Reserves of Oil and Natural Gas, Most Recent Estimates*, 3 March 2009, available from: <http://www.eia.doe.gov/emeu/international/ reserves.html>, accessed 10 June 2010.

US Department of Housing and Urban Development, *New Residential Sales in October 2009*, 25 November 2009, available from: <http://www. census.gov/const/newressales_200910.pdf>, accessed 9 July 2010.

Velde, F., 'Government Equity and Money: John Law's System in 1720 France', Federal Reserve Bank of Chicago working paper WP – 200331, November 2003.

von Peter, G., 'Asset Prices and Banking Distress: A Macroeconomic Approach', Bank of International Settlements working paper no. 167, December 2004.

Whelan, K., 'Policy Lessons from Ireland's Latest Depression', paper presented at the MacGill Summer School, Glenties, Co. Donegal, 20 July 2009, mimeo.

White, B.T., 'Underwater and Not Walking Away: Shame, Fear, and the Social Management of the Housing Crisis', Arizona Legal Studies discussion paper no. 0935, University of Arizona, October 2009.

Women's Aid, *Annual Statistics 2009*, available from: <http://www.womens aid.ie/download/pdf/annual_statistics_report_2009.pdf>, accessed 9 August 2010, pp. 8–12.

World Economic Forum, *Global Competitiveness Report 2009–2010*, Geneva, World Economic Summit, 2009.

Books and Book Chapters

Alletzhauser, A.J., *The House of Nomura: The Inside Story of the Legendary Japanese Financial Dynasty*, New York, Arcade, 1997.

Arestis, P. and Sawyer, M., *A Handbook of Alternative Monetary Economics*, Cheltenham, Edward Elgar, 2006.

Beck, U., *Risk Society: Towards a New Modernity*, Newbury Park, CA, Sage, 1992.

Dale, R., *Risk and Regulation in Global Securities Markets*, New York, Wiley, 1996.

Dillard, D., 'The Theory of a Monetary Economy', in K.K. Kurihara (ed.), *PostKeynesian Economics*, London, George Allen and Unwin Ltd., 1955.

Fair, R., *Testing Macroeconometric Models*, Cambridge, MA, Harvard Univeristy Press, 1998.

Fisher, I., *The Purchasing Power of Money: Its Determination and Relation to Credit, Interest and Crises*, assisted by Harry G. Brown, New York, Macmillan Company, 1911.

Fisher, E., *Risk, Regulation and Administrative Constitutionalism*, Oxford, Hart Publishing, 2007.

Fitz Gerald, J., 'Wage Formation and the Labour Market', in F. Barry (ed.), *Understanding Ireland's Economic Growth*, London, Macmillan Press and New York, St Martin's Press, 1999.

Galbraith, J.K., *The Great Crash 1929*, London, Penguin, 1992.

Galbraith, J.K., *The Great Crash 1929*, New York, Penguin, 1954.

Garber, P., *Famous First Bubbles: The Fundamentals of Early Manias*, Cambridge, MA, MIT Press, 2000.

Gleeson, J., *Millionaire: The Philanderer, Gambler, and Duelist Who Invented Modern Finance*, New York, Simon & Schuster, 1999.

Godley, W. and Lavoie, M., *Monetary Economics: An Integrated Approach to Credit, Money, Income, Production and Wealth*, London, Palgrave Macmillan, 2006.

Goldstrom, J.M. and Clarkson, L.A. (eds.), *Irish Population, Economy and Society: Essays in honour of the Late K.H. Connell*, Oxford, Oxford University Press, 1981.

Gray, J. and Hamilton, J., *Implementing Financial Regulation: Theory and Practice*, London, Wiley, 2006.

Gunningham, N. and Grabosky, P., *Smart Regulation: Designing Environmental Policy*, Oxford, Oxford University Press, 1998.

Hastings, T. (ed.), *The State of the Unions: Challenges Facing Organised Labour in Ireland*, Dublin, Liffey Press, 2009.

Hawtrey, R.G., *Trade Depression and the Way Out*, London, Longmans, Green and Co., 1931.

Hicks, J.R., *A Contribution to the Theory of the Trade Cycle*, Oxford, Clarendon Press, 1950.

Johnson, S. and Kwak, J., *13 Bankers: The Wall Street Takeover and the Next Financial Meltdown*, New York, Pantheon, 2010.

Kennedy, K.A. and Dowling, B.R., *Economic Growth in Ireland: The Experience Since 1947*, Dublin, Gill and Macmillan, 1975.

Keynes, J.M., *The General Theory of Employment, Interest and Money*, New York, Prometheus Books, 1997.

Keynes, J.M., *The General Theory of Employment, Interest and Money*, London, Macmillan and Co., Ltd., 1936.

Keynes, J.M., *The General Theory of Employment, Interest and Money*, Cambridge, Cambridge University Press, 1936.

Keynes, J.M., *Treatise on Probability*, London, Macmillan and Co., Ltd., 1921.

Kindleberger, C. and Aliber, R., *Manias, Panics and Crashes*, Basingstoke, Palgrave, 2005.

Koo, R., *The Holy Grail of Macroeconomics: Lessons from Japan's Great Recession*, New York, Wiley & Sons, 2008.

Kulkarni, D. and Simon, H.A., 'The Processes of Scientific Discovery: The Strategy of Experimentation', reprinted as Chapter 5.3 in H.A. Simon, *Models of Thought – Volume II*, New Haven, CT and London, Yale University Press, [1988], 1989.

Lee, J.J., *Ireland 1912–1985: Politics and Society*, Cambridge, Cambridge University Press, 1989.

Lindahl, E., *Studies in the Theory of Money and Capital*, London, George Allen & Unwin Ltd., [1929], 1939.

Lipschutz, R., *Governmentality and Global Politics: Regulation for the Rest of Us?*, Abingdon, Routledge, 2005.

MacKay, C., *Extraordinary Popular Delusions and the Madness of Crowds*, Philadelphia, PA, Templeton Foundation Press, [1841], 1989.

Marmor, T.R., Mashaw, J.L. and Harvey, P.L., *America's Misunderstood Welfare State: Persistent Myths, Enduring Realities*, London, Basic Books, 1992.

Marx, K. and Engels, F., *Ireland and the Irish Question*, Moscow, Progress Publishers, 1986.

McBarnet, D., *Crime, Compliance and Control*, Oxford, Oxford University Press, 1994.

Mill, J.S., *Principles of Political Economy*, people's edition, London, New York and Bombay, Longmans, Green and Co., 1898.

Minsky, H.P., *Stabilising an Unstable Economy*, New York, McGraw-Hill, 1986.

Minsky, H.P., *Can 'It' Happen Again?: Essays on Instability and Finance*, Armonk, NY, M.E. Sharpe, Inc., 1982.

Minsky, H.P., 'The Financial Instability Hypothesis: A Restatement', 1978, reprinted as Chapter 5 of H.P. Minsky, *Can "It" Happen Again? Essays on Instability and Finance* Armonk, NY, M.E. Sharpe, Inc., 1982.

Moran, M., *The British Regulatory State: High Modernism and Hyper Innovation*, New York, Oxford University Press, 2003.

Morgan, B. and Yeung, K., *An Introduction to Law and Regulation*, Cambridge, Cambridge University Press, 2007.

Morgenroth, E. and Fitz Gerald, J. (eds.), *ExAnte Evaluation of the Investment Priorities for the National Development Plan (2007–2013)*, Dublin, ESRI, October 2006.

Morris, C.R., *The Two Trillion Dollar Meltdown: Easy Money, High Rollers, and the Great Credit Crash*, New York, Public Affairs, 2008.

Murphy, A., *Corporate Ownership in France: The Importance of History*, in R.K. Morck (ed.), *A History of Corporate Governance Round the World: Family Business Groups to Professional Managers*, Chicago, IL, University of Chicago Press, 2005.

Murphy, A., *John Law: Economic Theorist and PolicyMaker*, Oxford, Clarendon Press, 1997.

Myrdal, G., *Monetary Equilibrium*, London, William Hodge & Company, Ltd., [1931], 1939.

Nell, E.J., 'The Simple Theory of Unemployment', in A.W. Warner, M. Forstater, S.M. Rosen and W.S. Vickrey (eds.), *Commitment to Full Employment: The Economics and Social Policy of William S. Vickrey* (Columbia University Seminar Series), Armonk, NY, M.E. Sharpe, 2000.

Nell, E.J., *The General Theory of Transformational Growth, Keynes after Sraffa*, Cambridge, Cambridge University Press, 1998.

Nell, E.J. and Forstater, M. (eds.), *Reinventing Functional Finance: Transformational Growth and Full Employment*, Northampton, Edward Elgar, 2003.

Newell, A. and Simon, H.A., *Human Problem Solving*, Englewood Cliffs, NJ, Prentice Hall, Inc., 1972.

Ó Broin, D. and Waters, E., *Governing Below the Centre: Local Governance in Ireland*, Dublin, New Island and TASC, 2007.

Ohlin, B., 'Introduction' to the English translation of *Geldzins und Güterpreise* by Knut Wicksell, translated by R.F. Kahn as *Interest and Prices*, London, Macmillan, 1936.

O'Sullivan, M., 'Was John Law Irish?', forthcoming in *Economie en Irlande, Groupe de Recherches en Etudes Irlandaises*, Caen, Universite de Caen.

O'Sullivan, M. and Miller, R. (eds.), *What Did We Do Right? Global Perspectives on Ireland's Economic 'Miracle'*, Dublin, Blackhall Publishing, 2010.

Palley, T., *Post-Keynesian Economics: Debt, Distribution, and the Macro Economy*, Oxford, Macmillan, 1996.

Papadimitriou, D.B. and Randall Wray, L., 'Minsky's Stabilizing An Unstable Economy: Two Decades Later', in H.P. Minsky, *Stabilizing An Unstable Economy*, New York, McGraw-Hill, 2008.

Parker, C., *The Open Corporation: Effective Self-Regulation and Democracy*, Melbourne, Cambridge University Press, 2002.

Pettit, P., *Republicanism: A Theory of Freedom and Government*, Oxford, Oxford University Press, 1997.

Pozen, R., *Too Big to Save? How to Fix the US Financial System*, New York, Wiley & Sons, 2009.

Rees, J., *Hostages of Each Other: The Transformation of Nuclear Safety Since Three Mile Island*, Chicago, IL, University of Chicago Press, 1994.

Reinhart, C. and Rogoff, K., *This Time Is Different: Eight Centuries of Financial Folly*, Princeton, NJ, Princeton University Press, 2009.

Romer, D., *Advanced Macroeconomics*, third edition, New York, McGraw-Hill/Irwin, 2006.

Rose, N., *Powers of Freedom: Reframing Political Thought*, Cambridge, Cambridge University Press, 1999.

Schumpeter, J.A., *The Theory of Economic Development: An Inquiry into Profits, Capital, Credit, Interest, and the Business Cycle*, translated by Redvers Opie, Cambridge, MA, Harvard University Press, [1911], 1934.

Shackle, G.L.S., *Expectations, Investment and Income*, second edition, Oxford, Clarendon Press, 1968.

Shackle, G.L.S., *The Nature of Economic Thought: Selected Papers 1955–1964*, Cambridge, Cambridge University Press, 1966.

Shackle, G.L.S., *Expectations in Economics*, Cambridge, Cambridge University Press, 1949.

Shiller, R.J., 'Do Stock Prices Move Too Much to be Justified by Subsequent Changes in Dividends?', reprinted as Chapter 4 of R.H. Thaler (ed.), *Advances in Behavioral Finance*, New York, Russell Sage Foundation, [1981], 1993.

Simon, H.A., *Models of Discovery – and Other Topics in the Methods of Science*, Dordrecht, D. Reidel Publishing Company, 1977.

Solow, R.M., 'Lecture I: Guess Who Likes Workfare', in A. Gutmann (ed.), *Work and Welfare*, Princeton, NJ, Princeton University Press, 1998.

Solow, R.M., Lecture II: Guess Who Pays for Workfare', in A. Gutmann (ed.), *Work and Welfare*, 1998.

Staiger, D., Stock, J.H. and Watson, M.W., 'Prices, Wages, and the U.S. NAIRU in the 1990s', in A.B. Krueger and R.M. Solow (eds.), New York, The Russell Sage Foundation and the Century Foundation Press, 2001, pp. 3–60.

Taylor, L., *Reconstructing Macroeconomics: Structuralist Proposals and Critiques of the Mainstream*, Cambridge, MA, Harvard University Press, 2004.

Tirole, J., *Financial Crises, Liquidity and the International Monetary System*, Princeton, NJ, Princeton University Press, 2002.

Tobin, J., 'Real Balance Effects Reconsidered', in J. Tobin (ed.), *Asset Accumulation and Economic Activity*, Chicago, IL, University of Chicago Press, 1980.

Westrup, J., 'Ireland', in D. Masciandaro (ed.), *The Handbook of Central Banking and Financial Authorities in Europe*, Cheltenham, Edward Elgar, 2005.

White, E.N., 'Are There any Lessons from History?', in E.N. White (ed.), *Crashes and Panics: The Lessons from History*, Homewood, IL, Business One Irwin, 1990.

Wicksell, K. *Geldzins und Güterpreise: Eine Studie über die den Tauschwert des Geldes bestimmenden ursachen*, Jena, Gustav Fischer Verlag, 1898.

Woodford, M., *Interest and Prices: Foundations of a Theory of Monetary Policy*, New York, Princeton University Press, 2003.

Journal Articles

Alesina, A., Perotti, R. and Tavares, J., 'The Political Economy of Fiscal Adjustments', *Brookings Papers on Economic Activity*, Spring 1998, pp. 197–266.

Barry, F., 'Social Partnership, Competitiveness and Exit from Fiscal Crisis', *Economic and Social Review*, Vol. 40, No. 1, Spring 2009, pp. 1–12.

Berger, A.N. and Udell, G.F., 'The Institutional Memory Hypothesis and the Procyclicality of Bank Lending Behavior', *Journal of Financial Intermediation*, Vol. 13, No. 4, 2004, pp. 458–95.

Bernanke, B., 'Non-Monetary Effects of the Financial Crisis in Propagation of the Great Depression', *American Economic Review*, Vol. 73, No. 3, 1983, pp. 257–76.

Bernanke, B. and Gertler, M., 'Should Central Banks Respond to Movements in Asset Prices?', *American Economic Review*, Vol. 91, No. 2, 2001, pp. 253–7.

Black, J., 'Forms and Paradoxes of Principles Based Regulation', *Capital Markets Law Journal*, Vol. 3, No. 4, 2008, pp. 425–57.

Black, J., 'Critical Reflections on Regulation', *Australian Journal of Legal Philosophy*, Vol. 27, 2002, pp. 1–35.

Bloom, D.E. and Canning, D., 'Contraception and the Celtic Tiger', *Economic and Social Review*, Vol. 34, No. 3, Winter 2003, pp. 229-47.

Bordo, M. and Filardo, A., 'Deflation and Monetary Policy in a Historical Perspective: Remembering the Past or Being Condemned to Repeat It?,' *Economic Policy*, Vol. 20, No. 44, 2005, pp. 799–844.

Braithwaite, J., 'Meta Risk Management and Responsive Regulation for Tax System Integrity', *Law & Policy*, Vol. 25, No. 1, 2003, pp. 1–16.

Braithwaite, J., 'The New Regulatory State and the Transformation of Criminology', *British Journal of Criminology*, Vol. 40, 2000, pp. 222–38.

Clower, R.W. and Howitt, P.W., 'The Transaction Theory of the Demand for Money: A Reconsideration', *Journal of Political Economy*, Vol. 86, No. 3, 1978, pp. 449–66.

Corsetti, G., Pesenti, P. and Roubini, N., 'Paper Tigers? A Model of the Asian Crisis', *European Economic Review*, Vol. 43, No. 7, 1999, pp. 1211–36.

Currie, L., 'Treatment of Credit in Contemporary Monetary Theory', *Journal of Political Economy*, Vol. 41, No. 1, 1933, pp. 58–79.

Dell'Ariccia, G. and Marquez, R., 'Lending Booms and Lending Standards', *Journal of Finance*, Vol. 61, No. 5, 2006, pp. 2511–46.

DeLong, J.B., 'Should We Fear Deflation?', *Brookings Papers on Economic Activity*, Vol. 1, No. 1, 1999, pp. 225–52.

Dorf, M. and Sabel, C., 'A Constitution of Democratic Experimentalism', *Columbia Law Review*, Vol. 98, No. 2, 1998, pp. 267–473.

Eggertsson, G.B. and Woodford, M., 'The Zero Bound on Interest Rates and Optimal Monetary Policy', *Brookings Papers on Economic Activity*, Vol. 1, 2003, pp. 139–233.

Englund, P., 'The Swedish Banking Crisis: Roots and Consequences', *Oxford Review of Economic Policy*, Vol. 15, No. 3, 1999, pp. 80–97.

Ferri, P. and Minsky, H., 'Market Processes and Thwarting Systems', *Structural Change and Economic Dynamics*, Vol. 3, No. 1, 1992, pp. 79–91.

Fisher, I., 'The Debt-Deflation Theory of Great Depressions', *Econometrica*, Vol. 1, No. 3, 1933, pp. 337–57.

Forstater, M., 'Functional Finance and Full Employment: Lessons from Lerner for Today', *Journal of Economic Issues*, Vol. 33, No. 1, 1999, pp. 1–17.

Fostel, A. and Geanakoplos, J., 'Leverage Cycles and the Anxious Economy', *American Economic Review*, Vol. 98, No. 4, 2008, pp. 1211–44.

Freeman, J., 'The Private Role in Public Governance', *New York University Law Review*, Vol. 75, No. 101, 2000, pp. 543–651.

Friedman, M., 'The Role of Monetary Policy', *American Economic Review*, Vol. 58, No. 1, March 1968, pp. 1–17.

Gali, J. and Gertler, M., 'Inflation Dynamics: A Structural Econometric Analysis', *Journal of Monetary Economics*, Vol. 44, No. 2, 1999, pp. 195–222.

Goodstein, R.L., 'On the Restricted Ordinal Theorem', *Journal of Symbolic Logic*, Vol. 9, No. 2, 1944, pp. 33–41.

Goodwin, R.M., 'The Nonlinear Accelerator and the Persistence of Business Cycles', *Econometrica*, Vol. 19, No. 1, 1951, pp. 1–17.

Gordon, R.J., 'The Time-Varying NAIRU and Its Implications for Economic Policy', *Journal of Economic Perspectives*, Vol. 11, No. 1, 1997, pp. 11–32.

Gordon, R.J., 'Price Inertia and Policy Ineffectiveness in the United States, 1890–1980', *Journal of Political Economy*, Vol. 90, No. 6, December 1982, pp. 1087–117.

Gordon, R.J., 'The Theory of Domestic Inflation', *American Economic Review Papers and Proceedings*, Vol. 67, No. 1, February 1977, pp. 128–34.

Gunningham, N., 'Environment Law, Regulation and Governance: Shifting Architectures', *Journal of Environmental Law*, Vol. 21, No. 2, 2009, pp. 179–212.

Honohan, P., 'Resolving Ireland's Banking Crisis', *Economic and Social Review*, Vol. 40, No. 2, 2009, pp. 207–31.

Honohan, P. and Lane, P.R., 'Divergent Inflation Rates in EMU', *Economic Policy*, Vol. 18, No. 37, 2003, pp. 357–94.

Honohan, P. and Leddin, A., 'Ireland in EMU: More Shocks, Less Insulation?', *Economic and Social Review*, Vol. 37, No. 2, Summer/Autumn 2006, pp. 263–94.

Honohan, P. and Walsh, B., 'Catching Up with the Leaders: The Irish Hare', *Brookings Papers on Economic Activity*, Vol. 33, No. 1, 2002, pp. 1–78.

Humphrey, J., 'A Scientific Approach to Politics? On the Trail of the Audit Commission', *Critical Perspectives on Accounting*, Vol. 13, No. 1, 2002, pp. 39–62.

Kaldor, N., 'A Model of the Trade Cycle', *Economic Journal*, Vol. 50, No. 1, March 1940, pp. 78–92.

Kalecki, M., 'A Theory of Profits', *Economic Journal*, Vol. 52, Nos. 206–07, 1942, pp. 258–67.

King, M., 'Debt Deflation: Theory and Evidence', *European Economic Review*, Vol. 38, Nos. 3–4, 1994, pp. 419–45.

Kirby, L. and Paris, J., 'Accessible Independence Results for Peano Arithmetic', *Bulletin of the London Mathematical Society*, Vol. 14, 1982, pp. 285–93.

Kiyotaki, N. and Moore, J., 'Credit Cycles', *Journal of Political Economy*, Vol. 105, No. 2, 1997, pp. 211–48.

Kurihara, K., 'An Endogenous Model of Cyclical Growth', *Oxford Economic Papers – New Series*, Vol. 12, No. 3, 1960, pp. 243–8.

Kydland, F.E. and Prescott, E.C., 'Rules Rather than Discretion: The Inconsistency of Optimal Plans', *Journal of Political Economy*, Vol. 85, No. 3, 1977, pp. 473–91.

Lane, P.R., 'Disinflation, Switching Nominal Anchors and Twin Crises: The Irish Experience', *Journal of Policy Reform*, Vol. 3, No. 2, 2000, pp. 301–26.

Lane, P.R., 'International Diversification and the Irish Economy', *Economic and Social Review*, Vol. 31, No. 1, 2000, pp. 37–54.

Lawlor, J. and McCarthy, C., 'Browsing Onwards: Irish Public Spending in Perspective', *Irish Banking Review*, Autumn 2003, pp. 2–17.

Lerner, A.P., 'The Essential Properties of Interest and Money', *Quarterly Journal of Economics*, Vol. 66, No. 2, 1952, pp. 172–93.

Levi-Faur, D., 'The Political Economy of Legal Globalization: Juridification, Adversarial Legalism, and Responsive Regulation – A Comment', *International Organization*, Vol. 59, No. 2, 2005, pp. 451–62.

Lucas, Jr., R.E., 'Some International Evidence on Output Inflation Trade-offs', *American Economic Review*, Vol. 63, No. 3, 1973, pp. 326–34.

Lucas Jr., R.E., 'Expectations and the Neutrality of Money', *Journal of Economic Theory*, Vol. 4, No. 2, 1972, pp. 103–24.

Matsuyama, K., 'Credit Traps and Credit Cycles', *American Economic Review*, Vol. 97, No. 1, 2007, pp. 503–16.

Miles, D. and Pillonca, V., 'Financial Innovation and European Housing and Mortgage Markets', *Oxford Review of Economic Policy*, Vol. 24, No. 1, 2008, pp. 145–75.

Minsky, H.P., 'The Legacy of Keynes', *Journal of Economic Education*, Vol. 16, No. 1, 1985, pp. 5–15.

Minsky, H.P., 'A Linear Model of Cyclical Growth', *Review of Economics and Statistics*, Vol. 41, No. 2, Part 1, 1959, pp. 133–45.

Minsky, H.P., 'Monetary Systems and Accelerator Models', *American Economic Review*, Vol. XLVII, No. 6, 1957, pp. 860–83.

Morgan, B., 'The Economization of Politics: Meta-Regulation as a Form of Nonjudicial Legality', *Social & Legal Studies*, Vol. 12, No. 4, 2003, pp. 489–523.

Mosler, W., 'Full Employment and Price Stability', *Journal of Post Keynesian Economics*, Vol. 20, No. 2, Winter 1997–8, pp. 167–82.

Organisation for Economic Cooperation and Development, 'The Corporate Governance Lessons from the Financial Crisis', *OECD Journal: Financial Market Trends*, Vol. 1, No. 96, 2009, pp. 52–81.

O'Sullivan, K.P.V. and Kennedy, T., 'A Model for Regulatory Intervention in Irish Banking', *Journal of Banking Regulation*, Vol. 8, No. 2, 2007, pp. 113–30.

Paris, J. and Tavakol, R., 'Goodstein Algorithm as a Super-Transient Dynamical System', *Physics Letters A*, Vol. 180, Nos. 1–2, 1993, pp. 83–6.

Patinkin, D., 'Wicksell's "Cumulative Process"', *Economic Journal*, Vol. 62, No. 248, 1952, pp. 835–47.

Phelps, E.S., 'Money-Wage Dynamics and Labor Market Equilibrium', *Journal of Political Economy*, Vol. 76, No. 4, Part II, 1968, pp. 678–711.

Phelps, E.S., 'Phillips Curves, Expectations of Inflation and Optimal Unemployment over Time', *Economica*, Vol. 34, August 1967.

Phillips, A.W., 'The Relation between Unemployment and the Rate of Change of Money Wage Rates in the United Kingdom, 1861–1957', *Economica*, Vol. 25, No. 100, 1958, pp. 283–99.

Prammer, D., 'Expansionary Fiscal Consolidations? An Appraisal of the Literature on Non-Keynesian Effects of Fiscal Policy and a Case Study for Austria', *Monetary Policy & the Economy*, Q3/04, 2004, pp. 34–52.

Rajan, R.G., 'Why Bank Credit Policies Fluctuate: A Theory and Some Evidence', *Quarterly Journal of Economics*, Vol. 109, No. 2, 1994, pp. 399–441.

Reinhart, C. and Rogoff, K., 'The Aftermath of Financial Crises', *American Economic Review*, Vol. 99, No. 2, 2009, pp. 466–72.

Samuelson, P.A. and Solow, R.M., 'Analytical Aspects of Anti-Inflation Policy', *American Economic Review Papers and Proceedings*, Vol. 50, No. 2, 1960, pp. 177–94.

Scott, C., 'Speaking Softly Without Big Sticks: Meta-Regulation and Public Sector Audit', *Law & Policy*, Vol. 25, No. 3, 2003, pp. 203–19.

Shackle, G.L.S., 'Expectations and Employment', *Economic Journal*, Vol. 49, No. 195, 1939, pp. 442–52.

Shleifer, A. and Summers, L., 'The Noise Trader Approach to Finance', *Journal of Economic Perspectives*, Vol. 4, No. 2, 1990, pp. 19–33.

Simon, H.A., 'A Behavioral Model of Rational Choice', *Quarterly Journal of Economics*, Vol. LXIX, No. 1, February 1955.

Sraffa, P., 'Dr Hayek on Money and Capital', *Economic Journal*, Vol. 42, No. 165, 1932, pp. 42–53.

Taylor, J.B., 'Discretion versus Policy Rules in Practice', *Carnegie Rochester Conference Series on Public Policy*, Vol. 39, 1993, pp. 195–214.

Taylor, L. and O'Connell, S.A., 'A Minsky Crisis', *Quarterly Journal of Economics*, Vol. 100 (Supplement), No. 5, 1985, pp. 871–85.

Uchitelle, E., 'The Effectiveness of Tax Amnesty Programs in Selected Countries', *Federal Reserve Board of New York Quarterly Review*, Autumn 1989, pp. 48–53.

Velupillai, K. Vela, 'Reflections on Mathematical Economics in the Algorithmic Mode', in *New Mathematics and Natural Computation*, Vol. 6, forthcoming 2010.

Velupillai, K. Vela, 'Some Swedish Stepping Stones to Modern Macroeconomics', *Eastern Economic Journal*, Vol. XIV, No. 1, January–March 1988, pp. 87–98.

Walsh, B.M., 'Urbanization and the Regional Distribution of Population in Post-Famine Ireland', *Journal of European Economic History*, Vol. 29, No. 1, Spring 2000, pp. 109–27.

Walsh, B.M., 'Expectations, Information and Migration: Specifying an Econometric Model of Irish Migration to Britain', *Journal of Regional Science*, Vol. 14, 1974, pp. 107-20.

Walsh, F. and Strobl, E., 'Recent Trends in Trade Union Membership in Ireland', *Economic and Social Review*, Vol. 40, No. 1, Spring 2009, pp. 117–38.

Wray, L.R., 'Government Deficits, Investment, Saving, and Growth', *Journal of Economic Issues*, Vol. 23, No. 4, December 1989, pp. 977–1002.

Wulwick, N.J., 'History and Methodology of Econometrics', *Oxford Economic Papers*, new series, Vol. 41, No. 1, January 1989, pp. 170–88.

Newspaper and Magazine Articles

de Bréadún, D. and O'Halloran, M., 'Big Job Cuts in Public Service Are "Doable" – Gilmore', *Irish Times*, 18 July 2009.

Deeter, K. and Kinsella, S., 'Municipal Bonds Could Be the Solution to Many Problems', *Sunday Business Post*, 15 November 2009.

Economist, The, 'Safe as Houses: Compare Countries' House-Price Data Over Time', *The Economist*, 8 July 2010.

Economist, The, 'Why Worry' in 'The Luck of the Irish: A Survey of Ireland', *The Economist*, 16 October 2004, pp. 6–8.

Irish Independent, 'AIB Sells €750m Five-Year Bond After Ratings Downgrade', *Irish Independent*, 6 November 2009.

Irish Times, 'Database to be Established to Monitor House Prices and Market Trends', *Irish Times*, 11 August 2010.

Irish Times, 'Judge Says Cases Showing Falls in Property Values of up to 80 per cent', *Irish Times*, 20 October 2009

Irish Times, 'Warning that No Vote Will Deter Future Investment', *Irish Times*, 15 September 2009

McGee, H., 'IMF to Have Role if Cuts Are Not Made, says Harney', *Irish Times*, 17 October 2009.

O'Mahony, B., '15% Chance We'll Default on Debts', *Irish Examiner*, 16 May 2009.

O'Sullivan, M., 'We Need a Political System that Encourages Strategic Thinking', *Irish Times*, 14 April 2009.

Press Releases and Speeches

Burton, J., 'Ireland Urgently Needs Fiscal Stimulus Package to KickStart Economy', 2 December 2008, available from: <http://www.joanburton.ie/?postid=1009>, accessed 26 July 2010.

Financial Regulator, *New Data on Residential Mortgage Arrears and Repossessions Published'*, press release, 22 December 2009.

Fine Gael, *NewERA*, November 2009, available from: <http://www.finegael.org/upload/NewERA.pdf>, accessed 27 July 2010.

Gilmore, E., 'A New Deal for Ireland', speech delivered 29 November 2008, Labour Press Release, <http://www.labour.ie/press/listing/1227990873132673.html>, accessed 26 July 2010.

Honohan, P., 'Financial Regulation in Ireland: Past, Present and Future', speech to the Financial Services Ireland Annual Dinner, 1 December 2009, Dublin.

Honohan, P., 'Opening Address to the ESRI/Foundation for Fiscal Studies Conference', Dublin, 13 October 2009.

Labour Party, *Building a New, Better Fairer Future: Labour's Priorities for the Emergency Budget*, 2 April 2009.

Sants, H., Chief Executive, FSA, 'Delivering Intensive Supervision and Credible Deterrence', speech given at the Reuters Newsmakers event, 12 March 2009, available from: <http://www.fsa.gov.uk/pages/Library/

Communication/Speeches/2009/0312_hs.shtml>, accessed 10 January 2010.

Datasets and Online Resources

Bureau of Labor Statistics, 'Current Employment Statistics – CES (National)', <http://www.bls.gov/ces/>, accessed 9 July 2010.

Burke, S., 'My Fantasy Health Budget', SaraBurke.com, 19 November 2009, available from: <http://saraburke.wordpress.com/?s=My+Fantasy+Health+Budget>, accessed 1 July 2010.

Central Statistics Office, CSO Database Direct: Details on Taxation by Item and Year, CSO, see <http://www.cso.ie/px/pxeirestat/Database/Eirestat/Eirestat.asp>, accessed 26 July 2010.

Central Statistics Office, *Economy*, CSO, 2009, available from: <http://www.cso.ie/px/pxeirestat/database/eirestat/eirestat.asp>, accessed 9 July 2010.

Central Statistics Office, *Labour Market and Earnings*, CSO, 2009, available from: <http://www.cso.ie/px/pxeirestat/database/eirestat/eirestat.asp>, accessed 9 July 2010.

Central Statistics Office, *People and Society*, CSO, 2009, available from: <http://www.cso.ie/px/pxeirestat/database/eirestat/eirestat.asp>, accessed 9 July 2010.

Department of Education and Science, *Key Statistics 2008–2009*, available from: <http://www.education.ie/servlet/blobservlet/stat_key_stats_2008_2009.pdf>, accessed 6 August 2010.

Doyle, D., 'Irish Bonds "Great Bargain", Debt Chief Somers Says', *Bloomberg*, 27 March 2009, available from: <http://www.bloomberg.com/apps/news?pid=newsarchive&sid=asadtlDx3UnA&refer=worldwide>, accessed 26 July 2010.

Halifax, 'Halifax House Price Index', December 2009, available from: <http://www.lloydsbankinggroup.com/media1/research/halifax_hpi.asp>, accessed 9 July 2010.

Knight Frank, 'Knight Frank Global House Price Index', 9 December 2009, available from: <http://www.knightfrank.com/news/Knight-Frank-Global-House-Price-Index-082.aspx>, accessed 9 July 2010.

Maddison, A., Database, University of Groningen, available from <http://www.ggdc.net/maddison/>, accessed 30 August 2010.

Marian Finucane Show, The, Interview with Sean FitzPatrick, RTE Radio One, 4 October 2008, available from: <http://dynamic.rte.ie/quickaxs/209-rte-marianfinucane-2008-10-04.smil>, accessed 30 August 2010.

Prime Time, 'Fight for Financial Survival', *Prime Time*, 26 February 2009, available from: <http://www.rte.ie/news/2009/0226/primetime.html>, accessed 30 June 2010.

Prime Time, Interview with Patrick Neary, 2 October 2008, available from: <http://www.rte.ie/news/2008/1002/primetime.html>, accessed 10 January 2010.

Stewart, J., 'Current Policies Set to Exacerbate Economic Crisis', *ProgressiveEconomy.ie*, 12 May 2009, available from: <http://www.progressive-economy.ie/2009/05/current-policies-set-to-exacerbate.html>, accessed 27 July 2010.

Taft, M., "What the Markets are Telling Us (and What our Commentators are Not)', *Notes on the Front*, 16 May 2010, available from: <http://notesonthefront.typepad.com/politicaleconomy/2010/05/what-are-the-markets-really-trying-to-tell-us——we-are-not-spain-we-are-not-italy-we-are-not-portugal-repeat-we-are-n.html>, accessed 1 July 2010.

Taft, M., 'Shock! Horror! McCarthy Vindicates Public Sector Efficiency!', *Notes on the Front*, 20 July 2009, available from: <http://notesonthe-front.typepad.com/politicaleconomy/2009/07/shock-horror-mccarthy-v indicates-public-sector-efficiency———-noel-whelan-wants-you-to-read-the-report-he-wants-you-to.html>, accessed 1 July 2010.

INDEX

Figures are indicated by **bold** page numbers, tables by *italic* numbers.